D1686011

# The Beginnings of Buddhist art, and Other Essays in Indian and Central-Asian Archæology

# THE BEGINNINGS OF

# BUDDHIST ART

## AND OTHER ESSAYS
## IN INDIAN AND CENTRAL-ASIAN ARCHÆOLOGY

BY

### A. FOUCHER
OF THE UNIVERSITY OF PARIS

REVISED BY THE AUTHOR AND TRANSLATED BY

### L. A. THOMAS AND F W. THOMAS
WITH A PREFACE BY THE LATTER

*PARIS*     *LONDON*
PAUL GEUTHNER     HUMPHREY MILFORD
13, RUE JACOB, 13     AMEN CORNER E C

MCMXVII

# THE BEGINNINGS

OF

# BUDDHIST ART

Printed for PAUL GEUTHNER by

A BURDIN — F GAULTIER and A THÈBERT, Succ<sup>rs</sup>, Angers, France

Demoulin frères. Sc

PAINTING FROM TURFAN

NOW IN MUSEUM FUR VÖLKERKUNDE, BERLIN

# THE BEGINNINGS OF

# BUDDHIST ART

## AND OTHER ESSAYS
## IN INDIAN AND CENTRAL-ASIAN ARCHÆOLOGY

BY

### A. FOUCHER
OF THE UNIVERSITY OF PARIS

REVISED BY THE AUTHOR AND TRANSLATED BY

### L. A. THOMAS AND F. W. THOMAS
WITH A PREFACE BY THE LATTER

*PARIS*
PAUL GEUTHNER
13, RUE JACOB, 13

*LONDON*
HUMPHREY MILFORD
AMEN CORNER, E C

MCMXVII

Foucher, Alfred Charles
         Auguste, 1865-

*DEDICATED*

WITH PROFOUND RESPECT AND AFFECTIONATE REGARD

TO

M. AUGUSTE BARTH

*Member of the Institute* ·

MASTER OF PENETRATING AND CREATIVE CRITICISM
IN ALL BRANCHES OF SANSKRIT LEARNING

*June 1914*

# PREFACE

To the rather limited circle of scholars interested in Indian Art and Archæology the work of M Foucher requires no introduction. His numerous studies devoted to these subjects, and in particular his comprehensive treatise on the Græco-Buddhist Art of Gandhâra, have fully established his position as a leader in this sphere A collective edition of his essays and addresses, dispersed in various serial and periodical publications, will therefore be sure of a warm welcome.

The translators do not disavow a hope that this English version may appeal not only to those readers, chiefly in the East, to whom the author's original presents a difficulty, but also to a rather wider public in England and America Aware of the interest which in Paris attended the delivery of M Foucher's lectures, they would regret if the charm had so far evaporated in translation as to forfeit a share in the growing appreciation of Oriental art.

Buddhism — for it is especially Buddhist monuments that are here surveyed — is of course, a subject of vast extent We may add that it is a highly organic subject, and that the study of it is still at a specially interesting stage, the stage of discovery We cannot touch it in any part without evoking responses from distant and unexpected quarters We might compare it to a magic carpet, we fix upon some well defined topic, relating, let us say, to the Græco-Buddhist school of Gandhâra, and promptly, even without our volition, some analogy or connection transports us to the Central Asia, China or Japan of many centuries later, even if we have not to continue our flight to Java in the ninth century or Cambodia in the twelfth The reader will find in these pages abundant examples of such transitions. The first essays reach back by a highly ingenious and probable hypothesis to the very origins of Buddhist art in India itself, and give us the measure of its possibilities by what it has achieved at Sânchî and Barhut Already we detect some traces of foreign influence, from the Persia of the Achæmenids Soon an abrupt irruption of Hellenistic art

overwhelms the native schools, and creates a repertory of religious compositions, which the Buddhist propaganda carries to Central Asia, the Far East,
and the Malay islands  Thus is established a genetic connection between the
religious art of Europe and Asia, a double efflorescence from one root, most
strikingly exemplified in the case of the Buddha type, which closely resembles
the earliest sculptural type of Christ, and most curiously in that of the 'Tutelary Pair', found throughout the whole Buddhist sphere and at the same time
in ancient Gaul . or shall we claim the highest degree of interest for the case
of the 'Madonna' group (Essay IX), which — ultimately derived, in all
probability, from ancient Egypt — has ended by conquering the whole world ?
This splendid generalization cannot fail to be fruitful, both on the European
and on the Asiatic side, in inspiration for future researches . in the meanwhile it may be welcomed as reestablishing by the aid of art that feeling of
solidarity and sympathy between India and Europe, which flourished during
the palmy days of Vedic studies, but latterly has been somewhat discouraged
by specialism.

   Need we remark that, where religious art and archæology are the theme,
literature and literary history cannot be far away ? M  Foucher has commented
upon the predominantly narrative character of the bas reliefs with which he is
dealing . it may indeed be said that, apart from purely decorative figures and
symbols, the great bulk of them are illustrations of scenes from the life of the
Buddha  The life must, indeed, be conceived in an ample sense, according to
that grandiose Indian conception whereby, as M. Foucher opportunely reminds
us, the biography is not confined to a single span, but covers the whole series of
countless births, under all forms of existence, which were necessary for the
accumulation of the positive and negative characteristics manifested finally in
the Great Being, the Perfectly Illuminated  The scenes therefore need to be
read, and at first the very alphabet was wanting  The problem was of far
greater obscurity than in the case of what M  Foucher terms the magnificent
illustrated bible constituted by the sculptors of the cathedral of Chartres. The
texts of the Buddhist religion have only gradually been made known : those
events in the life which were specially marked out for illustration — the
twelve acts of Buddha and so forth — had not been separated out ; the Jâtaka
book, recording the tales of previous births, was not at first available  The
names of those scholars to whom we are indebted  for the first tentatives at
decipherment, such as the inspired, if not impeccable, archæologist, General Sir
Alexander Cunningham, Prof. Grunwedel of the Berlin Ethnographical
Museum, Dr  Serge d'Oldenburg, Perpetual Secretary of the Imperial

*Academy of St Petersburg, and others will be found recurring in M. Foucher's pages. But undoubtedly the matter has in M. Foucher's own work made a long step forward : the reader will remark not only the artistic insight which gives so much ease and certainty to the identifications in this volume, but also the emergence of principles fitted to serve as a guide for future discovery and criticism in this field of study. In a word, we see taking shape, not only an art, but also a science of discovery and interpretation in regard to Buddhist, and by consequence to Indian, illustration*

*A history of Buddhist Art is a task for the future , may we some day have the pleasure of welcoming a systematic treatise upon the subject from M Foucher's own pen. For the present we are only at the commencement Nothing guarantees us that in its beginnings the Art shall be found on a level with the doctrine, or that it shall follow a parallel course, or again that it shall develope with a proportional rapidity. On the contrary, we see already that at Sânchî and Barhut, after centuries of active speculation, it makes its appeal primarily to a community characterized by naive and simple piety In the case of Christianity how many centuries of dogmatic strife precede the age of the primitives ! Nevertheless the reader who turns from the essays on Barhut and Sânchî to those dealing with the Great Miracle and with Boro-Budur — much clearer would be his impression, if he embraced in his view the mediæval and modern art of China, Japan, and Tibet — cannot fail to note the metaphysical contemplation which has grown upon the decay of the older popular piety Yet even here we have a warning as to the partial reversions which may result from the transplanting of religion to a less sophisticated society : since in the sculptures of Boro-Budur we find again — in an atmosphere, it is true, of hypertropical softness — no small admixture of that frank pleasure in mere story-telling which is the special charm of Sânchî and Barhut*

London. June, 1914

F. W THOMAS.

We are indebted for the use of photographs to the Secretary of State for India, Dr J Burgess, and Prof. A A Macdonell (England), to Prof. Ed Chavannes, Mr Henry H Getty and M V Goloubew (France), to Prof A Grunwedel and Dr A von Le Coq (Germany), to Mr J H (now Sir John) Marshall, Sir Aurel Stein and Mr (now Prof ) J Ph Vogel (India) ; to Major Van Erp (Java)  — and for the loan of blocks to the Académie des Inscriptions et Belles-Lettres, the Société Asiatique and MM Espérandieu, Guimet, Hachette et Cⁱᵉ, E Leroux (Paris), and to the Ecole française d'Extrême-Orient (Hanoi)

In the body of the work and in the descriptions attached to the plates will be found indications in detail of what we owe to this kind coöperation We tender here our grateful thanks for help in the absence of which the majority of these essays either would never have come into being or could not have been combined to form of a volume

Some faults of impression and minor errata will perhaps be judged excusable in an English book printed in France

*P S.* — It should moreover be stated — in view of some few details which the reader himself may notice — that this volume, with exception of the index and tables, has been in print since June 1914 Through the enforced postponement of its appearance, the dedication to M A Barth has become (since April 15, 1916) unfortunately only a tribute to his memory.

# CONTENTS

|  |  | Pages |
|---|---|---|
| I — The Beginnings of Buddhist Art | | 1 |
| II. — The Representations of « Jâtakas » on the Bas-Reliefs of Barhut | | 29 |
| III. — The Eastern Gate of the Sânchî Stûpa | | 61 |
| IV. — The Greek Origin of the Image of Buddha | | 111 |
| V — The Tutelary Pair in Gaul and in India | | 139 |
| VI — The Great Miracle at Çrâvastî | | 147 |
| VII. — The Six-Tusked Elephant | | 185 |
| VIII — Buddhist Art in Java | | 205 |
| IX — The Buddhist Madonna | | 271 |
| Index | | 293 |

# ILLUSTRATIONS

Hâritî, the Buddhist Madonna : painting from Turfan... *frontispiece*

Page

PLATES I-IV. — BEGINNINGS OF BUDDHIST ART. .       28
    I    Buddhist symbols on ancient Indian coins
    II    The three last Great Miracles :
        1° *at Sânchi* ; 2° *at Amarâvatî*
    III    The first Great Miracle
        1° *in Gandhâra* , 2° *at Amarâvatî*.
    IV.    The four Great Miracles
        1° *in Gandhâra* , 2° *at Amarâvatî* , 3° *at Benares*

PLATES V-VI. — JÂTAKAS AT BARHUT . . . .       60
    V.    In medallions.
    VI    On the rail-coping

PLATES VII-X — THE EASTERN GATE OF THE SÂNCHÎ STÛPA       110
    VII, 1.  General view taken from the East.
        2.  Back-view of Lintels of Eastern Gate.
    VIII, 1  Eastern Gate (*front view*).
        2.  Divine guardian at entrance
        *Interior face of left jamb.*
    IX, 1.  The Conversion of the Kâçyapas.
        *Interior face of left jamb.*
        2  The Return to Kapilavastu.
        *Interior face of right jamb*
    X, 1.  The Vocation, or Great Departure
        *Front view of middle lintel*
        2  A Procession to the Bodhi-Tree
        *Front view of lower lintel*

Page

PLATES XI-XVI. — GREEK ORIGIN OF THE BUDDHA TYPE      138

XI, 1. Buddhas in the Lahore Museum.
    2  Buddha in the Guides' Mess, Mardân
XII, 1  The Village of Shâhbâz-Garhî
    2  The Ruins of Takht-ı-Bahaı
XIII, 1  The Village of Sahrı-Bahlol
    2  Excavations near Sahrı-Bahlol
XIV, 1  Shâh-jî-kî-Dherî (Kanıshka Stûpa)
    2  Indo-Greek and Indo-Scythıc Coıns
XV, 1  The Relıc-casket of Kanıshka.
    2  The Bodhısattva Type
XVI, 1  Types of Bodhısattva, Buddha and monk
    2  Græco-Chrıstıan Chrıst and Græco-Buddhıst Buddha


PLATES XVII-XVIII — THE TUTELARY PAIR      146

XVII.   In Gaul.
XVIII   In Gandhâra.


PLATES XIX-XXVIII — THE GREAT MIRACLE OF ÇRÂVASTÎ      184

XIX     At Benares
XX      At Ajantâ.
XXI, 1  At Ajantâ . after a wall-paıntıng.
    2  In Chına · in the Ta-t'ong-fu Caves.
XXII.   On the Boro-Budur, Java
XXIII, 1  In Magadha.
    2. In the Konkan
XXIV.   In Gandhâra
XXV     In Gandhâra
XXVI.   In Gandhâra
XXVII   In Gandhâra
XXVIII, 1  In Gandhâra
    2. At Barhut


PLATES XXIX-XXX. — THE SIX-TUSKED ELEPHANT .      204

XXIX, 1  At Barhut
    2  At Amarâvatî
XXX, 1  In Gandhâra
    2  At Ajantâ

Page

PLATES XXXI-XLIV. — BUDDHIST ARCHÆOLOGY IN JAVA        270

XXXI, 1    Boro-Budur : General view (*from the north-west*)
      2    —         First Gallery (*part of west façade*)
XXXII      —         Section and plan
XXXIII, 1  —         Silhouette
      2.   —         Staircase (*north side*)
XXXIV, 1   —         Story of Sudhana, no 3   Incantation against the Nâga (*central portion*)
      2    —         Story of Sudhana, no 11  Manoharà's flight
                     *Above*   The Bodhisattva's farewell to the gods.
XXXV, 1.   —         Story of Sudhana, no 12 The Prince's return.
                     *Above* · The Bodhisattva's descent upon earth
      2    —         Story of Sudhana, no 16  At the fountain (*right hand portion*)
XXXVI, 1   —         Story of Mândhâtar, no 12 . The rain of garments
                     *Above* · The Bodhisattva chooses his bride.
      2    —         Story of king Çibi, the Dove and the Hawk
                     *Above*   The first of the Bodhisattva's four promenades.
XXXVII, 1  —         Story of Rudrâyana, no. 6  Presentation of the cuirass (*left-hand portion*)
      2    —         Story of Rudrâyana, no 9 · Mahâkâtyàyana's visit
                     *Above*   The Bodhisattva with his first Brahman teacher
XXXVIII, 1 —         Story of Rudrâyana, no 10 · The nun Çailâ's sermon (*left-hand portion*).
      2.   —         Story of Rudrâyana, no. 11  Queen Candraprabhâ's ordination (*central portion*).
XXXIX.     —         Story of Rudrâyana, fragments of nos. 12, 13 and 14
XL, 1.     —         Story of Rudrâyana, no. 16 · After the parricide.
                     *Above* : The ascetic Bodhisattva declines the aid of the gods
      2    —         Story of Rudrâyana, no 19  The rain of jewels (*left-hand portion*).

Page

XLI, 1  Boro-Budur   Story of the pair of Kinnaras (*central por-
                       tion of the second scene*).

        2      —       Story of Maitrakanyaka, no. 1 : The purse-
                       offering (*central portion*).

XLII, 1        —       Story of Maitrakanyaka, no. 2  The mother's
                       supplication (*left-hand portion*).

        2      —       Story of Maitrakanyaka, no 7 : In the
                       Inferno city (*right-hand portion*).

XLIII, 1  The unfinished statue of Buddha
          *Under the central cupola, Boro-Budur*

        2  Trailokya-vijaya
          *Bronze in the Batavia Museum*

XLIV      The Goddess Cundâ between two Bodhisattvas.
          *On the south western wall of the Chandi Mendut.*


PLATES XLV-L — THE BUDDHIST MADONNA              . 292

XLV.      After a wall-painting from Domoko (Chinese Turkestan).
          1 *Side view before removal*, 2  *As set up in British Museum.*

XLVI.     Suckling Madonna : 1. Romanesque, 2. Coptic.

XLVII     Indo-Greek images of Hâritî

XLVIII, 1  Hâritî and her partner in Gandhâra.

        2  Hâritî in Java

XLIX      Japanese images of Ki-si-mo-jin

   L      Chinese images of Kuan-Yin


*N B — A detailed description of each plate will be found either in the body of the
work or on the* page de garde *opposite the plate.*

# The Beginnings of Buddhist Art.[1]

Buddhism is a historical fact; only it has not yet been completely incorporated into history: sooner or later that will be achieved. Meanwhile its initial period remains, we must confess, passably obscure. To add to our difficulty, the little that we think we know of the social and political state of India in the times of its birth has been learned almost entirely through its medium : thus the frame is no better defined than the picture  But the task, arduous though it may be, is not impossible. The fifth century B. C is not so remote a period that it must always elude archæological research , the interval between the death of Buddha and the first information transmitted to us concerning him is not so considerable that we cannot flatter ourselves with the idea of discerning across it the veritable physionomy of the work, if not — in conformity with the pious, but too tardy wish of later generations — the « actual features » of the worker. This hope is still more confident, and the ambition less audacious, when it is a question of the beginnings of Buddhist art. The appearance of the latter is a relatively late phenomenon, since it presupposes not only the development of the community of monks, but also a certain organization of worship on the part of the laity. If among the productions of this art the sculptures are almost the sole survivors, we have at least preserved to us, notably in the labelled bas-reliefs

(1) *Journal Asiatique*, Jan.-Feb 1911.

1

of Barhut, documents of the very highest rank  Certainly the stones are by no means loquacious : but they
atone for their silence by the unalterableness of a testimony
which could not be suspected of rifacimento or interpolation. Thanks to their marvellous grain, they are to-day as
they were when they left the hands of the image-makers
(*rûpakâraka*) two thousand years ago; and upon this immu-
table foundation we can construct inferences more rigo-
rous than upon the moving sand of the texts. In the ever
restless and changing play of the doctrines we are never
quite certain that the logical sequence of the ideas is exactly parallel to the historical succession of the facts. On the
other side, the routine character of all manual technique
will allow us to detect with certainty, in the still existing
monuments, the material traces of the procedures which
must have been usual earlier . inversely, and by a kind of
proof backwards, the correctness of these postulates will
be verified in that they alone will be found to render a
satisfactory account of the often uncouth character of that
which has been preserved to us  All these reasons seem
to us to justify the task which we have undertaken. In the
assault delivered from various quarters upon the origins
of Buddhism we believe even that the attempt to go
back to the very beginning of its art is, among all the
methods of approach, that which has for the moment the
most chances of success

I

None, indeed, of the monuments known at the present
time, building or sculpture, takes us further back than the
Maurya dynasty Does that mean that art was created entire

in India towards the year 250 before our era, by a decree of
the Emperor Açoka? Of course it would be absurd to
believe this. From the Vedic times Indian civilization had
at its disposal the services not only of the carpenter, the
wheel-wright and the blacksmith, of the potter, the wea-
ver and other fabricators of objects of prime necessity, but
also of those whom we call art-workers, painters, goldsmiths, carvers in wood or ivory. If the texts were not there
to tell us this in words, the evidence of the sole surviving
monuments would be sufficient to establish it. Fergusson has proved once for all that the oldest constructions in
stone, by the servile manner in which they copy the fra-
ming and joining of timber work, testify to the previous
existence of wooden buildings On the other hand — as
we know from a reliable source by means of an explicit
inscription — it was the ivory-workers of Vidiçâ who carved, in the immediate vicinity of their town, one of the
monumental gates of Sânchî Besides, it is obvious that the
finished and well polished bas-reliefs, which for us are the
first in date, represent not by any means the first attempts
of beginners, but the work of sculptors long familiar with
their business and changing their material, but not their
technique. The whole transformation which was accomplished during the third century before our era is limited to
the substitution, in religious and royal foundations, of the
reign of stone for that of wood Unfortunately, there are
no worse conditions, climatic and historical, for the preservation of monuments than those of India. All that was of
wood was condemned beforehand to fall into dust, all, or
nearly all, that was of stone and that the climate might
have spared has been destroyed by the vandalism of man.
Thus is explained why the most ancient remains of Buddhist art are at once so late and so rare. If we leave aside

the great monolithic pillars dear to Açoka, as well as the caves excavated for the benefit of all the religious sects in every place where the geological formation of the rocks lent itself thereto, we find on the ground level, and pending more systematic excavations, scarcely anything to mention, except the debris of the balustrades of Bodh-Gayâ and of Barhut, and the four gates of Sânchî The mention of the kings Brahmamitra and Indramitra, inscribed on the first, on the second that of the dynasty of the Çungas, and on one of the last that of the reign of Sâtakani suffice to date them generally, but with certainty, as belonging to the second, or first, century before our era It is doubtless to the same epoch, if we may judge by the style, that we must refer the oldest fragments of the balustrades exhumed both at Amarâvatî and at Mathurâ. If to these few stray remnants of sculptures we add the remains of the most archaic paintings of Ajantâ, we shall very soon have finished compiling the catalogue of what may be styled — in opposition to the later school, of the north-west frontier, much more penetrated by foreign influences — the native school of Central India

Let us go straight to the most striking feature of this old Buddhist school. Although well known to specialists, it will not fail to surprise uninformed readers. When we find the ancient stone-carvers of India in full activity, we observe that they are very industriously engaged in carrying out the strange undertaking of representing the life of Buddha without Buddha We have here a fact which, improbable as it may seem, Cunningham long ago demonstrated. It is established on the written testimony of the artists themselves. Those of Barhut inform us by an inscription, that such and such a person on his knees before a throne « is rendering homage to the Blessed One ». Now, without exception, the throne is vacant; at the most, there is a symbol indicating the invisible presence of Buddha ([1]). The latest researches have only opened our eyes to the extent of the field of application of this constant rule, it holds good for the years which preceded as also for those which followed the *Sambodhi*, for the youth as also for the old age of the Master The façade of the middle lintel of the eastern gate of Sânchî illustrates his departure on horseback from his house : the embroidered rug which serves as a saddle for his steed is empty ([2]). A medallion of Bodh-Gayâ represents his first meditation : empty again is the seat before which the traditional ploughman is driving his plough ([3]) Some panels of Amarâvatî show us his birth and presentation to the sage Asita, only his footprints — a direct ideographic transcription of the formula which was in use in India to designate respectfully a « person » — mark the swaddling clothes on which in one place the gods, in another the old *rishi* are reputed to have received him into their arms ([4]). These selected examples suffice to demonstrate that the ancient Indian sculptors abstained absolutely from representing either Bodhisattva or Buddha in the course of his last earthy existence ([5]). Such is the abnormal, but indisputable fact of which every history of Buddhist art will have at the outset to render account

---

(1) A CUNNINGHAM, *Stûpa of Barhut*, pl XIII-XVII.

(2) See below, pp 75 and 105, cf pl X, 1.

(3) *Art greco-bouddhique du Gandhâra*, fig. 177 and p 345

(4) See on the staircase of the British Museum, nᵒˢ 44 and 48, or FERGUSSON, *Tree and Serpent Worship*, pl. XCI, 4, and LXI, 2

(5) Let us add, in order to be quite correct, « at least under his human form », for we know that a bas-relief at Barhut represents the Blessed One descending into the bosom of his mother in the form of an elephant (cf. below, p 20)

As far as we know, no perfectly satisfactory explanation of this fact has until now been given. First of all we tried to dispose of the matter more or less by the supposition, as evasive as gratuitous, that the ancient school had either not desired or had not been able to figure the Blessed One; neither of these two reasons appears to us to have the least value in proof. Shall we speak of incapacity? Assuredly, one can see that the concrete realization of the image of the « perfect Buddha » was not an easy task . and the difficulty could not but increase with the years, in proportion as the time of the Master grew more distant and his features faded more and more into the mists of the past Nevertheless, we must not form too poor an opinion of the talent of the old image-makers, and the argument becomes moreover quite worthless, when one attempts to apply it to the youth of Buddha. What was he, in fact, up to the time of his flight from his native town, but a « royal heir apparent »? Now the type of *râja-kumâra*, or crown-prince, is common on the gates of Sânchî, as also on the balustrade of Barhut (¹), what material hindrance was there to their making use of it to represent the Bodhisattva? It is clear that they could have done so, and yet they carefully abstained from doing so. Shall we fall back, then, upon the other branch of the dilemma and say that they did not dare? Assuredly the gravest members of the order must long have held to the letter the stern saying that « the master gone, the law remains (²) », and we are quite willing to believe that the law alone was of import for them The reverend Nâgasena still teaches king Menander that henceforth the

(1) See CUNNINGHAM, *Stûpa of Barhut*, pl XXV, 4 (*Mûgapakkha-jâtaka*, n° 538 cf *infra*, p 56 and pl V, 6) and p vi (mention of the *Viçvantara-jâtaka*), north gate of Sânchî, lower lintel (Viçvantara), etc
(2) *Mahâparinibbâna-sutta*, VI, 1.

Blessed One is no longer visible except in the form of the
*dharmakâya*('), of the « body of the doctrine », but of any
express prohibition of images we have in the texts no
knowledge Since when, moreover, and in what country
does popular devotion trouble itself about the dogmatic
scruples of the doctors ? Certainly it was not so in ancient
India for otherwise we could not at all understand the
enthusiasm with which the valley of the Ganges and the
rest of the peninsula welcomed the Indo-Greek type of
Buddha From Mathurâ to Bodh-Gayâ, and from Çrâvastî
to Amarâvatî, we see it installed in triumph on the circumference of the *stûpas* as in the interior of the temples. So
rapid a conquest is a sufficient proof that the objections of
conscience, if any such existed, were far from being insur-
mountable.

But, it will be said, if it is true that the ancient Indian
image-makers asked for nothing better than to represent
the Blessed One, and that, on the other hand, they were
capable of it, why then have they so carefully abstained ?
To this we see but one reply, in appearance, we must confess,
simple-minded enough, but one which, in India, is
still sufficient for all : « If they did not do it, it was because
it was not the custom to do it ». And, no doubt, it would
be easy to retort : « But you confine yourself to putting off
the question, if it does not arise with regard to the sculptors
whose works we possess, it still holds good entirely
with regard to their predecessors.. » — Certainly, and far
from contradicting, that is just the point at which we
wished to arrive. We hold that this monstrous abstention,
such as we observe on the monuments of Barhut and
Sânchî, remains perfectly incomprehensible, unless we

(1) *Milindapanha*, ed TRENCKNER, p 73, trans RHYS DAVIDS, p. 113.

enquire into the traditional habits which it supposes and
which, for that very reason, it is capable of revealing to
us. Like certain anomalies in animal species, it can only
be explained as an inheritance from a nearly obsolete past, which this survival helps us to reconstitute. In
other words, it is vain for us to seek a solution of the
problem in the few relatively late specimens at present
known to us, it is to the anterior history, to what is
still the prehistoric period of Buddhist art that we must
go to discover it. To such a typical case of artistic tera-
tology it is the evolutionist method of embryology that
it is proper to apply.


II


To begin, we have the best reasons for thinking
that the habit of adoring human images, and even the art
of fabricating them, were still less general in the India of the
Brahmans before Alexander than in the Gaul of the Druids
before the time of Cæsar. Certainly this absence of idolatry properly so-called did not in any way exclude the existence of more rudimentary forms of fetichism ( ) · nevertheless, the fact remains that Buddhism did not develope,
like Christianity, in a world long infected by the worship
of images and prompt to contaminate it in its turn. Not

(1) We allude to the golden *purusha* which formed a part of the altar of
sacrifice (*Çat.-Brahm* , 7, 4, 1., 15) and to the effigy *krtya* of the magic
rites (*Ath Veda*, X, 1), etc. — For what is to be understood by the Gallic
*simulacra* of Cæsar (*Bell Gall* , VI, 4), see the article of M S REINACH
on *L'art plastique en Gaule et le druidisme* (*Revue Celtique*, t XIII, 1892,
pp 190 sqq .), where are cited also corresponding testimonies of Hero-
dotus (I, 131) and Tacitus (*Germ* , IX) as to the non-existence of idolatry
among the Persians and the Germans

only did the first century already know symbolical or allegorical representations of Christ ; but from the second century we meet with his portrait on the paintings of the catacombs ([1]). When that of Buddha makes its appearance in India, the religion which he had founded was already four hundred years old : even so it had required the contact of the civilisation, and the influence of the art, of Hellenism. On the other hand, Buddhism was not born, like Islam, in an environment beforehand and deliberately hostile to idolatry. We do not find that the Vedic texts breathe a word about it, either for or against : and their silence is explained precisely by the fact that the idea of it had not even presented itself to the Indian mind. As soon as the time for it shall have come, the grammarians will not fail to mention in the employment of the learned language the mode of designating the new fact of the Brahmanic idols ([2]). Likewise, when the question of the images of the Master presents itself to the faithful Buddhists, their writings will supply explicitly the opportune solutions, and if these successive solutions are, moreover, contradictory, it is simply that in the interval the needs of the religious conscience have changed at the same time as the conditions of artistic production. But, as far as concerns the most ancient period with which we have to deal, investigations into the literature have remained from an iconographical point of view as sterile as the researches on the spot. For the moment the history of religious art in India, previous to Buddhism, is,

---

(1) M. BESNIER, *Les Catacombes de Rome*, Paris, 1909, pp 204, 208, 223-224.

(2) Cf *Scholia to Pânini*, V, 3, 99, excellently discussed by Prof Sten KONOW in his interesting *Note on the use of images in ancient India* (Ind Ant , 1909) but they have no value as proof for the pre-Mauryan epoch with which we are here concerned.

whether it must remain so or not, philologically a blank page, archæologically an empty show-case.

That in Buddhism, as in all religions, art is at first only a simple manifestation of worship, every one will willingly admit. The only question is to know what branch of Buddhist worship has supplied this special excrescence with an opportunity for its production. It is evidently not in the periodical reunions of the monks that we shall find the smallest decorative pretext  The veneration shown to the mortal remains of the Blessed One explains the leading role of the funeral tumulus in Buddhist architecture. It will not escape us that it is still the same veneration which, thus advantaged, has offered in the obligatory surroundings of those reliquary monuments the natural support to the sculptures, the sole destination of which for a long time was to decorate the balustrades of the *stûpas*. We might even suspect a mark of its influence in the almost entirely biographical character that this decoration has assumed, just as, by the rite of circumambulation, it has fixed the direction in which the scenes must succeed one another and be read. But, beyond this general orientation, we discover at the basis of this kind of devotion nothing that could have determined the mode of compositon of the bas-reliefs. There remains the third and last ancient form of Buddhist worship, that which Buddha himself is supposed to have taught on his death bed to his well-loved disciple, « There are four places, O Ânanda, which an honorable worshipper should visit with religious emotion. What are these four? »... They are, as we know, those where the Predestined One for the first time received illumination and preached and those where for the last time he was born and died ([1]). Now

(1) *Mahâparinibbâna-suta*, V, 16-22

just in this devout practice of the four great pilgrimages resides any hope which we have of at last coming upon the long-sought point of departure. In order that we may grasp at once the germ and the directing principle of Buddhist art, it is necessary and sufficient to admit that the Indian pilgrims were pleased to bring back from these four holy places a small material souvenir of what they had there seen

We can scarcely believe that the reader will refuse to grant us this small postulate. Can he be so ignorant of the outer world that he does not know the universal empire of the mania, innocent in itself, for souvenirs of travels? The innumerable manufacturers and shopkeepers who everywhere live by it would quickly demonstrate it to him. Has he never in the course of his migrations, whatever may have been the object or the cause of them, bought curios, collected photographs, or sent away picture post-cards? These are only the latest modes and a profane extension of an immemorial and sacred custom If he doubts this, let him lean, for example, over one of the cases at the Cluny Museum (¹) which contain the emblematic metal insignia of all the great pilgrimages of the Middle Ages, as they have been fished out of the Seine in Paris. Mediæval India has also left by hundreds evidences of this custom Most frequently they are simple clay balls, moulded or stamped with a seal, and without doubt within the reach of all pockets, which served at the same time as *memento* and as *ex-voto*. They are to be picked up nowadays on all Buddhist sites, even

---

(1) Unless it is more convenient for him to try the same experiment at the British Museum, where a case in the *Mediæval Room* also contains a collection of these *signacula*.

in the peninsula of Malacca and in Annam ('). Do we compromise ourselves very much by conjecturing that these sacred emblems are in Buddhism the remains of a tradition which goes back to the four great primitive pilgrimages? The worst that could result from it would be that Buddhist art must have owed its origin to the satisfaction of a need everywhere and always experienced, and, we may almost say, of one of the religious instincts of humanity It would be difficult to imagine a theory more humble and more prosaic : it is in our opinion only the more probable for that, nor do we see what other we can substitute, if, at least, we are unwilling to attribute to that art any but a rational origin

In fact, this point once gained, all the rest follows. Nothing is more easy than to guess what must have been the souvenirs brought back by the pilgrims from the four great holy places To take the modern example most familiar to the French reader, what is represented by the images or medals offered for sale and bought at Lourdes? First and foremost the miraculous grotto. What must have been represented on stuffs, on clay, wood, ivory, or metal by the first objects of piety manufactured at Kapilavastu, at Bodh-Gayâ, at Benares, or at Kuçinagara? Evidently the characteristic point towards which, at the approach of each of these four towns, popular devotion was directed. Now we know these points already from the picturesque expressions of the texts. What was first visited at Kuçinagara was the site, very soon and quite appropriately marked by

---

(1) For specimens from India, see CUNNINGHAM, *Mahâbodhi*, pl XXIV; J R A S , 1900, p 432, etc , from Burmah, *Archæol Survey of India, Annual Feport*, 1905-1906, pl LIII, from Malacca, *Bull de la Commission Archeologique de l'Indo Chine*, 1909, p 232, from Annam, B E. F E·O , 1901, p 25, etc.

a *stûpa* ('), of the last death of the Master In the same way, the essential miracle of Benares having taken place at the « Mṛiga-dâva », the Gazelle-park, it was inevitable that its consecrated description as « putting the wheel of the law in motion » should be translated in concrete terms by a wheel, usually accompanied by two gazelles. What was contemplated at Bodh-Gayâ, on the other hand, was the evergreen fig-tree, at the foot of which the Blessed One had sat to attain omniscience Finally, what would be worshipped at Kapilavastu ? Here the answer is less certain : undoubtedly the great local attraction consisted in the recollection of the nativity of Buddha , but, without mentioning his paternal home, the most ardent zeal might hesitate between the place of his material birth and that of his spiritual renaissance, between the park of Lumbinî, where he issued from the right side of his mother, and the no less famous gate, through which he escaped from the miserable pleasures of the world Whatever might in this case be the difficulty of choice, with regard to the three other sites at least no hesitation was possible. A tree, a wheel, a *stûpa*, these suffice to recall to our memory the spectacle of those holy places, or even, by a constant association of ideas and images, to evoke the miracles of which they had been the theatre. Again, these things could be indicated as summarily as one could wish : if human weakness cannot dispense with the material sign, imagination makes up for the poverty of artistic means.

---

(1) « A Stûpa of Açoka », says Hiuan-tsang , that is, of archaic form , cf also Fa-hian ( BEAL, *Records*, I, p LII, and II, p 32)

## III

Such is the sole part which hypothesis plays in our theory. The whole subsequent development of Buddhist art flows logically from these premises; and henceforth there are none of the still surviving documents which do not successively corroborate the various stages of its evolution The oldest monuments which have come down to us from Indian antiquity are a few rectangular coins of copper or silver. Now it is very remarkable that, among the symbols with which they are punch-marked, the tree, the wheel and the *stûpa* play a considerable, and indeed, on many of them, a predominant part ([1]). Thanks to the chance of their discovery, the existence of the *signacula,* which we imagined to have been made for the use of pilgrims, ceases to be, for as far back as we can go, a pure conjecture (see pl I, B, C, D) Better still, we can clearly discern in the infantile simplicity of these emblems the style of the most ancient manifestations of the religious art of the Buddhists. They are, properly speaking, less images than hieroglyphics endowed for the initiated with a conventional value : and, at the same time, we succeed in explaining to ourselves what we have already more than once had occasion to note, that is, the abstract and *quasi* algebraical character of this art at its commencement ([2]) Moreover, we easily conceive that, in consequence of being conveyed beyond the great centres of pil-

---

([1]) To quote only the latest study, cf. D. B. Spooner, *A new find of punch-marked coins,* in *Arch Survey of India, Annual Report 1905-1906,* 1909, p. 150 According to the excellent analysis which Dr Spooner has given of this discovery, out of 61 coins 22 bear all three symbols at once and 22 others associate the two last together

([2]) Cf for instance, *Art greco-bouddhique du Gandhâra,* p. 608

grimage, artistic emblems of this sort may have seen
their initial signification modified. They came, by degrees,
to be regarded less as mementos of sacred spots than as
figurative representations of miracles, the memory of which
was connected with those places  In other words, in proportion as they were propagated further and further from
their place of origin, their topographical and local character
diminished more and more, to the advantage of their symbolical and universal value, until they ended by becoming
the common patrimony of the image-makers and being
fabricated everywhere without distinction where a Buddhist
donor ordered them. It is just this state of diffusion and
subsequent generalisation that is proved to us even in the
IV[th] century by the banality and dispersion of the so-called « Buddhist » coins.

But we must hasten, in this rapid sketch, to come to the
monuments whose Buddhist character can no longer be
disputed  We know what impulse was towards the middle
of the third century given by the imperial zeal of Açoka
to the religious foundations of the sect  It is, therefore, only
the more curious to observe how, even a hundred years after
him, the school of Central India continues to follow faithfully in the beaten track of the past. From this point of view,
the four gates of Sânchî, which we have had the good fortune
to retain almost intact, may furnish a fairly safe criterion of
the degree of persistence of the ancient usages. Now Fergusson long ago remarked there the extreme frequency of
what he called « the worship » of the tree, the *stûpa* and
the wheel. According to statistics hardly open to suspicion,
since they were drawn up in support of theories quite different from ours, the first emblem is repeated no less than
67 times, the second 32 times ; and if the last does not
reappear more that 6 times, this number suffices, never-

theless, to assure it the third place in the order of importance of the subjects([1]). We have not, of course, to follow
Fergusson in the strange anthropological speculations
which he has engrafted on to these observations. All that
we should be tempted at first to read in his table would
be the preponderance of the miracle of the *Sambodhi*, or of
the *Parinirvâna*, over that of the *Dharmacakra-pravartana*.
In reality the larger number of the first two symbols de-
pends upon another cause. The artists proceeded to apply
to the Buddhas of the past the formulas which had
at first served for the Buddha of our age. People
were pleased to level all the seven by representing them
at one time by their funeral tumulus, at another, and
much more frequently, by their empty throne under
their Tree of Knowledge ([2]) . the wheel alone had remained the special apanage of our Çâkya-muni, and consequently was repeated only at rarer intervals But these
are only subsidiary details, taking these figures all together,
their imposing total testifies loudly enough to the constant repetition in traditional form of what we know, from
the evidence of the coins, to have been the first attempts
at Buddhist art. Being forced to cover the relatively
extensive surfaces placed at their disposal, the sculptors of

---

(1) Cf FERGUSSON, *Tree and Serpent-Worship*, 2nd edition, 1873, pp 105
and 242 Here is the table, in which he has included the data of the sole
gate of one of the small neighbouring *stûpas*

|  |  | Tree, | Stûpa, | Wheel |
|---|---|---|---|---|
| Great *Stûpa*. | South Gate | 16 | 5 | 1 |
|  | North Gate | 19 | 8 | 2 |
|  | East Gate | 17 | 9 | 1 |
|  | West Gate | 15 | 10 | 2 |
| Small *Stûpa* | Only Gate | 9 | 6 | 4 |

(2) See below, *Eastern Gate of Sânchî*, pp 72 and 104 The decisive reason
for the predominance of the inspired compositions of the type of the *Sambodhi* over all the others will be given a little further on, p 19

Sânchî evidently commenced by re-editing profusely, right in the middle of the second century before our era, the summary and hieroglyphic compositions which they had inherited from their direct predecessors, the makers of religious objects in the fifth century (see pl. II)

## IV

This is a first and certainly very important, but purely material, verification of our hypothesis. There are proofs more subtle than the proof of statistics, which open up deeper views of the development of the ancient Buddhist school. The years have passed, technical skill has increased, the iconographic types of gods and genii have been formed, the gift of observation and a sense of the picturesque have awakened in it . but it remains nevertheless, as regards the capital point of the figuration of Buddha, the docile captive of custom. Around the old themes of the studios, it embroiders, it is true, some variations · it embellishes the *stûpas,* surrounds the wheels with wreaths, or, careless of the anachronism, gives beforehand to the tree of the *Sambodhi* the curious stone surround which, more than two and a half centuries after the miracle, it owed to the piety of Açoka ([1]); but for all that it does not go beyond the ancient formulas. Weary of eternally repeating the sacred miracles, does it risk treating some still unpublished episode? The idea of taking advantage of this, in order to break free from routine, never occurs to it It cannot but know that its business is no longer to supply pilgrims with a memento of what they had seen with their own eyes in the course of their visits to the sacred places;

---

([1]) See below, *Eastern Gate of Sânchî,* p  102

it is fully conscious that what it has now to do is to illustrate on a permanent monument the biography of Buddha, but it appears hardly to grasp clearly the fact that for this new purpose the old procedures, formerly perfectly appropriate to their object, are no longer suitable. Evidently, it was too late to rebel and to shake off the yoke of an artistic tradition which had ere long been strengthened by religious legends, at least it is about this same time that the texts, until then silent on the question, suddenly decide to proclaim — with an excessive precipitation to be contradicted soon after by posterity — the previous incapacity of the artists to portray during his lifetime the ineffable lineaments of the Blessed One ('). And how otherwise, in fact, explain the persistent absence of his image, whilst so many of the popular divinities were paraded on the pillars of Barhut and Sânchî ?

Henceforward there is only one way, in conformity with the living reality, of conceiving the study of the ancient Indian school. Its history is that of a struggle, more or less surreptitious, between the two tendencies which divided it against itself, an irrepressible desire for new scenes and a superstitious respect for its precedents. On the one hand, it experiences a growing need for the form of Buddha to serve as a centre or pivot for the scenes of his life, and on the other hand, it accepts as an axiom that, in order to represent the Blessed One, it suffices to do what until then had always been done, that is, to evoke him by the sight of one of his three speaking emblems. Watch it at work. The tumulus of the *Parinirvâna*, the ultimate end of the career of the Master, was *ipso facto* beside the point, when it was a question of representing some incident in that career. The

---

(1) *Divyâvadâna*, p 547

symbol of the wheel, specialized in the representation of the
« First Preaching », could scarcely be employed again,
except on the occasion of the similar miracle wrought at
Çrâvastî for the greater confusion of the rival sects ([1]).
There remained for ordinary employment in miracles of
the second rank the heraldic emblem already utilized for the
*Sambodhi*. And, in fact, we can well see how the studios of
Central India resign themselves once for all to this procedure and accommodate themselves more or less success-
fully thereto. All the same, they cannot resist slipping in
here and there a few variants, or even trying on occasions
some different course. It is under an empty throne, surmounted by a tree, that at Barhut Buddha receives the
visit of the *nâga* Elâpatra, when he preaches in the heaven
of the Thirty-three Gods, the motif is in addition graced
with a parasol; and this latter, in its turn, takes the place
of the tree on the occasion of the visit of Indra or Ajâtaçatru. At times the throne by itself does the work. In two
cases, on the eastern gate of Sânchî, the school even ventures
so far as to avail itself solely of the « promenade »,
or *cankrama*, of the Master in order to suggest his presence ([2]). But the boldness of its innovations goes no
further, and we very quickly reach the limits of its audacity. We have indeed sketched them above (pp. 4-5), and
it would have been superfluous to return to the matter,
did we not now believe that we have divined the *raison d'être*,
and actually the manner of production, of the strange anomalies which at the beginning of this study we had to
confine ourselves to stating.

    We have, likewise, explained above how — and now we

---

(1) See below, Essay VI

(2) Cf CUNNINGHAM, *Stûpa of Barhut*, pl XIV, 3, XVI, 3, XVII, 1;
XXVIII, 4 etc , and below, *Eastern Gate of Sânchî*, pp. 93 and 100

understand why — the artists came into collision with the impassable barrier of ancient usages, when they had to represent the form of the Predestined One in the course of the first twenty-nine years of his life, at the time when his princely surroundings still hid under a mundane cloak the Buddha about to appear. In truth, we were not able as yet (p. 13) to determine exactly, by the aid of the texts, which episode of his youth the faithful had chosen as the principal object of commemoration, nor in what manner the old image-makers must have set to work to commemorate it It is curious to note that the sculptors of the second century shared our perplexities in this regard. Those of Barhut adopted the precise moment when the Bodhisattva descended into the bosom of his mother, when, at least, the latter dreamed that he descended there in the form of a little elephant (¹) Those of Sânchî do not represent the Conception, save incidentally; on the other hand, they complacently detail all the circumstances of the prince's entry into religion, that is, of his flight on horseback from his native town : they portray the gate of the town and several times the horse, the groom and the Gods. they leave to be understood only the hero of this Hegira (²). As to those of Amarâvatî, on the stelæ where they have set one above another the four grand miracles, they employ indifferently, in order to fill the panel reserved for Kapilavastu, — side by side with the tree of Bodh-Gayâ, the wheel of Benares and the *stûpa* of Kuçinagara (see pl. II, 2) — now the same « great abandonment of home », where we see nothing but the horse passing under the gateway, now a « nati-

---

(1) CUNNINGHAM, *Stûpa of Barhut*, pl XXVIII, 2
(2) See below *Eastern Gate of Sânchi*, pl 75 and p 105 (cf pl X, 1)

vity », where we see only the mother, to the exclusion of the new-born child ('). Which of these three compositions (see pl. III) is the most archaic and best preserves for us the aspect of the « souvenirs » which the pilgrims of the fifth century were already able to purchase at Kapilavastu? This is a question which we at present find very difficult to answer If, again, on this point we confide ourselve to the numismatic documents, they will persuade us that from the beginning a certain wavering manifested itself in the choice of the artists and the faithful. Most of the Buddhist coins devote two abbreviations, instead of one, to the Nativity alone, at least, of the five usually associated symbols, the lotus, the bull, the tree, the wheel and the tumulus, the two first must correspond simultaneously to the first of the four great miracles. Apparently, the lotus recalled those which had sprung up spontaneously under the seven first steps of the Master, whilst the bull, almost always flanked by his zodiacal emblem, incarnated the traditional date of the birth, the day of the full moon of the month Vaiçâkha (see pl. I, A). On other occasions, but more rarely, the bull is replaced by an elephant, a plastic reminder of the Conception (²). It may be

(1) FERGUSSON, *Tree and Serpent-Worship*, pl XCIII-XCVIII. With regard to this we may note that much later stelæ of Benares continue to groupe in the scheme of Kapilavastu the birth (with or without the conception, the seven steps, or the bath) and the great departure (see pl IV, 3 A and cf *Anc. Mon Ind.*, pl 67-68, etc )

(2) Cf the tables of D B. SPOONER, *loc. cit*, pp 156-157 As for the above mentioned interpretations of the lotus and the bull, we, for our part, give them as simple conjectures In any case, we may at this point observe that in later Buddhism the lotus has retained the symbolical signification of « miraculous birth », and that the bull appears again with its astronomical value on one of the best-known bas-reliefs of the Lahore Museum (cf A. GRUNWEDEL, *Buddhistische Kunst in Indien*, 2d ed., p. 121, or *Buddhist Art in India*, p. 129). The lamented Dʳ Th. Bloch in one of his last

also, although we possess no concrete proof of this, that the gate through which the Bodhisattva had been cast by his vocation out of the world may, at an early date, have found copiers and amateurs. But these are merely accessory questions   what is important here is that only the traditional avoidance of images, inherited from the humble pioneers of former days, can give us the key to the later improbable compositions, child-births without children, rides without riders

V

This is not all  The sculptors of the second century verify our hypothesis not only in what they reproduce and in what they imitate of the works of the past : we may maintain that they do this, also, indirectly, in what they innovate. However unreflecting and mechanical their submission to custom may have been, the forced absence of the protagonist from the scenes of his own biography could not help but inconvenience them considerably. Let the career of the Blessed One be no more than a monotonous tissue of conversations more full of edification than movement, yet only a small number of episodes allowed of being portrayed independently of the principal personage. With the aid of what subjects were the artists to cover the numerous medallions, the long stretches, or the high gates of the *stûpa* balustrades? The first expedient of which they

articles (Z D M G 1908, vol LXII, pp 648 and sqq ) thought he recognised in a defective photograph of this bull with the hanging tongue the image of a wild boar, and he built up a whole theory on this mistake · it suffices to refer the reader anxious to clear up this matter with his own eyes to BURGESS, *Anc Mon. Ind* , p  127

bethought themselves was to turn to the previous
existences of the Master, at the time when under all animal
forms, and later under all social conditions, he was quali-
fying by means of perfections for the final attainment of the
Bodhi. Thereby we explain why the sculptors of Barhut
preferred to dip into this treasure of tales and fables (¹)
In treating this new matter they were no longer trammel-
led, as when illustrating the last life of the Master, by a
custom which had been elevated into a law. Accordingly
they have no scruples in representing the Bodhisattva in
each scene, and it is with a perfect liberty of mind that,
at the time of his penultimate terrestial existence, they give
to Viçvantara the features which they so jealously abstained
from lending to Siddhârtha (cf. above, p. 6). Representations of *jâtakas* are far from being unknown at Sânchî but
the decorators of the gates had recourse once again to another stratagem in order to slip between the links of tradition. It goes without saying that in all the scenes posterior
to the *Parinirvâna* the absence of the figure of the Blessed
One became perfectly justified and at the same time ceased
to be an inconvenience to the artist Thus, they soon took
pleasure in cultivating this part of the Buddhist legend.
According to all probability they began by illustrating the
famous « war of relics », which the death of the Blessed One
nearly precipitated. Encouraged, apparently, by this trial,
they did not fear to attack even the cycle of Açoka and to
represent at one time his useless pilgrimage to the *stûpa* at
Râmagrâma, and at another his solemn visit to the tree of
the *Sambodhi* (²). Thus, under the pressing incentive of
necessity, the native school, incapable of openly shaking

---

(1) See below, *Representation of Jâtakas on the Bas-reliefs of Barhut* (Essay II)
(2) See below, *Eastern Gate of Sânchî*, pp. 78 79 and 108 109

off its slavery, had artificially created for itself a double means of escape, in the legends previous to the last renaissance or posterior to the final death of Buddha. For our part, we do not doubt that, if it had continued to develop normally and according to its own rules, we should have seen the number of these sham historical pictures or these illustrations of popular stories increase at the expense of the old fund of pious images.

It is no longer a secret to anyone that the regular sweep of this evolution was brusquely interrupted by a veritable artistic cataclysm. The Hellenized sculptors of the north-west, strangers to the native tradition of Central India, satisfied to the full, and even outwent, the wishes of their Buddhist patrons by creating for their use the Indo-Greek type of Buddha Immediately their colleagues of the low country, seduced by this wonderful innovation, greeted with no less enthusiasm than the laity the rupture of the magic charm which had weighed so heavily and so long upon the ancient Buddhist school We have already remarked upon the fact of the rapid diffusion of the new type (p  7) : it is now clear to us that its adoption did not come into direct collision with any dogmatic prejudice Always docile interpreters of current ideas, the texts set themselves henceforth to guarantee, by the aid of apocryphal traditions or an abundance of miracles, the authentic ressemblance of those portraits whose possibility they were a moment ago denying ([1]). The reason is

---

(1) By apocryphal traditions we mean those relative to the statue of sandal wood, carved even during the life-time of Buddha and attributed by
Fa-hian (trans LEGGE, p  56) to Prasenajit of Çrâvastî, and by Hiuan-tsang
(trans Stan JULIEN, I, pp 283 and 296) to Udayana of Kauçâmbî, whose
example had only been imitated by Prasenajit (cf BEAL, *Records*, I, p  XLIV
and 235, II, p  4) As regards the miracles, see those which are related to us

that, in reality, the new mode (see pl IV) did not expressly infringe any ritualistic prohibition it did nothing but overthrow the artistic procedures of composition, and the bonds which fell were of a purely technical kind. We have seen clearly enough how the image-makers of the basin of the Ganges had slowly suffered the spider's web of custom to weave itself around them, and how, not daring to tear it apart, they had already endeavoured to free themselves from it. Under the stroke of the revelation which came to them from Gandhâra their emancipation was as sudden as it was complete : but even through this unexpected development we are prepared to follow up the test to which we have submitted our theory and from which it seems to us to have so far issued with honour.

The history of the ancient régime in Buddhist art prior to the Gandhârian revolution may, in fact, be summed up somewhat as follows. We have every reason to suppose that there was, first, from the fifth century onwards, local production at the four great centres of pilgrimage, and conveyance into the interior of India, of rude delineations copying the « sacred vestiges » actually still visible above ground in the sites of the miracles. It was these naturally unpeopled tableaux which, thanks to time and distance, ended by being regarded as systematic representations of the four principal episodes in the life of the Blessed One, and which, joined to some routine variations composed in accordance with the same formula, served, before as well as after Açoka (middle of the third century B. C.), for the decoration of religious foundations ; finally, on the monuments of the second century (still before our era)

concerning the image of the temple of Mahâbodhi by Hiuan-tsang (trans Stan. JULIEN, I, p. 465; BEAL, II, p 120) and Târanâtha (trans SCHIEFNER, p 20) we remark already tentatives towards freedom from the tyranny of the ancient customs by recourse to subjects previous or subsequent to the last existence of Buddha. However, the school of the north-west comes on the scene. By reason of the very fact that it has been almost entirely removed from these traditional influences, it must, in our system, present characteristic signs quite different from those of the ancient school. Now, the conclusions of an extensive study which we have long dedicated to the Greco-buddhist bas-reliefs, seem to have conspired in favouring, point for point, the reverse of the preceding propositions. What we have observed at Gandhâra is, first, the almost total disappearance of legendary scenes later than the cycle of the *Parinirvâna*, as also a marked diminution in the number of *jâtakas*, in the second place, there is an indefinite multiplication of episodes borrowed from the youth or the teaching career of the Master, whose corporeal image occupies now the centre of all the compositions; finally and correspondingly, there is an extreme rarity of symbolical representations ([1]). In any case — and this is our concluding argument — the old emblems do not disappear completely. Not only at Gandhâra, but even on the latest productions of mediæval India, not to mention the Lamaist images of the present day, these survivals of a former age continue to manifest themselves. If the *stûpa* is regarded as having on nearly all the new representations of the *Parinirvâna* become superfluous, the Tree of Knowledge never fails to rear itself behind the Buddha of the *Sambodhi*, whilst the wheel between the two gazelles, either back to back or face to face, continues to mark the throne of his First Preaching (see pl. VI, 2). And thus

---

(1) Cf *Art gréco bouddhique du Gandhâra*, pp 266, 270, 427 etc.

the decline of Buddhist art is linked to its most distant *visible* origins, the only ones (need we specify?), which have been taken into consideration here (¹).

Such, at least, is the theory which we could not refrain from submitting to the appreciation of Indianists. Taken altogether, it is only an attempt at synthesis, an effort first to coordinate logically, then to organize in accordance with the laws of an historical development, a series of facts already known. In this sense there is not one Buddhist archæologist, commencing with Fergusson and Cunningham, who has not contributed to it, and it may be found more or less devoid of originality. Our whole ambition would be precisely that it should give, when read, the impression of being already public property. That would be the best of symptoms, for none is better adapted to produce a belief that — except for the retouches which the progress of research will inevitably give to it — it is destined to endure

---

(1) Cf *Art greco-bouddhique*, figg 208 and 209 and *Iconographie bouddhique de l'Inde*, figg 29 et 30 : the latter is a representation of the *Parinirvâna*, still surmounted by a *stûpa*.

PLATE I

Cf. pp 14, 21

The elements of this plate have been obligingly-sketched by M Lemoine, Professor of Drawing at the Lycée at Quimper, from the following publications . A. Cunningham, *Coins of Ancient India* (London, 1891), Vincent Smith, *Catalogue of the Coins in the Indian Museum, Calcutta* (Oxford, 1906), D. B Spooner, *A new find of punch-marked coins* (in *Arch Surv of India, Annual Report, 1905 6*, pp 150 sqq ) cited respectively as C., Sm , Sp

A 1 (C , pl XI, 2, 4); 2 (C , pl I, 1, 5, 6), 3 (Sp , pl LIV *a,* 3, 14); 4 (Sm , pl XIX, 13) · variants of the lotus, the symbol of the miraculous birth of the Bodhisattva. The most characteristic form, with eight petals, is found on the coins of Erân (no 1) : we give here in addition two fantastic, but current, forms — composed of three parasols and of three « taurine» or *nandi-padas,* framed (no 2), or not (no 3) in petals — and one quite stereotyped form (no 4)

5 (C , pl I, 23 or pl II, 8 etc ), 6 (Sm., pl. XX, 8), 7 (C , pl. II, 20); 8 (Sm , pl XIX, 15, etc.) : variants of the « taurine » or *nandi-pada* symbol, denoting the zodiacal sign Taurus, the Bull (Skt *Tâvura*), which, during the month of Vaiçâkha (April-May), presided over the Nativity of the Bodhisattva. The most simple form, and the starting-point of the development, is composed of a point surmounted by a crescent (no 5) In the most elaborate form a *vardhamâna,* a *triçûla,* or even a *triratna* have in turn been detected : we do not perceive any reason why in becoming more complicated it should have changed its name and signification

9 (C , pl. III, 2), 10 (C , pl I, 26), 11 (C , pl. III, 3) , 12 (C , pl III, 2) from the Buddhist point of view these four sacred animals typify respectively, the elephant the Conception, the bull the (date of the) Nativity, the horse the Great Departure, and the lion, generally, the « lion among the Çâkyas » (*Çâkya-simha,* that is Çâkya-muni)

B 1 (C , pl I, 1), 2 (Sm , pl XIX, 11), 3 (C , pl II, 7 8); 4 (Sm pl XX, 5) variants of the tree of the Perfect Illumination (*Sambodhi*) Nos 1 and 2 present fairly well the form of the leaf of the *açvattha,* or *ficus religiosa* ; the foot of the tree is always surrounded by a railing

C. 1 (Sm , pl XIX, 1, etc ); 2 (C., pl. III, 13) variants of the Wheel of the Law (*Dharmacakra*) On no 2 it is surrounded by small parasols

D 1 (C , pl. 1, 4, 5), 2 (Sp , pl. LIV *b,* 1, 13), 3 (C , pl II, 15), 4 (Sm , pl XX, 11, 12) . variants of the *stûpa,* or tumulus, of the *Parinirvâna.* Later the form of no. 1 was mistaken for a bow with its arrow , we seem to recognize in origin a *stûpa* crossed by the staff (*yashti*) of its parasol (*chattra*) . we need only compare the parasols which enter into the composition of the lotuses of nos A 2 and 3

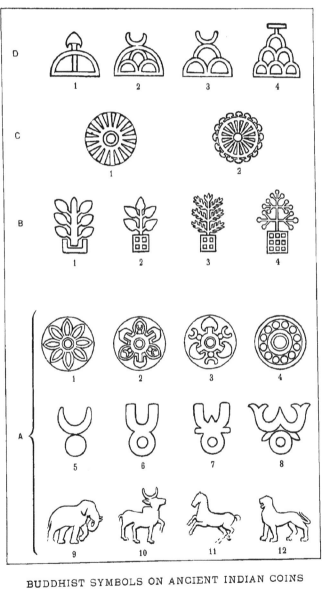

BUDDHIST SYMBOLS ON ANCIENT INDIAN COINS

PLATE II

Cf pp 17, 20, 73, 148

The three Sânchî panels belong to the western gate of the great stûpa, B to the front façade, C and D to the rear . the photographs were kindly lent to us by Mr. J. H MARSHALL — The stele of Amarâvatî is reproduced from the photograph published by FERGUSSON, *Tree and Serpent Worship*, 2nd ed., pl. XCIV.

B Miracle of the Perfect Illumination (*Sambodhi*), near to Gayâ; represented by a tree above a throne Note the characteristic leaf of the tree of Çâkya-muni (cf. pl I, B)

C Miracle of the First Preaching, or Putting in motion the Wheel of the Law (*Dharma-cakra-pravartana*), near to Benares; represented by a wheel above a throne

D. Miracle of the Final Extinction (*Parinirvâna*), near to Kuçinagara, represented by a *stûpa*
Worshippers — on the earth human and of both sexes, in the air divine — press round each of these symbolical representations. Those in the top corners of B 1 and D 1 have a human bust terminating in the stereotyped body of a bird We are not long in remarking the constant contrast, both in the material objects and in the persons, between the still heavy and clumsy style of Sânchî and that of Amarâvatî, almost too elegant and affected. What here concerns us most is that the fundamental identity of the subjects is not in the slightest degree compromised by these differences of treatment

THE THREE LAST GREAT MIRACLES

1° AT SÁNCHI                             2° AT AMARÁVATI

PLATE III

Cf pp 21, 148.

1 The three Gandhâra panels are reproduced · A¹, from a photograph taken by the author in the Lahore Museum; A², from a photograph in the Lahore Museum, copy kindly lent by Prof. A A MACDONELL; A³, from a photograph by Mr A E CADDY in the Calcutta Museum. — 2 The three Amarâvatî panels A¹, from a photograph taken by the author in the Madras Museum (Cf BURGESS, *Buddhist Stûpa of Amarâvatî*, pl XXVIII, 1), A², from FERGUSSON's photograph, *Tree and Serpent Worship*, pl LXV, 3 ; A³, from the same source, pl XCVI, 3

The locality of the scene is in all cases Kapilavastu We shall not here insist further on the differences of type, costume, furniture and ornamentation

A¹. The Conception (*Garbha-avakrânti*) : the Bodhisattva descends into the right side of his mother's bosom in the form of a little elephant The school of Amarâvatî always places at the four cardinal points of the room the four *Lokapâlas*, or Guardians of the World, but sometimes, as here, it forgets to represent the elephant, and, as little as at Barhut (CUNNINGHAM, pl XXVIII, 2) and at Sânchî (see *infra*, pl IX, 2, at the top), does it think of making Mâyâ lie in such a manner that she can properly present her right side to the Blessed One The school of Gandhâra is never guilty of these negligences, which are contrary to the letter of the texts (*Art g b du Gandh*, I, figg 149 and 160 a, cf however *ibid*, fig 148, from Amarâvatî)

A². The Nativity (*Jâti*) . the Bodhisattva issues from the right flank of his mother, who is standing and holding a branch of a tree Therefore in both views we see in the centre of the composition Mâyâ standing, with one arm raised, between the gods on the right and her women on the left But it will be noticed that on this occasion also her attitude is in Gandhâra more rational, leaving free the right hip, by which the child is supposed to issue As regards the latter, who on the panel at Lahore is perfectly visible, we perceive at Amarâvatî only the imprint of his sacred feet on the cloth, which is held by the four *Loka-pâlas* together, and no longer by Indra alone

A³ The Great Departure (*Mahâbhinishkramana*) the Bodhisattva leaves his native town on horseback. At Amarâvatî we perceive only the gate of the town (cf the gates at Sânchî on our pll VI-VII) and the riderless horse, preceded by a god and followed by a squire holding the parasol. In Gandhâra the indication of the gate has in our reproduction (but cf *Art g -b du Gandh*, I, fig 187) been cut away, yet Chandaka is to be seen holding high the parasol, while Yakshas raise the horse's feet and Mâra, armed with his bow, stands at its head Above Chandaka, again, is seen a half-length figure of Vajrapâni, armed with his thunderbolt, and above Mâra, between two divinities, the personification (recognizable by the turreted crown) of the town of Kapilavastu Finally and above all, the Bodhisattva is this time shown on the back of his horse.

THE FIRST GREAT MIRACLE
(CONCEPTION, NATIVITY OR VOCATION)
1. IN GANDHĀRA                              2. AT AMARĀVATĪ

PLATE IV

Cf pp 25-26, 148.

The sources of the various pieces are as follows : 1. A Museum für Volkerkunde, Berlin, (from a photograph lent by Dr Burgess) ; B British Museum, C-D Lahore Museum (from photographs by the author) — 2 . Stele in the Madras Museum (Cf Burgess, Amarâvatî, pl XLI, 6), from a photograph lent by M V. Goloubew — 3 Stele in the Calcutta Museum, from a photograph by the author

A *Jâti* — 1 The Nativity is here represented according to the usual formula of Gandhâra — 2 At Amarâvatî the *Jâti* has here been replaced by the *Mahâbhiniṣkramana*, the physical birth by the spiritual one (cf. pp 13 and 148, n 2), but this last episode is now conceived in the Gandhâran manner (cf. pl III, A²) — 3 The panel of Benares groups on the right, the Nativity, with Indra kneeling to receive the child (notice the analogy of Indra's tiarâ with that which he wears on pl IV, 1, A), in the middle, the Seven Steps of the Bodhisattva, who at the same time receives the Bath, poured from vessels by two Nâgas; on the left, at the bottom, the Great Departure on horseback ; and above, the Cutting of the Hair and the Farewell to Chandaka.

B *Sambodhi* — 1 The Illumination is here symbolized by the assault of Mâra (*Mâra-dharṣhana*) and his army (cf *Art g -b du Gandh* , I, fig. 201) — 2 At Amarâvatî this army is no longer represented, except by three dwarf Yakshas in front of the throne it is the daughters of Mâra who now play the principal rôle in the scene of the temptation. We shall remark the omission of the *Bodhi-druma* and the absence of

the *bhûmi-sparça-mudrâ* — 3 At Benares, on the other hand, we find again, in addition to the same femme and demoniacal persons, these two essential elements, namely the indication of the tree and the gesture of taking to witness the Earth, whose figure is only half seen

C. *Dharma-cakra pravartana* — We shall notice likewise that, for his First Preaching, the Buddha of Gandhâra and of Amarâvatî has not yet adopted the gesture consecrated to reaching (cf no 3 C.) On the other hand, we see on no 1 C the wheel and a gazelle, and on no 2 C two gazelles If from no 3 C (where, by an exception, Buddha is seated in European fashion) these accessories are absent, the omission is repaired on other stela of the same school (cf. *Iconogr bouddh de l'Inde*, I, fig 29, and Burgess, *Anc. Mon. India*, pll. 67 68)

D. *Parinirvâna* — 1 The episode of the Death of the Master is treated in accordance with the usual formula, including the despair of Vajrapâni, the grief of the Mallas and the Gods, and the ultimate conversion of Subhadra — 2 The curious circumstances that on this point the school of Amarâvati has remained obstinately faithful to the ancient device of the *Stûpa* (cf pl II, D), nevertheless, the entrance through the railing is now adorned with a standing figure of Buddha — 3 Finally, we shall notice, even more clearly than in the other compartments, that on the stele of Benares the image of the Blessed One tends to invade the whole disposable space to the detriment of the attendants : instead of legendary the scene becomes iconographic

3. AT BENARES

THE FOUR GREAT MIRACLES

2. AT AMARĀVATĪ

1. IN GANDHĀRA

# The Representations of "Jâtakas" on the Bas-reliefs of Barhut([1]).

Ancient India has bequeathed to us a considerable mass of texts and a very restricted number of sculptures : this means that for our instruction concerning its civilization we possess many more written documents than carved monuments  The latter deserve all the more to attract our attention. Their most ancient remains may, in fact, furnish us, as regards the external appearance and the material side of Indian life in the second century before our era, with a number of concrete and precise details which we should never have been able to expect from the most extensive or the most profound study of the literature  I hasten to add that I do not conceive the identification of these works of art as possible without their confrontation with the texts. These latter alone can help us to understand the mute language of the stones and, even in the absence  of any explanatory inscription, to assign names to the characters, speech to the gestures, in one word titles to the subjects. In practice it is precisely thus that matters fall out. We find ourselves possessing in the holy scriptures of Buddhism a ready made commentary for the greater part of the surviving ancient bas-reliefs , and these pieces of sculpture, rare or scattered though they be, are, for their part, a mine of illustrations quite appropriate to as many episodes of the Buddhist legend. You divine without difficulty the interest

(1) Lecture at the Musée Guimet, in *Bibliothèque de vulgarisation du Musée Guimet*, vol XXX, 1908.

of this intimate accord between the written and the figured
versions of the same stories and the advantage still to be
obtained from it for the comprehension of both. This is
what I should like to verify experimentally by study-
ing, in accordance with the texts and the monuments,
the traditions relating to some of the previous existences
of the Buddha Çâkya-Muni. For this purpose we will
make use, on the one hand, of the Pâli collection of the
*Jâtakas* (¹) and, on the other, of the bas-reliefs of the *stûpa*
of Barhut(²) From their rapprochement will quite naturally emerge for our convenience a small illustrated collection of some twenty-five Indian tales, and you shall judge
if I exaggerate their charm.

I

*The Jâtakas* — I owe however (by way of preface)
some explanations which may allow you better to understand the meaning and more to enjoy the flavour of these
tales and images, as amusing as naïve. But these necessary
explanations may be extremely brief, and it will suffice if I rapidly recall to your mind three essential notions.

The first is that, according to Indian ideas, every living
being, whoever he may be, is not only sure of dying it
is no less certain that he must be born again in one of the
five conditions of lost soul, ghost, animal, man or

(1) *Jâtaka*, éd Fausbøll, 6 voll in-8° and one volume of index, London,
1877-1897, translated into English under the direction of Professor E B Co-
WELL, 6 voll in-8°, Cambridge, 1895-1907.

(2) CUNNINGHAM, *The Stûpa of Barhut*, London, 1879 (published by order
of the Secretary of State for India, who has kindly authorised the reproductions given in this book) — Cf S D'OLDENBURG, *Notes on Buddhist
Art*, St Petersburg 1895 (in Russian, translated into English in the *Journal
of the American Oriental Society*, XVIII, I, Jan. 1897, pp 183-201)

god, after which he will have to die again, in order to be
born once more, and so on for ever, unless he attains salvation, which is nothing else than the final escape from
this frightful circle of transmigration.

The second point is that not only the attainment of this
deliverance, but the conditions even of each of the ephemeral existences are regulated automatically by a moral
law as general and as unavoidable as the physical law of
gravity, the law of « works », or (to employ a Sanskrit
word, the use of which has been popularized by the theoso-
phists) of *Karma* At the death of each being there is
drawn up a kind of debit and credit account, with assets and
liabilities, between the sums of the merits and demerits
accumulated by him in the course of his anterior existences : and an immediate sanction, resulting mechani-
cally from this simple mathematical operation, fatally
decides his future destiny.

In the third place, it is a belief no less generally admitted
in India that whoever has attained to sanctity possesses,
among other supernatural faculties, the privilege of remembering his past existences and even those of others This
gift of extra-lucid intuition, or, as it was called, of « divine
sight », no one, of course, was considered to possess
in a more eminent degree than Buddha. Now it was, we
are told, his habit, with regard to incidents arising in the
bosom of his community, to point or justify his prohib-
itions or his precepts by the opportune reminiscence of
some analogous occasion which had already confronted
him in the course of his previous lives.

These three points agreed, all becomes perfectly clear.
We admit fully henceforth that Çâkya-Muni, like all
others, must have traversed a long series of successive rebirths. We understand, also, why he accomplished on the

way so many good actions, displayed so many virtues, realized so many superhuman perfections : nothing less was
required to enable him to acquire merits capable of conveying him to the supreme dignity of Buddha. Nor could
we get our information concerning his past lives from
a better source, since — if we believe the tradition —
it is from the mouth of the Master himself that the story
had been gathered before being consigned in writing to the
works which have come down to us and which it would
be useless to-day to enumerate and criticize. If we proceed
to make use of the Pâli collection, it is not that I am
under any illusion as to the antiquity of the prose commentary on the versified, the only canonical, part ([1]) :
the reason for this choice is simply that, as containing
nearly five hundred and fifty narratives, that collection is
by far the most considerable of all

II

*The Bas-reliefs of Barhut.* — Thus familiarized afresh with
the *jâtakas*, you will not be surprised to note that the sculptors charged with the decoration of the ancient Buddhist
edifices of central India have drawn copious inspirations
therefrom. Not only did they, as we believe we have
demonstrated above ([2]), feel themselves under less restraint
in the treatment of subjects of this kind, but moreover
no subject could answer better to the needs and the
aim of the artist. Seeing that it was a question of religious
foundations, that aim was quite naturally the edification
of the faithful, both sedentary and pilgrim . and what could

---

(1) On this subject see below, essay VII on the *Saddanta jataka*
(2) See, p 23

be more edifying, in default of scenes derived from the last
life of the Master, than narratives of which he himself had
previously been the hero before becoming the narrator? On
the other hand, their familiar and picturesque character fitted in marvellously — certainly much better than moral
considerations or metaphysical speculations — with the
exigences of an art so concrete as sculpture and necessita-
ting so much precision in material detail. Thus the good
stone-cutters of Barhut and Sânchî have had recourse, like
the sculptors of our cathedrals, to the treasure of their « Gold-
en Legend », and have created, by the very force of things,
a plastic art at once narrative and religious, which recalls in
many ways the formulas of our artists of the Middle Ages.
Thus it is, for example, that they did not, any more than
these latter, prohibit the juxtaposition of episodes and repetitions of persons in the framework of one and the same
panel. We shall have many opportunities of remarking this
naive proceeding.

But it is well to form beforehand some idea of the
monuments which these bas-reliefs adorned. The Buddhist
sanctuary was preeminently the *stûpa*, that is the « tumulus », and its principal role was to cover up a deposit of
relics. As we see it in India from the third century before
our era, it was already a stereotyped edifice of brick or
stone, which presupposed the art of the architect and utilized that of the sculptor. Its chief feature was a full hemispherical dome, usually raised on a terrace. This dome,
which was called the egg (*andâ*), supported a sort of kiosk
(*harmika*), itself surmounted by one or several parasols, an
emblem of which you know the honorific signification in
the East. The whole was surrounded, like all sacred
places in India, by a high barrier, at first of wood, then
directly imitated in stone from its wooden prototype. This

enclosure was flanked at the four cardinal points by monumental gates (*torana*), with triple curved lintels of which
we have fine examples at Sânchî (¹). On the most ancient
specimens from the basin of the Ganges the decoration was
strictly limited to the doorways and railing. At Barhut
medallions were strewn over the upright pillars and cross-
bars of the latter, whilst all along the inner face of the
coping further motifs were ensconced in the intervals of
the undulations of a serpentine garland. You will recognize
one or other alternative of this double provenance in all
the reproductions which are about to defile before your
eyes (Pl V-VI).

One last question : Why have we chosen by preference
the bas-reliefs of Barhut? The answer is easy : because most
of them are accompanied by an inscription written in the
oldest alphabet of central India, the one which towards the
middle of the third century before our era was used by the
famous king Açoka for his pious edicts On one of the
jambs of the eastern gate, found *in situ*, we read, in a
somewhat later script, a mention of the ephemeral suze-
rain dynasty of the Çungas, which succeeded the Mauryas towards the year 180 B C ; it relates to the
erection of the gate, or, to be more exact, the replacement
an old wooden model by a « stone work », and thus we
feel certain that towards the end of the second century
the final touch must have been given to the decoration of
the *stûpa*, commenced, no doubt, during the third. This is
not all. Among the hundred and sixty *graffiti*, more or less,
observed on the recovered debris of the balustrade more
than half are restricted to giving merely the name of
the donor, male or female, of such and such a pillar or

---

(1) See below, pp 65-66, and cf pl VII and VIII, 1

such and such a transverse bar; but the rest give us explicit information concerning the subjects which the sculptures claimed to represent. Thus we have to deal with bas-
reliefs sufficiently dated and identified beforehand by their
authors for the benefit of their contemporaries and of the
most distant posterity. In the moving sands of Indian antiquity we can find no better data, nor firmer ground on
which to work.

## III

*The animals* — After this indispensable preparation we
may with full knowledge broach the examination of the
twenty-five *jâtakas*, of which, possessing the text, we recognize also the representation A perfectly natural plan will be
imposed upon us : it will be, if we may so express it, the biographical sequence of these successive lives, as well as the
hierarchical order of the conditions into which the future
Buddha had successively to be born. We shall see him
mount one by one the rungs of the ladder of beings, first
animal, then woman, and finally man. And indeed, putting
aside all one's complacency as Indianist, I do not think that
the imagination of any race has ever created a finer or
vaster subject for a poem than this destiny of a single being
in whom are shown all aspects of life, in whom is concentrated all the experience of past ages, in one word, in whom
the evolution of the entire human race is reflected. Unfortunately, as usually happens in India, the execution comes
infinitely short of the conception. To sum up in one work,
spacious and substantial, in view of the immense and varied
career of the Predestined One, the original Indian system of
the universe, would have required the powerful constructive
genius of a Dante : Buddhism had not that good fortune.

And this is why we do in Indian literature not meet with
more than scattered fragments of the epic of the Bodhisattva, or future Buddha.

To-day we are concerned only with the period of
his previous lives, beginning with the most humble of
them : but even within these limits we cannot help but
regret the manner in which the monks, more solicitous for
edification than for poetry, have bungled the subject. In the
same way as, according to the naturalists, the embryo of
mammalia reproduces in the course of its development
the divers characteristics of the inferior species, so we should
like to follow through the course of the animal forms
which he remembered having assumed one after the other
— fish, reptile, bird, quadruped, quadruman — the whole
embryology of a Bodhisattva  But for that we should
have to give ourselves up, in the midst of the disorder — or
of the still more outlandish order(¹) — of the texts, to a
veritable task of patchwork, joining together here and there
the scattered portions of a poem which was never written.
Evidently the idea of following out any series and grada-
tion whatever did not occur to the minds of the compilers
of these stories. We must say in excuse for them that the
theory of evolution troubled them, for reasons easy to
guess, much less than it does us  Furthermore, if they
are incapable of composing a harmonious whole, they
make up for it in detail by the naive savour and, at times,
humourous attractiveness of their style : it is impossible to
deny them a veritable talent as narrators. Once we have
renounced for them higher ambitions, the compensation
will appear to us very appreciable. Their stories of ani-

---

(1) We know that in the Pâli collection of *Jâtakas*, for example, these are
classed solely according to the increasing number of verses which they
contain, without regard to subject

mals form in fact a veritable « Jungle Book » long before
that which did so much for the reputation of Rudyard
Kipling : moreover, the latter was, in his, directly inspired by popular Indian tradition

Let us examine first the stories which present animals only, and which, consequently, are pure « fables »
There were related in India two thousand years and
more ago tales with which we are still to-day familiar
from infancy. I will cite, for example, that of « the Tortoise and the two Ducks », which is depicted already on the
ancient balustrade of Bodh-Gayâ. Among the fragments of
Barhut which have survived until our time we do not find
any equally celebrated. On the other hand, when we see the
Bodhisattva appear there, he has already arrived at the state,
or if you prefer, at the genus of bird

I. Here (CUNNINGHAM, XXVII, 11) in his character of
royal swan he refuses, if we may so express it, the « hand »
of his daughter to the peacock, in spite of his magnificent
plumage and because of his indecent dance (*Jât.* 32).

II. There (CUNNINGHAM, XLV, 7) under the form of a
pigeon, he reprimands the lazy and gluttonous crow, whom
the cook punishes so cruelly for an attempted raid upon
his pots (*Jât* 42, cf. 274 and 375).

III. Elsewhere (CUNNINGHAM, XLVII, 5) he is the cock
perched on a tree, who wisely resists the treacherous
seductions of a she-cat (*Jât.* 383 ). — La Fontaine (*Fables*,
II, 5) says of a fox

IV Still further on (CUNNINGHAM, XXV, 2), born an
elephant, he exterminates, with the help of his faithful wife,
a terrible enemy of his race, an enormous crab, « as broad
as a threshing-floor », which, in order to devour them,
had hidden itself at the bottom of the lake in which the
pachyderms were accustomed to bathe (*Jât.* 267)

V  As we cannot see all in detail, I will detain you
only a moment with the fifth *jâtaka*, spoken (and even
written) of as « of the Quail ». As usual, the text (*Jât* 357)
indicates first of all on what occasion the fable was related.
It was not the first time that Dêvadatta, the traitor cousin
of Buddha and the Judas Iscariot of his legend, proved the
hardness of his heart. At that time the Bodhisattva was
born in the form of an elephant, chief of a troop of
80,000 others — India is very fond indeed of this round
number. A quail, which had made her nest within their
pasture ground and whose young, scarcely hatched, were
still incapable of moving, begs him to spare her offspring
He willingly consents to this, and by his orders his
80,000 subjects respect the young birds as they file past :
doubtless, this is what they are in the act of doing on the
right lower part of the medallion (pl V, 1). But he warns
the quail that a fierce solitary is following him. The latter,
deaf to all prayers, crushes the nest : you perceive one of
the young ones under his right hind foot, exactly on the
edge of the break in the stone, whilst the weeping mother
is perched on a tree in front of him. But vengeance is not
long delayed · for already on the bulging forehead of the
cruel elephant a crow is busy, pecking out his eyes with its
beak, whilst a big « blue fly » deposits its eggs in the
sockets. A third ally of the quail, its gossip the frog, is seated at the top of the medallion in a conventional rocky
landscape Its role, in the story as on the bas-relief, is by its
croaking to attract the enormous animal, which is blind
and burning with fever, by making it believe in the proximity of water. Thus it leads him right to the edge of a
sharp precipice, where he falls headlong · only his hind
part has not yet quite disappeared into the abyss Application   the Bodhisattva was the leader of the troop of

elephants, Dêvadatta was the solitary. — « Well, what about the quail », you will ask. — You desire to know too much.

## IV

*The Bodhisattva under an animal form and mankind.* — In these five fables man does not intervene. Here are five others in which he is seen and, at first, hardly to his credit.

VI. In order to follow up the two preceding births, let us take a new one in the form of an elephant and even of an elephant « with six tusks » (*Jât.* 514) The wonderful animal is standing in the foreground, leaning against the banyan tree (pl XXIX, 1) which the oldest tradition assigns to him for a shelter. Behind him, likewise in profile, is his first wife, her left temple adorned with a lotus, whilst, seen full face in the background, his second wife, furious at not having herself received any such flowery ornament, is showing unmistakable signs of jealous anger She goes so far as to suffer herself to die of hunger, while forming the aspiration of being born again as a woman and becoming queen of Benares. Scarcely has her double wish been fulfilled than she charges the cleverest hunter in the country to carry out her vengeance Hidden at the bottom of a pit, the latter discharges a poisoned arrow into the bowels of the elephant, as is written and is elsewhere found figured, on the sculptures of Amarâvatî and of Gandhâra. But at Barhut, when we again (on the left of the medallion) see the hero of the story, it is already the moment when, wounded to death and practising the virtue, which was Buddhist before becoming Christian, of pardoning all offences, he docilely stoops down, in order to allow his enemy to cut off his triple tusks with the help of an enormous saw. We must turn to the Pâli collection or to the paintings of the Ajaṇṭâ Caves to learn that the wicked queen, at the sight of the tusks of her former husband, which her emissary brought back to her, felt nevertheless a revulsion of conscience, of which she died heart-broken (¹).

VII. No less naively illustrated is the ne-birth as an antelope, *kurunga*. On pl. V, 2 we read as plainly as in the text (*Jât.* 206) that there were once an antelope, a tortoise and a wood-pecker, which, united by friendship, lived together on the shores of a lake in the depths of the woods. The antelope has just been caught in a trap : and, whilst the tortoise exerts itself to gnaw through the fetters, the wood-pecker, represented a second time on the right, does all that it can, in its character of bird of ill-omen, to delay the coming of the hunter. Soon — but no room could be found in the picture for this second adventure — the antelope will in its turn deliver the tortoise .

> Ainsi chacun en son endroit
> S'entremet, agit et travaille,

as we are told by La Fontaine, who to our trio of friends has added also a rat (*Fables*, XII, 15).

VIII Another medallion (pl. V, 3) contains no less than three episodes At the bottom the tender-hearted stag, *ruru*, saves the son of the merchant, who was going to drown himself in the Ganges, and brings him on his back to the bank, where one of his roes is stooping to drink at the river. At the top, on the right, the king of Benares, guided by the young merchant, who is evidently acting as his informant, is preparing with bent bow to kill the great rare stag, the object of his desires as a hunter But the words ad-

---

(1) We shall have an opportunity later (Essay VII) of recurring more in detail to the *Saddanta-jâtaka* (cf pl. XXIX and XXX)

dressed to him by the latter quickly cause the weapons to fall from his hands, and we find him again in the centre in edifying conversation with the wonderful animal, whilst the treacherous informer seems to be hiding behind the royal person. We know from another source that the Bodhisattva, always charitable, intercedes with the king in favour of his perfidious debtor (*Jât.* 482 ; not to be confused with 12).

IX. Of the two births as ape, which we meet next, the one (*Jât.* 516) contains a story with a quite analogous moral, but the bas-relief is very much damaged (CUNNINGHAM, XXXIII, 5). A Brahman, saved by the Bodhisattva, who rescues him from the bottom of a precipice, repays him with the blackest ingratitude, attempting to assassinate his benefactor during his sleep. On this occasion also the magnanimous animal forgives.

X. More original and much better preserved is the other *jâtaka* of Mahâkapi (*Jât.* 407; pl. V, 4). At that time the Bodhisattva was in the Himâlayas, king of 80.000 monkeys, and he took them to feed upon a gigantic mango-tree — others say a fig-tree, and the bas-relief agrees with this — whose fruits were delicious, but the branches of which unfortunately spread over the Ganges. In spite of the precautions prescribed by the foreseeing wisdom of the « great monkey», a fruit, hidden by a nest of ants, escapes the investigations of his people, ripens, falls into the stream of water, and is caught in the nets which surround the bathing-place of the king of Benares. The latter finds it so much to his taste that, in order to procure others like it, he does not hesitate, when he has obtained information from the « wood-rangers », to follow the river to its source, until he arrives at the wonderful tree. At night the monkeys gather together as usual . but the king of Benares has the tree surrounded

by his archers, with fixed arrows and only awaiting the day
to begin the slaughter. There is alarm in the camp of the
Bandar-log, as Kipling expresses it. Their leader reas-
sures them and promises to save their lives. With a
gigantic spring, of which he alone is capable, he clears a
hundred bow lengths as far as the opposite bank of the river,
there cuts a long rattan, the one end of which he fixes to
a tree on this bank, whilst he attaches the other to his foot,
and with another spring returns to his own people. But
the vine which he has cut is a little too short, and it is only
by stretching out his hands that he can reach the branches
of the fig-tree. Nevertheless, the 80,000 monkeys pass over
this improvised bridge and descend in safety on the other
side of the river. This latter is, as usual, indicated by
sinuous lines, in which a tortoise and some fish are swim-
ming But already two men of the court of the king of
Benares are holding by the four corners a striped coverlet,
into which the Bodhisattva, exhausted with fatigue, has only
to let himself fall when the last of his subjects has been
saved. At the bottom (and this is the second picture within
the frame) we find him sitting in conversation with his
human colleague, who is amazed at his vigour, his ingenuity, and his devotion to his people. Between them a
person, of whom we see only the bust and the hands
respectfully joined together, is, if we may judge from the
absence of the turban, a man of low caste, apparently that
one of the « wood-rangers » who guided the royal caravan
towards the Himâlaya.

V

*The Bodhisattva in human form and animals.* — In this
last narrative the king of Benares gives a proof of good

feeling : therefore he is presented to us as an ancient incarnation of Ânanda, the well-beloved disciple. In the four
preceding fables man appears to us in the odious form of
a hunter, except when he reveals himself as a monster of
ingratitude, whilst the brute continues to show an example
of the most difficult virtues. However, we must not be in
too great a hurry to conclude that, in the *Jâtakas*, the better
part always belongs to the animals · in fact, it only falls to
them when they incarnate the Bodhisattva. In other words,
in the Buddhist adaptation to which these tales have been
subjected the Bodhisattva has been incarnated in animal
form only in those cases where it was decidedly more
flattering to be beast than to be man. Here are four other
examples which will abundantly prove to us that ingratitude, foolishness, the aggressive instinct, and dishonesty are
not, in the minds of our authors, the privilege of humanity
alone, as you might have been led to believe. The stories
ought indeed to come a little later in the plan which we
have adopted, since the Bodhisattva is there already clothed in the human form *par excellence*, I mean that of a man :
but for the advantage of warning ourselves against a wrong
idea it is worth while slightly to disarrange the hierarchical
order of the sexes

XI. Do you desire further simian stories? Look on the
left of pl. VI, 1 at this young novice, or Brahmanic student,
who is giving a thirsty monkey something to drink. Now
he goes away towards the right, having loaded on his
shoulders, at the two ends of a stick placed like a balancing
beam, his two round pitchers, suspended in nets of cord
after the manner of the time and of the present day ; meanwhile the animal, who has mounted into the tree again,
makes grimaces at him as a reward for his charity . « Oblige
a villain, and he will spit in your face », says our proverb.

If we are to believe the text, the monkey did worse still on the head of the Bodhisattva, a thing which is quite among the habits of these horrid beasts. It is needless to repeat to you that he was none other than Dêvadatta (*Jât.* 174)

XII. Another time (*Jât* 46 and 268), a gardener, wishing to take his holiday, has charged the monkeys which haunt his garden to water it in his stead. And in fact they set about it with pitchers (pl. VI, 2), but on a suggestion of their king, who by nature prefers to do things methodically and does not intend his water to be wasted, they begin by pulling up every shrub in the nursery, so as to measure by the length of its roots the exact quantity of water which it will require. The Bodhisattva is the « wise man », who enters by the left and surprizes them while thus occupied He does not restrict himself to stating that hell is paved with good intentions · there is no lack of moralizing, also, about the stupidity of the king of the monkeys · if he is the most intelligent, what must be thought of the rest of the troop?

XIII. On another fragment of the coping (CUNNINGHAM, XLI, 1-3) is figured in two successive scenes the story of a stupid fighting ram, who is inspired by his warlike instincts to charge a Brahmanic ascetic : we must say in his excuse that the latter was wearing a garment of skin (*Jât.* 324) The whole humour of the affair is that the monk imagines, at the moment when the ram stoops, ready to rush upon him, that even the beasts bow before his worth. It is in vain that a young merchant, no other than the Bodhisattva, warns him of his imprudent mistake : there he is soon on his back, upset along with the double burden which he was balancing on his shoulder.

XIV Again in another place it is the turn of the Bodhisattva to carry the water-vessel and wear the big chignon

and the summary costume of an ascetic (pl. VI, 3), and it is
in this guise (and not that of a tree-god, as the commentary
gives it, *Jât.* 400) that he is present as a simple spectator
at a very amusing scene. Two otters, by uniting their efforts,
have dragged a big fish to the dry ground on the bank of a
river, the one holding it by the head, the other by the tail;
but, their united exploit accomplished, they quarrel about
the sharing of the booty and take a passing jackal as arbiter.
The latter is represented twice, first seated between the
litigants, then walking proudly away to the right · he is
carrying the best piece in his mouth and leaving to the two
deceived otters only the head and tail of their prey. The
moral is easily guessed The text states very explicitly that
the best law-suits in the world only serve to enrich the
coffers of the king; and you, for your part, have in the
« Jackal and the two Otters » already recognised an Indian
variant of the « Oyster and the Litigants » of La Fontaine.

XV. For the rest we must not in the presence of the
extreme variety of these tales claim to set up too general
rules. A little further on (pl. VI, 4) animals reappear
side by side with another identical incarnation of the
Bodhisattva, and this time they play a most honou-
rable part The bas-relief is here much simplified in
comparison with the version of the *Jâtaka* (488), which
gives to the hero a sister, six brothers and two servants. At
Barhut we see at his side only a woman — likewise clothed in the ascetic costume — who may very well in the
intention of the sculptor be the wife of his lay years,
and of whom the Pâli prose, with its accustomed and
perhaps excessive modesty, will have made his sister: has
it not been bold enough (*Jât.* 461) to give us Râma as the
brother, and not the husband, of Sîtâ? On the other hand, a
monkey and an elephant likewise take part in this scene,

unless the latter is merely the mount of Çakra . for the
« Indra of the Gods » looks upon it as a duty to bring
back the bundle of lotus stalks (rather similar to our
bundles of asparagus and just like those which I have seen
sold, nowadays, in Kashmir, in the market of Srinagar),
which gave its name to the story. That is all the food of
the ascetic, and on three days in succession Çakra, in order
to prove him, has stolen it, but without succeeding in
moving him. At the moment when he repents, each one
of the characters, both human and animal, was about to
exonerate himself from this theft by a veracious oath, even
the monkey declaring himself incapable of it, for, it is said
somewhere, « in the company of saints everyone becomes
a saint ».

## VI

*The Bodhisattva and women.* — With these reservations, these two series of examples, preserved by chance,
suffice to prove what I was just now saying concerning
the double attitude of the *Jâtakas* with regard to animals.
If from the beasts we now pass — without any idea of
comparison, be it said — to the women, we observe that
at the very first the same distinction seems necessary.
Either we are in the presence of one of those beautiful
types of faithful wife which are an honour to Indian literature, and then we may safely wager that the Bodhisattva
is this time incarnated in the feminine form; or else it is
a masculine role which is assigned to him, and in this case
the texts, giving free scope to an instinct for satire worthy
of our Gaul of the Middle Ages, becomes inexhaustible on
the subject of the malice and perversity of the fair sex.
The stories which they tell of it (we shall, of course,

adduce only those which are figured, more or less, at Barhut) lack neither raciness nor verve. In fact, whilst the stories which have come before us up till now were properly fables, we have now to do with the kind of jolly tales which in the Romance languages of mediæval Europe were called « fabliaux » or « fableaux ».

XVI. On a medallion which can hardly with propriety be reproduced (CUNNINGHAM, XXVI, 7), we witness the conception and birth of the *rishi* Rishyaçringa (Antelope-horn) or Ekaçringa (Unicorn), as celebrated in the Brahmanic epic as in the Buddhist legend Son of an anchorite and a roe, he knows nothing of a sex to which he is not even indebted for his mother, and consequently he will be an easy prey to the first women he meets. On this common trunk are grafted two groups of stories. In the first, the young hermit is scarcely adolescent and lives with his father A neighbouring king, in order to put an end to a famine, or simply because he has no son, forms the design of taking him for his son-in-law and his own daughter, or, in the less ancient versions, some courtesans charge themselves with the task of leading him astray and bringing him back to the court (*Jât.* 526; *Mahâvastu*, III, 143; *Mahâbhârata*, III, 110-113 etc), Without great difficulty they succeed, as soon as the father has turned his back, being helped as much as they could desire by the naive candour of the young man, who as yet has seen nothing of the world, for whom a rebounding ball seems a marvel, who takes cakes for delicious fruits without pips, and who calls carriages « moving huts ». He apprehends still other causes of amazement, not less ingenious, but already less innocent, at the aspect, so new to him, of his feminine visitors: and you can easily conceive that this theme of the spontaneous awakening of the sexual instinct

in the most ignorant of young men should have served as
an example to Boccacio and for a story to La Fontaine
(*Contes*, III, 1, « The Geese of Brother Philip », taken from
the preamble to the fourth day of the *Decameron*).

Of the second form of the legend the clearest summary
that we at present possess has been preserved to us by the
Chinese pilgrim Hiuan-tsang with reference to a ruined
convent of Gandhâra, in the extreme north-west of
India. « It was in this place, he tells us, that formerly there
lived the *rishi* Unicorn; this *rishi*, having allowed himself to
be led astray by a courtesan, lost his supernatural powers,
the courtesan mounted on his shoulders and thus returned
to the town » (cf *Jât.* 523, *Daçakumâracarita*, II, 2 etc ). Here
there is no longer any question of the father of the hermit,
and the age of the latter is left undetermined. On the other
hand, what we are told of him reminds us of the fables
detailed in our relations of animal stories, the so-called « Bestiaria » of the Middle Ages, concerning the Unicorn which
only a young girl is able to capture . « And she (says
their source, the Physiologus) commands the animal and it
obeys her, and she leads it away to the king's palace ». Why
there rather than elsewhere? This unexpected trait forms, on
the contrary, an integral part of the adventure of the shy
anchorite Unicorn, whom the king's daughter very naturally leads to her father, or whom the courtesan has wagered
that she will bring back to the court. And, again, the
piquant detail that this latter mounts astride on the shoulders
of the wise *rishi* awakens invincibly the memory of the
celebrated « Lay of Aristotle ».

XVII. A fragment of another medallion, found only by
the greatest chance, bears as title the three first words of
the one stanza which constitutes the ancient nucleus of
*Jâtaka* 62 · « The music that the Brahman . » : and, in fact,

it shows us a caste man seated, with his eyes bandaged and playing the harp, whilst a couple dance before him (CUNNING-HAM, XXVI, 8). He is the chaplain of the king of Benares, and had, we are told, a habit of gaming with his master. But the king, each time he threw the dice, used, in order to bring himself good luck, to hum four verses, taken from some popular song, which were not very respectful to the virtue of women, and by force of this truth he won every time  The Brahman, in a fair way to being ruin-ed, gives up playing and decides to rear a new-born girl-child without her ever seeing any other man than himself. She has scarcely reached marriagable age when he, in his turn, challenges the king, whose word, having become false, is no longer efficacious, so that he loses game after game. Thwarted, and guessing what is the snake under the rock, he charges one of his agents to seduce the only real virtue in his kingdom. This plan does readily succeed; and it must be believed that intelligence comes to a girl still more quickly than to a boy. The young novice's mind is so readily and so effectually enlightened, that she consents to organize the little scene of comedy represented by the bas-relief, and it is with her lover that she is dancing to the sound of the harp played by the blinded Brahman. I lay no stress upon the rest of the story or how she succeeds in exonerating herself by making a false oath true, a device equally well known to our folk-lore   the important thing is that in this Indian heroine you have been allowed to salute in passing the type of the eternal Agnes.

XVIII. Even the single story consecrated to the praise of woman fails not to be well-known to our mediævalists under the name of « Constant du Hamel ». Certainly, we must immediately deduct from this last story some details which truly smack too much of its native soil : I refer to the vengeance exercised by the villain on the wives « of the provost, the forester and the priest ». This manner of applying the law of retaliation, and even with interest — for the peasant does to another what the other has merely had the intention of doing to him — is a trait eminently Gallic ; and you will not be in any way astonished to observe that it was evidently the part which La Fontaine desired to retain of the story, when he put it into verse in his tale of « the people of Rheims » · you will understand no less clearly that the Indian versions contain nothing of the kind. For the rest, the accord would be truly too astonishing, if it were not a case of a borrowing by European literature from that of India (*Jât.* 546, *Kathâsaritsâgara*, I, 4 etc.). Taken on the whole, it is the Pâli text which most nearly approaches the bas-relief of Barhut (pl. V, 5) · there also Amarâ, the virtuous wife, whose husband is absent, has four suitors to whom she assigns an interview for each of the watches of the same night, and it is also in great esparto baskets that she causes her tricked lovers to be packed by her servants At the moment chosen by the sculptor we are in the midst of the court : the king is seated on his throne, surrounded by his ministers, and at his right side one of the women of the harem is waving a fly-flapper. Amarâ is standing on the other side, her left hand on the shoulder of her attendant, and at her order the covers of three of the baskets have already been raised and the heads of three of the delinquents uncovered, whilst two coolies bring the fourth But the Singhalese compilation dismisses this story in ten lines, as an episode in a long narrative, and consents to see in Amarâ only the wife of the absent Bodhisattva for it is quite resigned to represent the latter as an animal, a pariah or even a bandit, but never, no ! never, a woman, be she, as in this case, a paragon of all the virtues. If, however, we come to realize that the *jâtaka* in question has the honour of a complete medallion and that these representations have no edifying interest except on the condition that the future Buddha there appears in person, it will soon be granted that there are great chances that the sculptor regarded him as incarnated here in the feminine form. Even if the author had not himself made this identification, everything invited the spectator to do so. The inscription on the bas-relief (*yavamajhakiyam jâtakam*) does not contradict it for the Pâli tradition also makes Amarâ to be born in one of the four suburbs *Yavamajjhaka*, situated at the four gates of the capital of Mithilâ.

However it may be as regards this particular point, the tremendous buffoonery of the situation could not escape the worshippers, and they must have been at least as much amused as edified. If we ourselves look at it more closely, we shall not be able to avoid the impression that, with all her virtue, Amarâ was not exempt from mischief. Doubtless she had recourse to the arsenal of her tricks only for a good motive; but we tremble at the thought of what would happen to her husband, if this astute woman employed in deceiving him a quarter of the malice that she displays in keeping herself faithful. In one word, and with all taken into account, whether the story be written in praise of the fair sex or not, it is always the same creature of perfidy, if not of voluptuousness, with whom we have to deal : or, to put it better, we observe that the quite monastic mistrust and aversion which Buddhism professed towards woman are (we may say) never disarmed. Of all the snares of Mâra the Malignant, is she not the worst ? And was it not solely in the rupture of all family ties, commencing with the conjugal tie, that the assured pledge of salvation was supposed to be found?

XIX Among our bas-reliefs we find still another fairly
picturesque illustration of this moral conception. It is taken
from the history of Mahâjanaka (*Jat* 539). A son, born in
exile, of the widow of a king of Mithilâ, I will pass over
the adventures which finally re-establish him on the throne
which his uncle has usurped, and at the same time win
for him the hand of his beautiful cousin Sîvalî What is of
importance to us here is the resolution, which he soon forms,
of taking to the religious life and the useless efforts to which
his wife resorts in order to retain him in the world. At
last he departs, but his wife belongs to that variety of
woman which our writers of vaudevilles call « clinging » ;
and she obstinately adheres to his steps Vainly does a
remnant of politeness lead him to make use of various
symbols in order to mark his decided intention to deprive
himself henceforth of a companionship which he looks
upon as an obstacle to his deliverance : she will listen
to none of them, not even the plainest, such as the one
represented, with the names of the persons to vouch for
it, on the railing at Barhut (pl VI, 5) The king, who has
already cast aside his diadem, is standing, still followed by
the queen, in front of an armourer's bench and with the
two first fingers raised is speaking in parables The arti-
zan is about to straighten an arrow which he has just put
through the fire, and, closing one eye, is examining with the
other whether it is straight. To a premeditated question
from Mahâjanaka he replies that one can judge the straightness of things much better with a single one eye than with
two for, except in solitude, there is no salvation for man.

XX. This monkish moral is, however, susceptible of a
quite touching revulsion, or rather of quite gracious over-
sight. Evidently it was impossible for the compilers of this
great collection of folk-lore to bring all the narratives

within their narrow range of edification · and thus it is that
a delightful story of love must have found grace in their
eyes It is not preserved to us at Barhut, except by a
miserable sketch (CUNNINGHAM, XXVII, 12), but it is still
in existence on the Boro-Budur of Java ('), where the
human bust of the *kinnara* is no longer terminated by
foliage, but by the body of a bird. The king of Benares,
while out hunting, perceives a couple of these marvellous beings covering each other with caresses and tears
He questions them, and learns from the mouth of the
woman — always the more talkative — that they were once
separated by the storm and had to spend the night on
either side of the river. Now it will soon be seven hundred years since this mischance, and their life is a thousand years . however, they have not yet quite conso-
led each other for the separation of a few hours, and
since then have been unable to help mingling tears with
their caresses. — What an example for lovers, thinks the
king ; and it will not surprise you to learn that, with the
help of this simple legend, Buddha forthwith reconciled
the king and queen of Kosala, very much in love with one
another, who were sulking (*Jat.* 504 ; reject 481 and 485)

VI

*The Bodhisattva and the castes* — This last story is less a
« fableau » than a fairy tale As for the preceding one, it
should rather be classed in the category of those « examples », wherewith our preaching friars of the Middle
Ages were accustomed to stud their sermons. The five that
still remain to be reviewed are all edifying stories which

––––––––––

(1) See below, Essay VIII.

similarly served the needs of the Buddhist preaching. They
will perhaps seem to you only moderately amusing :
but in India morality must always have its turn. In them
the Bodhisattva is constantly reborn in the state of man,
that state so difficult to attain, we are told, which, while
the one most favourable of all to the acquisition of
merits, is also the only one in which the candidate for
the Bodhi ever has a chance of attaining his object. Each
time this marvellous being, whatever may be his caste,
astonishes us with the proofs of his skill, wisdom and
disinterestedness : but it is especially in his royal births
that he gives free course to his virtue. Let us not forget
that the Buddhists professed to place the class of the *Kshatriya*, or, as we should say, the nobility of the sword, to
which their Master belonged, above that of the Brahmans :
naturally, we shall have to follow the order established by
them in the hierarchy of the castes

XXI The Bodhisattva knew all social positions, even
that which consists in being under the ban of society,
as is the case with the pariah  However, in the lowest position in which we recognise him on the bas-reliefs of
Barhut, he has already arrived at the third class, that of the
Vaiçyas, that is to say, of peasant proprietor or town shop-
keeper  It is as a son of a citizen of Çrâvasti that by an
ingenious stratagem he consoles his father, who was still
inconsolable for the death of his grandfather (*Jât.* 352, CUN-
NINGHAM, XLVII, 3)  He brings water and food to the dead
body of an ox, abandoned at the gates of the town ; and
when his father, informed by friends, runs up to remons-
trate with him, he answers him in the same tone and has
not much trouble in proving to him that the more foolish
of the two is not the one whom people think. For it is
folly, according to Buddhist ideas, to weep for the dead

XXII. Elsewhere the Bodhisattva has become the Pandit Vidhura, minister of the king of Indraprastha. The fame of his wisdom and eloquence is so great, that the wife of a Nâga conceives a fancy for hearing him speak. In order to make more sure of him being brought to her, the undine pretends to have a « desire », that of eating his heart Behold the husband much disturbed « As well ask for the moon », he remarks (*Jât.* 545). But what is there that women cannot do ? The four panels of one pillar are consecrated to the description of how the daughter of the Nâga was not long in finding a young captain of the genii, who, for love of her « beaux yeux », charges himself with the commission, how the young gallant challenges the king of Indraprastha to play, and with one cast of the dice wins his minister from him , how he vainly endeavours to kill the latter by throwing him down from the top of a mountain; and how, in the end, he decides to take him alive to the house of the Nâga, to the great satisfaction of his future mother-in-law, who thus obtains from the mouth of the sage the little private lecture which she desired (CUNNINGHAM, XVIII). And, as is always the case with these Buddhist tales, all is well that ends well

XXIII But, as I have told you, it is especially when the Bodhisattva is born again as a *Kshatriya* that his acts foretell the great renunciation of which he is to offer a perfect model in the course of his last existence. Once, at a time when human life was exceedingly long, he renounces the throne and the world from the moment of the appearance of his first white hair (*Jât.* 9). His barber is ordered to show it to him as soon as he perceives it · and it is for that reason that, on pl. VI, 6, he interrupts the combing of his master's long hair King Makhâdêva, although he still has 84.000 years to live, abdicates at once in favour of his

son — apparently the third person in the scene — and
retires to lead in his own park of mango-trees the ascetic
life

XXIV. Another time he does not wait so long to abandon
his throne, and he is still in full youth when he yields place
to his youngest brother (*Jât.* 181, *Mahâvastu*, II, 73). The
jealousy and suspicions of the latter soon force him to go
into exile, and, thanks to his talent as an archer, he earns
his living in the service of a neighbouring king. The bas-
relief represents this Asadisa at the moment when, by
means of an arrow skilfully shot, he gathers for his master
a mango from the very top of a high tree (CUNNINGHAM,
XXVII, 13) The continuation of the story makes him again
protect his ungrateful brother against the seven hostile
princes who were besieging him, and finally he enters — or
rather, according to the Indian expression, he « departs »
— into religion.

XXV. Once even it is from his earliest infancy that he
gives evidence of his resolution to know nothing of
this world, and he feigns to be dumb, deaf and para-
lyzed (*Jât.* 538) In vain are many experiments tried
to prove him, neither privations nor delicacies, nor toys,
nor noises, nor lights, nor fear, nor suffering, nor (when
he is nearly sixteen years old) voluptuous temptations can
draw from him a gesture, a cry, or any sign whatever of
sensibility or intelligence. That is why you see him lying
so stiff in the lap of his father, the king of Benares (pl. V, 6)
The latter ends by becoming weary of such a son, and
orders his chariot-driver to take him out of the town and
bury him, dead or alive. Thus, at the bottom, we see Prince
Sêmiya standing near an empty quadriga, whilst on the
right the driver is busy with a hoe, hollowing out a grave.
However, the prince suddenly decides to move and speak:

but when his father, informed by the driver, runs up with his suite, full of joy, it is only to find him already transformed by the providential intervention of the king of the gods into an ascetic, and sitting in the shadow of the trees of his hermitage . and this forms the subject of the third and last episode, on the right top border of the medallion.

The texts specify elsewhere that in this last existence the Bodhisattva had realised the perfection of « determination », in the life of Vidhura (XXII) that of « wisdom », in that of Mahâjanaka (XIX) of « heroism », in that of the ascetic with the lotus stems (XV) of « detachment », in that of the king of the monkeys (X) of « truth », in that of the stag (VIII) and the elephant with six tusks (VI) of « generosity »; and we know from a detached fragment that at Barhut also was seen the birth in which, under the name of Prince Viçvantara, he attained by the gift of his goods, his children and even his wife, the acme of « charity » Thus we recognize on our bas-reliefs some of the most celebrated *jâtakas*; and of the ten cardinal virtues only « patience », « benevolence » and « equanimity » are not represented by name Further, we must not forget that the researches of Cunningham have collected scarcely more than a third of the railing : the rest had been carried away and destroyed by neighbouring villagers, and this vandalism justifies the precaution, taken by the English archæologist, of transporting all that had survived to the Museum at Calcutta Inversely, it is only right that I should warn you that we are far from having identified all the bas-reliefs which have been exhumed We might draw up another list, almost as long, of those which still await (the greater number, but not all, for want of an inscription) a satisfactory explanation. Some motifs are evidently taken from *jâtakas* not to be

read in the Pâli collection . and this is a salutary warning
to us that the latter, considerable though it may be, is far
from being complete. Besides, we might have drawn attention in passing to a number of discordances in detail, as
regards the treatment of subjects certainly identified, between the prose part of this collection and the bas-reliefs,
whilst we have remarked the almost literal harmony between
a lapidary inscription and the text of one of the versified
refrains known under the popular title of *gâthâ* ([1]). But
these are remarks which are of interest chiefly to specialists.
I would mention only one point, namely, that they autho-
rize us to believe that the sculptors of Barhut worked not
in accordance with a given text, as did those of Boro-
Budur, but according to a living tradition, as it echoed in
their memory or was transmitted among them.

I will add that they worked also according to nature :
you have been enabled to judge for yourselves of their ho-
nest care for true detail  Each photographic reproduction of
their works has shown you, as through a window opening
upon the past, the costumes, weapons, tools, furniture and
vehicles employed in India two thousand years ago ; and
thus in one hour they have given you through your eyes
more concrete ideas about that civilization than you would
have been able to acquire in a year's reading. But the greatest
service that they have rendered us — for from it flow all
the others — was when they carried their foresight to the
point of engraving by the side of the majority of their compositions the titles of the subjects which they had intended
to represent  What gratitude ought we not to feel towards
them for that just distrust of their own talent, so rare
among artists! It has given us the key to ancient Indian

---

([1]) See below some remarks on the *Saddanta-jâtaka* (Essay VII).

art. So much modesty, sincerity and conviction, do they not go far towards making up for the lack of technical skill? I am sure you will not be severe towards them in this respect : and if these fables, these fabliaux and moralities, have interested your eyes no less than your ears, you will thank not only the narrators of them, but also the worthy old image-makers of India.

# PLATES V-VI

The Barhut sculptures here reproduced are borrowed, with the permission of the Secretary of State for India, from the beautiful publi cation of General A. CUNNINGHAM, *The Stûpa of Bharhut* (London, 1879).

| Pl. V | 1 (C , pl. XXVI, 5) | described on p | 38 |
|---|---|---|---|
| » | 2 (C , pl XXVII, 9) . | » | » 40 |
| » | 3 (C., pl XXV, 1) | » | » 40-41 |
| ,, | 4 (C , pl. XXXIII, 4) . | » | » 41-42 |
| » | 5 (C., pl. XXV, 3) : | » | » 50 |
| » | 6 (C , pl. XXV, 4) . | » | » 56 |
| Pl. VI. | 1 (C., pl XLVI, 8) | » | ,, 43 |
| » | 2 (C , pl XLV, 5) · | » | » 44 |
| » | 3 (C., pl. XLVI, 2) | » | » 45 |
| » | 4 (C , pl XLVIII, 7) | » | » 45-46 |
| » | 5 (C , pl. XLIV, 2) | » | » 52 |
| ,, | 6 (C , pl XLVIII, 2) | » | » 55 |

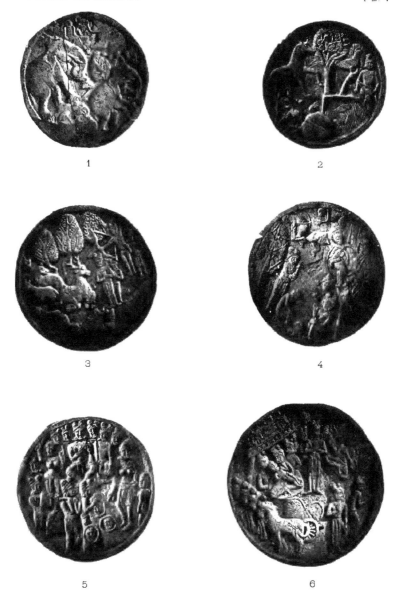

1

2

3

4

5

6

IN MEDALLIONS

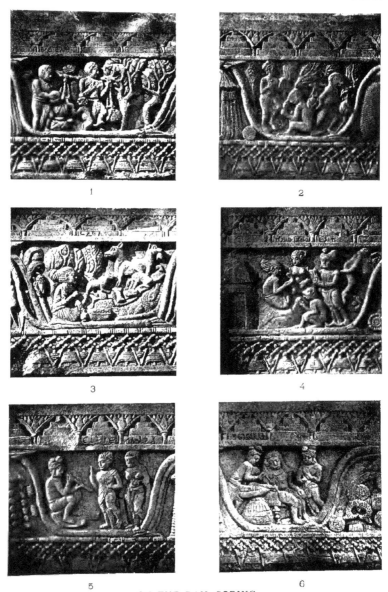

ON THE RAIL COPING

# The Eastern Gate of the Sânchî Stûpa [1]

The visitor to the Indian Museum in London, the Musée Guimet in Paris, or the Museum fur Völkerkunde in Berlin, cannot fail to notice among the objects therein exhibited a monumental gate covered with bas-reliefs, but there is every chance in the world that he will confine himself to casting a quick, heedless glance towards it in passing A reproduction of a remote Indian original, this moulding naturally cannot have any claim to speak to our European eyes or to awaken in our minds the remembrance of any traditional legend. But then let us bring before it any native of India, he will remain as puzzled and, if he is candid, as silent as we Do not, however, hastily conclude from this that these sculptures have never had any meaning for anyone, because to-day their compatriots themselves no longer understand anything about them. Only imagine a similar experiment to be tried with us, and that we were set down, for example, before one of the porches of the cathedral of Chartres, how many would be able to read without preparation in the magnificent illustrated Bible so suddenly opened before them ? You know that in the eighteenth century no one would have been found capable of this and in the nineteenth it required a whole phalanx of patient investigators to rediscover the lost meaning of the scenes and figures painted on the windows, or carved under the vaults, by

(1) Lecture at the Musée Guimet, in *Bibliothèque de Vulgarisation du Musée Guimet*, vol. XXXIV, 1910

our image-makers of the Middle Ages  The conditions are
exactly the same for this Gate of Sânchî, with time the
subject of its bas-reliefs has ended by becoming, even for
the descendants of those who once built or carved it, a
veritable enigma. I invite you to join me in investigating
its meaning.

I will add that, disagreable or not, this research is a
kind of obligation, which we may no longer with decency
shirk  It was in fact the original building, and not
the reproduction, that just missed coming to Paris.
In 1867–8 the Begum of Bhopâl was instigated to
offer to the Emperor of the French one of the four great
gates of the *stûpa* of Sânchî, that is to say, a portion of
the most beautiful, and even of the unique architectural
whole that we have retained from Ancient India  The
Begum, indifferent, desired nothing better, but the English
resident intervened, and this act of vandalism — we are
all the more ready after this lapse of time to designate it as
such, since the project fell through — was fortunately
not perpetrated(') However, the Anglo-Indian government
understood that there were there archæological remains
capable of arousing the interest of artists and scholars. From
1869 it caused to be executed at great cost several mouldings
of the eastern gate, one of the only two which had remained standing, and with great liberality it divided them
between London, Edinburgh, Dublin, Berlin, Paris, etc.
The one which fell to our share had already known some
vicissitudes, till at last it found an asylum — if not a shelter — in the courtyard of the Musée Guimet  On the
other hand, this costly and somewhat embarrassing present

---

(1) See ROUSSELET, *L'Inde des Rajahs*, pp 522-25 and cf H  COLE, *Great
Buddhist Tope at Sanchi*, introd  (*Tope* is the  Anglo-Indian equivalent of the
Sanskrit *stûpa*)

has not yet been made in France the object of any special study. It is this too prolonged neglect that we are about to endeavour to repair.

I

*The Great Sânchi Stûpa.* — The numerous ruins which are scattered over the environs of the village of Sânchî-Kânâ-keda (in Sanskrit Kâkanâda), near to Bhilsa, are situated right in the heart of Central India, on the ancient commercial highway between Pâtaliputra (Πα/έσθρα, Patna), the capital of the Maurya emperors, and Bharukaccha (Βαρυγαζα, Bharotch or Broach) by way of Ujjayinî ('Οζήνη, Ujjain). Sânchî has now become a station of the *Indian Midland Railway,* and the expresses stop there by request to set down a few tourists But it is doubtless to the abandonment of the ancient route and to the subsequent thinning of the population that the ancient Buddhist sanctuaries with which the rocky hill is crowned have owed their exceptional escape from the fanaticism of the Musalman invaders as well as the cupidity of the modern Hindus Whilst at 300 kilometres to the North-East the contemporary and quite analogous *stûpa* of Barhut, with which we shall so often have to compare it, had been three parts destroyed by the villagers of the neighbourhood, who made a business of exploiting it, the principal monument at Sânchî was still in an excellent state of preservation when it was visited for the first time, in 1818, by General Taylor and described in 1819 by Captain Fell. In compensation, it had much to suffer three years later from the brutal excavations inflicted upon it, without mercy for art and without profit to science, by some English amateurs (¹). From 1881 to 1883 the Archæological Department exerted itself to repair as well as possible this grievous devastation. They closed up the enormous, gaping breach, which had been made in one third of the central dome, under pretext of ascertaining whether it were solid or hollow; they reerected (placing, it is true, several of the lintels so as to face backwards and overlooking in the debris some fragments of the jambs) the southern and western gates, the second of which had fallen only under the weight of the rubbish thoughtlessly thrown upon it, finally, with a zeal almost excessive, they cleared the whole site, without sparing a single tree. Fig. 1 in pl. VII, a kind of horseback view taken from the east in the rising sun, will explain to you better than long descriptions the state and general aspect of the building (²)

Like every old *stûpa*, it is composed essentially of a massive hemispherical dome, raised upon a pediment likewise circular, which was reached by a flight of steps. The whole was made of bricks covered with a stone facing, which in its turn was overlaid with a thick layer of mortar, still existing in places. The terrace, in this case $4^m,25$ high and $1^m.70$ wide, served evidently as a promenade for the perambulations of the faithful  The dome — a kind of giant reliquary, though in the particular case the deposit of relics has never been discovered — measures $12^m,80$ in height, with a diameter of $32^m,30$. The only element to-day lacking to this developed tumulus is the architectural motif which served as a crown : but in thought

---

(1) On all these points, see the *Journal of the Asiatic Society of Bengal*, III, 1834, p 489, and IV, 1835, p 712.

(2) I owe the communication of this photograph and the following ones to the kindness of Mr. J. H. MARSHALL, the distinguished Director General of Archæology in India

it is easy to complete the whole by the aid of the bas-reliefs (see pl VII, 2) They frequently reproduce the characteristic silhouette of this pinnacle, with the honorific parasol surmounting it, which must have raised the total height to about 25 metres

According to the invariable custom in India this sanctuary is surrounded by a stone railing, which protected it from profanation, and which, in spite of its massive weight, is evidently an imitation of a wooden fence In form slightly oblong, it measures across from east to west 43$^m$,60, and from north to south 1$^m$,10 more, in order to leave room for the flight of steps In the uprights, 3$^m$,10 high, were fixed with mortises and tenons three cross-bars and one coping, the latter 0$^m$,68 high At the four cardinal points an opening was arranged in such a way that the breach was not apparent to the eye, masked as it was in each case by a double elbow in the enclosure When it was thought to add fronting doors to these slanting entrances, it was necessary to attach the right jamb of each of these latter to the railing by a joint at right angles : in this way were formed four rectangular vestibules, shut in at the sides, and with the front and back faces corresponding alternately as regards rail and opening.

These four gates, or *toranas*, of almost unvarying dimensions and arrangements, are likewise the work of carpenters rather than of masons, and it is even surprising that they should have had the boldness to execute them in stone. They rest on two square pillars, 0$^m$,68 broad, 4 metres in height, with an interval of 2$^m$,15. These two jambs are surmounted by two great capitals, 1$^m$,25 in height and decorated in one case with dwarfs, in another with lions, and in two with elephants. These latter in their turn support no less than three lintels slightly curved, projecting

on the two sides, these lateral projections becoming smaller
and smaller, doubtless in order to accentuate the impression of height in the whole (cf pl. VIII. 1) The entire
construction attains a height of about 10 metres, without
reckoning the mystic symbols at the summit. Caryatides
of a fairly successful outline connect the outer side of the
capitals with the first architrave, other figures of men,
women, horses with their riders, elephants with their
drivers formerly adorned the spaces of the blocks which
separate the lintels. It should be remarked at once that
these statues are almost the only pieces of sculpture
finished in full relief that ancient India has bequeathed to
us, most frequently the images even of divinities, such as
those which here decorate the bases of the uprights, were
not entirely detached from the stone whence the artists'
chisel had elicited them. Then again, lintels, coins and
jambs have all their visible faces covered with bas-reliefs.
The question is to discover what these sculptures represent.

## II

*Means of Identification.* — At first sight the problem seems
to be susceptible of the most simple solution In fact one
sees almost everywhere *graffiti*, deeply incised in the ancient
Indian alphabet, which, like ours, reads from left to right;
it seems then that we have only to come close and decipher
them But, in proportion as we advance in this task, our hope
of finding the kind of information which we are seeking
diminishes. All that we can learn from each of the *circa* 375
inscriptions cut in the railing and in the gates (') is

(1) These inscriptions have last been studied by G. Buhler in *Epi-
graphia Indica*, vol II, pp. 87 sqq. , 366 sqq.

that a certain individual or a certain guild made a gift of
such and such an upright or cross-bar, in short, of the piece
on which, precisely in order that no one might be ignorant
of the fact, they have taken care to have their names inscribed As a type we may take the one displayed right in the
middle of the façade of the left jamb of the eastern gate, it
tells us simply ·

*Korarasa Nâgapiyasa Acchâvade sethisa dânam thabo* . « (This)
« pillar (is the) gift of the banker of Acchâvada, Nâgapiya,
« a native of Kurara »

Certainly these indications are far from being entirely
devoid of interest. First of all, they tell us that, if not the
monument itself, at least its enclosure was built by public
subscription, with special appropriation of the contribu-
tions, as in certain modern religious foundations. Moreover these votive and somewhat ostentatious epigraphs
enlighten us indirectly on many points — for example, as
regards the social condition of the individual subscribers,
who nearly all belong to the middle class, merchants
and bankers, the class from which the Buddhist laity were
most freely recruited, or again, concerning the details of the
artistic execution, as when one of the jambs of the southern
gate is given us as an offering in kind, the chef-d'œuvre,
and at the same time the *ex-voto*, of the carvers in ivory
of the neighbouring town of Vidiçâ; or lastly, concerning
the date of the sculptures, which the incidental mention
on this same gate of the reigning king Sâtakani allows us
to connect with the second, or first, century before
the Christian era. But, as regards the subject of the scenes
represented, the inscriptions and their engravers are aggra-
vatingly silent. Evidently the sculptors of Sânchî, as a
means of ensuring at all periods the comprehension of their
work, counted on their artistic talent as illustrators: wherein

they showed themselves much less far-seeing and less mo-
dest than their confreres who had just decorated the balustrade of Barhut, and who had not considered it futile to
engrave on the stone the titles of their bas-reliefs

It is as well to state at once that an analogy with a later
and well-known motif, a characteristic detail awakening
the remembrance of a text, a determinate number of objects
forming a traditional group, all these helps and others
besides would, no doubt, in the end have opened a way to
the interpretation of some of the Sânchî panels, but it is
doubtful if these isolated discoveries would ever have gone
beyond the stage of ingenious hypotheses, or have deserved
to be looked upon as anything but *jeux d'esprit*. If in
this matter we are able to arrive at certainties of a scientific character, we owe it to the worthy image-makers
of Barhut It is they who, thanks to the perfectly explicit
indications which they themselves have transmitted to
us on the subject of their compositions, have furnished
us with a key to ancient Buddhist art (¹) In the case
of Sânchî, where we have to explain a monument closely
connected in spirit, as in space and time, with Barhut, it
may easily be conceived that these precious and trustworthy data will necessarily be our first and constant
resource While forming a fund of interpretation acquired
in advance, they will at the same time furnish a firm
starting point for fresh research, for we may expect that
one identification will lead to another, and that the panels
will mutually explain each other, were it only by reason
of their proximity. On the whole, we must not despair of
seeing the majority of these pictures in stone come to life
by degrees under an attentive gaze; and, thanks to their

(1) See above, Essay II, p 29

expressive mimicry, they will end by making us understand the message which it was their mission to transmit to
posterity

## III

*Decorations, images and symbols.* — If we approach in a practical manner the task thus defined, it will immediately
appear to us that we could not have entirely dispensed
with the information, or the confirmations, furnished by
the written evidence of Barhut, except so far as
concerns the purely decorative bas-reliefs It is a matter
of course that the natural intelligence is always and everywhere sufficient to understand the sense and appreciate the
æsthetic value of motifs designed solely for the pleasure
of the eyes. Nothing is more simple than to classify these
ornaments into different categories, according as they
are borrowed from the fauna, flora, or the architecture, either local or foreign Our archæological knowledge
will not need to be very extensive in order to enable us
to recognize the Iranian origin of a certain number of them,
lions or winged griffins, bell-shaped capitals surmounted
by two animals set back to back, honey-suckle palmettes,
merlons, serrated ornamentation, etc We shall find, on
the contrary, a smack of the Indian soil in the balustrade
ornaments, in the horse-shoe arches, in the garlands of
lotuses, or even in the elephants so ingeniously sketched
according to nature. But neither these identifications, which
are within the reach of children, nor those more learned
distinctions tell us anything whatever concerning the
scenes any more than concerning the idols to which after
all these decorations only serve as a framework.

From the first moment that we find ourselves in the
presence of our fellow-creatures the problem of iden-

tification becomes infinitely more complicated. Even as regards isolated persons we cannot content ourselves, as in the case of animals, with a simple designation of species. We must at least discern their real nature, whether human or divine; next, try to determine their social rank on earth or in heaven, then finally, if possible, assign a proper name to each It is a great deal to ask Certainly we have very little difficulty in recognizing in a frequent feminine figure, seated on a lotus and copiously doused by two elephants, the prototype of the modern representations of Çrî, the Hindu Goddess of Fortune ('). On the other hand, we should scarcely have known what to say concerning the beautiful ladies who connect the jamb with the first lintel, if it were not that we find them again on the Barhut pillars They have retained, here as there, in addition to their opulent charms and somewhat scanty costume, their eminently plastic pose, and they continue, as is written, « to bend their willow-forms like a bow » and « to lean, holding a mango-bough in full flower, displaying their bosoms like golden jars » (*Buddhacarita*, II, 52 and IV, 35, trans COWELL) But there, in addition to what we have here, they bear also a little label which teaches us to see in them, instead of simple bayadères, divinities, of an inferior order, it is true, belonging to those whom we should call « fairies ». At the same time, in the lay persons

---

(1) See below. *Catalogue*, § 4 *a* This resemblance does not at all prove that we have already to do with the goddess Çrî The frequency of this figure at Sânchî, where it recurs as many as 9 times (see above, p 18, n 1), the manner of its juxtaposition to the Bodhi-tree, the Wheel of the Law, and the *Stûpa* of the *Parinirvâna* suggest, on the contrary, that we are dealing with a symbolical representation of the Nativity, when the two *Nâgas* (here elephants, see below, p 109), simultaneously bathed the mother and the unseen child Accordingly, this scene should have been cited and discussed above, p. 20, had we not preferred to neglect for the moment a hypothesis still awaiting verification.

who, upright at the foot of the jambs, reveal to us for their part the masculine fashions of Central India in the centuries immediately preceding our era (pl VIII, 2), we learn to recognize demi-gods and genii, guardians of the four entrances to the sanctuary, as also of the four cardinal points ([1]).

Elsewhere, as we have said, numerical considerations may sometimes point out the way of interpretation. Let us take the right (or north) jamb of the eastern gate Its façade is divided into panels, in each of which a god, if we may judge by his attributes, is seen seated, like an Indian king, in the midst of his court. Each of these compositions taken by itself tells us absolutely nothing but, if we set aside for a while the last terrace, we ascertain that there are six of these compartments.. This number alone is a flash of light; and Prof. A. Grunwedel needed nothing further to lead him to conjecture with infinite probability that here we see, arranged one above another on this pillar, the first six stories of the 27-storied paradise of Buddhism, — the only ones, moreover, which belong to the domain of sensual pleasures and consequently to that of our senses It is with difficulty that we are able to discern also, on the balcony of the highest terrace, half-length figures of the Gods in the heaven of Brahmâ, who belong to already another sphere, one step higher, the superior divinities, like Dante's souls in paradise who have become pure lights, escape by definition the scope of the plastic arts. The identification justifies itself, then, admirably, and it is confirmed even by the uniformity and banality of the scenes · for we know very well that, if the torments of hell are usually very varied, there is, according to the

---

(1) See below, *Catalogue,* § 1 *b* and 9 *a,* and cf CUNNINGHAM, *Barhut,* pl. XXI-XXIII,

representations which have been attempted, nothing more
monotonous than the happiness of the heavens. However,
the hypothesis becomes quite convincing only after a comparison with inscribed pictures of the paradise of the Thirty-
three Gods at Barhut (¹)

One other example is from this point of view still more
characteristic On the posterior frontal of this same gate
(pl VII, 2) is figured a row of vacant thrones under trees,
between human and divine worshippers They were counted. There are seven of them   and thereupon an expert
student of Buddhism, the Rev S Beal, had not been long in
rediscovering in the legend of the Master seven miraculous
trees : unfortunately it would be easy to enumerate still
more of them. The analogy of certain series in Gandhâra or at Ajantâ would to-day furnish a much more
satisfactory explanation by suggesting that it was a
symbolical manner of representing the seven traditional
Buddhas of our æon, the last being Çâkya-Muni But
you perceive that this conjecture would remain suspended literally in the air .. Well, the inscribed bas-reliefs of
Barhut have made it a certainty In fact, they show us in
succession all these same trees, of easily recognizable
species, above these same seats of stone, between these
same worshippers, but in this case each of them bears as
on a label the name of the Buddha whose memory it
evokes, and thus we can no longer doubt that the intention
of the old image-makers was indeed to represent the
seven Enlightened Ones of the past by the seven trees under
which they sat in order to attain to enlightenment (²)

---

(1) See below, *Catalogue*, § 6, and cf CUNNINGHAM, *Barhut*, pl XVI, 1,
and XVII, 1, and FERGUSSON, *Tree and Serpent Worship*, pl XXX, 1

(2) See below, *Catalogue*, § 10 *b*, and cf CUNNINGHAM, *ibid*, pl XXIX-
XXX and FERGUSSON, *ibid*., pl IX and Xa (medial lintel of the north gate)·

You perceive already, and we may resume in a single
sentence, the immediate consequences of this important
observation  Following always the same trail, we shall
learn to recognize after the symbolism of the tree, which
betokens Buddha's attainment of *Sambodhi*, that of the
wheel, which signifies his preaching, and finally that of the
*stûpa* or tumulus, which is the emblem of his *Parinirvâna*.
A comparison with the stelæ on which the old school of
Amarâvatî in Southern India was pleased to group the
representations of the « four great miracles » will finally
settle our ideas on all these points ('). At the same time
we shall not only have identified roughly a good half of the
Sânchî bas-reliefs, we shall moreover be sufficiently familiarized with the secrets of the studio to be able to approach
with some chance of success the interpretation of the
remainder of the works

## IV

*The Legendary Scenes* — Kindly bethink yourselves that
in fact the Acquisition of Omniscience, the First Sermon
and the Final Decease are, with the Nativity or the Vocation, the four chief episodes of the Buddhist legend.
Now it is scarcely necessary to say that all the scenes at
Sânchî are dedicated solely to the illustration of this
legend. In their chronological order they will be divided
naturally into three categories, according as their subject is borrowed from the previous lives, from the last
life, or from times subsequent to the definitive death of
the Blessed One.

---

(1) See above, pl. II

To begin with the past rebirths, it is sufficiently well known that these *jâtakas*, as the Indians call them, are the favourite subjects of the ancient sculptors of Barhut ([1]) : and this time also we could not put ourselves to a better school to learn to read these riddles in stone. For we must constantly bear in mind that all these bas-reliefs are what our illustrators call « stories without words » · only, instead of depicting the successive episodes in a series of distinct pictures, the old Indian masters, like those of our Middle Ages, did not shrink from placing the incidents in juxtaposition or repeating the characters within one and the same panel Once we are aware of this procedure, it is a mere pastime to explain their works and to follow the edifying thread of the story through the apparent disorder of the actors and under the accumulation of genre details wherewith they like to crowd the subject. Let us add that the pastime is all the more attractive as, in spite of certain failings in technical skill, we cannot but admire the natural gifts of our sculptors ([2])

In the scenes of the last life of the Master we shall, of course, find employed the same method of composition. But there will be added to it another convention, a most unexpected one, and one capable of completely baffling our researches, were it not that we have already been made aware of it, or rather, to employ a better expression, it is

---

([1]) See above, Essay II

([2]) We have not noticed on the eastern gate any specimen of *jâtaka* , but, in order that it may not be thought that they were excluded from the repertory of Sânchî, let us point out those of the elephant Saddanta on the posterior face of the middle lintel of the southern gate (FERGUSSON, pl VIII), of the rishi Ekaçringa, recognizable at once by his one frontal horn, and of prince Viçvantara on the lower lintel of the northern gate (FERGUSSON, pl XI-Xa and XXIV, 3), of the Mahâkapi and Çyâma on the southern jamb of the western gate (FERGUSSON, pl XVIII XIX and XXXIV)

not that some element comes into increase the pictorial com-
plication of the scene; it is, on the contrary, something
which is wanting in it, and that something is nothing less
than the figure of the principal hero. In all these illustrations of the biography of Buddha we shall find everything
that the author desires, except Buddha himself It is
already a good number of years since the inscribed bas-
reliefs of Barhut, by informing us that a certain worshipper,
on his knees before a vacant throne merely surmounted
by a parasol or marked by a symbol, is in the act of « adoring the Blessed One », have placed beyond doubt this
invariable and surprising abstenance The Sânchî sculptures,
which on the whole are better preserved, tell us more on this
point than do the ruins of Barhut. From these latter we
already knew that the ancient school of Central India had
not at its disposal a type of the perfect Buddha : the façade
of the middle lintel of our eastern gate, which represents the
« Great Departure of the Bodhisattva » (pl. X, 1), proves
to us, in its turn, that it refrained no less rigorously from
figuring the Predestined even before the *Sambodhi*, when it
would have been so simple and so easy to lend him
the usual features of Viçvantara or some other « crown
prince ». We have here a new fact and one of prime importance in the limited sphere of Buddhist archæology To
the list of conventional representations of the Buddha by
a throne of stone, the imprint of two feet, a wheel or some
other emblem, we must now add the no less strange
representation of the Bodhisattva by a horse without a rider
under an honorific parasol (¹).

---

(1) See below, *Catalogue*, § 11 *a*, cf likewise, CUNNINGHAM, *Barhut*,
pl XX, 1, and FERGUSSON, *Tree and Serpent Worship*, Amarâvatî, pl XCVI,
3, etc. These are precisely the facts of which we have sought in our first
essay to explain the origin and significance

It is, however, episodes borrowed from the second part of the last existence of the Master that form|the bulk of the legendary scenes of Sânchî. The native artists did not, in fact, resign themselves to reproducing solely and always the same great miracles, symbolized by the tree, the wheel or the *stûpa* they have fulfilled their undertaking to illustrate in detail the career of Buddha without figuring him. As if this prime difficulty were not enough, they imposed upon themselves a further one, which has not up to now been sufficiently emphasized , we mean the law to which they submitted of not bringing on to the scene any among the disciples but laymen or any among the monks but heretics prior to their conversion Thus they deliberately proposed to make us spectators of the Master's work, which consists essentially in the foundation of a monastic order, not only without our seeing the founder, but even without our catching a glimpse of a single Buddhist monk When we observe the ingenuity which they have displayed in the accomplishment of this unpromising programme, we cannot too much regret the narrow limits within which they have restricted themselves. The eastern gate, to speak only of this one, does not limit itself to showing us typical specimens of this art, at once so natural and so distorted. The panels of the southern jamb supply us in addition with a characteristic example of the manner in which, as we have indicated, they explain by their propinquity each another On the interior face (pl. IX, 1) Beal had already recognized, and verified more or less satisfactorily in detail, three distinct phases of the conversion of the thousand Brahmanic anchorites, disciples of the three brothers Kâçyapa. Prof Grunwedel has included in the same series of wonders the picture of the inundation, which occupies the centre of the front face. Henceforth we believe it impossible not to conclude this series, in accordance with a fixed tradition, by recognizing in the king just below, who is leaving his capital to pay a visit to the Blessed One, Bimbisâra, the famous sovereign of the neighbouring town of Râjagriha (Rajgir) and the faithful friend of the Master There remains now at the top of this same face a representation of the *Sambodhi* : if we reflect that the site of this miracle, namely Bodh-Gayâ, is likewise very near to Uruvilvâ (Urel), where all the episodes of the conversion of the Kâçyapas take place, we shall be at last successful in penetrating the really very simple plan of the artist : whether on his own initiative, or in consequence of the express command of the banker Nâgapiya, his intention was evidently to group on the same jamb legendary events localized in the same district of the country of Magadha (').

However well the Indian school proper may have been served in its ungrateful entreprise by the monotonous character of this perpetual course of visits and preaching, of conversions and offerings, which forms the career of Buddha, it is self-evident that its system of composition accommodated itself infinitely better to subjects subsequent to the *Parinirvâna,* the only ones in which the absence of the Master's figure became quite plausible If its regular development had not been very soon interrupted by the adoption of the Indo-Greek type of Buddha, which came from the north-west of India, it would probably have been led by the natural course of things to assign a growing importance to this sort of historical pictures, side by side with the pictures of piety Therefore, we do not hesi-

---

(1) See below, *Catalogue,* § 8 et 9, also the interior face of the northern pillar of the same gate is consecrated to Kapilavastu (*Cat* § 7), the front face of the eastern pillar of the northern gate to the Jetavana of Çrâvastî (FERGUSSON, pl X and XI), etc

tate to recognize at once a few attempts of this kind at
Sânchî, notably among the bas-reliefs which are freely displayed over the whole width of the lintels. It is scarcely
necessary to state that these scenes are not less legendary in
fact, or less edifying in intention, than the others We shall
recall, first of all, on the southern gate that vivid representation of the famous war of the relics, which by an ironical
return of the things of this world came near to being precipitated by the death of the Apostle of Benevolence. We
know that fortunately it was averted ([1]): the « Seven before
Kuçinagara » at last obtained from the inhabitants of the
town a portion of the ashes of the Blessed One, and each of
these eight co-sharers, keeping his portion or carrying it in
triumph to his native land, built a *stûpa* in its honour  It
was these eight original deposits — or rather seven of
them — that towards the middle of the third century B. C.
the famous Açoka, piously sacrilegious, violated, with
the sole aim of distributing their contents among the innumerable Buddhist sanctuaries which were then beginning to
be scattered all over India  As to the eighth, that of Râmagrâma, it seems to have been already lost in the jungle ;
and a well-known tradition (although not known to be
so ancient) will have it that in regard thereto the royal
pilgrim was confronted by the courteous, but definite refusal
of the Nâgas, who were its guardians. Now such, surely, is
the spectacle offered to us, a century after the event, by the

---

(1) See FERGUSSON, pl VII et XXXVIII (and comp  western gate, *ibid* .
pl XVIII et XXXVIII, 2)  this scene was originally carved on the face of
the lower lintel, and such is indeed the position assigned to it by the drawing
of COLE, reproduced by FERGUSSON , but in the restoration this lintel a nd the
higher one were replaced back to front  — It was the same with the three
lintels of the western gate  on the other hand COLE had in his drawing
inverted the order of the first and the third

central lintel of this very southern gate ([1]). A hundred
years are amply sufficient, especially in India, to create a
complete cycle of legends Reflect, on the other hand, that at
a few paces from the future site of the gate Açoka had
already caused his famous « edicts » to be engraved upon a
column. According to all probability the erection of this
column was contemporary with the building of the *stûpa*,
which may very well be one of the « 84 000 » religious foundations ascribed to the devout emperor. Finally,
we have reasons for thinking that the latter had remained a kind of local hero in the district · at least it is in
the immediate neighbourhood of Sânchi that the *Mahâvamsa* places the romance of his youth with the beautiful
daughter of a rich citizen of Besnagar All this may help
us to understand that two other pseudo-historic scenes
on our eastern gate may in the same way be borrowed
from his cycle. The one on the reverse side of the lower
lintel (pl VII, 2) must have some connection with the
Râmagrâma *stûpa*, if it is not simply another version of
the legend which we have just cited. As for the other on
the front of the same block, we cannot help believing that
the solemn procession to the Bodhi tree (pl. X, 2) is the
figured echo, if it is not the direct illustration, of a passage
in the *Açokâvadâna* ([2])

# V

If at the point at which we have now arrived we cast a
general glance over the gate which is the particular object of

----

(1) FÉRGUSSON, pl. VII, for the tradition compare *Divyâvadâna*, p 380,
FA-HIAN, ch xxiii, and HIUAN-TSANG, xi, 3ᵈ Kingdom
(2) See below, *Catalogue*, § 12 *a* and *b*, and cf *Divyâvadâna*, p 397
and sqq.

our studies, we shall be as surprised as any one to observe that we are beginning to understand its mute language. There is now scarcely a part of it whose meaning or intention escapes us, from the genii which mount guard at the foot to the Buddhist symbols which decorate the summit. We may, therefore, consider that we have accomplished the bulk of our task, and I shall confine myself in conclusion to endeavouring to unite your impressions : this will be the best way of summing up the various kinds of interest which these sculptures may present.

The keenest is to be found, perhaps — at least for those among us who have a taste for antiquity — in the very expressive and complete picture that they give us of the ancient civilization of India Architecture both urban and rural, furniture, tools, weapons, instruments of music, standards, chariots, harness for horses and for elephants, costumes and ornaments for men and women etc., all these concrete and precise details merely await to be detached by a draughtsman, in order to serve as authentic illustrations to a future Dictionary of Indian antiquities. And side by side with this information, which is purely material, but in itself so precious, how much more may we gather concerning even the life of the courts, towns and hermitages, if we glance successively at these anchorites, so busy around their sacrificial fires (cf. further on, page 98), these women who attend to their domestic occupations (page 95), these kings seated in their palaces or proceeding with great pomp through the streets of their capitals, before the curious eyes of their subjects (pp 91 and 93), etc What is to be said then of the no less important information which these sculptures furnish concerning the external forms of worship and even of the beliefs, the features worn in popular imagination by genii and fairies, as also concerning the manner in which the religious conscience of the time conceived the written tradition of Buddhism!

But these are questions reserved for specialists, and, doubtless, many of you are more concerned for the æsthetic value, than for the documentary interest, of these old monuments From this point of view you cannot have failed to appreciate the perfect naturalness of the artists who worked at them, and I do not hesitate to praise above all the justness of their observation — so remarkable especially in their animals and trees — and the freedom of their execution, in spite of a certain clumsiness and a very pardonable ignorance of *our* perspective. You divine also what a delicate problem is raised as to the determination of the exact place of their works in the general history of art I do not think that anyone can reasonably contest the statement that this school of Barhut and of Sânchî is a direct expression of Indian genius, with all the spontaneousness and conventionality to be found in either. And in making this statement I am not thinking only of fundamentals, of the thoroughly indigenous character of the subjects which the art proposed to treat even as regards its specially technical proceedings, that extremely deeply incised relief, that constant search for swarming effects, that systematic overcrowding of the whole available space in the panel by accessory details, it is in the hereditary habits of the wood and ivory carvers of ancient India, not forgetting its goldsmiths, that I should seek their origin But, if ancient Buddhist art is thus attached by all its roots to its native soil, we should have to be wilfully blind not to see the foreign shoots which have already ingrafted themselves on this wild stock. A quantity of decorative motives have appeared to us so directly borrowed from Persia that their importation can scarcely be explained otherwise than by

an immigration of Iranian artisans  But this is not all
here and there, in bold foreshortenings, in the skilful placing of three-quarter length figures, in the harmonious
balancing of groups — in a word, in the detail of the work-
ing process, as also in the general arrangement of the composition — we detect growing traces of an influence more
subtle and more difficult to disentangle, but incomparably
more artistic, which in fact had by the vicissitudes of political history been brought much nearer, the influence of
Hellenistic models  Moreover, we now know from a reliable
source that this influence had already penetrated as far
as there, and the native artists of Vidiçâ could see quite
close to their town the column which had been raised on
behalf of a local râjah in the reign of the Indo-Greek
king Antialkidas (about 175 B  C.) by the envoy Heliodoros, son of Dion, a native of Taxilâ (¹)

But, if these bas-reliefs have deserved to hold your attention for an instant, it is not solely for what they teach us
or inspire us with a desire to know of the civilization and
art of India ˙ it is also and especially for the curious comparisons with our own religious art to which they lend
themselves. You have surely observed among them an
employment of symbols, in every way analogous to that
exhibited by the first Christian artists of the Catacombs at a
time when they also had not at their disposal an universally
accepted image of the Saviour  The parallelism of the two
developments might be pursued still further . and later on,
when in both cases the type of the Master had been definitely fixed, it would be no less easy to find in Buddhist tradition written evidence of the tendency, so well known to

(1) The quite recent discovery of this inscribed pillar is due to Mr J
H MARSHALL, J R A. S. 1909, p 1053.

us, to authenticate the resemblance, as if it were a question
of a portrait made from a living model. Another feature
which you must also have noticed in passing is the narrative character of the bas-reliefs, forthwith employed to
relate edifying stories, and it will not have escaped you
either that we find again on the altar screens of the Middle
Ages, and even on certain panels of the first Renaissance
— for example on those with which Ghiberti decorated the
doors of the Baptistery at Florence — the same procedures
of juxtaposition of episodes and repetition of persons which
were already in use at Barhut and at Sânchî Thus these old
monuments, in exchange for the trouble which we have
taken to become familiar with them, offer us ample material for comparisons of an interest more general and more
closely connected with us than we could have expected. It is
of this that I wished in conclusion to remind you as a compensation for the perhaps rather too technical subject
which circumstances, as told in our preamble, have imposed upon us.

### SECOND PART

## SUMMARY CATALOGUE OF THE SCULPTURES

[We have not deemed it necessary to encumber this
short notice with a detailed account of the more or less successful attempts which have already been made with a view
to the interpretation of the sculptures of Sânchî. The principal publication treating of them, after the first essay of
CUNNINGHAM, *The Bhilsa Topes* (London, 1854), is that of
FERGUSSON, *Tree and Serpent-Worship* (2ᵈ ed., London, 1873,
reproducing the identifications proposed by BEAL, *Journ.
of the Roy As Soc.*, new series, V, 1871, pp 164 and sqq.) :

but the photographs, although annotated by numerous drawings, are almost unusable, because their scale has been too much reduced, and the text, ruined by strange theories, has lost nearly all value The same remarks apply to the photographs of Sir Lepel GRIFFIN, *Famous Monuments of Central India,* and of H COLE, *Preservation of National Monuments, India · Great Buddhist Tope at Sânchi* (1885), and to the text of F C MAISEY, *Sânchi and its remains* (London, 1892) Fortunately the moulding of the eastern gate, given to the « Museum fur Volkerkunde » in Berlin, attracted in a very special manner the attention of Professor Grunwedel in Chapter V of his celebrated *Handbuch* (*Buddhistische Kunst in Indien,* 2ᵈ ed., Berlin, 1900, revised and enlarged by Dr J Burgess, *Buddhist Art in India,* London, 1902, particularly pp. 72-74) We are in perfect agreement with the eminent archæologists of Edinburgh and Berlin as regards the method to be followed · at the same time, we must warn the reader once for all that on several points we have arrived at conclusions somewhat different from theirs If this treatise marks any progress whatever in the interpretation of the Sânchî bas-reliefs, it is entirely due to the excellent direct photographs which Mr J. H Marshall has put at our disposal ]

The sculptures which cover from top to bottom the eastern gate of the *stûpa* of Sânchî may be divided into two great categories, the decorative elements and the Buddhist scenes In reality the line of demarcation between these two orders of subjects is at times very difficult to trace. Many of the so-called ornaments have a traditional symbolical value, and, on the other hand, a great number of the edifying representations tend to pure decoration. The distinction is justified, however, in practice We shall avoid many useless repetitions, if we decide to classify

in the first category all those motifs whose character,
being before all ornamental, is sufficiently emphasized by
the fact that they are symmetrically repeated on the beams
or the uprights of the stone scaffolding which constitutes
the *torana* (cf above, pp. 65-6).

## THE DECORATIVE ELEMENTS

§ 1 *Decoration of the jambs* — Thus it is that the two jambs
of the gate, that of the north and that of the south, — or
more simply, of the right and left as you enter, — bear on
two of their faces motifs which are evidently complemen-
tary

*a*) Their *outer face* is simply decorated with those pink
lotus flowers (*padma* or *nelumbum speciosum*), which, as we
know, play a considerable part in Indian ornamentation
and symbolism  To the right a series of full-blown roses
is enclosed within two waved garlands of these same flowers, graced with buds and leaves. To the left the principal
subject consists of a similar garland, whose decoration
changes likewise between each undulation of the chief
branch : in addition Indian swans (*hamsa*) and a tortoise
are intermingled with the flowers

*b*) In the two male figures placed opposite each other at
the foot of the *inner face* of the two jambs we must, from
analogy with Barhut, recognize the protecting spirits of
the eastern region, that is, the Gandharvas or celestial
musicians, the chief of whom is Dhritarâshtra (cf above,
p. 71) Nevertheless, they are presented simply under the
appearance of great Indian lords, wearing turbans and
adorned with heavy jewels, earrings, necklaces and bracelets
of precious stones. The ends of their long loin-cloths hang
in close little pleats in front, as for the second part of their
costume, the scarf, whose usual function is to drape the

body, they wear it negligently tied round their loins
The one holds up the ends of it with his left hand,
whilst the other has placed his awkwardly on his hip (see
pl. VIII, 2) The latter holds in his right hand a *Bignonia*
flower, while the former has a lotus. Both are looking in
the direction of the sanctuary, and are leaning against a
background formed of a *Bignonia* in blossom and a mango-
tree bearing fruit

§ 2 *Capitals* — The great capitals which surmount the
two jambs of the eastern gate are decorated with tame elephants (pl. VIII, 1) Four of these animals are placed very
ingeniously about each pillar in such a way that their heads
form a round embossement to the four edges of the corners
Their harness consists of a rich head-stall (from which
hang in front of the ears two pendants of pearls, and
behind two bells) and a tasselled saddle-cloth, kept
in its place by cords which pass under their bodies and
form knots on their backs. The person of distinction was
seated astride in the most comfortable place on their
necks holding in his hand the special crook (*ankuça*), he
was his own driver and, in fact, we know that in ancient
India the art of driving elephants formed an integral
part of a complete education Right on the elephant's
hind quarters crouches a standard-bearer, who doubtless,
in the case of a rapid motion, held on to the knot of
the belly-band As for the elephants themselves with
their trunks and one of their fore-feet slightly bent back,
they are, as usual, admirably rendered. Formal leaves and
flowers decorate the upper part of the capitals An inscription on the inner face of that to the left invokes imprecations
on whosoever shall remove a single stone of the gate or
the railing. As regards the two caryatids, see below, § 5 *a*.

§ 3 *Decoration of the lintels.* — The three lintels likewise repeat on both their faces several symmetrical forms of decoration

*a*) On the *façade* (pl. VIII, 1) we shall note first three kinds of false capitals, of a character quite Iranian, which, continuing the two uprights, break through each lintel. On the two lower ones the decorative designs consist of winged lions, two of which are seated back to back, while a third protrudes its head and two front-paws through the space between them On the topmost one they consist of two great fully harnessed draught oxen, likewise seated back to back, but furthermore ridden by two men.

*a'*) On *the reverse side* (pl VII, 2) the corresponding subjects are in the same order : two pairs of goats, with or without horns; two pairs of two-humped camels, likewise seated; two pairs of horned lions, standing and passant All these animals serve as steeds for riders of both sexes and of different types, native and foreign. One of those at the summit has short hair, tied with a fillet, and carries in his left hand a piece of a vine-stock.

*b*) The extremities of the lintels are uniformly decorated both on the observe and on the reverse by a kind of long tendril, rolled seven times round itself and attached to the whole by an ornament of honeysuckle : this makes a total of twelve snails, and produces a somewhat unfortunate effect. If it were claimed that this is an attempt to imitate the Ionic volute, it would have to be acknowledged that it is inverted and executed in a most rudimentary fashion.

*c*) The whole surface of the lintels unoccupied by these decorations is, as a general rule, consecrated to legendary scenes. There is, it seems, no exception to be made, except upon the façade and only on the projecting portions of the

lower and middle lintels. The former are garnished with
two pairs of peacocks — a triumph of graceful design,
which is to be found also on the northern gate — and the
latter by wild elephants.

§ 4 *The supports* — We agree to designate by this term
the four cubical blocks placed in the prolongations of the
uprights and the six uprights set in between the three lintels to separate them from one another.

*a*) On the *façade* (pl VIII, 1) the lower support to the
right and the upper one to the left both represent a feminine
figure seated, with one leg hanging down, upon a lotus
issuing from a lottery vase (*bhadra-ghaṭa*) · she holds in
her hand this same flower, and on two other lotuses at
either side of her two standing elephants douse her, or are
in the attitude of dousing her, with two pitchers held at the
ends of their trunks We know that this motif is preserved
even to our days in the representations of the Indian Fortune but we have reasons for believing that this was not
the original denotation (1) The subjects of the two other
corresponding panels belong, in any case, to the category
of Buddhist miracles. The one on the left represents the
« preaching of Buddha » by means of the Wheel of the Law
placed on a throne under a parasol among the usual worshippers, human and divine. The one on the right shows
us — as is proved by the characteristically twisted floweret
of his tree, — the Messiah of Buddhism, Maitreya, symbo-
lised by this *campaka* or *nâga-pushpa* (*Michelia champaka* or
*Mesua Roxburghi*).

*a'*) On the *reverse* side of the gate (pl. VII, 2) the lower supports are decorated only with lotuses issuing from a *bha-*

---

(1) See above, p 70, n 1

*dra-ghata*, but the upper ones return to the legendary scenes with two *stûpas* emblematic of the *Parinirvâna* of the Master, and quite similar to those on the front, of which, as we shall see below (§ 10 *a*), they complete the number

*b*) One may connect with these the symbols on the *front* of the six uprights, symbols usually enclosed between a railing and merlons : namely, formal Bodhi-trees and columns surmounted by the Wheel of the Law or by a lion simply

*b'*) *Behind* they are all covered with the same ornamentation, in which the lotus is united with the honeysuckle.

§ 5. *The detached figures.* — To exhaust the list of symmetrical subjects, nothing further remains for us than to enumerate the detached figures in full relief (cf above, page 66, and pl. VIII, 1).

*a*) The most interesting are the fées (*yakshinî*, cf above, p. 70), who, with the curve of the mango-tree from which they hang by the two arms, form so ingeniously decorative a bracket. Only the figure on the right is preserved. Like the men, she wears a long *dhoṭi*, only it is made of a more transparent material. Her hair, curiously erected in the form of a brush on the top of the head, is spread over the back (instead of being gathered in a plait, as is the case, for instance, with the female dancers of § 6 *a*). In addition to earrings, necklace and bracelets for the wrists, she wears ankle-rings, which come nearly up to her knees, and the characteristic feature of an Indian woman's toilet, the rich belt of jewelry which covers the loins. In conformity with the custom of the ancient school, the sex is indicated.

*b*) The few smaller figures to be found on this gate — which we may complete in our thoughts by analogy

with the northern gate — comprise also another fairy in a
different pose, three elephants, in each case mounted by two
persons, and a miserable vestige of a lion

*c*) As for the symbols at the summit, they were three in
number. At the top of each upright two, of which one is
still in its place, represented the top of a flag-staff. In the
middle — on a pedestal probably formed of four lions,
flanked by two worshippers bearing fly-flappers — stood
finally the ancient solar symbol of the wheel, placed at the
service of the Good Law

### The Legendary Scenes.

After this rapid sketch of the decorative elements we
enter upon a necessarily much more detailed examination
of the religious scenes. For it is self-evident that it is eminently these that need explanation.

We will begin with those which are figured on the two
faces, namely the front and the interior ones, which hold
the place of honour in the jambs. We have already seen
that their exterior faces bear only one decorative motif
(§ 1 *a*). As regards their rear faces, they left no space
above the balustrade, except for two little bas-reliefs,
analogous to those which we have already noticed on
the supports (cf. § 4 *a* and *a*')   taken all together,
they represent in the same stereotyped manner, by the
pretended adoration of the tree, the wheel and the *stûpa*,
the three great traditional miracles of the Illumination,
the Preaching, and the Death of Buddha

§ 6. *Front face of the right jamb*. — This façade is decorated
with four superposed buildings . the lower one has only
one story, the middle ones have two, both covered with a
rounded roof, in which are open bays in the shape of a

horse-shoe; the top one has one story, surmounted by an uncovered terrace, which is surrounded on three sides by a group of buildings It is difficult in the present state of the stone to judge of the distribution of the persons on the lower panel, but the five following ones, divided likewise into three compartments by columns with or without Persepolitan capitals, are all composed in the same manner The centre is occupied by a divine personage, as is proved by the thunderbolt which he holds in his right hand and the vase of ambrosia in his left. God though he be, he is for the rest conceived in the image of an Indian king. Behind him stand the bearers of his parasol and fly-flapper, insignia of his royalty, on his right, in the same surroundings, but on a slightly lower seat, is his viceroy (uparâja) At his left are seen the musicians and dancers of his court. It is well known that this concert-ballet is according to Indian ideas the indispensable accompaniment of a happy mundane life. Indications of trees form the background. On the upper terrace, as on a balcony, lean two other gods, likewise fanned by women.

We have enumerated above (p. 71) the reasons which militate in favour of the identification of this series of stories with those of the Buddhist paradise They would therefore serve respectively as dwelling-places, (1) for « the Four Great Kings », guardians of the four cardinal points (the necessity of housing all four of them would explain the absence of bayadères in the compartment to the right of the lower panel, at the same time that their subordinate character would justify the line of demarcation traced by the roof of the palace between them and the following ones); — (2) for the Thirty-three Gods over whom Indra reigns, and (3) for those ruled by Yama; — (4) for the Satisfied Gods ( Tushita), among whom the Bodhisattva resided before

his last re-descent upon earth, (5) for the Gods who dispose
of their own creations, — (6) and finally, for those who
even dispose of the creations of others, and whose king
Mâra, God of Desire and Death, extends his empire over
the five lower heavens  As for the two persons on the
terrace, they would represent the last divinities still visible
to our human eyes, those of Brahmâ's world.

§ 7. *Inner face of the right jamb.* — This face, according to
Fergusson, presents an exceptional interest, « being the
only subject at Sânchî that we can, with certainty, attribute to Buddhism, as it is known to us »  To-day it is better
known, but the representation, on the upper extremity of
the middle bas-relief, of the « dream of Mâyâ », — otherwise, the « conception of the Bodhisattva », who descends
into his mother's bosom in the form of a little elephant —
remains certainly in this case the pivot of all identification
We know that this scene, so strange to our eyes, in which
it is a pachyderm which plays the part of the dove in our
« Annunciations », is itself certainly identified by the Barhut inscription : « The Descent of the Blessed One ».
Consequently, we might be tempted to see in the upper
bas-relief a picture of the Bodhisattva in the heaven of
the Tushita gods at the moment when he prepares to be
born again in the royal family of Kapilavastu  But the
sculptor prevents us from going astray in that direction by
the care which he has taken to represent before and behind
the empty throne obviously the same king and the same
tree which we find again at the bottom of the lower panel.
He could not more clearly indicate that he is referring us to
the latter to find the solution of the enigma

a) If we turn then to that (pl IX, 2), we shall find, first of
all, in the centre of the composition this same king, about

to set out with great pomp from one of the gates of his good town of Kapilavastu. He is in his chariot, accompanied by the three usual servants, the driver, holding the reins and the whip, the parasol and fly-flapper bearers. As is customary, the horses, whose head-adornment is very high, have their long tails carefully tied up to the harness, doubtless in order that they may not inconvenience the occupants of the chariot. At their left the archers of the guard stand out along the ramparts of the city, and in front march the herald and the seven musicians of the royal orchestra, blowing oblique flutes and shells or beating drums. Behind we perceive, emerging from the streets of the town, a brilliant suite mounted on horses and elephants. Through the balconies of the verandas spectators, mostly women, protrude their heads, curious to see the procession of the feudal cortège of king Çuddhodana and his peers, the noble lords of the race of Çâkya.

Where are they going? Not far, it seems, into a park near the town, where all have dismounted; and the first idea is that they are going to the famous park of Lumbinî, theatre of the « Nativity », which may be presaged by the scene (at the top of the panel) of the « Conception » But there is nothing to corroborate this hypothesis. The king and the Çâkyas appear indeed all occupied in contemplating with clasped hands some miraculous event, but their eyes are raised into the air, and the object towards which they are turned is a small rectangular slab, stretched exactly above their heads. It cannot take us long to recognize in this slab the « promenade of precious stone » (Skt *ratna-cankrama*) which Buddha created by magic « in the air », on the occasion of his first return to his native town of Kapilavastu (¹)

_____

(1) *Mahâvastu*, III, p 113, Commentary on the *Dhammapada*, ed Fausböll, p 334, *Mahâvamsa*, XXX, st. 81, etc

7

The legend is well known : on the occasion of this meeting
between the father, who had remained a king, and the son,
who had become Buddha, a most delicate question of
etiquette had arisen which of the two should salute the
other first? The Blessed One escaped the difficulty by the
miracle which the sculptor has endeavoured to represent as
well as he could with his limited means and without
representation of Buddha himself.

*b*) Apparently he was still somewhat distrustful of the
intelligence of his spectators; for, in order to give more precision, he has been careful to put in the first row at the left a
*nyagrodha* tree surrounded by a balustrade. This *Ficus indica*
(clearly distinguished from the *açvattha* or *Ficus religiosa*, as
it is represented, for instance, on the face of the left jamb)
is evidently intended to symbolise by itself the *nyagrodha-
ârâma* at the gates of Kapilavastu, which on the same occasion king Çuddhodana assigned to his son for a residence. Henceforth the meaning of the upper bas-relief
becomes, reciprocally, clear enough. It represents in the
same elliptical manner the Buddha seated upon a throne,
under this same *nyagrodha*, in the before-mentioned hermitage, and the said king, his father — always to be recognized by the spindle-shaped object kept in its place by a
buckle of gems on the top of his turban — « renders
homage to him for the third time », whilst the Çâkyas,
whose pride has been broken by the miracle, imitate his
example. As always, the tree is adorned with garlands and
surmounted by a parasol of honour, whilst in the heavens
two divinities, mounted on griffons, and two others, half
man and half bird, bring still more garlands or cause flowers
to rain down.

But what now is the point of the motif of the « Conception », thus intercalated between two episodes which

took place more than forty years after? The answer is
simple, it is there solely to say : « the action takes place at
Kapilavastu », and it is just this which explains why, in
spite of its traditional importance, it is treated in so secondary a manner. What else could our sculptor do, unless
he attached a label, as at Barhut? He has taken care to
supplement by the addition of the *nyagrodha* the somewhat
summary indication of the *ratna-cankrama* For the rest, that
is for the royal procession, he has given free play to his
spirit of observation and his taste for the picturesque,
trusting in the means which otherwise he has put at our
disposal for localizing the event and identifying the prota-
gonists : and, if on this point we have, as we believe, arrived
at a definite interpretation, it is solely owing to the docility
with which we have followed his indications.

For the person standing at the foot of the jamb and the
one opposite to him we must refer to § 1 *b* above

§ 8. *Inner face of the left jamb* — For the general sense of
the bas-reliefs of this jamb and the link which connects
them we must refer to what was said above on pages 76-7

*a)* We will begin this time with the upper panel of the
inner face. Apparently it represents the rural country town
of Uruvilvâ, whose immediate approaches had been a few
months previously the scene of the *Sambodhi*, and later —
after Buddha's first journey to Benares — of the conversion
of the Kâçyapas. Above, at the left, women are doing their
household work on the thresholds of their huts; one is husk-
ing rice in a wooden mortar with a huge pestle, another
winnows it with a fan in the form of a shovel, two neigh-
bours are one of them rolling out pastry-cakes and the other
grinding curry-powder. The attention of the latter seems
to be distracted by the (perhaps amorous) conversation of

the man seated beside her  Further down to the right two
more women with round pitchers upon their hips are
going in the direction of the river Nairañjanâ (now the
Lilañj), where a third is already stooping to fill her *ghati*
Some men are coming and going, the bamboo-pole on their
shoulders laden or empty  It is the village life of two thousand years ago . it is also the village life of to-day, and there
is not one of the utensils represented there that we have
not somewhere seen in use. Troops of oxen, buffalos, goats,
sheep add life to the picture. In what does its edification
consist ? Simply in this, that the invisible Buddha is felt
to be seated under a parasol and on a throne, behind
which two devotees are standing  Before the gate of the
village a third person is likewise to be seen, with his hands
clasped , and the attitude of this villager is the only connecting link between the genre scenes, so complacently treated, and the religious subject, which is decidedly a little
sacrificed  As for the two worshippers, we believe, after carefully weighing everything, that we must recognize in them
the gods Indra and Brahmâ, paying a visit to the Blessed One in his residence, which was near to, but distinct
from, that of the oldest of the Kâçyapas, the Kâçyapa
of Uruvilvâ. This interpretation not only has the advantage of connecting the subject with the series of wonders which in the end determined the conversion of the
Brahmanical ascetics . it also provides a place moreover for
the third and fourth of those *prâtihâryas*, besides containing
an implicit allusion to the second, in the order in which the
*Mahâvagga* (1, 16-18) counts them  If it is objected that
these miracles are given in the text as taking place during
the night, we shall reply that our sculptors have systematically ignored this detail, for the very good reason that it was
not within their competence (cf. below, § 11 *a*).

*b*) However the case may be, the panel immediately
below represents patently the miracle of the « victory over
the wicked serpent », the first in the version of the *Mahâvagga*, the last in that of the *Mahâvastu* Buddha has been
allowed by the oldest of the Kâçyapas to pass the night, at
his own risk and peril, in a fire-temple, in spite of the
redoubtable *nâga* which inhabits it (pl IX, 1) The latter
at once attacks him, and the two struggle together for a
long time, smoke against smoke, flame against flame,
until the final defeat of the dragon This is why we here
see flames escaping by the horse-shoe bays in the rounded
roof of the temple, « as if it were a prey to fire ». Through the
pillars supporting the roof, between the fire altar (or rather
vessel of fire) and the five-headed hood of the serpent you
see the throne of the invisible Buddha On either side Brahmanic anchorites, characterised by their high conical-sha-
ped head-dresses and their bark-garments, are contemplating
with surprise or respect the victory of the Blessed One,
whilst below, to the left, three young novices are hastening
to go and fill pitchers at the Nairañjanâ Their intention, if
we are to believe the analogy of Gandhâra (cf. *Art gréco-
bouddhique du Gandhâra*, fig 224, 225 *b*, etc ), is to use
them in extinguishing the fire. On the right an ascetic
has just made his report to the old Kâçyapa, seated on a rol-
led-up mat (*brishî*) on the threshold of his round hut, with
its roof of leaves (*parnaçâlâ*), a band is passed round his
knees and loins, and his head is leaning upon an esparto
cushion. In front is a row of trees along the bank of the
river. The instruments of the Vedic sacrifice, an elephant,
antelopes, two buffalos, which lift their heads with an air
of alarm, trees swarming with monkeys, complete or close
the picture of the hermitage On the whole, the miracle
is related as minutely as was possible to the sculptor. The

whole question is to find out whether he has not sought, in accordance with his habit, to combine two subjects At the middle bottom, in the river — indicated as usual by waved lines, lotuses and aquatic birds — an adult anchorite, who is about to bathe, seems to be watching a fire-cauldron, placed in unstable equilibrium on the edge of the water. If we remember that one of the wonders accomplished by Buddha consisted precisely in creating fires, in order to allow the Brahmans to warm themselves on leaving the bath, we cannot help asking ourselves whether we have not here at least one allusion to this further *prâtihârya* (cf. *Mahâvagga*, I, 20, 15)

*c*) In any case, two, or even three, miracles are grouped on the next small panel Here again, it is understood, the intention of edifying does not prevent the scene from being treated in a picturesque manner After the life of the village it is the life of the hermitage that we have before our eyes. On the right two anchorites are splitting wood by means of axes which, if we may judge from their massive appearance and the form of their handles, must be made of stone, two others are occupied in lighting fires, and a fifth holds in his hand a sacrificial spoon, whilst two novices are carrying on their shoulders the one a fagot of logs and the other a double basket of provisions. Among the trees at the back a sacred tumulus, as is proved by the balustrade surrounding it, must enclose the relics of some superior of the community, and thus gives the last touch of local colour (¹)

_____

(1) We may notice that the form of this *stûpa* is the most ancient of which Indian art has preserved the image In the objects decorating its circumference (a long shell, a double basket (?) and a large conch) we should be disposed to see — like the oar planted by the companions of Ulysses on the tumulus of Elpenor — the implements used by the deceased during his lifetime.

But for the initiated all the details of the decoration have at the same time an edifying signification. The texts tell us, in fact, that according to the will of the Blessed One these logs and these fires alternately refused and consented, the former to allow themselves to be split and the latter to let themselves burn. That is why, on the right, one of the anchorites continues to hold his axe in the air, without being able to lower it ('), whilst his neighbour has just succeeded by a lucky stroke in splitting his piece of wood It is also for the same reason that, of the two Brahmans who are lighting their fires by fanning them with esparto screens, the one in the second row cannot succeed in obtaining any flame whatever, whilst the one in the first row sees his fire blaze up brightly. These two miracles are related to us by the *Mahâvagga* (1, 20, 12-13) in the same breath But what then would be the role of the anchorite on the left? We imagine that we must turn to the *Mahâvastu* (III, p 426, l. 15-18) for the answer. His attitude suffices by itself to indicate the twofold marvel, which is perfectly analogous to the preceding ones, of the offering which at first will not be detached from the spoon, then at last consents to fall — in the shape of a snail doubled up — into the sacrificial pile (pl IX, 1).

§ 9  — *Front face of the left jamb.*

*a)* Nevertheless, in order to overcome the arrogance of the old Brahman, there was need of another miracle, whose decided importance was of sufficient value to cause it to be

---

(1) We borrow this interpretation from the *Mahâvastu*, III, p 428, 1 4-8, but without concealing from ourselves the fact that it may just as well have been conceived afterwards in view of a bas relief analogous to the one at Sânchî.

placed upon the front of the pillar, as it forms the dénoument of the episode in the *Mahâvagga* (I 20, 15 , wanting in the *Mahâvastu*) : « At this time there fell out of season a heavy rain, and a great flood followed ». You will understand henceforward why the Nairañjanâ has risen to the point of washing the lower branches of the trees, to the greatest terror of the monkeys who have taken refuge there, and also to the evident satisfaction of the water birds and even of a crocodile. On the swollen waters of the river old Kâçyapa hastens in a curiously jointed canoe, attended by two ascetics with paddles, to the assistance of the Blessed One But the latter has left his seat (relegated to the bottom at the right of the composition), and has formed for himself a « promenade », which allows him to walk about with dry feet in the midst of the wild waters This time the anchorite cannot but recognize the transcendent superiority of his host : when we see him again below, standing on the bank with his disciples, he is turning his back towards us, in order to make in the direction of the master's *cankrama* the gesture of submission or *añjali* (¹).

*b*) There remains then to be explained the panel immediately below Once more it represents a king leaving his capital chariot, music, guards, suite, spectators, everything, even the architecture, is similar to § 7 *a* Only we notice the way in which the rampart of bricks goes right to the top of the panel, in order to separate the city from the

---

(1) It appears to us that the ingenious suggestion that he has prostrated himself must be put aside for in that case we could not understand how his disciples could remain standing ; besides, the flowers placed near him are scattered almost everywhere in the picture and are found likewise on one of the preceding bas-reliefs (§ 8 *b*) Also, the analogy of § 7 *a* is in opposition to the identification of the *cankrama* of the Blessed One with the great washing-stone brought to him on another occasion by the god Indra

scene which takes place on its outskirts. The first thing is to
know the name of the town : but this time it is to the neighbouring scenes that we must address our questions. We have
already seen above (p. 77) that they reply unanimously   it
is the capital of Magadha  The texts for their part agree in
telling us that immediately after the conversion of the Kâçyapas and their thousand disciples the Blessed One, at the
head of his new community of saints, repaired to Râjagriha, and at the gates of the town received the solemn visit
of King Bimbisâra (¹). In accordance with the usual custom the king advanced in his good chariot as far as the
road would allow a carriage to pass, then he descended and
went on foot towards Buddha. This is what he is doing at
the top on the left, followed by one sole companion, whose
duty is to represent in his own person the king's innumerable cortége. Before the empty throne of the Blessed One
conventional indications of water and rocks succeed, in
default of a wood of bamboos, in particularizing the location
of the scene on the hill Antagiri near the famous hot springs
of Râjgir (²)  As for the rest of the story, it must naturally
be supplemented by the help of the texts : the king and the
people of Magadha wonder at first concerning Buddha and
old Kâçyapa, which is the master and which the disciple,
the public homage of the old anchorite will soon decide the
question. If we see nothing of all this, it is because the
Sânchî bas-reliefs systematically omit all representation

---

(1) *Mahâvagga*, I, 22 , *Mahâvastu*, III, p 441-449 , *Divyâvadâna*, p 393,
etc.
(2) Cf. Cunningham, *Arch. Reports*, III p 140 . « I fixed the position of
the Bamboo Forest to the south-west of Râjgir, on the hill lying between
the hot-springs of Tapoban and old Râjagriha ». It is precisely by the « Gate
of the Hot Springs » (*tapoda dvâra*) that the *Lalita-Vistara*, xvi, makes
Buddha for the first time enter Râjagriha

not only of Buddha, but also of his monks (cf above,
p. 75). It is easy to observe how infinitely clearer the sole
representation of the latter makes the same series of episodes on one of the pillars of the balustrades of Amarâvatî
(FERGUSSON, pl. LXX, or *Art gréco-bouddh. du Gandh.*,
fig 228)

   *c*) Finally, every one must recognize at the top of this
same face, in the religious fig-tree (*açvattha*) surmounted,
as usual, by a parasol and inhabited by winged genii, the
tree and the symbol of the perfect « Bodhi of the Blessed
One Çâkya-Muni ». of this the inscription on an analogous bas-relief at Barhut convinces us  In both cases we
find at the foot of the same tree the same throne, surmounted by the same symbol (which is double at Barhut), and,
about the offshoot of the branches, the same temple open
to the sky  We may safely aver that this strange sanctuary is, at the earliest, that which Açoka had piously
built around the sacred tree, more than two centuries after
the death of the Master : but this flagrant anachronism is
one of those to which we are perfectly accustomed in the
religious art of all times and all countries, and does not in
any wise prevent the picture from relating to the very
miracle of the Illumination of Buddha. Perhaps it has not
been observed with sufficient attention that the analogy of
Barhut forces us to establish a close connection between
this scene and the double row of people contiguous to it :
the whole difference consists in the fact that here they are
above it, while in the former case they are below, but the
inscriptions prove that they are different categories of Gods,
and must be regarded as grouped in adoration at the four
cardinal points of the tree, as happened at the moment of
the *Sambodhi*(¹). Henceforward we must here also recog-

---

(1) For the bas-reliefs see CUNNINGHAM, *Barhut*, pl. XIV, 1, and for the

nize in the four worshippers at the bottom « the four
great kings », who live in our atmosphere, to the right those
of the east and the south, to the left those of the north and
west The ten persons of the first row, counting two for
each heaven, would then indicate the kings and viceroys
of the five other paradises of the Kâmâvacaras, just as on
the face of the other pillar (§ 6) they happen to be represented in their heavenly palaces, then the eight gods in the
row above, of whose bodies (as in the case of the two who
form their counterpart on the upper terrace on the right) only
half is seen, would represent in twos the inhabitants of the
four stages of Brahmâ's heaven, the last that we may ask the
sculptor to show us (cf. above, p. 71). Thus a close examination reveals, under the evident striving after variety in
the outer forms, a striking carefulness in balancing the
intrinsic importance and the religious value of the subjects
on the symmetrical faces of the two jambs.

§ 10 *Upper lintel.* — We shall find traces of the same
carefulness on the two faces of the lintels, where, side by
side with symmetrical decorations (cf above, § 3), great
Buddhist compositions also are to be found We will begin
our study of them at the top, a method which will apparently allow us to follow a certain chronological order in
reviewing the scenes

*a)* Thus it is that the *frontal* of the gate is occupied from
one end to the other by a symbolical representation of the

---

inscriptions HULTZSCH, *Ind Antiquary*, XXI, p. 235 Let us notice also on
the front face of the lower lintel of the western gate (the back face of the
same lintel in the restoration of to day, and the front face of the upper lintel
in the plan of COLE *ap* FERGUSSON, pl. XVIII) that the defeat of Mâra's
army by Buddha is represented beside a Bodhi tree, which is already surrounded by his temple.

seven last Buddhas of the past, typified alternately by the
tumulus of their *Parinirvâna* and the tree of their *Sambodhi*
(pl. VIII, 1). The sculptor, having only two trees at his disposal, considered it his duty to give the honour of being
placed on the fronton to the first and the last Buddha of
the series    in fact, by comparison with the reverse side,
one can distinctly recognize on the right of the central
*stûpa*, the *Bignonia* of Vipaçyin, and on the left the sacred
fig-tree of Gautama, otherwise called Çâkya-muni  On the
other hand, the two missing tumuli are restored on the two
upper supports (cf § 4 *a'*) of the reverse side, so as to complete the traditional number  This observation allows us to
suppose that some æsthetic scruple alone prevented the
artist from placing the seven *stûpas* in a row on the façade,
as on the other face he did not hesitate to do with the
seven corresponding trees (cf above, p. 72).

*b*) For the *rear façade* (pl. VII, 1) it will be sufficient to
give, according to the text and the inscribed bas-reliefs at
Barhut, a list of the seven Buddhas and their respective
*Bodhidrumas*. Here they are, in the order in which they are
presented, going from right to left of the spectator :

| | |
|---|---|
| Vipaçyin (*Pâli* Vipassin) | Pâtali *(Bignonia suaveolens)*. |
| Çikhin (*P* Sikhin). | Pundarîka (*Mangifera* . . . [and not *nymphæa*]). |
| Viçvabhû (*P.* Vessabhu). | Çâla (*Shorea robusta*) |
| Krakucchanda (*P.* Kaku-sandha). | Çirîsha *(Acacia sirissa).* |
| Kanakamuni (*P*. Kona-gamana). | Udumbara (*Ficus glome-rata*) |
| Kâçyapa (*P* Kassapa) | Nyagrodha (*Ficus indica*) |
| Gautama (*P* Gotama) | Açvattha (*Ficus religiosa*). |

It will be well likewise to connect with this series the

representation, on one of the upper supports of the façade,
of the tree of the eighth and future Buddha of our age,
Maitreya (cf. § 4 a)

§ 11. *Middle lintel* — The middle lintel, which is closer
to the eye of the spectator, replaces these symbolical
pictures by two episodes, borrowed, the one from the youth,
the other from the career of Çâkya-muni

a) *Front face*. — We have already stated (above p. 75)
what from the point of view of Buddhist iconography
constitutes the chief interest of the central panel (pl X, 1)
On the left we perceive the stereotyped representation of
a town, proved by the context to be Kapilavastu, in its
streets and at its windows the customary animation is to be
seen (cf. § 7 a and 8 b) : it is clear that the sculptor has
not troubled himself in the least about the fact — which of
course he knew as well as we do — that the escape of the
Bodhisattva took place during the night. The latter, on his
good horse Kanthaka, is passing through the city gate for
« the great departure » (*Mahâbhinishkramana*), and we
can follow, to the right, in no less than four successive
editions, the progress of his miraculous course . but on
each occasion the embroidered rug which serves as a saddle
to his steed is presented to us without a rider. Each time
also the cortège is the same : Chandaka, the faithful attendant, holds, as usual, the parasol; four Gods are lifting the
horse's feet, in order, it was thought, that the sound of his
shoes might not give the alarm, another has taken possession of the fly-flapper · two others, who at first are dwarfs,
but for the sake of variety, strangely enough, grow bigger
by degrees as they advance towards the right, are carrying
the ewer and the sandals , next, others are throwing flowers,
waving their scarves, or beating the heavenly drums. When

the right jamb of the gate forces the sculptor to end the series of his repetitions, the attendant and the horse are, as it is written, taking leave of their Master. But the latter is figured only by the gigantic imprint of his feet, marked by the wheel and surmounted by the fly-flapper and the parasol. Finally, at the bottom on the right, Chandaka is returning to the house, leading with him Kanthaka and bringing (in his right hand and in a kind of wallet slung over his shoulder) the jewels which the young prince has just taken off for ever, in order to embrace the religious life The three persons, at once both edified and contrite, who follow, are, doubtless, the emissaries whom king Çuddhodana vainly charged to bring back his son.

Such is the manifest meaning of this long scene . but we still have to account for the sacred tree — the parasol surmounting it, and the railing which surrounds it, are a proof of this sacredness — which occupies the centre of the panel Assuredly it is there for reasons of symmetry , but this position of honour demands also that it shall have a meaning and this meaning will come to us the very moment that we recognize in it (thanks always to the comparison with the inscribed bas-relief of Barhut, CUNNINGHAM, pl XLVIII, 11) a *jambu* tree (*Eugenia jambu*) A *jambu* tree so close to Kapilavastu cannot be, in Buddhist art, anything but the one whose shadow ceased one day to turn to the sun, in order to continue to shelter « the first meditation » of the still young Bodhisattva We shall notice how three persons, without ceasing to associate themselves with the principal action, form around the tree of the miracle the necessary group of worshippers. Thus the artist has been able to combine most ingeniously in one and the same picture a summary indication of the commencement, and a detailed representation of the dénoue-

ment, of the religious vocation of the Predestined. And who
can say even whether the quadruple repetition of the horse
and the procession leaving the town were not connected
in his mind with the intervening episode of the famous
« four outgoings », which by the successive encounter
with an old man, a sick person, a dead man and a monk,
revealed to the future Buddha the miseries of life and the
only way of salvation?

*b) Rear face.* — In case the good sculptor had still
further intentions, may we be pardoned by his ashes, if we
cannot perceive them! May he pardon us above all, if we
cannot grasp exactly with what episode of the legend we
must connect the scene that covers the whole reverse side
of the middle lintel. It is, no doubt, the Buddha Câkya-
muni who is supposed to be seated on this empty throne,
since the tree which shelters it is a Holy Fig-tree, exactly
similar to the one which decorates the left projection of the
upper lintel. On the other hand, the Blessed One is evidently
far in the jungle, in the sole companionship of the beasts
assembled to do him homage and belonging as much to
the kingdom of phantasy as to the kingdom of nature First
of all, there are four lions guarding his throne, two seen in
full face and two in profile, then buffalos and antelopes,
observed and rendered in a marvellous manner, and furthermore birds, some with, and some without crests, bearing
flowers and fruits in their beaks. Side by side with these real
animals we see dream-monsters : on the right, bulls with
human faces and — forgetting their natural enmity in the
contemplation of the Blessed One — a great polycephalous
serpent by the side of an enormous vulture Garuda, whose
ears are adorned with earrings; on the left Tibetan dogs,
with manes and claws. To sum up, nearly the whole of the
sculptor's decorative menagerie was mobilized in this scene.

Now there was indeed a celebrated occasion on which, after the great internal quarrel of Kauçambî, Buddha left his community, in order to retire into solitude : and he was among the beasts and the beasts even served him (*Mahâ-vagga*, x, 4, 6-7). But here we find none of the traditional details of the episode, at least as it is related in the Pâli text

§ 12 *Lower lintel.* — Then the last lintel seems to us to bear on its two faces scenes subsequent to the death of Buddha.

*a) Front face.* — In the centre stands the tree now so well known to us as that of his Illumination (cf § 9 c) · but here this tree receives a royal visit. It is quite certain that the Blessed One was not visited by any king at Bodh-Gayâ for the texts give us a detailed account of the manner in which he employed the days, and even weeks, which preceded and followed his attainment of omniscience. It remains, therefore, that it can only have been in commemoration of Buddha that the ceremony here represented took place. Let us remind ourselves, however, of what is told us of Açoka, how the great emperor evinced a special devotion to the tree of the Bodhi, and continually showered presents upon it, so many and so often that his favourite queen, Tishyarakshitâ, looking upon it as a rival, became jealous and caused a pariah sorceress to cast a spell upon it The tree began to wither, and Açoka declared that he would not survive it; fortunately the queen, being undeceived, was able in time to arrest the effect of the witchcraft, whereupon the emperor decided to do « what none of the sovereigns of the past, neither Bimbisâra nor the others, had done », that is, to come in procession and, with a view to giving back to the tree all its first splendour, « to water it with pitchers of scented water » (*Divyâvadâna*, p 397-398). Now what is it exactly that we see here (pl. X, 2)? On the right a king, accompanied, as usual, by his wives, his orchestra, and his guards, dismounts languishingly from his elephant, encouraged, it seems, by his queen and helped by a young dwarf  The latter is probably a *Yaksha*, exactly like those who frequent the interior of the sanctuary, for we are told that, like Solomon, Açoka commanded the genii  Immediately on the right of the sacred tree we see again the same king, preceded by his queen, and both with their hands devoutly clasped render homage to it. On the other side there advances likewise, to the sound of another orchestra, a solemn procession of faithful laymen, bearing banners, flowers, and further (in their midst and in the front rank) pitchers, evidently intended for the watering of the tree  This last detail has won our conviction (cf. above, p. 79). Finally, from this identification it would result that this time the indication of the temple round the tree open to the sky would not be an anachronism (cf. p. 102)

*b) Rear face.* — Besides, as we have already said, this is not the only legend belonging to the cycle of Açoka that seems to us to have inspired the image-makers of Sânchî. Concerning the tumulus of Râmagrâma two other stories were still current among them; or rather two versions of the same story. According to one this *stûpa* was honoured by mythical serpents (*nâga*); in the other it was wild elephants (*nâga*) who paid their devotions to it : we are not far from believing that this simple pun gave rise to the two forms of the tradition. However that may be, the first is figured on the southern gate : the other, we believe, is here. Besides, whatever may be the name by which the *stûpa* is called, there is no doubt as to the meaning of the

8

story written in stone. Those are, in fact, wild elephants, which are marching in procession towards the sanctuary from the two extremities of the lintel, and it is indeed as votive offerings that they lift in their trunks, or are still dragging with their tusks, flowers torn from the lotuses in the nearest lake.

We shall here end these notes, already, perhaps, too long and nevertheless most summary. If we wished to describe in detail and one by one the five hundred and more characters, who, without counting the animals, figure on this one gate alone, we should never have finished ; and we might just as well undertake to write an encyclopædia of Indian Antiquities. The little that we have said will, at least, be sufficient to justify the double allegation which we believed might be put forward regarding this gate (p. 80) : it seems in fact upon investigation that these sculptures are for the most part deciphered ; and no one will think of disputing the fact that they offer a certain amount of interest for the history of civilization in general, and more especially for that of art applied to religion

# PLATES VII-X

All the photographs of which plates VII-X are composed have been kindly lent to us by the Director General of Archæology in India, Mr J. H MARSHALL, and all the stereotypes by M. E. LEROUX

Pl VII, 1 :   described on pp  63-64
Pl. VII, 2 .          »          72, 79, 87-8, 104, 107-8, 109-110
Pl VIII. 1          »          65-66, 86 89
Pl VIII, 2 ·          »          71, 85 86
Pl IX, 1          »          76, 97 99
Pl IX, 2          »          92-95
Pl X, 1          »          75, 105-7
Pl X, 2 .          »          79, 108 9

1. — GENERAL VIEW, TAKEN FROM THE EAST

2. — BACK VIEW OF LINTELS OF EASTERN GATE

2.   DIVINE GUARDIAN AT ENTRANCE
(INTERIOR FACE OF LEFT JAMB)

1.—EASTERN GATE
(FRONT VIEW)

2. THE RETURN TO KAPILAVASTU
(INTERIOR FACE OF RIGHT JAMB)

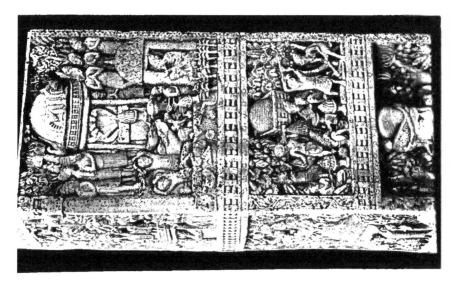

1. THE CONVERSION OF THE KÂÇYAPAS
(INTERIOR FACE OF LEFT JAMB)

1     THE VOCATION, OR GREAT DEPARTURE
(FRONT VIEW OF MIDDLE LINTEL)

2     A PROCESSION TO THE BODHI TREE
(FRONT VIEW OF LOWER LINTEL)

# The Greek Origin of the Image of Buddha [1].

One of the advantages of the Musée Guimet most
appreciated by its orientalist lecturers is that they are free
to dispense with the oratorical precautions which they
must take everywhere else Generally, wherever they venture to open their mouths, they believe themselves obliged
to begin by asking pardon of their auditors for the great
liberty which they take in speaking on subjects so far
removed from their usual occupations and for drawing
them into surroundings so different from those in which
they are accustomed to move. Such a formality would
in this case be entirely superfluous. You could not but
be aware of the fact that on crossing the threshold of
this Museum you would immediately find yourself transported from Europe to Asia, and you would hardly expect
me to apologize for speaking of Buddha in the home of
Buddha For, if he is not the sole inhabitant of this hospitable house, haven of all exotic manifestations of religious art, I dare at least to say that he is its principal tenant
To whatever gallery your steps may lead you, be it consecrated to India or to China, to Indo-China or to Tibet, to
Japan or to Java, him you will never fail to meet again and
again, in room after room, with the dreamy look of his half-
closed eyes and his perpetual smile, at once sympathizing
and disillusionized. If the distraction of your gaze, wandering

(1) Lecture at the Musée Guimet (*Bibliothèque de Vulgarisation du Musée Guimet*, vol XXXVIII).

from image to image, does not too much dissipate your attention, and if your minds succeed by degrees in disregarding the
diversity of the dimensions and the variety of the materials,
you will not be long in noticing that always and everywhere,
minute or gigantic, carved in wood, cut in stone, modelled
in clay, cast or beaten in metal, he continues to be astonish-
ingly like himself Soon, by dint of verifying the justness
of this first observation, you will arrive at the reflexion that
so great an uniformity supposes, at the origin of all these
idols, the existence of a common prototype, from which
they will have been more or less remotely descended.
And thus in the end you are inevitably confronted by the
question which I have to-day set myself the task of answer-
ing If it shall appear that the reply brings us back straight-
way and in a rather unexpected manner towards the
familiar horizons of our classic antiquity, well¹ that will
simply be one more element of interest.

But before interrogating the images of Buddha concerning their more distant origins, it is well to define exactly
what we mean by the name. Europeans commonly make
the strangest abuse of it. How many times have I not
heard — and usually on the most charming lips — the
very elementary principles of Buddhist iconography out-
raged, and no matter what statuette, Chinese, Tibetan,
or Japanese, however monstrous it might be, thoughtlessly designated by the name which ought to be reserved
for Çâkyamuni and his peers! What would you think of an
Asiatic who should designate en bloc, by the one name of
« Christ », not only Our Lord, God the Father, the Holy
Ghost, and the Blessed Virgin, but also all the angels, all
the saints, and even all the devils of Christianity? After
having first laughed, you would soon cry out at the sacri-
lege . and yet that is what we calmly do every day by lump-

ing together under the name of the one Buddha all the inhabitants of the Buddhist heavens and even hells. Therefore, let me implore you, once for all — especially the ladies — no more thus to profane the name of the Blessed One by applying it indifferently at one time to savage or even obscene demons, at another to extravagant divinities, bristling with manifold heads and arms, and at another to simple monks.

In strictness, the title of « Illuminated » — for such is very nearly the equivalent of « Buddha » — ought to be reserved for a personage whom, for my part, I should not hesitate to regard as historic, for that scion of the noble family of the Çâkyas, who was born in the north of India, at the foot of the central Himâlaya, towards the middle of the VIᵗʰ century before our era , who about his thirtieth year gave up his possessions, his parents, his wife, his child, in order to embrace the wandering life of a mendicant monk; who, after six years of vain study and austerities, finally at the foot of the ever-green fig-tree of Bodh-Gayâ discovered the secret of liberating human beings from the evils of existence; who during more than forty years preached in the middle portion of the basin of the Ganges salvation by the suppression of desire, the root of all suffering; who died and was cremated , whose ashes, regarded as holy relics, were distributed to the four quarters of India and deposited under vast tumuli, where we still find them to-day ; whose image, finally, is still enthroned above the flower-adorned altars, mid clouds of incense and murmurs of prayers, in all the pagodas of the Far East. And, doubtless, this effigy served in its turn as a model for those of the mythical predecessors, or of the transcendent hypostases, which Indian imagination was not long in creating for him in unlimited numbers, through infinite time and space, in the depths of our terrestrial past as well as in the abysses where at this moment move all the other universes. But such is the servile fidelity of these copies that from the iconographic point of view one may say : « There is no Buddha but Buddha ». Now the essential character of this figure is precisely that always and everywhere, through all the differences of gesture and pose, it assumes only one form, simply and purely human. This is the most important fact to be borne in mind. As for the particular signs which prevent our ever failing to recognize the type, the first statue or photograph to your hand will familiarize you with them.

## I

Here then we are agreed : together we seek the origin of the image of the Indian mendicant who, by the prestige of his intelligence, his goodness and, perhaps, also of his personal beauty, exercized over his contemporaries an influence capable of forming a basis for one of the three great religions of the world, that which from his epithet we call Buddhism. At the first view the problem does not seem so very complicated. Granted that all these representations seem to descend from a common prototype, the question resolves itself into discovering the place, time, and occasion of the first appearance of this type In other words, it will be necessary, but sufficient, to determine which are the most ancient known images of Buddha. Theoretically, nothing is more simple, in practice we quickly perceive that the thing is sooner said than done.

It is in Ceylon, the first Buddhist stage on the maritime high road of Asia, that the European usually finds himself for the first time in the presence of veritable idols of the Blessed One. Most often he restricts himself to an excursion, along red roads losing themselves in the distance under a slowly diminishing arch of green palmeries, to the singularly modernized temple of Kelani, a little to the north of Colombo. But, even if he pushed on as far as the ancient ruined towns of the interior, he would be no more successful in finding in their old statues the original type which we are seeking. With still greater reason would he renounce the idea of encountering it in the other terrestrial paradise, that of the austral hemisphere, for the not less luxuriant island of Java was also only an Indian colony, and, doubtless, it became so later than did Ceylon. The hundreds of Buddhas who have given a name to Boro-Budur are attributed only to the IX[th] century of our era. The even more recent character of the majority of the idols which are still venerated in Cambodia, Siam and Burmah shows only too clearly through their tinsel and their gilding. The most ancient Lamaic images could hardly be anterior to the official proclamation of Buddhism in Tibet towards the year 632 In Japan everyone will tell you that the figure of the Master was not introduced there until the VI[th] century, and that it came from China through the intermediacy of Corea. Nor do the most ancient Chinese images known to us, those of the grottoes of Long-Men or of Ta-t'ong-fu, which M. Chavannes has just made known by reproductions, go back beyond the IV[th] century ([1]). Finally, the last archæological missions in Central Asia have succeeded in proving, as had already been supposed, that their model came from India by the two routes which

---

([1]) E  CHAVANNES, *Mission archéologique dans la Chine septentrionale*, Paris, 1909.

on the north and the south skirt the desert of Turkestan (').

Thus clearly were we directed in advance to seek the plastic origins of Buddha in the very places which saw the beginning of his doctrine. And, were it not of interest to prove the diffusion and permanence of the type through the whole of eastern Asia, we might have spared ourselves this vast circuit. The point clearly marked for the serious commencement of our quest is the country of Magadha, otherwise that province of Behar which the latest imperial proclamation of Delhi has just officially detached from Bengal But the numerous statues in black basalt, which we there find — to begin with that which has been set up over the altar of the temple of Bodh-Gayâ, at the very spot where the Illuminated received his Illumination —, go back for the most part only to the dynasty of the Pâlas, which was overthrown by the Musalmans in the XII[th] century of our era. The excavations of Sârnâth, the site of the First Preaching, in the northern suburb of Benares, have furnished us with more ancient examples, carved in a grey sandstone of an uniform tint, which mark at the time of the Gupta Kings (IV[th] and V[th] centuries A. D ) a kind of renaissance of Indian art More to the north-west the ruins of Mathurâ, far to the south-west those of Amarâvatî have supplied us with still older ones, which the mention on the former of the Indo-Scyths, on the second of the Ândhras carry as far back as the II[nd] century of our era But whether carved in the yellow-spotted red sandstone of

---

(1) See, for example, in GRUNWEDEL, *Bericht über archäologische Arbeiten in Idikutschari und Umgebung im Winter* 1902-1903 (Munich, 1906), pl. IV, fig. 1, a specimen from Turfan, and in M. A STEIN, *Ancient Khotan*, pl. LXXXII, 2, another example from the environs of Khotan

Mathurâ or in the white marble of Amarâvatî, they are as like as brothers, and everyone will agree that they are descended from a common ancestor of blue slate and native to the north-western corner of India

Thus, following our thread, we have already remounted in the scale of years nearly twenty out of the twenty five centuries which separate us from the time of Buddha. The result is appreciable, and can only encourage us to continue But just at this moment the thread which guided us step by step through the chaos of Buddhist art breaks off sharp in our hands. While statues of the Master, dated with certainty from the first century after, if not before, Christ, are to be found abundantly in the Upper Panjâb — as is proved by the collections of the provincial capital (pl. XI, 1) — we vainly seek their archetype in the still older monuments of central India, prior to the second century of our era One significant fact robs us even of all hope of ever finding it by means of some excavation either better carried out or more successful. While on all the bas-reliefs of the Panjâb the Blessed One is represented standing in the middle of the panel, on the balustrades or the gates of Barhut or of Sânchî he is totally absent even from the scenes of his own biography This fact is too well known to be again dwelt upon, especially as we have already made an experimental verification of it (') All that I wish to insist upon to-day is that the oldest known Buddhas are those which we have encountered in the « House of Marvels », as the natives call the museum of Lahore. To complete the geographical part of our quest, it remains only to find out exactly whence these Buddhas come. The former keeper — whom many of us know from the fine portrait drawn by

_____

(1) See above, pp. 4-5 and 74-5

the filial piety of Rudyard Kipling at the beginning of
« Kim » — is no longer there to tell us, we regret to have
heard last year of his death, and moreover he retired long
ago. But his successor will answer you that all these carvings came originally from the district of Peshawar, on the
right bank of the Indus, at its confluence with the Kabul-
Rûd . And, doubtless, your first astonishment will be
that, after having vainly sought not only throughout the
whole of still Buddhist Asia, but in the very places which
saw the birth of Buddhism, the cradle of the images of the
founder, we have finally discovered it in a Musalman country and on the western confines of India.

What this district is at present I would only too willingly
stop to describe to you; for I have trodden it in every direction during happy months of archæological campaigning.
Gandhâra — for such was its Sanskrit name — shows us
after all only a vast, gently undulating plain, bristling in
places with rugged hills, and three parts encircled by a belt
of fawn-coloured or bluish mountains, which nearly everywhere limit the horizon But the opening left by them on
the south-east over the Indus is the great gate of India, and
to the west the winding Khyber pass remains the principal
route of communication between the peninsula and the
Asiatic continent; and the towns which formerly guarded
this ancient route of invading armies and merchant caravans were Purushapura (now Peshawar), Pushkarâvatî,
the Peukelaotis of the Greeks; Çalâtura, the natal town of
Pânini, the great legislator of Sanskrit grammar , Udabhân-
da (now Und), where the great river was passed, in
winter by a ford, in summer by a ferry, and whence in
three days one reached Takshaçilâ, the Taxilâ of the historians of Alexander . And immediately you feel how in this
country, which one might call doubly classic, memories

associated with the two antiquities, Hellenic and Indian, arise from the ground at each step. Even if history had not preserved for us any remembrance of the memorable encounter between the two civilizations, the mute witnesses in stone, which we have come purposely to interrogate, would be sufficient to establish it. To cut as short as possible ('), let me lead you straight to the centre of the country, into the little garrison town of Hoti-Mardân : and there, at the hospitable mess of the regiment of the Guides, I will show you, leaning against the wall of the dining-room and no longer inhaling any incense but the smoke of the cigars, the most beautiful, and probably also the most ancient, of the Buddhas which it has ever been granted to me to encounter (pl XI, 2).

Look at it at leisure Without doubt you will appreciate its dreamy, and even somewhat effeminate, beauty; but at the same time you cannot fail to be struck by its Hellenic character. That this is a statue of Buddha there is not the least doubt: all the special signs of which I was speaking a short time ago bear witness to its identity / Is it necessary to make you lay your fingers upon that ample monastic robe, that pretended bump of wisdom on the crown of the head, that mole between the eyebrows, that lobe of the ear distended by the wearing of heavy earrings, and left bare because of the total renunciation of worldly adornments? These are all traits which we might have anticipated from the perusal of the sacred texts. But, if it is indeed a Buddha, it

---

(1) Here, of course, we can only note the principal points Those who are anxious for details concerning the country, its archæological sites, and the results of the excavations, will pardon us if we refer them to our works *Sur la frontière indo-afghane* (Paris, 1901), *La Géographie ancienne du Gandhâra* (B E. F E-O, I, 1901), *L'Art gréco-bouddhique du Gandhâra* (Paris, 1905-1914).

is no less evidently not an Indian work. Your European eyes have in this case no need of the help of any Indianist, in order to appreciate with full knowledge) the orb of the nimbus, the waves of the hair, the straightness of the pro-file, the classical shape of the eyes, the sinuous bow of the mouth, the supple and hollow folds of the draperies. All these technical details, and still more perhaps the harmony of the whole, indicate in a material, palpable and striking manner the hand of an artist from some Greek studio If the material proofs of the attribution constitute what I should be prepared to call the native contribution, neither will you hesitate to ascribe to an occidental influence the formal beauty of the work Thus the statue of Mardân, with all its congeners, appears to us as a kind of compro-mise, a hybrid work, which would not in any language have a name, had not the no less heteroclite term of « Greco-Buddhist » been forthwith invented for it

II

Such is the — I must confess unexpected — result of our researches on the spot. It is only in the country which from our point of view we might quite correctly call the vestibule of India, that we finally discover the archetype of Buddha, and when at last we find it, it is to acknow-ledge that its appearance is at the least as much Greek as Indian. The fact is, doubtless, sufficiently surprising to call for some commentary. What historical circumstances can have rendered possible, and even spontaneously engen-dered, this creation of the Indo-Greek type of Buddha? What attracts us most in the question is, I will warrant, how the Hellenic influence could thus have reached as far as the

banks of the Indus. Allow me to call your attention to the
fact that Gandhâra is scarcely further, as the crow flies, from
the mouth of the Hellenized Euphrates than from that of
the Buddhist Ganges  In reality the problem has two faces,
like the images which we have to explain  To account for
the birth of such a statue, it is necessary to justify the pene-
tration not only of Greek Art, but also of the Buddhist religion, into the country which was to be the theatre of their
prolific union. And it is indeed with the latter that it will be
best to undertake the historical part of our quest.

At the present time not only is this unfortunate Gandhâra, which had always so much to suffer from its situation on the high road of the conquerors of Asia, no longer
Buddhist, it has become more than half Afghan in race,
Iranian in language, and withal Musalman. It is a curious
fact that, according to Strabo, at the time of the rude and
passing conquest of Alexander, the « Gandaritis » did not
form a part of India, which at that time commenced only
at the Indus. Seleukos, after his fruitless attempt at invasion in 305 before our era, is said to have ceded it by
treaty, together with the hand of his daughter, in exchange for 500 elephants, to the first historical emperor
of India, that Candragupta whom the Greek historians call
Sandrakottos Fifty years later this district still formed part
of the domains of the latter's grandson, the famous Açoka; and he caused to be engraved on a huge rock, half-way
up a hill near the present village of Shâhbâz-Garhî (pl. XII,
1), the pious edicts in which he recommended to his people the practice of all the virtues, beginning with kindness
to animals. From the fifth of these edicts it quite clearly
appears that for him Gandhâra was a frontier country, still
to be evangelized. We know, on the other hand, the zeal of
this « Constantine of Buddhism » for the propagation of the

Good Law. Then again, according to the Singhalese chronicle, the *Mahâvamsa*, it was precisely during his reign that the apostle Madhyântika converted Gandhâra as well as Kashmir Thus the religion of Buddha would have taken more than two hundred years to spread from Magadha as far as the frontiers of northern India. We see no reason for contesting the authenticity of a tradition in itself so probable.

Besides, whatever may be the exact date of the introduction of Buddhism into Gandhâra, it must there have been specially successful. We shall end by finding there, duly acclimatized and deeply rooted, a quantity of legends which the missionaries had brought with them from the low country. Some did not hesitate to bring Buddha himself on the scene. It was, they said, the Master in person, who had overcome the terrible Nâga of the Swât river, and had limited the disastrous inundations, whence this aquatic genius derives all his subsistence, to one in every twelve years In the same way it was no longer at Râjagriha, but at one stage to the north-west of Pushkarâvatî, that the Blessed One is now supposed to have converted the insatiable ogress of Smallpox. Thanks to the want of orthodoxy on the part of mothers, when the health of their children is in question, this last superstition has in the minds of the present inhabitants of the country almost alone survived the total wreck of Buddhism. A small quantity of earth from a certain tumulus, placed in the *taviz*, or amulet-case, usually suspended round the neck of the new-born, is still considered an infallible preservative against the terrible infantile epidemic , and it is owing to this curious property, joined to the topographical information of Hiuan-tsang, that I was able to recognize the traditional site of this miracle.

However, it was to be feared that these narratives of a

personal intervention of the historic Buddha in Gandhâra might justly meet with the same incredulity as those which, in my native province, begin with the words  « At that time, our Lord Jesus Christ was travelling in Brittany... » For the purpose of localization in the country they preferred, it seems, to fall back upon the numerous previous lives in the course of which the future Buddha attained the summit — or, as we should say to-day, established a record — in all perfections. The monks of several convents in the neigh-bourhood of Shâhbâz-Garhî had, for instance, divided among themselves, by very clever adaptation to the pictur-esque accidents of the landscape, the various episodes of the romance of Viçvantara, that monomaniac of charity. Others had, so to speak, specialized either in the touching story of the young anchorite Çyâma, sole support of his old blind parents, or in the galant adventure of the wise Ekaçringa, whom the seductions of a courtesan reduced to the role of beast of burden, etc... But they did not stop there, an exceptionally holy tetrad of great *stûpas*, situated in Gandhâra proper, or in the bordering territories, soon marked the place where the Sublime Being had formerly, in one existence after another, made a gift of his flesh, his eyes, his head, and his body — the first to buy back a dove from a hawk, the last to satisfy a famished tigress, and the two others with an intention whose practical utility, if not its edifying character, escapes us  And thus northern India came to possess, like central India, its « four great pilgri-mages ». It is not in any way an exaggeration to say that Gandhâra thus became (after Magadha) as it were a second Holy Land of Buddhism, and we see that certain Chinese pilgrims were quite content with a visit there, without feeling the necessity of pushing as far as the basin of the Ganges.

Only this local prosperity of Buddhism can explain to us the number and the richness of the ancient religious foundations of the country. Some repose under the tumuli which dot the plains on every side, and are used by the present inhabitants as stone-quarries Others are hidden in the folds of the mountains, or with their crumbling walls cover the sharp crest of some spur. Among the former I will name to you in particular those which underly the enormous mound of Sahri-Bahlol (pl XIII) : though excavated long ago, they still with their artistic spoils enrich the museum which has lately been established in Peshawar, as capital of the new « North-West Frontier Province » Among the second I will show you as a specimen the celebrated ruins of Takht-i-Bahai with their equally inexhaustible reserves (pl XII, 2); on the platform above the imposing retaining walls rise the dismantled chapels where once were enthroned the statues which have since taken the road to our museums, those mortuaries of dead Gods. You are free to restore them in thought with the splendour borrowed from the colours, and even from the gold, with which in former days care was taken to increase in the dazzled eyes of the faithful their appearance of life. But, above all, you must grasp the fact that in this country you literally walk on ruins, and there is scarcely a corner where a few strokes with the pick-axe will not bring to light some Buddhist bas-relief or statue. Evidently Hiuan-tsang was scarcely exaggerating, when he estimated approximately, and in round numbers, at a thousand the number of monasteries which once constituted the ornament, as also the sanctity, of Gandhâra. If you will now reflect that this anti-chamber of India has from all times been the region most open to western influences, moral as well as artistic, you will understand the double role which it was naturally called upon to play in the evolution of the religion which it had embraced with so much zeal   The numerous doctors whom it has produced have taken a preponderating part in the transformation of the Buddhist egoistical « salvation » into the theory of a charity more widely active, but also of a character more metaphysical and pietistic, which its adherents adorned with the name of Mahâyâna. But the important thing for us here is not so much the abstruse depth of its theologians as the pious generosity of its donors. It was they who, according to all probability, took the initiative in utilizing for the satisfaction of their religious zeal the talent and resource of the Hellenistic artists, whom historical circumstances had led as far as Ariana. And thus they made their country the creative home whence Buddhist iconography was by degrees propagated throughout the rest of India and the Far East.

Of the two elements, the Greek and the Buddhist, which concurred in the production of our Gandhâra statues, we comprehend then already the second. It remains to explain the intervention of the first. But this is a story already familiar to you, and it will be sufficient if I recall it in a few words, or rather I should like to give you an illustration and, as it were, a direct apprehension of it, by putting before your eyes the most artistic of the documents — or, if you prefer, the most documentary of the works of art — I mean the coins.

In the first place, I shall mention only by way of reminder Alexander's forced entrance into India in the spring of the year 326 before our era. We too much forget that it was on his part a notable folly to venture during the hottest months of the year on the burning plains of the Panjâb, that he was soon forced to retire, and that

his retreat across the deserts of Gedrosia (the present Be-
luchistan) ended disastrously — so that this expedition
into India, if only we replace the cold by the heat, the
snow by the sands, was, as it were, the Russian campaign of the Macedonian conqueror Much more fruitful of
results was the constitution of the Greek kingdom of Bactria, on the confines of the north-west of India, about 250
B. C., in open revolt against the Seleucides The beautiful
coin of Alexander, son of Philip, which you see in pl XIV, 2,
was struck not by Alexander himself, but in imitation of
his by king Agathokles, whose name and titles you read on
the reverse, encircling the image of Zeus Everything in
this medal is still purely Greek.

Fifty years later Demetrios, son of Euthydemos, profiting by the break-up of the empire of the Mauryas, con-
quers and annexes the whole of northern India, and
immediately you see in that helmet, made from the
head of an elephant, as it were a trace of the Indian orientation of his policy (pl XIV, 2). This latter must, besides, have ended by costing him his original kingdom. Another valiant condottiere, Eukratides, rebelled in his turn,
and made himself master of Bactria, so that, as Strabo tells
us, there remained to Demetrios nothing more than his
Indian conquests, and he was henceforward known under
the name of « King of the Indians ». This is a capital fact, to
which I could not too strongly draw your attention.
During a century and more the Panjâb was thus a Greek
colony, in the same way as it afterwards became Scythian,
then Mogul, and finally English That is to say, a handful
of foreigners, supported by mercenary troops, in great part
recruited in the country itself, became masters there, and
levied the taxes You may easily perceive that/this kingdom
was a centre of attraction for Greek adventurers of all kinds,

beginning with soldiers of fortune and mountebanks, and passing by way of merchants to the artists who took upon themselves, among other tasks, that of making the superb coins to which we are indebted for the survival of the classically sounding names and the energetic features of those so-called « Basileis », changed into very authentic râjahs.

Of all these Indo-Greek kings I will name only Menander (pl. XIV, 2), since he is known to us not merely from the narrative of Plutarch, but also from Indian texts. A curious apologetic treatise, entitled « The Questions of Milinda » and composed as a dialogue in the Platonic manner, brings before us in the town of Sâgala on the one hand Hellenism, represented by Menander, the king of the Yavanas (Ionians), and, on the other hand Buddhism, in the person of Nâgasena, one of the patriarchs of the church. According to native tradition the monk even converted the king. However, on the reverse of his coins, Pallas Athene continues still to brandish the paternal lightning of Zeus. She does not seem in any way to care how little her image squares with the exotic surroundings of the language and the writing in which Menander, generalizing a usage inaugurated by his predecessors, is always careful to have the Greek legend of the face translated for the use of his Indian subjects. Never, in truth, were the circumstances more favourable than during his reign (between 150 and 100 B. C.) for planting the germ of the whole subsequent development of Greco-Buddhist art by the creation of the Indo-Greek type of Buddha What, in fact, is that beautiful statue which I showed you just now (pl. XI, 2), but an Asiatic coin struck in European style? And what more simple for artists initiated into all the secrets of Hellenic art, as were the authors of those magnificent medals, than to adopt for the representation of the Indian Saviour the most intellectual type of their beardless Olympians? Thus we arrive quite naturally at the strange and quaint mixture which we were analysing a short time ago, at this statue, which is a Hellenized Buddha, unless you prefer to describe it as an Indianized figure of Apollo.

Thus must have been created under the industrious fingers of some *Graeculus* of more or less mixed descent — and perhaps, also, who knows? at the command of a Greek or an Eurasian convert to Buddhism — the earliest of the images of Buddha. Yet, since we are forced to touch upon the question of chronology, it is only, I must confess, in the first century of our era, that the type of Buddha at last makes its appearance on the reverse of the coins. And certainly his name is still written there in Greek characters « Boddo ». But on the observe, instead of an elegant Greek, we perceive the figure of another invader, of a bearded Scythian, grotesquely accoutred in his high boots and the rigid basques of his tunic (pl. XIV, 2) His name is given in the inscription he is the « Shah of the Shahs » Kanishka, he who was after Açoka the second great emperor of the Buddhist legend, and whom M. S. Lévi has in his turn so well surnamed the « Clovis » of northern India : for he also — either from conviction or from calculation — became converted to the religion of the country vanquished by his arms But, just as the Frank Clovis had no part in the development of Gallo-Roman art, you may easily imagine that the Turk Kanishka had no direct influence on that of Indo-Greek art, and, besides, we hold now the certain proof that during his reign this art was already stereotyped, if not decadent.

All the Chinese Buddhist pilgrims who from the IV[th] to

the X[th] centuries of our era visited the holy places of India
agree, in fact, in testifying, that Kanishka had built by the
side of his winter capital Purushapura « the highest pagoda
of the country ». Now in the course of my journey on the
Indo-Afghan frontier, on the 21st of January 1897, among
the numerous tumuli — simple refuse of brick kilns or vestiges of ancient monuments — which are scattered over
the flat outskirts of Peshawar, I thought I recognized in one
(pl. XIV, 1), by reason of its site, its form, its composition,
its surroundings, finally of a number of concordant indications — not to count that secret voice of things, which soon
whispers to the heart of the archæologist —, the remains
of the great religious foundation of Kanishka  That dusty
mound, which, if in circumference it measured three hun-.
dred metres, was not more than 4 or 5 metres above the
present ground surface, did not look very promising. However, when the Anglo-Indian government did at last reorgan-
ize its archæological service, Messrs. Marshall and Spooner
were pleased to consider that the proposed identification
was at least worth the trouble of verification by digging.
The results of the first campaign, during the cold season 1907-1908, were most disappointing. Fortunately
the English archæologists were not discouraged, in March
1909 they at last determined the dimensions of the base of
the sanctuary — the vastest, indeed, that has ever been discovered in India — and soon they were fortunate enough
to unearth in the centre the famous relics of Buddha, which
Chinese evidence assures us were deposited there by
Kanishka himself, and which to-day Burmah is so proud of
possessing. They were enclosed in a golden reliquary, about
18 centimetres high, of which you have before your eyes
(pl XV, 1) a view. All that I wish to take note of here is
first, that this box does in fact bear in dotted letters the

name, and in repoussé the image, of our Kanishka, the one perfectly legible and the other a good resemblance. Now, in point of execution the reliquary already betrays signs of artistic decadence, and this stylization is especially notable in the Buddha whom you see seated between two standing divinities on the top of the lid. This votive document is sufficient, then, to carry back at least a hundred years, and consequently, to the 1st century *before* our era, at the latest, the creation of the plastic type of the Blessed One.

### III

Thus, then, we are on the whole well informed as to the where and when, from the rencontre of the two inverse expansions, that of Hellenism towards the east consequent upon the political conquests of Alexander, and that of Buddhism towards the west by favour of the religious missions of Açoka, was born once for all the Indo-Greek type of Buddha. Our geographical and historical quest may, therefore, be considered as ended. But we have as yet accomplished only two-thirds of our task, and the iconographic question awaits almost in its entirety an elucidation. We have indeed from the first glance at the Museum at Lahore seen that, in opposition to the old native school, the image of Buddha is like a trade-mark of the workshops of Gandhâra It remains to learn how it was itself manufactured. We are agreed that at the time of its composition the Indian material was poured into a western mould : among all the possible results of this operation, which one definitely emerged from the foundry? This we have still to analyse, at the risk of passing from one surprise to another.

What in fact did I tell you? Here is a creation which the experience of centuries and the exploration of Asia have taught us to regard as one of the most widespread and the most durable successes that the history of art has ever chronicled It is proved to have been adopted with enthusiasm by the entire Buddhist world : it was, and has remained, for the faithful the sole manner of conceiving and figuring the Master. . And yet we cannot hide the fact that, if from the beginning the people must have felt the attractive charm of its ideal and serene beauty, it must at its first appearance have been the object of just and bitter criticisms on the part of the old champions of orthodoxy. To-day even, if we, Buddhists or students of Buddhism, could free ourselves from long custom and create for ourselves new eyes, we should be the first to be shocked by the ambiguous character of the Gandhâra type of Buddha For in fact, what is it that Buddhist scriptures are never tired of repeating? It is not we, it is tradition which poses for the new-born Bodhisatwa the famous dilemma : « Either thou wilt remain in the world and reign over the universe, or else thou wilt enter into religion and become a Saviour of the world » We all know that the second alternative was the one realized  Now what do we see here (pl. XI, 2)? This person is not a prince, for he wears neither the costume nor the jewels of one; but how could one maintain that he is a real Buddhist monk, since his head is not shaven? If he were a *bhikshu*, he would not have retained his hair : if he were a *cakravartin*, he would not have donned the monastic gown. A monk without tonsure or a king without jewels, decidedly these strange images, from whichever side one approaches them, are frankly neither flesh nor fish. From the artistic point of view we have already seen that, properly speaking, they were neither

Greek nor Indian, from the iconographic point of view we must admit that they are neither cleric nor layman, but still and always a hybrid combination of two heteroclite elements.

Shall we lean over the crucible in which the formula of this new compromise was elaborated, and try to reconstitute from the monuments themselves how things happened? Let us take the princely heir of the Çâkyas (pl. XV, 2) at the critical moment when he is realizing his religious vocation. The moral crisis which has just cast him out of the world, and, as a beginning, has made him flee by night from his native town, must, in fact, be translated occularly by a complete transformation of his exterior aspect. Now we read, and we see, that on the dawn of his escape, judging himself beyond capture, he stops and sends back horse and squire. At the same time he charges the latter to carry back to his home all his princely jewels, including the rich turban which encircled his long hair, gathered up in a chignon on the top of the crown. Thus he appears to us, his head bare and already in the act of changing his silken clothes, which are no longer suitable to his new state, for the coarse garment of a hunter. In all these details the figured tradition conforms with a good grace to the written. There is only one point on which the Indo-Greek artists have shown themselves intractable. At that instant all the texts will have it that the Bodhisattva himself with his sword cut off his hair. but to this last exigency of Indian custom the school of Gandhâra has never given its consent. Whether it represents the Master at the height of his ascetic macerations, or whether it shows him in all his splendour, at the moment when he has just attained to Illumination, his chignon continues to remain such as it was before his entrance into religion. When at last he begins to convert his first disciples, there is only the more striking contrast between his wavy hair and the shorn crowns of his *bhikshus* : for these latter, evidently sketched from life, wear the full tonsure, exactly like the bonzes of the present day Accordingly, we may say that by systematically refusing in the case of the Blessed One to complete the expected transmutation of layman into monk, the Gandhâra sculptors have not only put themselves in intended contradiction to the sacred writings : they have also obstinately closed their eyes to the data supplied by the direct observation of a number of their own clients.

Visit afresh the collections, or turn over at your leisure the reproductions, of Greco-Buddhist bas-reliefs. The sole distinction between the Bodhisattva, or any other great lay person, and Buddha consists in this, that the latter appears without jewels and draped to the neck in the monastic gown. On the other hand, the only characteristic difference between the Master and the monks of his order lies in the privilege, which he alone enjoys, of retaining his hair. At this point the recipe for fabricating a Buddha after the mode of Gandhâra presents itself spontaneously to you (pl. XVI, 1) You take the body of a monk, and surmount it with the head of a king (or what in India comes to the same thing, a god), after having first stripped it of turban and earrings. These are the two necessary and sufficing ingredients of this curious synthesis, and you divine immediately the advantages of this procedure. Were it not for the head, confusion with any other monk would be almost inevitable : and this simple consideration may help to explain why the ancient native school abstained from representing the disciples as well as the Master (¹) On the other hand, were

---

(1) See above, p 76

it not for the monastic cloak, you might be a little  puzzled
to distinguish the Perfect Buddha from the future Buddha,
whenever the second is shown without a headdress, or
even when the lips of the former continue  to wear that
little moustache which you still find on the remote Japanese images. But join together the two elements, however
incongruous, a layman's head on the body of a cleric : and
this combination will at once give you an individuality sufficiently marked to answer all the practical needs of iconography. The result has shown it well.

But, however complex the Indo-Greek type of Buddha
may be, you doubtless consider that we have examined
and dissected it more than sufficiently for to-day; and you
tremble to perceive the endless  conclusions which we
might at once draw from this analysis, however superficial
and summary First of all, it would be sufficient to prove,
even if history did not so state, that this type was created
as an afterthought and, let us say, *de chic,* by strangers more
artists than theologians, more solicitous for esthetics
than for orthodoxy. I would go further : Not only at  the
moment of its conception had the face of the Master long
been blurred in the mists of the past, and all precise iconographic data concerning him been lost, but among the
vapours of incense which the worship of posterity caused
to mount towards his memory, while waiting for the latter
to be materialized in his image, he had already assumed
a superhuman and, as is written, a « supernatural » (*lokot-
tara*) character  At least, we could  scarcely otherwise
explain the success of that stroke of audacity whereby the
school of Gandhâra assigned to him from the beginning a
special physionomy, derived from, and at the same time
remaining at an equal distance from, that of a monk and

that of a god. It results, further, that this type issues from the fusion of a double ideal, that of the Greek Olympian and that of the *Mahâpurusha*, or Indian « Great Man », with no borrowing from living reality, if we except the detail of the distended lobe of the ears. And this would to some extent excuse the defect that many of these images are not exempt from some academic frigidity. Finally, we comprehend the reason for the retouches which later generations thought it necessary to apply, notably as concerns the hair. We can even see in how mechanical a manner through uniformly covering bandeau and chignon with the short traditional curls, their want of skill has suddenly caused to stand out on the top of the crown the boss called *ushnîsha*, a word which formerly meant only headdress.. ..

And this is not yet all . what should I not have to tell you concerning the diffusion in India and the Far East of the idolatrous worship of Buddha, parallel to that of the images ! But reassure yourselves : sufficient for each hour its subject, and I will not further abuse your patience. Moreover, as we remarked at the beginning, nothing is easier than to see how much better preserved — or, if you prefer, less deformed — at all times and in all places was the face of the Blessed One than his doctrine. I shall not, therefore, insist to-day on the conquest of upper and lower Asia by this irresistible propagator of the Indo-Greek school of Gandhâra. But you would not forgive me, if I did not show in conclusion how this Buddhist school finds itself by its origins in contact with our Christian art. Look at these two statues (pl. XVI, 2), the one represents Christ, and the other Buddha. The one was taken from a sarcophagus from Asia Minor, and is to-day to be found in Berlin; the other comes from a ruined temple in Gandhâra, and is at present in Lahore Both, with the pose of the right arm similarly draped in their mantles, are direct descendants of a common ancestor, the beautiful Greek statue of the Lateran Museum, called the Orator, in which we have long recognized a Sophocles It is not to be doubted that, plastically speaking, they are cousins-german. The one is a Greco-Christian Christ, the other is a Greco-Buddhist Buddha. Both are, by the same right, a legacy left *in extremis* to the old world by the expiring Greek art

After this last experience it will, doubtless, seem to you proved that this figure of Buddha, which, smiling at us from the depths of the Far East, represents for us the culmination of what is exotic, nevertheless came originally from a Hellenistic studio Such, at least, is the truth to-day — I mean the conclusion arising from the documents at present known — and such, at the point at which archæological researches have arrived, will probably be the truth to-morrow Must we be glad or sorry for this ? Facts are facts, and the wisest thing is to take them as they come. It was recently still the custom to triumph noisily over the artistic inferiority of the Indians, reduced to accepting ready made from the hands of others the concrete realization of their own religious ideal. At present, owing to æsthetic bias or to nationalist rancour, it is the fashion to make the school of Gandhâra pay for its manifest superiority by a systematic blackening of its noblest production. We for our part refuse in this connection to share either the unjustifiable contempt of the old criticism for native inspiration, or the ill-disguised spite of the new against the foreign make It is not the father *or* the mother who has formed the child , it is the father *and* the mother. The Indian mind has taken a part no less essential than has Greek genius in the elaboration of the model of the Monk-God. It is a case where the East and the West could have done nothing

without each other  It would be childish to associate ourselves, in a partizan spirit and turnabout, with the exaltation
or the contempt, whether of Europe or of Asia, when so
fine an opportunity offers for saluting in the Eurasian pro ·
totype of Buddha one of the most sublime creations wherewith their collaboration has enriched humanity

I Photograph taken by the author in 1896 at the Lahore Museum (cf p 117) In the upper row reposes a colossal head with a moustache, obtained from the excavations of Kharkaï (cf *Art g-b du Gandh.*, I, p. 18); in the middle one two Buddhas, seated in the pose of meditation, on the lowest and on the ground three others in the attitude of instruction It will be observed that a great number of them had, before being collected for the museum, already lost their heads (cf. *ibid*, p. 14)

II- Photograph taken by the author in 1897; for the description cf pp 119-120 This magnificent Buddha is, moreover, not the only masterpiece possessed by the English officers of the native regiment of the *King's Own Corps of Guides* Their collection is one of the finest that we have met with, and there is nothing surprising in the fact, if we reflect that their garrison is placed in the centre of ancient Gandhâra (cf *ibid*, p. 27, or *Sur la frontière indo-afghane*, p 39, and the maps at the end of those works)

2. BUDDHA IN THE GUIDES' MESS, MARDÁN

1. BUDDHAS IN THE LAHORE MUSEUM

PLATE XII

Cf pp 121, 123, 124

I. An engraving borrowed from *Sur la frontière indo-afghane* (Paris, Hachette et Cⁱᵉ, 1901, fig 11, cf *Tour du monde*, Nov 1899, p. 543), executed from the author's photographs. On the left, beyond the ploughed land, is seen the village of Shâhbâz-Garhî. In the background rises the hill of Mekha-Sandhi, once sanctified by the legend of prince Viçvantara (cf *ibid*, p 55, *Notes sur la géographie ancienne du Gandhâra*, in *B É F E -O* , I, 1901, pp 347-59, and above, p 123) Quite to the right stands the rugged hill-side, on which is still to be found the inscription of Açoka (cf. p. 121)

II A photograph taken by the Archæological Survey and placed at our disposal by Dr J Ph. Vogel (cf p. 124) In the foreground we see the central spur, on which stands the principal monastery the view extends towards the north east above the hills of the little range of Takht-i-Bahai as far as the Swât mountains For other views of the same site cf *Sur la frontière indo-afghane*, fig 14, or *Tour du monde*, *ibid*, p. 545, and *Art g -b. du Gandh*, figg 1 and 63-4 (with plan and description of the buildings, pp. 160-163)

1.    THE VILLAGE OF SHAHBAZ-GARHI

2.    THE RUINS OF TAKHT-I-BAHAI

PLATE XIII

Cf. p 124

I — An engraving borrowed from *Sur la frontière indo-afghane*, fig 15, (or *Tour du monde*, Nov. 1899, p 544), after a photograph taken by the author. The eminence, increased in height by the slow accumulation of the dust of the past, is still surrounded by a magnificent wall, now buried in the earth  The people of the country continue to maintain a connection between the village and the hill of Takht-i-Bahai, situated at a distance of less than a league to the north, which would represent respectively the capital and the « throne » of one and the same râjah (cf p 124)

II — An Archæological Survey photograh, communicated by Dr J Ph VOGEL, representing a corner of the recent excavations of Dr. D B SPOONER in one of the neighbouring tumuli of Sahri-Bahlol (cf p 124) These excavations have been described by their author in the *Archæological Survey of India, Annual Report, 1906-7*, pp 102-118 For previous explorations of the same district see H W. BELLEW, *General Report on the Euzufzai* (Lahore, 1864) and *Punjab Gazetteer, Peshawar District* (1897-1898), pp. 46 sqq , for the more modern researches (1912) of Sir Aurel STEIN see, on the other hand, *Annual Report of the Archæological Survey of India, Frontier Circle, 1911-12* (Peshawar, 1912, with map).

1.    THE VILLAGE OF SAHRI-BAHLOL

2.    EXCAVATIONS NEAR SAHRI-BAHLOL

PLATE XIV

Cf pp. 126-129

I — An engraving borrowed from *Sur la frontière indo-afghane,* fig 40, (or *Tour du Monde,* nov 1899, p 556). The identification of this tumulus with the « Pagoda of Kanishka » (cf above, p 129) was first developed in our *Notes sur la géographie ancienne du Gandhâra* (*B. É F. E -O* , I, 1901, pp. 329-333, with maps) Of the excavations by which it was verified an account has been given by Dr D B Spooner in *Archæological Survey of India, Annual Report, 1908-9,* pp. 38-59.

II — The four coins reproduced are borrowed from the *Catalogue of Indian Coins in the British Museum, The Coins of the Greek and Scythic Kings of Bactria and India,* by Percy Gardner (London, 1886), pll. IV, 1 ; II, 9 , XI, 7 , XXVI, 8  *a* Head of « Alexander, son of Philip », wearing a lion's skin, like Heracles, on the reverse, mention of the « reigning king, Agathokles the just », inscribed round a Zeus seated on a throne with a back, holding in his raised left hand the long sceptre and on his extended right hand the eagle (cf p 126) — *b* Head of a king, wearing a diadem and a helmet in the form of an elephant's head, on the reverse, mention of « King Demetrios », inscribed on both sides of a standing Heracles, bearing in his left hand the club and the lion's skin and with the right hand crowning himself with an ivy-wreath (cf. p. 126) — *c* Diademed head of the « Saviour King Menander » , on the reverse, Pallas Athene, bearing the aegis and hurling the thunderbolt : round her the same inscription, but this time in the Indian alphabet and language of the north-west (cf. p. 127). — *d* Full-length portrait of the « Shah of Shahs, Kanishka the Kushan », spear in the left hand, the right extended above a pyre , on the reverse, a standing Buddha, having an aureole and a nimbus (cf p 128)

1.    SHÂH-JÎ-KÎ-DHERÎ (KANISHKA STÛPA)

2.    INDO-GREEK AND INDO-SCYTHIC COINS

PLATE XV

Cf pp 129-132

I — Archæological Survey photograph, supplied by Sir Aurel Stein (for other reproductions cf *A S I*, *Annual Report*, 1908-9, pll XII XIII). At the top a Buddha is seated on the slightly expanded stem of a lotus, whose petals decorate the upper face of the lid, between two standing lay persons, probably Brahmâ and Indra On the lip of the lid is a frieze of geese (*hamsa*) On the main body of the casket itself a Buddha seated in meditation and two half-length deities repose in the waves of a garland supported by frolicking Cupids On the left we see the profile of the standing figure of Kanishka. It will be observed that not only is the design superior to the execution, but also the mantles of the Buddhas cover them right to the neck and hide their crossed feet, and that their hands as yet know only two *mudrās*, that of meditation and that of reassurance It is therefore permissible already to speak of stylization and even of decadence, but not yet of the ultimate decline of the school (cf p 130).

II — Statue of Bodhisattva, obtained from Shâhbâz-Garhî, at present in the museum of the Louvre (cf p 132) With its costume formed of two pieces of material, one for the trunk and the other for the lower limbs, with its turban, its sandals, its rich adornments, and finally its nimbus, this statue represents that ideal type of the great lay noble which in India serves for kings and gods. (For a heliogravure and a detailed description of this particular one cf. *Sculptures gréco-bouddhiques du Musée du Louvre* in *Monuments et Mémoires*, vol VII, part I, 1900) On the pedestal is represented the worship of Buddha's alms-bowl.

2.    THE BODHISATTVA TYPE

1. — THE RELIC-CASKET OF KANISHKA

PLATE XVI

Cf pp 133-136.

I — The type of Bodhisattva and that of Buddha are borrowed from a frieze in the museum of the Louvre (cf *Art g.-b. du Gandh*, fig 134), that of the monk from a bas-relief in the British Museum For the reason of their being placed together cf. pp. 133-134.

II. — The image of Christ is reproduced from a plate in Professor STRZYGOWSKI's *Orient oder Rom*, let us not omit to confess that it has been artificially isolated from the rest of the sarcophagus In contrast to its slender figure the image of Buddha (no 527 of the Lahore Museum; height m 0,60) is noticeably squat. The gesture of the left arm we shall find again in the Buddha of this same plate XVI, 1, and in the sixth of the seven which are ranged on the base of plate XXVI, 1 For comparison the Sophocles of the Lateran museum may be found reproduced in most manuals of classical archæology (Cf pp 135-136)

1.   TYPES OF BODHISATTVA, BUDDHA AND MONK

GRÆCO-CHRISTIAN CHRIST AND GRÆCO-BUDDHIST BUDDHA

# The Tutelary Pair
# in Gaul and in India [1]

When turning over the leaves of the monumental and valuable *Recueil des bas-reliefs, statues et bustes de la Gaule romaine* of M Espérandieu, we see again and again a figure usually entitled « Abundance » or « Goddess Mother ». Rare in Provence, where apparently it is better concealed under the purely classical features of Demeter and Fortune, it shows itself from time to time in Aquitaine with an appearance already more indigenous , then multiplying itself, it passes into « Lyonnaise », where we have counted it no less than forty times (vols III-IV) : the sequel of the publication will tell us whether it enjoyed the same favour in Belgian Gaul Its most usual type, very close to that of the pullulant *Matres*, holds in the left hand a horn of abundance, and in the right a patera In no. 3225 (Langres) we see moreover on either side of the goddess two little genii, one of whom « dips into a purse placed between her feet ». If it is not she, then it is one of her sisters, who elsewhere is represented with a child in her arms, like a Madonna (nos. 1326-1334, Saintes), or with a sack on her knees, from which drop coins (no. 1367, Ruffec). At times fruits are also placed actually on the lap of the goddess (nos. 2350, Mont Auxois , 3237, Langres). Lastly, the patera is occasionally replaced by a cake (nos. 1528,

(1) *Revue archéologique*, 1912, II, pp. 341-9

Bourges), or, in the more debased pieces, by a goblet of the special form called an *olla* (nos. 1161, Puy-de-Dôme; 2112, Beaune) These last attributes seem to be only borrowings from another Gallic divinity, or rather two others who are masculine and likewise of frequent occurence Their usual attributes are the *olla* and the purse, often difficult to distinguish from one another , but local and barbarous variants represent them as holding likewise the cake and the sack of money (no. 1555, La Guerche, Cher), or even a child (no 2882, Auxerre), when they do not in their turn borrow the patera full of fruits (no. 2263, Entrains) or the horn of abundance (nos. 2162, Mâcon; 2166, Chalon-sur-Saône) One of the types is bearded like Jupiter, whose long sceptre it replaces, as we know, by the handle of a mallet. The other, beardless, most often hides his personality under the figure of Mercury The intimate relationship of both with the goddess, or goddesses, of « Abundance » is certain for a proof we require only the numerous groups in which they appear in company, standing on the same stele or seated side by side on the same seat. Some represent the god without a beard, and indicate clearly — from the wings on his feet up to the petasus, taking the caduceus *en route* — his assimilation to Mercury (nos. 1800, Fleurieu-sur-Saône ; 1836, Autun), or give him the appearance of a « local Mars » (no 1832, Autun). The majority resort to the model of the bearded god with a mallet (nos 2066, Nuits ; 3441, Dijon etc ). Often they assign to the husband, as mark of office, the same horn of abundance as to his companion, unless they lend to the latter the purse (no. 3382, Châtillon-sur-Seine), or make both place their hands on the same *olla* (no. 2118, Beaune) In one case a child is playing at their feet (no. 1830, Autun). For the necessities of our case we will restrict ourselves to borrowing from M Espérandieu's collection an almost complete specimen of each of the two principal variants of the subject (pl. XVII, 1 and 2) (¹)

No one expects from an Indianist that he shall undertake more closely to identify Gallo-Roman divinities or even to distinguish very carefully between them, but perhaps he may be allowed to point out the existence, on the opposite confines of the world known to the ancients, of perfectly analogous figures and even groups (pl. XVIII, 1 and 2). As far as one can judge of the popularity of gods by the always fortuitous result of excavations, this divine pair was in Gandhâra no less in vogue than in Lyonnaise, but there we possess more precise information concerning it. The Buddhist community showed itself more receptive to popular superstitions than the Christian clergy. It assigned a place in its convents, and dedicated passages of its scriptures, to this conjugal association of the fairy with the children and the genius with the purse . for, after all, they are only demi-gods of fairly low extraction, created for the use of the middle classes, and on a level with them. In the man it has long been proposed to recognise Kuvera, the « King of the Spirits » (²), but the texts merely designate him as their « general », by his name Pâñcika, and it is in virtue of this title that he is nearly always leaning upon a lance. These *Yakshas* of India, like the dwarfs of our mythologies, are essentially guardians of treasures; and doubtless this is how Pâñcika must have commenced

---

(1) In addition to the specimens represented or quoted in the texts, see also nos 1564, 1573, 1828, 1837, 1849, 2129, 2249, 2252-2253, 2255-2256, 2271, 2313, 2334, 2353, 2878-2881, 2911, etc It seems that the same two gods are again found in the company of the same goddess on the « triades » of nos 2131 (Autun) and 2357 (Asile-Sainte-Reine)

(2) Cf. Dr J Ph. VOGEL, *Note sur une statue du Gandhâra*, in *B E. F E -O.*, III, 1903

his career, but the « purse of gold », which he holds in
his right hand, would sufficiently prove, even if we were
not expressly told, that he had already transformed himself from a jealous gaoler into a generous dispenser of
riches Whilst the miserly demon was thus changing into a
liberal genius, his wife Hâritî was undergoing a parallel
evolution, and from an ogress was becoming a matron.
Originally she personified some terrible infantile epidemic;
and, although herself a mother of five hundred little
elves, she found her food in the children of men; but
when she is depicted for us by religious art, she is supposed to have been already converted by Buddha, and her sole
function is to accord to the vows of the faithful a numerous
progeny If we care to translate the myth into Greco-
Roman terms, Lamia was metamorphosed into Lucina
Most often she is represented as holding on her knees, or
even suckling, her last-born, which has caused her to be
called the Buddhist Madonna ([1]), whilst numbers of
her sons frolic around her or, climbing about her person,
make her look like an Italian allegory of Charity. The
authors of pl XVIII, 1 and 2 have expressed the traditional
conception of the fruitful and fructifying Hâritî in a manner more sober than usual, being content with putting a
*cornucopia* into her left hand. They forget only one point,
namely that according to Indian ideas a horn or any other
remnant of a dead animal (except the black antilope) is an
unclean thing, and that only people of the currier caste,
the least fastidious and the most despised of men, can touch
such an object For us Europeans, who are not disturbed
by such refinements of delicacy, this attribute, far from
shocking, only awakens in the delighted mind ideas of fer-

---

(1) Cf *infra*, the last essay

tile maturity and maternal prosperity. This is, indeed, how the Indo-Greek sculptors understood it, and the mere choice of this symbol would be sufficient to prove that they were more Greek than Indian · but the meaning of these abridged versions remains evidently the same as that of the more ornate replicas, which encumber with urchins the pedestal, the knees, and even the shoulders of these same persons (cf. pl. XLVIII, 1). The mere sight of the god leaning lovingly on the arm or the shoulder of his companion, and the latter not fearing to caress his knee in public, leaves us in no doubt that popular imagination and cult have in fact united in matrimony the genius who dispenses riches and the fairy who grants posterity.

We should be willing to believe that the Gallic groups, like their Indian prototypes, must practically answer to the same eternal desires of humanity for offspring and for money — although our modern civilization seems to detach itself from the one to the advantage of the other. As far as the god is concerned, whether it be a question of the Gallic Mercury, who, we are told by Caesar, controlled the gains of commercial transactions, or of that *Dis Pater*, who seems to be the native double of Plutus, as well as of Pluto, the purse which he holds in his hand is in all languages an expressive emblem  and as for the goddess, by whatever name she may be called, Rosmerta, Maia, Tutela, Nanto-svelta, or simply Bona Dea, her horn of abundance signifies fecundity. According to all appearance, whilst her husband was more particularly destined to fulfil the aspirations of the men, her task was to satisfy those of the women ; and thus in Gaul, as in India, both sexes must have found satisfaction in the worship of this divine pair. Besides, it is sufficient or four purpose that their tutelary character should be incontestable. What chiefly interests us is the analogy between the procedures followed by the artists of such distant countries, in order to picture before our eyes ideas on the whole analogous.

Between the two groups reproduced in our plates the only contrast at all striking consists in the respectively inverse positions of the two spouses. But, inverted as it is, it retains the same intention of reserving for the goddess the place of honour in relation to the man — that being according to the old Indian custom on the left, and not on the right as with us (¹) The stool placed beneath the left foot of the persons in pl XVII, 1 is lacking in pl. XVIII, 1 and 2, but it exists on other replicas, and, besides, the group of pl XVII, 2 dispenses with it likewise. The scaly decoration of the pedestal of pl. XVIII, 1, made of coins half covering each other, is only a paraphase of the signification of the purse. The double seats on pl. XVIII allow a sight of their four feet, turned on the lathe in the Indian manner. but, on the other hand, the nimbus which emphasizes the divine character of the pair is perfectly familiar to our western eyes. Then, beside these small local differences, what resemblances are to be observed! If we leave aside the leggings and the large earrings of the Indian genius, his costume even, consisting of a tunic and a cloak, is not so very different from that usually worn by his Gallo-Roman equi-

---

(1) For other conjugal pairs thus placed cf *Art gréco-bouddhique du Gandhâra*, figg 160-162 A curious fact to be noticed is that two Gallo-Roman groups, to be classed among those which have best retained the accent of their birthplace, also place the goddess on the left of the god, they are nos 1319 (Saintes) in which the god with the purse is crouched down « à l'indienne » near the goddess with the horn of abundance, who is seated in the European manner, and 2334 (Auxois) We may ask ourselves if the custom of the Gauls was not the same as that of the Indians on this point, exactly as we know that it was the common custom of the two nations to count past time by nights and not by days, etc,

valents. To the mallet of the one corresponds well enough the long sceptre of the other, with its end rounded in the form of a mace (pl. XVIII, 1). As for the beardless god of pl. XVII, 2, he, we are told, « holds in his left hand a lance, and in the other an object scarcely recognizable, perhaps a purse » : these are precisely the insignia of the corresponding person in pl. XVIII, 2. Last but not least, the women have the same pose, the same attributes, the same draperies, even the same headdress in the form of a « bushell », or « basket » : between them a quasi-identity asserts itself, and there would be no exaggeration in saying that, from the banks of the Indus to those of the Seine, it would have cheated even the eyes of the donors.

Such is the testimony of the monuments  What does it prove ? Let us hasten to say, nothing very new  for certainly no one will venture to imagine direct influences between Gaul and India. Moreover, the connection, as far at least as the goddess is concerned, is already established in the memory of instructed readers by a number of intermediary figures : at need it would soon be discovered among those tiny mercantile and travelling folk, the Mediterranean terracottas. We shall be excused for holding in this case also to prudent generalities and confining ourselves to the introduction of our Indian replicas into the discussion. If it were not sufficient to indicate this new fact, and if we ought further to essay an interpretation of it, that which we should propose is a very simple one. It has long been ascertained that the art of Gandhâra borrowed its technique from Hellenistic art · it is impossible then that it should not have features in common with Greco-Roman, and consequently with the Gallo-Roman art. This kind of relationship, however distant the degree may be, is justified principally, in archæology as well as in linguistics, by the same construc-

tion of the forms and the employment of the same grammar, verbal or decorative. and in this particular case no
specialist could turn over the leaves of M Espérandieu's
collection without noticing, in support of the cousinship
of these distant schools, a number of details of composition
and the constant return of the same ornamental subjects,
amorini, griffons or tritons, garlands, acanthuses or flowers.
But, after all, nothing is more striking and more persuasive
for the public than a comparison bearing on vocabu-
lary, especially if it is a question of a common significant
word. This is just the kind of contribution that we
believed we could supply here by noting the suggestive
correspondence of the oriental and occidental expressions of the same ideas, or, better, of the same religious
needs. In truth, these works, however complex they may
be, only transcribe quite rudimentary notions ; but notions
only the more deeply grounded in human nature. Such
as they are, these groups — which, besides, are nearly
contemporaneous — seem to us to furnish for the moment
one of the most palpable verifications of the fact that in the
first centuries of our era the sculptors of the Gauls and
those of Ariana had each learned at the school of the Greeks,
and spoke from one end of the ancient world to the other
the same common language, the same artistic « koiné ».

PLATE XVII

Cf. pp 141-145

These two bas-reliefs are nos 80 (height m 0, 46) and 81 (height m 0, 30) of the Archæological Museum of Dijon, they were both found on Mount Auxons, the first in 1803, the second in 1834. With the kind consent of Major E. Espérandieu, our plate reproduces the two stereotypes of nos 2347 and 2348 of his *Recueil général des bas reliefs, statues et bustes de la Gaule romaine*, whence, for the sake of greater impartiality, we content ourselves with reproducing the descriptions.

I — « God and Goddess, seated facing us, booted and each with the left foot on a footstool. The god, on the right, is bearded, and wears a long tunic and a mantle, he holds in his right hand a naked sword, and with the other he leans on the iron of a mallet, the handle of which rests on the arm of his seat. The goddess, crowned with a tower, has a long tunic, which leaves her right shoulder and part of her breast bare ; with her left hand she holds against her shoulder a horn of plenty, filled with fruits, with the other hand a slanting patera ».

II — « God and Goddess seated facing us, their feet shod. The god, on the right, is beardless, his body naked, and he has a mantle over his knees, in his left hand he carries a lance, in the other an object which is scarcely recognizable. perhaps a purse. The goddess. clothed in a long robe which leaves a part of her breast and her right shoulder uncovered, holds in her right hand a patera and in the other a horn of plenty. filled with fruits ».

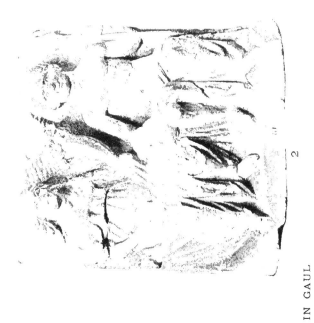

1         IN GAUL         2

PLATE XVIII

Cf. pp 141-145

I — Archaeological Survey photograph, supplied by Dr J Ph VOGEL, who himself published it in the *B É. F E -O*, VIII, 1908, p 488 The original, bought at Sahri-Bahlol, is at present to be found in the Peshawar Museum, it measures m 0, 21 in height The genius, curiously clothed with a tunic, a chlamys and leggings, holds a long sceptre and a purse, the fairy, whose head is unfortunately lost, rests her right hand on her husband's knee, and with the other holds up the horn of plenty At the two corners of the plinth two gaping vessels pour out streams of gold coins

II — The original (height m 0, 18) is found in the Museum fur Völkerkunde in Berlin (I C 32805), and for the photograph we are indebted to Prof. GRUNWEDEL and Dr von Le COQ This time the genius bears the customary lance and purse As in the preceding group, his left arm leans on the shoulder of his wife, whose right hand likewise caresses his knee As to the latter, she clearly has for head-dress the *modius* or *κάλαθος* (like the goddess on pl XVII, 1 [1]

2

1

# The Great Miracle at Çrâvastî (¹).

## I

The narratives of the death of Buddha assert that after his cremation eight kings or ruling clans shared his ashes, and that they deposited their several portions under as many *stûpas*. We see no reason for disbelieving tradition on this point · the important thing is not at times to confuse these first eight sanctuaries with the historical « eight grand *caityas* » (²) We know, indeed, for certain that eight towns of Madhyadeça had finally divided among themselves, not the relics, but the legend, of Buddha. In their immediate neighbourhood were eight specially holy places, supposed to preserve the vestiges of the eight principal miracles of the Master. This implies that they formed as many centres of attraction for pilgrims, the organized exploitation of whom — one of the few industries which still survive in India — must have constituted an appreciable source of income It may easily be imagined that the definite choice of scenes and sites was not accomplished without rivalries

---

(1) *Journal asiatique*, Jan -Feb 1909

(2) That there is no lack of opportunity for these confusions we find proved at once in *Une poésie inconnue du roi Harsa Çîlâditya*, restored from Chinese transcription by M. S Levi (*Actes du Xᵉ Congrès int des Orient* , 1894, I, p 188, Leiden, 1895) and entitled « Hymn to the Eight Great *Caityas* », which enumerates still more The « eight reliquaries » of stanza 5, followed by the *stûpas* of the « urn » and the « ashes », are evidently the 8 + 2 *stûpas* of the *Mahâparinibbâna-sutta*, VI, 62, and have nothing to do with the « eight great *caityas* » of the title

and hesitations. At least four cities, indeed, received from the first an undisputed recognition. A relatively ancient text, the *Mahâparinibbânasutta*, already recommends the pilgrimages to the four sacred places of the Birth, the Illumination, the First Preaching, and the Death, of Buddha (¹). On the square bases of the little *stûpas* of Gandhâra and the stelæ of Amarâvatî these four scenes are invariably associated (pll. II-IV) : only we must draw attention to the fact that in the latter case Kapilavastu is usually represented not by the nativity of the child Buddha, but by what might be called his birth into the spiritual life, we mean his « abandonment of home » (²). However, neither the cities of Gayâ and Benares, nor certainly the obscure frontier market towns of Kapilavastu and Kuçinagara could pretend to monopolize between them the Buddhist legend and the advantages accruing therefrom. Through the disconnected accounts of

---

(1) V, 16-22, the *Jâti*, the *Abhisambodhi*, the *Dharmacakrapravartana*, and the *Parinirvâna* are similarly associated in the *Divyâvadâna*, ed COWELL and NEIL, p 244 and p 397, l. 18.

(2) For the little *stûpas* of the north-west, cf. *Art greco-bouddhique du Gandhâra*, fig 208 For the stelæ of Amarâvatî see J BURGESS, *The Buddhist Stûpas of Amarâvatî and Jaggayyapeta*, pll XVI, 4, XXXII, 4; XXXVIII, 5; XLI, 6 (with the departure on horseback, cf J FERGUSSON, *Tree and Serpent-Worship*, pl. LXXV on the right), and pl XVI, 3 (with the farewell to Chandaka, cf FERGUSSON, *ibid*, pl LXXV, to the left) On all those stelæ which are complete the *Parinirvâna* is constantly symbolized by a simple *stûpa*. With these one may connect others, in which the *Abhisambodhi* and the *Dharmacakrapravartana* are figured by an empty throne under a tree or a wheel (BURGESS, *ibid*, pll XXXVIII, 3 and 6, XLV, 2 and 4, XLVI, 1-3, XLVII, 3, XLVIII, 1, FERGUSSON, *ibid*, pll XCIII, XCIV, 1, 4) The most curious of this kind are those which shrink from representing not only the Buddha, but even the Bodhisattva, and wherein the *Mahâbhinishkramana* is no longer represented, except by a horse without a rider (FERGUSSON, *ibid*, pll XCIII, to the left, XCVI, 3 and XCVIII, 2) It will be observed besides that on several stelæ of Benares (*Anc Mon Ind*, pl 67, 2 and 68, 1) the *Mahâbhinishkramana* is associated with the *Jâti* in the same framework.

the documents we seem to catch the play of the two domi-
nant forces which brought the number of the great pilgrimages up to the sacred figure of eight. Sometimes the preponderant element seems to be the prestige which a certain
miracle had very early acquired in the popular imagination.
Thus we see the « descent from heaven » separate itself
very early from the crowd of traditional marvels; but its
localization continues fluctuating, at least if we keep to
the letter of the texts (¹) On the other hand, the ancient
capital of Magadha, Râjagriha, and the wealthy free town of
Vaiçâlî easily, by reason of their preeminent rôle in the Buddhist scriptures, eclipsed the titles of Kauçâmbî or Mathurâ :
there is, however, no consensus of testimony as to which
among all the edifying scenes which had there come to
pass it was right more particularly to commemorate. At
Çrâvastî even, where the interest is at once concentrated
upon the Jetavana, the Master's favourite sojourn, unanimity of choice does not fall, as might have been expected, on
the « great miracle », the triumph whereby its immediate
environs had been rendered famous (²). In the face of the

(1) It is known that the *Divyâvadâna* and Fa-hien localize the *Devâvatâra*
at Sânkâçya, Hiuan-tsang at Kapitha and Fa-t'ien (cf S LEVI, *loc cit*, p 190)
at Kanyâkubja, the *Mahâvyutpatti* (§ 193) and Wou-k'ong (trans. S LEVI
and Ed. CHAVANNES, *Journal Asiatique*, sept-oct 1895, p 358) do not give
definitely the place of this « Descent » of Buddha
(2) The *Mahâprâtihârya* is indeed mentioned by the text of Harsha and
placed, somewhat incorrectly, by Fa-t'ien in the Jetavana of Çrâvastî (the
*Divyâvadâna* [pp 151 and 155, ll 12-14 and 17-18] specifies, in fact, that the
theatre of the scene was situated between the town and the park), but
Wou-k ong associates with the Jetavana the preaching of the *Mahâprajñâpâ-
ramitâ-sûtra*. In the same way, at Râjagriha, in direct antithesis to the vague
« teachings » of Fa-t'ien, he places the preaching of the *Saddharmapundarika*
on the neighbouring hill of the Gridhrakûta At Vaiçâlî both agree to call by
different names the touching episode of the rejection of life (*âyur°* or *âyuh-
saṃskâra-utsarjana*), which supervened three months before the *Parinirvâna*.
But we shall see that, guided by considerations of a pictorial and technical

capricious divergencies of the texts the concordant precision of the figured monuments has fortunately permitted
us to make out the list, and to sketch the traditional scheme,
of the four supplementary great scenes, the miracle of Çrâvastî, the descent from heaven at Sânkâçya, the monkey's
offering at Vaiçâlî, the subjugation of the savage elephant
at Râjagriha (¹). It is true that, in order definitely to fix this
scheme, we have availed ourselves chiefly of miniatures
in Nepalese and Bengali manuscripts of rather late date
(XIᵗʰ-XIIIᵗʰ centuries). At the most we had been able to
compare with them only a few carved slabs, which came
from the scene of the « first preaching », at Sârnâth, in the
northern suburb of Benares, and which date back approximately to the Vᵗʰ century of our era. Unfortunately, these
slabs were quite incomplete   we may be permitted, therefore, to emphasize the interest of the recent discovery at
the same place of a stele in fairly good condition, divided
into eight panels and consecrated precisely to the eight great
scenes (pl XIX, 1) Let us say at once that seven of these
bas-reliefs only confirm what we already knew of the subjects which they represent and the conventional manner of
treating them. Besides, Mr. J H Marshall has completely
identified them. He has no hesitation, except as regards
one single scene, « of which the identification », he says,
« is doubtful, but which appears to have taken place at Çrâvastî » (²) And it is, in fact, concerning the traditional

---

order, the artists made from the mass of the traditional accounts a quite
different choice from the men of letters

(1) See *Et sur l'Iconogr. bouddh de l'Inde*, I (1900, pp 162-170), sum-
marized, corrected and completed, *ibid* , II (1905), pp 113-114.

(2) See Mr MARSHALL's (article in *J. R A S* 1907, pp 999-1000, and
pl. IV, 1) We take pleasure in here thanking the very distinguished Director-General of Archæology, India, for his extreme kindness in putting at

manner of representing the « Great miracle » of Çrâvastî
that this new document will furnish us with useful evidence.

## II

The canonical importance of the *mahâ-prâtihârya* of Çrâvastî is incontestable. The *Divyâvadâna* gives it expressly
as one of the ten acts of which every perfect Buddha must
necessarily acquit himself before dying (¹) It is likewise
in this text — that is to say, as MM. S Lévi and Ed Huber
have shown, in the *Vinaya* of the Mûla-Sarvâstivâdins —
that we find the most ancient and most detailed account
of the miracles whereby on this occasion Çâkyamuni
triumphed over his rivals, the six chiefs of sects. Thanks to
the translation of Burnouf, this account is too well known
to need citation here (²). We shall restrict ourselves to
bringing out the essential points After having wrought a
few minor miracles, which were mere preliminary trifles,
and refusing to allow anyone, monk or layman, man or

---

our disposal a photograph of the stele in question and authorizing its
reproduction

(1) *Divyâvadâna*, pp, 150 151 ; no Buddha of the past has failed in it *ibid.*,
p 147, ll. 24-27); according to the Tibetan testimonies the Buddha of our
age accomplished it in the sixteenth year of his ministry (ROCKHILL, *Life of
the Buddha*, p 79)

(2) *Divyâdâna*, XII and BURNOUF, *Introduction à l'hist du Bouddh indien*,
pp 162 sqq The XIII<sup>th</sup> story of the *Avadânakalpalatâ*, deplorably edited
indeed in the *Bibl Indica*, V, 1895 (see, below, p 174, n 5), adds, in accordance with the usual custom of Kshemendra, nothing but poetic graces;
ROCKHIL (*Life of the Buddha*, pp 79-80, following the Dulva) and SCHIEFNER
(*Eine tibet. Lebensbeschr. Çâkyamuni's*, p. 293) restrict themselves to a reference to BURNOUF. For the connections of these various authors with the
tradition of the Mûla-Sarvâstivâdins see also the very clear conclusions of
Prof S LÉVI, *Journal Asiatique*, July-August 1908, pp 102 and 104

woman, to be substituted for him, so as to confuse the *Tîrthyas* by the exhibition of a supernatural power, the Blessed One accomplishes successively, on the direct and twice repeated invitation of king Prasenajit, two kinds of miracles. At first he displays what in technical terms is called the *yamaka-prâtihârya*, which consists in walking the air in various attitudes, while emitting alternately flames and waves from the upper and lower parts of his body, in the second place, multiplying images of himself up to heaven and in all directions, he preaches his law A violent storm, raised by a chief of the genii, completes the overthrow of the heterodox. An immense multitude is converted to the good law.

If now after the Sanskrit version we consult the Pâli tradition, we find that the *mahâ-prâtihârya* of Çrâvastî is there usually designated « the miracle at the foot of the mango-tree ». The *Mahâvamsa* and the commentary of the *Jâtaka*, for example, give it no other name. According to the latter, as also according to the Singhalese and the Burmese (¹) accounts, Buddha did, in fact, begin by accomplishing the magical operation which the jugglers of India are always endeavouring to imitate . from the stone of a mango planted in the ground he is supposed to have forthwith grown an enormous tree, covered at once with flowers and fruits But then this is merely a simple extra, scarcely even a curtain-raiser. When the great day has come, the divinities assemble, and the introduction to *Jâtaka* no. 483

---

(1) Cf *Mahâvamsa*, ed. TURNOUR, pp 107, 181, 191, ed GEIGER, pp 137, 241, 254, *Jâtaka*, ed FAUSBØLL, I, p 77, l 23, 88, l 20, etc , *ambamûle*, or *gandamba-mûle*, is written, Ganda has become in the commentary of the *Jâtaka*, no 483, and Gandamba in Sp HARDY (*Manual of Buddhism*, 1ˢᵗ ed. pp 295-296), the name of the gardener who supplied the mango see also BIGANDET, *Life of Gaudama*, Rangoon, 1866, p 205.

tells us in a single sentence that « The Master, having accomplished the *yamaka-pâtihâriya*, and having recognized the believing dispositions of a great number of people, redescended, and, seated on his Buddha seat, taught the law » (¹) If we analyse this brief résumé of the scene, it is not difficult to recognize in it, exactly as in the overelaborate version of the *Divyâvadâna*, the distinct and successive enunciation of the same two moments, that of the « pair of miracles » and that of the preaching.

Of these two manifestations the first strikes one immediately as the more original and the more picturesque · one would have wagered that it must have thrust itself on the choice of the artists whose duty it was to decorate the Buddhist monuments with edifying scenes, or to compose pious *ex-votos* for the use of the laity As a matter of fact, we have found in the ancient school of Gandhâra at least one indubitable representation of the « twin miracles » ; and even at the present moment the special attribution of this bas-relief to the *mahâ-prâtihârya* of Çrâvastî seems to us not in the least untenable, on the sole condition that we mark well its exceptional character (²). It was, besides, the accidental circumstance of this find that prevented our carrying still further our researches on this point. Nevertheless, as we had already observed, it was the scene of the manifold

----

(1) See *Jâtaka*, IV, p 265, ll. 13-14 , the English translation (IV, p. 168, l. 13) of *oruyha* $=$ *avaruyha* by « then arose » seems to us to be a *lapsus calami*, going directly against the meaning It will be noticed that the Pâli, like the *Mahâvastu*, makes use of the technical term of *yamaka-p°*, BIGANDET, *loc cit* , p. 207, gives us a very clear description of it (perhaps even two descriptions, cf below, p 157); it is also easily recognized through the *tejo°* and *apokasina samâpatti* of Sp. HARDY, *loc cit* , p 297

(2) See *Art g -b du Gandh* , pp 516 and 535, and fig 263 ($=$ *Anc Mon India*, pl 115, 5), where we give the reasons which led us us to prefer this identification to the equally possible one of « the arrival at Kapilavastu »

preaching of the Master that later, if we may judge from
the miniatures of the manuscripts, inspired the traditional
image of the « great miracle » : at least, they represent it
regularly by three Buddhas teaching, seated side by side
upon as many lotuses (¹). Now the stele recently exhumed
from the ground of the ancient Mrigadâva testifies, five or
six centuries earlier, to this same manner of conceiving
the subject . the compartment which we know beforehand
to have been reserved for the miracle of Çrâvastî shows us,
in fact, like the miniatures, three Buddhas seated on lotuses
in the attitude of teaching This is the new fact supplied
by this discovery, and it will not be long before its consequences unfold themselves before our eyes.

But, first of all, a question arises as to whether we must
restrict ourselves to merely stating, or whether we can succeed in explaining, the unexpected choice of the artists. If
we consider only the stele in question (pl. XIX, 1), it seems
that we may immediately see a reason, although an external
one, for the course taken by its author Let us observe, in
fact, that of the four great supplementary scenes of the
legend of Buddha there are two which absolutely necessi-
tate a standing posture . they are the subjugation of the
wild elephant and the descent from heaven. A legitimate
care for symmetry in the alternation of the poses would
have demanded a sitting posture in the corresponding
scenes, not only in the monkey's offering, but also in the
great miracle of Çrâvastî Such, at least, is the idea impe-
riously suggested by an examination of the apportion-
ment of the subjects on the new stele — the only one,

(1) See *Icon bouddb de l'Inde*, I, pl X, 1 (cf BENDALL, *Catalogue of the
Buddhist Sanskrit Manuscripts in the University Library, Cambridge*, 1883,
pl II, 1), and cf *ibid* p 205, no 82, and II, pp 114, no 4

let us remember, that we possess with the eight scenes complete (cf. the table below)

| | |
|---|---|
| *First Preaching*<br>BUDDHA SEATED | *Parinirvâna*<br>BUDDHA LYING DOWN |
| *Descent from Heaven*<br>BUDDHA STANDING | *Miracle of Çrâvastî*<br>BUDDHA SEATED |
| *Offering of the monkey*<br>BUDDHA SEATED | *Subjugation of the elephant*<br>BUDDHA STANDING |
| *Nativity*<br>MÂYÂ STANDING | *Perfect enlightenment*<br>BUDDHA SEATED |

It is scarcely necessary to remark that this reason, valid for the whole, is inapplicable to an isolated panel The reading of the texts will furnish an argument of wider bearing It does not, in fact, take us long to perceive that they use and abuse the *yamaka-prâtihârya*. The general introduction of the *Jâtaka* makes it to be wrought by Buddha as early as the eighth day after the Bodhi, and specifies that he repeated it under three other circumstances, (1) at the time of his visit to Kapilavastu and of his meeting with his father and his relatives, the Çâkyas, (2) at the time of his encounter with the heterodox monk Patikaputta, and last, (3) at Çrâvastî, at the foot of the mango-tree ('). The *Divyâvadâna* attributes it further to a simple monk; the *Mahâvastu* to Yaçoda or Yaças, the converted son of the banker of Benares; the *Sûtrâlankâra* to the five hundred *bhikshunis*, companions of Mahâprajâpatî, the *Jâtaka-*

---

(1) *Jâtaka*, I, pp 77 and 88, trans Rhys DAVIDS, *Buddhist Birth Stories*, pp. 105 and 123, on the first of the three other occasions cf. *Mahâvastu*, III, p. 115, and on the second the *Manual* of Sp HARDY, p 331.

*mâlâ* to a Pratyeka-Buddha ; finally, the *Mahâvamsa* twice
places it to the account of simple relics of the Blessed
One, etc. (¹). We receive the impression that the *yamaka-
prâtihârya* has become hackneyed in consequence of being
classic Moreover when, after having accomplished it, Buddha returns and seats himself in his place, he informs king
Prasenajit in a moment of proud modesty that « this
kind of magical power is common to all the disciples of the
Tathâgata » (²) Hence it may be conceived that artists and
worshippers were of one mind in no longer finding in
this banal wonder anything to characterize with sufficient clearness the great scene of Çrâvastî, and preferred
the multiplication of the teaching images of the Master :
for it is written that this last miracle is realizable only by
the special power of the Buddha and the gods (³).

Finally, if we must conceal nothing, we seem to
detect in the texts themselves a tendency to confuse the
two kinds of wonders, and even to eliminate the former
in favour of the latter. First of all, there seems to have
been at times a misapprehension as to the real meaning
of the expression *yamaka-prâtihârya*. This technical term
« twin miracles » does in fact lend itself to confusion
We know now from the very explicit descriptions of the
*Divyâvadâna* and the *Mahâvastu* that it must be understood

---

(1) *Divyâvadâna*, p. 378 , *Mahâvastu*, III, p 410 ; *Sûtrâlankâra*, trans.
Ed Huber, p 399, *Jâtakamâlâ*, IV, 20 , *Mahâvamsa*, pp. 107 and 191 (Turnour), 137 and 254 (Geiger)

(2) *Divyâvadâna*, p 161, l 13  *sarvaçrâvaka-sâdhârana*. The text of the
commentary of *Jâtaka*, n° 483, IV, p  265, ll 12-13   *Asâdhâranam sâva-
kehi yamaka-p°*, which seems to mean the contrary, becomes in consequence
most suspicious, at least if the two texts are speaking of the same miracle.

(3) *Divyâvadâna*, p  162, *ad fin*  The power of holding a dialogue with a
magic double is likewise stated a little further (on p. 166, l. 11) as a privilege of perfect Buddhas only and inaccessible to simple *çrâvakas*.

as the combined alternation of the two opposite wonders
of water and fire : but it was not without reason that in
1880 Prof. Rhys Davids understood it to mean « making
another appearance like unto himself » In the Burmese
narrative translated by Bigandet (¹) Buddha does, indeed,
begin by making flames or streams gush forth alternately
from the upper and lower parts of his body : but very soon
he hastens to create a companion for his conversation
and his walks, and sometimes it is his turn, and sometimes that of his double, to walk or to sit down, to question or to reply. It is curious to notice that the *Divyâvadâna* also makes the magically multiplied images of the
Blessed One assume varied attitudes, and whilst some
repeat afresh the marvels of water and fire, « others either
ask questions or give answers to them ». It even goes so
far as to introduce most unexpectedly, as an ending to the
chapter, a dialogue between Buddha and another self, created expressly for this purpose (²). Thus it manifests at
least a certain propensity to amalgamate the two successive
moments which it at first endeavoured to distinguish, and
to confuse the reduplication of the miracles with that of
the images (³) But this is not all. In another passage of the
same collection the reverend Pindola Bhâradvâja relates to
king Açoka this same miracle of Çrâvastî, of which he

_____

(1) See RHYS DAVIDS, *Buddh Birth Stories*, p. 105, n 4, and BIGANDET,
*loc cit*, p 207

(2) *Divyâvadâna*, p 162, ll 17-20, and 166, ll 3-11, cf. the description
of plate XXI, 2.

(3) The same confusion seems to be reproduced with regard to the miracles
attributed to the monk Panthaka, as regards these last I am indebted to the
obliging friendship and incomparably extensive information of Prof S. LEVI
for the following references *Divyâvadâna*, p 494, *Anguttara-Nikâya*, I, 14
(p. 24) ; *Visuddhi-magga*, analysed in *J Pâli Text Society*, 1891-1893, p 114;
*Vinaya* (Chinese) of the Sarvâstivâdins (c. 11), of the Mahiçâsakas (c 7),
of the Dharmaguptas (c 12), etc.

represents himself as an eye witness. Now he no longer
even mentions the *yamaka-prâtihârya* : « And when, o¹
Great King, in order to triumph over the Tîrthyas, the
great miracle was accomplished at Çrâvastî by the Blessed
One, and there was created an array of Buddhas which
mounted up to the heaven of the Akanishtha gods, at that
time I was there, and I saw these sports of Buddha (¹) ».
Here it is no longer a question of anything but the second
miracle. Finally, we again find this latter, reduced to its
most simple expression, in the *Buddhacarita* of Açvaghosha,
whose descriptions are always so close to the figured monuments According to him (so far as we can trust the English
translation made by the Rev. S. Beal from the Chinese
translation of the original Sanskrit) Buddha restricts himself
to rising into the air and there remaining seated, and
« diffusing his glory like the light of the sun, he shed
abroad the brightness of his presence ». In this version —
by a strange coincidence, but one which in our opinion it
would be vain to seek to press further — the *mahâ-prâtihârya*
quite assumes the characteristics of a Transfiguration · « His
face did shine as the sun, and his raiment became white as
the light (²) »

III

These waverings of tradition, as they are thus indicated in
the texts, may help us to understand the at first somewhat
surprising choice of the Indian image-makers. Regarding

(1) *Divyâvadâna*, p 401 (cf BURNOUF, *Introd* , p 398) it will be noticed
that these are exactly the same terms as are employed on two occasions
in the previously quoted *sûtra* (*Divyâvadâna*, p 162, ll 16 and 26) —
P 401, l 15, read probably *aham* instead of *mahat*
(2) *Sacred Books of the East*, XIX, p 240, *Gospel according to St Matthew*,
XVII, 2

the fact of the choice itself there is, as we said above, no
room for doubt. Let us resume the examination of the new
panel, no. 5 of plate XIX, 1 : On a lotus, whose peduncle
issues from a ripple of waves rolled into volutes, Buddha
is seated with crossed legs in the hallowed posture, and his
hands are joined in the gesture of instruction; on his
right and left, again, there rises a *padma* with a long stalk,
bearing another smaller Buddha, similar in all respects to
the first... Now it is written in the *Divyâvadâna* that at
that moment — namely, at a second invitation from Prasenajit and when the first series of miracles was already
accomplished — « Buddha conceived a mundane thought »
Immediately the Gods rush forward to execute it : Brahmâ
takes a place at his right and Çakra at his left, while the
two Nâga kings, Nanda and Upananda, create entire a
wonderful lotus, on the corolla of which the Blessed One
seats himself. Then by the force of his magic power,
« above this lotus he created another, and on this one also
a Buddha was seated with his legs crossed : and thus in
front, behind, at the sides... » The crowd of Buddhas, holding themselves in the four consecrated attitudes (erect,
walking, seated, or recumbent), soon rise to the highest
heavens ([1]). The bas-relief, unable to juggle, like the text,
with numbers and forms, shows us just three of them, all
alike seated : but by now there is for us no question that
we must see in this restricted space an attempt, however
timid, to realize the legendary phantasmagoria.

---

([1]) Cf *Divyâvadâna*, p. 162 We know that the heaven of the Akanishthas
is the highest heaven of the *Rûpadhâtu*, at the 23rd story of the Buddhist
paradises We remember also that the two kings of the serpents, « Nanda
and his junior », play a part in a number of episodes in the life of Buddha,
beginning with the bath which followed the nativity We shall find information concerning them extracted by M Ed HUBER from the *Vinaya* of the
Mûla-Sarvâstivâdins in the *B É F E -O.*, VI, 1906, pp. 8 sqq

With this abridged version we may connect immediately other more developed pictures, such, for example,
as that which totally covers another stele originating from
Sârnâth (¹), and in which are staged no less than four
rows of Buddhas, seated or standing pl (XIX, 2). On seeing
the upward-branching lotus stems which bear these small
figures, we might believe ourselves in the presence of a
genealogical tree of Buddhas  Thus we are invincibly led
to recall those which, either carved or painted, entirely
cover great stretches of the walls of several of the subterranean temples of Ajantâ. One of these frescoes, of which
a copy has been published, very gracefully combines
wreaths of flowers and foliage with the dreamy figures of
the seated or standing Buddhas (²)  it decorates the wall
on the right, in the antechamber of the sanctuary of Cave I;

---

(1) Again let us cite no  (Sârnâth) 1 of the Calcutta Museum (ANDERSON,
Catalogue, II, p. 4, Anc Mon India, pl 68, 1), the left upper division of
which unfortunately broken) represents similarly the « great miracle » of
Çrâvastî opposite to the « descent from heaven » (cf below, p 164, n 1).
It will be observed that on two other stelæ of the same origin (Anc Mon.
India, pll 67, 3 and 68, 2 · Art g -b du Gandh , fig 209, and Iconog. bouddh.
de l'Inde, I, fig 29, to the right) analogous representations of the same
miracle decorate the borders of the stone and enclose the scene

(2) See GRIFFITHS, The Paintings of Ajanta, pl XV (cf on the plan of the
grotto the letter O and X, ibid , pl IV and pl VIII) and BURGESS, Notes
on the Bauddha Rock Temples of Ajantâ, p 17; the paintings of this cave are
usually attributed to the VIᵗʰ century — In Cave II the walls of the antechamber of the sanctuary are likewise adorned with figures of Buddha,
of a very inferior make to those of the preceding ones  M Griffiths counted 1055 of them, measuring about o m 20 high and covering a surface of
22 square metres  he has reproduced some of them, pl. XXIV (cf p 28,
and BURGESS, loc cit , p 35, § XVIII ad fin ) — One may immediately
connect with these frescoes the « thousand Buddhas » painted on the vault
of the grotto no 1 of Murtuk, a specimen of which Prof GRUNWEDEL has
reproduced in his interesting Bericht uber Archæologische Arbeiten in Idikutschari und Umgebung im Winter 1902-1903, pl XXX  notice the strangely
stereotyped character of the support of this Buddha, affecting both a cloud
and a lotus.

and no one will be surprised to learn that there it forms a
pendant to another of the eight great scenes, « the Perfect
Illumination », symbolized on the left wall by the *Mâra-
dharshana*. The high reliefs of plate XX merely reproduce it
in stone . in imitation of the painting the sculptor has not
failed to fill the space between his characters with leaves
and buds of pink lotuses, of the same kind even as those
which bear his superposed rows of Buddhas ([1]). Only it
will be observed that the stem of the seat of the central
figure, at the bottom, is supported with both hands by two
kneeling *nâgarâjas*, both wearing head-dresses of five serpent heads. As we have just been reading the *Divyâvadâna*,
their names immediately occur to our minds · they are
Nanda and Upananda. Thus we find ourselves in possession
of an explanation satisfactory down to the details of the compositions. We have not, as was thought, to do with simple
debauches of piously decorative imagery : we must here
recognize representations on a vast scale, by reason of the
space which the artist had at his disposal, of the « great
miracle » of Çrâvastî ([2]). This is indeed, if one reflects
upon it, the only orthodox method of explaining the
simultaneous presence of several Buddhas in the same picture, when an absolute law says that there shall never be

---

([1]) All the necessary particulars concerning this sculpture are given opposite to plate XX In the *Arch Survey of Western India*, vol IV, pl XXXVII,
2 (cf *ibid* , p. 52), will be found a drawing of the opposite wall of the
same vestibule of the sanctuary, with its eight rows of Buddhas, seven of
which are rows of seven . the *nâgarâjas* are not missing

([2]) Is it worth while to observe that nowhere, either in these representations or in those considered above, have we found any trace of an attempt
at an artistic realization of the fancies imagined by the editor of the *Hien-yu-
yin-yuen king* ? Never, in particular, do we see rays which open out into lotus
bearers of illusory Buddhas burst from the « pores of the skin », or from
the « navel », of the principal character, as is written in SCHMIDT's translation
from the Tibetan *Dzang-lun* (*Der Weise und der Thor*, pp 82 and 84).

more than a single one at one time in each world-system.

It follows that we must at the outset suspect the existence of this subject every time that we find ourselves in the presence of multiple images of Buddha : not, certainly, where they are isolated in separate sections or merely juxtaposed, but where they are evidently associated in the same action (¹). If from this point of view we examine the reliefs and the frescoes of Ajantâ, we shall not fail to discover a whole series of replicas, somewhat less prolix, but not less surely identifiable, than the preceding. Here we will restrict ourselves to citing the most typical of these variants. It seems that we shall have to look for them in the immediate neighbourhood of the inner sanctuaries : « On the back wall, between the left chapel and antechamber [of the adytum of cave II], a large Buddha has seated himself under an *âmba* (mango) tree with an Indra on his right and a Bodhisattva on his left (²). His feet rest on a

---

(1) This restriction is necessary for three reasons First, we must reckon with the progressive crowding together of images of Buddha on the façade or inner walls of the same sanctuary at the expense of various donors -– Secondly, we must not forget the relatively ancient juxtaposition (cf pl XXVI, 1) of the seven Buddhas of our age but we are prepared to believe that there may be a close connection between this motifs and the « grand miracle », either because in the latter the Buddhas prefer to affect the number 7 in rows (cf p. 161, n 1 and p 163), or because the representations of the « seven Buddhas » are strongly influenced by those of the *mahâ-prâtihârya* (as is notably the case at Ajanta for the pl XCI of GRIFFITHS, in contrast to pl LXI) Finally, we do not pretend do deny that at a fairly late period there may have been sought, in a mechanical repetition of images of the Master, an automatic accumulation of merit . but it is our opinion that the origin of this inept procedure must be sought in the single motif where its employment was canonically justified

(2) Dr BURGESS, *loc cit*, p 34, § XVII we think it necessary to make a choice and say, « between Brahmâ and Indra », or « between two Bodhisattvas » but that can be decided only on the spot Let us remark also that a mango-tree cannot be a Bodhi-druma The letters E-F mark the place of this panel on the plan of Cave II, given by Mr GRIFFITHS, pl. XX e Wmust

white lotus · a worshipper is below a little to the left  Across
the top are seven Buddhas in various *mudrâs*, each on a
lotus, the stalks being brought up from below  On each
side of the *Bodhi-druma*, or sacred tree, are two Buddhas...
Below these, on each side, were two pairs more », etc. We
borrow this description from the notes of Dr. Burgess :
it would not be possible to find a better one for the « great
miracle » of Çrâvastî, including the mango-tree of the Pâli
tradition. It is again the same subject which in Cave XVII,
on the right wall of the vestibule of the sanctuary, forms
a pendant to the no less famous miracle of « the descent
from heaven » ('), and this replica, unfortunately very
much damaged, contains also a topical and rather exceptional detail : « The right end of the antechamber », says
Dr. Burgess (²), « is painted with standing and sitting
Buddhas ; the lower portion, however, is destroyed, except
a fragment at each end. The portion remaining at the
right side is very curious, representing a number of Digambara Jaina *bhikshus* helping forward an old fat one,
and carrying the *rajoharana* or *pichi*, a besom to sweep
away insects, etc. Most of them are shaven-headed and
stark naked. One or two, who wear their hair, are clothed.
On the extreme left are an elephant and a horse with two
men. The intermediate painting is completely destroyed ».
By now it is not difficult for us to recognize — exactly as

___

add that the fresco is approximately dated « by an inscription painted in the
alphabet of the VI[th] century »

(1) The *Devâvitâra* is there represented in three stages, as on the pillar ot
Barhut (CUNNINGHAM. *Stûpa of Barhut*, pl  XVII) : at the top is seen the
« Preaching to the Trayastrimça Gods », in the middle the « Descent from
Heaven », at the bottom the « Questions to Çâriputra ». Only these last
two episodes are represented on GRIFFITHS' plate LIV ; for the plan of
Cave XVII cf his plate LIII.

(2) *Loc. cit.*, p. 69, § XXXIII.

on plate LXVIII of the *Anc. Mon. of India* (¹) — at the
left at least an indication of the royal presence of Prasenajit,
to the right the demoralized troop of Tîrthyas, and doubtless the obese and naked old man, whose steps these have
to support, is the Pûrana Kâçyapa whom the Buddhist
legend denotes as their leader and whose defeat is about
to have for penalty an ignominious suicide (²). It is again
he whom we believe we can identify on the left side of
the new panel of plate XIX, 1, by his shaven head, his naked-
ness and, especially, by his strange backward posture, in
striking contrast to the devout attitude of the Buddhist
monk who forms a pendant to him on the other side. But,
on the whole, representations of monks belonging to other
sects are rather rare in Buddhist art, even where their
presence would be most expected · and the pictures of the
Master's triumphs willingly dispense with the not very
edifying spectacle of the vanquished. It would be only the
more desirable that we should possess a good reproduction
of what is still to be found of this Ajantâ fresco. Lacking
this, we must content ourselves with giving a sketch of
one of those which adorn the principal archway of
Cave IX (pl XXI, 1). We know the curious aspect of that
little subterranean chapel, with its three naves, its portal
gallery and its *stûpa* marking the position of the altar : the
warm, ruddy tones of its frescoes give the finishing touches

---

(1) At the bottom of the upper compartment on the left we perceive,
indeed, in addition to the two *nâgarâjas* who are holding up the stem of
the central lotus, 1st, at the left of the spectator, King Prasenajit, who is
recognizable by his parasol-bearer and his elephant, and 2nd, facing him,
also seated upon a stool, Pûrana Kâçyapa, in the form of a fat, naked man,
with shaven head, who is supported from behind under the arms by one of his
companions We may connect with this type that of the same person in *Art
g -b du Gandh* (fig 261 and 225 *c*), and read, *ibid*, pp. 529 and 537,
remarks on the rarity of these representations of « sectarians »

(2) *Divyâvadâna*, p. 165

to the illusion of an ancient basilica. Above the pillars, where the triforium should be, ranges a series of paintings representing hieratic groups (¹). One, almost complete, which is represented by our plate, has the advantage of uniting only the essential elements of the subject, namely, the three Buddhas with their feet placed on lotuses, and — at each side of the one in the centre of the picture, who is teaching, and of whom the two others are, and can only be, illusory emanations — the two traditional divinities, voluntarily reduced to the humble role of flyflap-holders Is it necessary to observe that this is exactly the same distribution of persons (²) that we find again on the lower row of plate XIX, 2 ?

All the specimens of which we have just been speaking, both from Benares and from Ajantâ, can in bulk be dated, in accordance with the alphabet of the inscriptions on some of them, as of the V$^{th}$ or VI$^{th}$ century of our era We shall not hesitate, in spite of time and distance, to connect with them the numerous groups which decorate the principal wall of the highest sculptured gallery of Boro-Budur (IX$^{th}$ century). Almost the whole of this wall is covered with variations on the theme of the « Great miracle » of

---

(1) Cf GRIFFITHS, *Paintings of Ajantâ*, pll XXXVIII and XXXIX

(2) The only differences to be observed consist, 1$^{st}$ in the somewhat capricious detail (cf p 167) of the orientation of the acolyte Buddhas, turned or not towards the central Buddha , 2$^{nd}$ in the fact that the latter has a lotus not for a seat but only for a footstool. This kind of throne and this sitting position « in the European mode » are current peculiarities of the local style, although they are not unknown to the school of Benares and although we may have found them even so far as in the great Buddha of the Chandi Mendut near Boro-Budur in Java They constitute all the less an obstacle to the proposed attribution since the central lotus, while treated as a simple little bench, is nevertheless usually supported by the two classical *nâgarâjas* (cf for example, in *Arch. Survey West. India*, IV, pl XXXVI, 2, the Buddha craned on the *stûpa* of cave XXVI of Ajânta, and below, p 168).

Çrâvastî ; and this profusion of replicas is sufficiently justified by the enormous surface which the sculptors of the
monuments had received instructions to decorate   We
content ourselves here with reproducing the group placed
at the left of the eastern staircase, which we know was
that of the façade (pl. XXII). On the other side an analogous group forms a pendant thereto, except that it is still
more complex and contains no less than seventeen images
of the Blessed One. The general arrangement of these
compositions is a compromise — doubtless imposed by
the dimensions of the rectangular panels, which were
much wider than they were high — between the line taken
by plates XIX, 2 and XX and that by plate XXI, 1 · but on
one side or the other all the topical features are to be found.
This symmetrical reduplication of Buddhas, supported by
lotuses and surrounded by divinities, suffices to establish
not only the undeniable relationship of the schools, but
also the fundamental identity of the subjects.

Inevitable, again, is the connection with many of the
great rock-sculptures of northern China, less remote in time,
but not less distant in space, from their Indian prototypes.
We shall note especially, among the gigantic images which
decorate the grottos of Ta-t'ong-fu (V^{th} century), those
recently published by M. Chavannes, which, as he informs
us, owe the possibility of their being so clearly photographed to the fact that the crumbling of the rocky façade has left
them open to the sky (pl. XXI, 2). The presence of a
second Buddha standing at the left of the great seated one,
— the acolyte on the right has disappeared in the fallen débris
— is sufficient to recall the *mahâ-prâtihârya* : and the innu-
merables figures of the Blessed One, superposed upon a
kind of band, which form nimbuses and aureoles on the
flamboyant background of the *tejas*, finally convince us

that we have to deal with a representation of this miracle in the traditional form of the multiplication of Buddhas (¹)

All these works of art, painted or carved, whether Chinese, Japanese, or Indian, represent more or less, in fact, — to make use of the expression employed in literature, — the *vaipulya* method of sculptured tradition. Let us return to our starting point, I mean to the quite summary lesson presented to us by the stele of the Archæological Survey (pl. XIX, 1) : we shall see connected with it also a series of replicas no less sober than itself A carving, which we believe to be unpublished, will furnish us with a type of them, at least as far as Magadha is concerned (pl XXIII, 1). A great Buddha, seated, in the attitude for teaching, on a lotus whose stem is flanked by two Nâgarâjas, is inserted between two other images of himself, with feet also resting on lotuses. The only novelty introduced is that the two acolyte Buddhas, instead of confronting the spectator, as in plate XIX, 1, or being turned towards the central person, as in plate XXI, 1, or slightly turned from him, as in plate XIX, 2, are looking in exactly opposite directions. This slab, of rather rude workmanship and late date (²), will serve as a perfectly natural transition to the miniatures of the Nepalese or Bengal manuscripts of the XI^{th}-XIII^{th} centuries,

---

(1) We should like to connect with these groups from Ta-t'ong-fu others somewhat later, which decorate the grottos of the pass of Long Men (Ho-nan), of which also M. CHAVANNES has brought back photographs taken in the course of his last mission in China (see, already, *T'oung Pao*, Oct 1908, fig. 4 , cf *Journal asiatique*, July-August 1912, figg 1 4, *Bull École fr Extr -Or.*, V, 1905, fig 36) but here the two acolyte Buddhas have been changed into two simple monks ! The transformation might in strictness be explained by scrupulous orthodoxy (cf above, pp 161-162)

(2) For a reproduction of an analogous group, of the same provenance and likewise preserved in the Museum of Calcutta, see *Ét sur l Iconogr. bouddh de l'Inde*, I, fig. 28, where these three Buddhas are placed just below a representation of the Nativity

where the representation of the « great miracle » of Çrâvastî by three Buddhas back to back has become the constant rule (¹) The identification of our plate XXIII, 1, which already flowed naturally from the analogy of the new stele of Sârnâth, receives, on the other hand, an interesting confirmation *in extremis* from these latest indigenous manifestations of Buddhist art.

Whilst definitely taking this turn in eastern India, our subject became in the West by degrees stereotyped under a form equally abridged, but sensibly different. The place occupied by Elias and Moses in the Christian pictures of the Transfiguration is now, in the representations of the Buddhist « great miracle », no longer held by the two acolyte Buddhas, but by two divine attendants. The imagery of the valley of the Ganges had reduced their part to almost nothing, or even omitted it entirely : here, on the contrary, they end by figuring alone at the side of the Master, standing on lateral lotuses and retaining in their hands their fly-flappers As to the central Buddha, at one time he continues to sit in the Indian manner upon a *padma* like that of plates XIX-XX, at other times, and more frequently, he is installed on a throne after the manner of Europeans, as in plate XXI, 1, and only uses the necessary lotus as a footstool . but nevertheless the two traditional Nâgarâjas continue to hold up its stem. We borrow from a mural sculpture of Kudâ the most reduced type of the first variant (pl. XXIII, 2) a no less summary specimen of the second would be furnished by one of the caves of Kondivté (²) But, above all, we must recognize that all the cave-

_____

(1) Cf above, p 154, n 1
(2) See Burgess, *A S W I*, IV, pl XLIII, I, left part (cf *ibid*, p 71). Cf the fuller replicas of Kanheri, *ibid*, fig 22, *Buddh Art in India*, fig 60, and *Cave Temples of India*, pl LVI (cf *ibid*, p 358), etc

temples of western India are covered with representations of this kind. On this point it is sufficient to refer to the testimony, which no one will think of challenging, of Fergusson and Burgess Along with them we might gather an ample harvest of replicas of the « great miracle » If we do no undertake to draw up a list from their descriptions or from the too cursory notes which we formerly found occasion to take, it is because on these sculptures of a late period there is always reason to fear contamination of subjects (¹).

## IV

We have followed up the evolution of the subject and its variants from the V^{th} century of our era to the final extinction of Buddhist art in India. Could we not now, after having brought the course of its history as far down as possible, endeavour to remount towards its origin and seek in the preceding schools, beginning with that of Gandhâra, the prototypes of the monuments which we have just identified? The enterprise imposes itself upon us, and there seems to be no way of escape Such fortunately is, so far as

---

(1) In fact these contaminations have not failed to take place The Buddha of the *mahâprâtihârya* of Çrâvastî makes the gesture of instruction, exactly as does the Buddha of the *Dharmacakra-pravartana* of Benares nothing further was required to provoque confusions and exchanges between the two motifs originally characterized, the one by the lotus with the Nâgarâjas, the other by the wheel with the gazelles On plate 164 of *Anc Mon India*, by the side of the subject of our plate XXIII, 2, we find some « First Preachings » treated as « Great Miracles », except that the gazelles have replaced the Nâgarâjas on each side of the lotus, on the façade of the great temple of Kârli (*ibid*, pl 168) the gazelles have even been intercalated above Nâgarâjas ¹ From this it may be conceived with what precautions we must surround ourselves before risking a firm identification from descriptions alone

Buddhist iconography is concerned, the routine force of tradition, that, in order to succeed in this second part of our task, it will suffice to determine with exactitude the distinctive feature common to all the verified representations of the *mahâprâtihârya*. Now, if you turn over the plates afresh, you will very soon observe that what characterizes them above all is the special form of this lotus « with a thousand petals (¹), as broad as a chariot wheel, of solid gold, with a diamond stem », standing out entirely from the plinth  Whether supported or not by the two Nâgarâjas, whose masterpiece it is, it constantly serves as a throne — or at least as a footstool — to a Buddha  eated in the attitude of teaching. By this sign we must henceforth retrospectively identify a whole series of Greco-Buddhist stelæ, the greater number of which have already been published, but not explained, and which for the convenience of the reader we have here collected together before his eyes (pll. XXIV-XXVIII, 1).

The most sober type (and the one which most closely resembles that of plate XXIII, 2) presents to us a Buddha, flanked simply, in addition to the usual worshippers, by two standing divinities (²), who, like him, are sheltered under

(1) *Divyâvadâna*, p 162, ll 9-11  Cf the epithet of Buddha in Kshemendra's *Daçâvatâracarita*, IX, 54 . *Bhûnirgata-pratata-kâñcana-padma-prstha-padmâsinastha*

(2) We may connect with this group that of the British Museum, reproduced by Dr Burgess (*Journ of Indian Art and Ind*, no 62, 1898. pl 8, 2 = *Anc. Mon India* pl 92, in the middle) the teaching Buddha and the two divinities are seated, or standing, on the enlarged pericarp of a lotus flower  In the acolyte at the right we recognise Brahmâ by his head-dress and his water vessel, in the one on the left Çakra by his diadem. The two worshippers are withdrawn to the bottom of the stele and separated by what is usually the stalk of the central lotus, but is here treated as a pyre — We pay no regard to another image (that of the Calcutta Museum) likewise published by Dr Burgess (*J  I  A  I* , no 69, Jan 1900, fig 24 = *Buddh  Art*

parasols, adorned with garlands (pl. XXIV, 1). On plate XXIV, 2 we scarcely divine the suggestion of the lotuses on which rest the seat of the Master and the feet of his two acolytes : on the other hand, two other busts of the Blessed One are interposed in the hollows delimited by the lines of their shoulders : except for the exchange of place between the two gods and the two magical Buddhas, it is evidently the same group as on plates XIX, 2 (first row) and XXI, 1 At other times the ingenious art of the sculptor erects graceful architectures (pl. XXV) above the three principal characters : doubtless we must here recognize the *prâtihârya-maṇḍapa*, built expressly for the occasion of the miracle, but we remain free to admire in it, together with the Mûla-Sarvâstivâdins, the royal munificence of Prasenajit, or, with the Theravâdins, the divine skill of Viçvakarman ('). At one time (²) it is a simple portico that presides above the three seated figures (pl. XXV, 2) At another time bolder constructions lodge beneath their domes or arches images of Buddha or even accessory episodes (pll XXV, 1 and XXVI, 1). On this last plate the two divinities, again standing, have each provided themselves with a long garland, which we shall find in their hands on all the reproductions that we still have to examine (pll. XXVI, 2-XXVIII, 1). The latter, like those first cited, place the scene — or rather, the vision — in the open sky : at the most, they

---

*in India*, fig 112) here Buddha is indeed seated between the two worshippers on the characteristic lotus, but — by an exception which, for the rest, is since the last excavations of Takht-i-Bahai (cf below, p 172, note 1) not unique — he is making the gesture of meditation, instead of that of instruction

(1) *Divyâvadâna*, p 155, l 18 . *Jâtaka*, IV, p 265, l. 10

(2) From the point of view of the arrangement of the attendants we may connect with this plate the fragment published by Dr J Ph VOGEL in *Archæol. Survey Report, 1903-1904*, pl LXVIII *b* (with the Nâgarâjas) and *c*.

shelter some small figures under aerial aediculæ. However,
the number of divine spectators increases in a striking manner. Now they are placed one above the other on their lotus
supports, profiting by all the liberty which a picture of
apparitions allows to be taken with the laws of perspective.
At the same time the central Buddha becomes bigger, and
his figure still more disproportionate to his surroundings.
The garlands which used to hang above his head no longer
suffice; there is now added a crown, borne by two little
genii, with or without wings, once even other marvellous
beings, with their busts terminating in foliage, hold still
higher a parasol of honour. Lastly, among the images which
have emanated from the Blessed One, some, as if better to
emphasize their supernatural and magical character, are
surrounded by an irradiation in the form of an aureole
composed of other Buddhas (¹)

These specimens are more than are required to prove
that we have not to deal with the fancy of some isolated
artist, but, in reality, with a traditional subject, constantly

---

(1) See the two upper corners of plate XXVIII, 1 and compare fig 78 of
*Art g -b du Gandh* , and especially the panel recently discovered by Dr D
B Spooner at Takht 1-Bahai and published by Mr J. H. Marshall in the *J
R A S* , Oct 1908, pl VI, 3 Here again we recognize the *mâha-prâtihârya*
The lotuses which once decorated the bottom of the slab have almost
disappeared through the defacement of the stone, but it is not so with those
which support the characters above, that is, five little seated Buddhas
(three of whom are at the top among foliage), and the two divine garland-
bearers By way of an exception the principal Buddha affects the pose of meditation The front of his parasol is curiously adorned with a crescent moon,
doubtless in order to emphasize the aerostatic character of the miracle But
the point which specially holds our attention is the indication on each
side of his body, between the knee and the shoulder, of four little Buddhas,
standing on lotuses and arranged obliquely like the outspread feathers of a
peacock's tail — It is known that Sir Aurel Stein found this procedure in
use also on the sculptures of Rawak in Chinese Turkestan (*Ancient Khotan*,
I, figg 62-65 , cf. *Sand-buried Ruins of Khotan*, frontispiece).

reproduced for the edification, and at the request, of the faithful. The series of these examples adjusts itself without effort in all its characteristic features — seat, attitude, gesture, surroundings of Buddha, etc. — to that in which we have already with certainty recognized versions of the « great miracle » of Çıâvastî. By virtue of the close relationship which we have often had an opportunity of noting between the Greco-Buddhist sculpture and the tradition of the Mûla-Sarvâstivâdins we must more than ever appeal to the *Divyâvadâna* for information concerning the identity of the various personages In the two « kings of the serpents », who at times support the stem of the great lotus (pll. XXV, 2, XXVII, XXVIII, 1), we naturally continue to greet our old acquaintances « Nanda and his junior », either accompanied or not by their wives. From these « fallen beings » we pass to the human bystanders. It has been asked whether the two lay devotees without nimbuses and of different sexes, who on plate XXVIII, 1 surround the seat of Buddha, are not merely donors of the stele ([1]). But it will be noticed that their point of support is, like that of the rest of the figures, the enlarged pericarp of a lotus : they appear, therefore, to form an integral part of the scene. For the same reason we must refuse to see in them anonymous worshippers : rather should we seek here — exactly as in their kneeling counterparts on plate XXIV, 1 — that Lûhasu-

---

[1] This identification was proposed incidentally by Dr. J Ph. VOGEL, *A. S I Rep*, 1903-1904, p 257 . but, in a general way, we believe it safer to look for donors only on the bases of stelæ (cf. pll XXV, 1 XXVI, 1, and XXVII) or the pedestals of statues — On the other hand, the hypothesis of Dr VOGEL (*ibid*, n 3) which suggests the identity of the four nimbused figures seated on the lower row of the same stele (pl XXVIII, 1) with the four Lokapâlas, seems to us most probable and confirmed by analogy with plates XXVI, 2, and XXVII.

datta and his wife, « the mother of Rıddhila » (¹), who ın
turn and ın vain proposed to the Blessed One to accomplish
the miracle ın his stead. Lıkewise, on plate XXV, 2, the
text expressly invıtes us to recognıze ın the monk and nun
kneeling at each sıde of the Master the *agraçrâvikâ* Uıpala-
varnâ (²) and the *agraçrâvaka* Maudgalyâyana, who also
asked, and saw themselves successively refused, the same
authorizatıon. It ıs, then, these same four personages,
rather than commonplace worshıppers, whom we should
prefer to recognize on plate XXIV, 2. We should be equally
ready to find King Prasenajit, the ımpartıal (³) president
of this publıc manifestatıon · but, even where the number of spectators ıs increased, hıs royal equıpage never
appears, as later, to betray hıs incognıto (⁴). In front of the
four men of good caste seated at the bottom of plate XXVI,
2, ıt seems that we are rather, as on plates XXVII and
XXVIII, 1, ın the presence of the four guardian gods
of our terrestrıal horızon. Among the crowd of dıvınities
we shall recognıze ımmedıately on plate XXVII, above
the rıght shoulder of Buddha, hıs faithful companıon
Vajrapâni, to whom also by certaın texts a part ıs given
in the story, he beıng made to ıntervene in order to hasten the dénouement (⁵) The femınıne figure facıng hım

---

(1) On thıs *upâsaka* and *upâsıkâ* ınformatıon taken from the *Vınaya* of the
Mûla-Sarvâstıvâdıns wıll be found ın the already quoted artıcle of M Ed
Huber (*B É F E -O* , VI, 1906, pp 9 sqq.)

(2) For thıs tıtle gıven to Utpalavarnâ, cf for example, the commentary
on the *Dhammapada,* ed Fausbøll, p 213

(3) For thıs ımpartıalıty cf *Dıvyâvadâna,* p 146, 1 23.

(4) Cf above, p 164, note 1.

(5) Accordıng to the *Dıvyâvadâna* (pp 163-164) the *yaksha-senâpatı* who,
understandıng the ımpossıbılıty of otherwıse overcomıng the obstınacy of
the Tîrthyas, raıses a vıolent storm to dısperse them ıs called Pâñcıka, but
the *Bodhısattvâvadâna-kalpalatâ* calls hım Vajrapânı (XIII, 57). Only we must

would perplex us greatly, did not her crown of towers signalize her at once as the incarnate *nagara-devatâ* of Çrâvastî, an edified witness of the miracle which will henceforth assure her fame; it is in no other form that, for example, the native town of Buddha is seen on other Greco-Buddhist bas-reliefs (¹). But the most interesting feature to be observed is that, if we are to credit the *Divyâvadâna*, the two chief divine acolytes can be no other than Brahmâ on the right of Buddha and Çakra on his left As a matter of fact, on several replicas the sculptors obviously emphasize this identification by the aid of the usual procedures of the school : to the much bejewelled turban of Indra they oppose, as is the custom, the chignon of Brahmâ, or they even endeavour to designate the latter expressly by the indication of a water-vessel or of a book (²)

---

warn the reader that this stanza *vasantatilakâ*, as it is given in the *Bibl Indica*, I, v, p 427, has no kind of plausible meaning Prof S Lévi has kindly restored the text for us, by the help of the Tibetan translation on the opposite page It should read (the corrections are indicated by the italics)

Atrântare Bhagavatah satatam vipaks*ân*
Sarvâtmanâ ksapanak*ân* avadhâr*ya* Yaksah |
*K*siptogravâ*ta*vrtavarsavaraiç cakâra
Vidrâvya randhraçaranân bhuvi Vajrapânih ||

We should translate « In the meanwhile, perceiving that the Sectarians persisted in remaining obstinate adversaries of the Blessed One, the Yaksha Vajrapâni, raising a violent storm accompanied by rain, dispersed them, and forced them to seek a shelter in the hollows in the earth »

(1) See *Art g.-b du Gandh* , figg. 183-184 *a*, and p 360.

(2) Cf the procedure of distinction employed *ibid* , figg 152, 154-156, 164 *a* (cycle of the nativity), 197 (march to Vajrâsana), 212 (invitation to the preaching), 243 (preaching to the Trayastrimças), 264 (descent from heaven), where we know that we have to deal at the same time with Çakra, the Indra of the Gods (cf fig 246), and with Brahmâ, the *Çikhin* In the particular case with which we are concerned their positions are at times exchanged from one stele to another (cf plate XXIV with plate XXV and p. 170, note 2), either because on this point the tradition was uncertain or

It would take too long to enter further into the details of each variant; and besides on this point we may refer to the notices which accompany the plates  only, we should wish to be allowed to make three remarks of a general character. The first bears on the importance which already in the school of Gandhâra we have been led to attribute to the *lakshana,* or sign of recognition · it seems indeed that here we find a fresh proof of the antiquity and wide extension of this proceeding (¹) In this very case it is a lotus with a stem rising from the ground or from the waters, that serves as a distinctive mark for a whole series of monuments ands has allowed us to follow the series for more than a thousand years, through the four corners of the peninsula. It is quite exceptional that, as on plate XXV, 2, the peduncle of the flower should be hidden and its pericarp covered by a cushion  and, if the artists of western India prefer that Buddha should cause his teaching to be heard from the height of a throne (*simhâsana*), the typical *padma* is retained at least as a stool for his feet. Henceforth, therefore, we may rank this « lotus emergent and usually attended by two Nâgarâjas », to use heraldic terms, side by side with, for example, the « wheel flanked by two gazelles, either back to back or face to face », among the specific symbols of the great events of Buddha's life  In the second place, this identification seems to us to confirm another rule which we had thought ourselves in a position to lay down, and in accordance with which there is scarcely any Gandhârian bas-relief, however passive and motionless the characters therein may be, wich does not, even under

---

because there had been a confusion, which is always easy, between the right and the left of the statue and those of the spectator.

(1) *Art gr -b  du Gandh* , p  607

the most strictly iconographic appearances, conceal the
story of some episode in the legend of Buddha. We shall
be the more readily excused for recalling the fact, inasmuch as we are the most to blame for having once ranged
among the simply decorative motives, in default of finding a better place, several of the stelæ which now assume
for us a definite meaning and one of legendary value,
as being versions of the « great miracle » at Çrâvastî ([1])
But at the same time — and this third observation is
the most important of all — it is to be feared that we
must relinquish the idea of indubitably distinguishing,
in the whole repertory of the Greco-Buddhist school, an
iconolatric group of « Buddha between two Bodhisattvas ».
As far as concerns the great scene of the descent from
heaven at Sânkâçya, the texts had already forced us to recognize in the two divine acolytes of the Master the gods
Brahmâ and Çakra  Here again ought not the same evidence
to constrain us to accept the same identification? Then
will disappear our last hope of discovering by the side of
the Blessed One an Indo-Greek Avalokiteçvara or a Mañjuçrî, as plates XXIV, 1 and XXVI, 1 seem specially to invite
us to do. In fact, all that we can say is that we beliewe we
discern already on these stelæ in the type, head-dress, attributes, meditative or pensive pose of the attendants the suggestion of the procedure which later served to represent,
and to differentiate from one another, the great Mahâyâ-
nic divinities : but methodically we may not go further and
light-heartedly oppose to the peremptory assertions of the
texts any quasi-gratuitous conjectures. Even the sign of the
ûrnâ, so distinctly marked on the forehead of the acolytes
in plates XXIV, 1 and XXV, 2 fails to induce us to lay

(1) Cf. ibid., figg. 76-79 and p  479

aside this prudent reserve So long as the sculptures do not
furnish us with an image bearing a written inscription, the
verbal statements of the Scriptures will always take prece-
dence over their mute velleities of expression. Likewise, the
more we advance in familiarity with the old artists of the
north-west of India, the nearer are we to believing that the
names of Avalokiteçvara and Mañjuçrî were as strange to
their thought as to that of the compilers of the *Divyâvadâna*
and the *Mahâvastu*

V

It will be felt how far this question passes beyond the
limits of the present article, and we will not here insist upon
it further  All that remains to ask ourselves, in order to
complete the study of the representations of the *mahâ-prâtihârya*, is whether it was represented or not on the most
ancient monuments of central India. Now it seems indeed
that the old native school had already essayed in regard to
it one of those conventional and summary pictures of
which it possessed the secret. The pillar of the southern
entrance in the railing of the *stûpa* of Barhut has three
of its faces decorated. Of the three upper bas-reliefs ('), the
first represents, we believe, by the symbol of the Bodhi-
tree, the « perfect illumination », the second, by the symbol
of the *stûpa*, the *parinirvâṇa*; the third, by the symbol of
the garlanded wheel, the « great miracle ». This, at least, is
suggested by two inscriptions on the last named, from
which we are not certain that all the admissible inferences
have hitherto been drawn (see pl. XXVIII, 2). At the bottom
a king issues from his capital, mounted in his quadriga : the

---

(1) CUNNINGHAM, *Stûpa of Barhut*, pl XIII

epigraph, by informing us that he is called « king Prasenajit of Koçala », gives us at the same time the name of the
town and localizes the scene at Çrâvastî Now this king and
his suite are going in the direction of a building of imposing appearance, which shelters a wheel surmounted by a
parasol, and bearing a heavy garland suspended from its
nave For all students of ancient Buddhist art the allegory
is clear · but, for fear the spectator should conceive the
slightest hesitation, a second helpful inscription informs
him that it is indeed « the wheel of the Law of the Blessed
One » which is represented The symbol, therefore, if
translated into the style of the later schools, is the exact
equivalent of an image of an instructing, and consequently
converting, Buddha On each side, standing in a devout
attitude with joined hands, is a personage in splendid
lay costume, such as India has always indifferently conceived its kings or its gods (¹) Accordingly it is impossible
for us in the presence of this group not to think of Buddha
attended by Indra and Brahmâ, in the presence of this edifice
not to think of the *mandapa* constructed for the purpose of
the « great miracle » Cunningham, with his accustomed
instinct, has already connected with this bas-relief the
passage in the *Divyâvadâna* translated by Burnouf, which
does precisely on this occasion make the king of Koçala
betake himself « in his good chariot » to the presence of
the Master: but he did not follow out the identification to the
end (²). In truth, we see no reason for stopping half way.

---

(1) For some quite similar images of gods on this same balustrade of
Barhut see also CUNNINGHAM, *loc cit.*, pl XVII

(2) *Ibid* , pp 90-91 — It will be noticed that the visit of Ajâtaçatru to
Buddha, which on the pillar of the western entrance forms a pendant to this
one. is likewise of importance from a legendary point of view (*ibid* , pl. XVI
and p. 89).

Evidently it was not a question of an ordinary visit, but of
a meeting having a solemn character. We know from a sure
source, namely the inscriptions, the exact locality of the
scene, that is Çrâvasti, the capital of Koçala, and the names
of the two principal actors, Prasenajit and the Blessed
One ; the bas-relief shows us the devout ardour of the one,
and suggests the converting gesture of the other ; finally,
the accessory details of the two attendants standing beside
the invisible Buddha and the great hall which shelters him
harmonize equally well with the traditions relative to the
« great miracle ». We shall not escape the conclusion that
such indeed was the subject which the sculptor had proposed to himself. The counter-proof is easy   let us imagine
that precisely this task had been set him; granted the customary procedure of the old school, we do not see how he
could have accomplished it otherwise (¹).


Thus we should end by restoring to this subject of the
*mahâ-prâtihârya* the sphere which legitimately belongs to it
and which until now had been too parsimoniously measured out. We are now in a position to sketch its history
from the earliest to the last surviving monuments. Treated allegorically — and with good reason — by the old
native school, it is not long in utilizing for its own advantage the type of Buddha created by Indo-Greek art. From

---

(1) Again an interesting replica of our plate XXVIII, 2 will be found on
plate XXXI, 1, of CUNNINGHAM  We should be quite willing to connect with
it the representations of wheels on pillars, like that of plate XXXIV, 4 (cf
at Sânchî, FERGUSSON, *Tree and Serpent Worship*, pl XLII, 1)  Perhaps it would
even be necessary to see a reference to the *mâha-prâtihârya* in the wheel
which, according to the evidence of Fa hien and Hiuan-tsang, surmounted
one of the two columns raised at the entrance to the Jetavana

the outset it adopts that *mudrâ* of instruction (¹) and especially that particular *lakshana* of the lotus with a stem, both
of which it will retain as characteristic signs from end to
end of its evolution  Under its most restricted aspect, as at
Barhut, it counts only two attendant divinities · but on
other replicas these latter multiply themselves and mingle
with apparitions of Buddhas It is chiefly these latter
that are retained by the stelæ of Benares, and, after their
example, by the later productions from the basin of the
Ganges, whilst western India to the very end reserves the
best place for the divine acolytes. At the same time, the
composition, which had finally on the vast walls of Ajantâ
attained a disproportionate development, returns, with
the ultimate decadence, to the soberness of its commence-
ments. All being taken into account, without going
outside the Indian publications, and leaving aside the
already identified miniatures of the manuscripts, we propose henceforward to inscribe the rubric of the « great miracle of Çrâvastî » under the following reproductions

1. Barhut, pl XXVIII, 2 ; *Stûpa of Barhut*, pl. XXXI, 1,
perhaps XXXIV, 4, etc. (Ancient Indian style, 2ⁿᵈ century
B. C.);

2. Gandhâra : pll. XXIV-XXVIII, 1 , *J. Ind Art. and Ind* ,
no. 62, 1898, pl. 8, 2=*Anc. Mon. India*, pl 92 (in the middle);
*Arch. Survey Report*, 1903-1904, pl. LXVIII, *b* and *c* ; *Art g -b.
du Gandhâra*, fig. 78 ; (with an exceptional *mudrâ*) *J I. A. I.*,
no. 69, 1900, fig. 24 = *Buddh. Art in India*, fig. 112, and *J.
R A. S.*, Oct. 1908, pl. VI, 3 (Indo-Greek style, 1ˢᵗ and 2ⁿᵈ centuries A. D.);

3. Benares : pl. XIX ; *Anc. Mon. India*, pl. 68, 1 (in the

---

(1) For the only two exceptions known to us cf p 170, n 2, and 172,
n 1

left upper compartment); (on the lateral borders) 67, 3, and 68, 2 (Gupta Style, 4$^{th}$-6$^{th}$ centuries),

4. Ajaṇṭā : pll XX-XXI, 1, *Paintings of Ajaṇṭā*, pll 15, 24, 39, *Arch Survey. West. India*, IV, pl. XXXVII, 2 (Câlukya style, 6$^{th}$-7$^{th}$ centuries),

5 Magadha : pl XXIII, 1; *Ét sur l'Iconogr. bouddh. de l'Inde*, I, fig 28 (Pâla style, 8$^{th}$-10$^{th}$ centuries),

6. Konkan    pl. XXIII, 2, *Arch. Surv. West. India*, IV, pl. XLIII, 1, and fig. 22 = *Buddh. Art in India*, fig. 60; *Cave Temples of India*, pl. LVI (Râshtrakûta style, 8$^{th}$-10$^{th}$ centuries).

Henceforward the picture of the *mahâ-prâtihârya* would not be missing from any school . we await only that of Mathurâ. This is just what might be expected from the importance assumed by the episode in the legend, as a compulsory prodigy of every « Blessed One » worthy of his name It would have been too astonishing, considering the constant parallelism between the two forms, written and figured, of the tradition, if no ancient illustration had corresponded on this point to the texts. Our hypothesis fills a real gap, and it is only just that « the great miracle of Çrâvastî » should advantageously, as far as the number of known replicas is concerned, bear comparison with the three other great scenes from the teaching career of Buddha.

Why then — and this is the last point on which we are conscious of owing the reader some explanation — why has it been so tardily and so laboriously recognized, whilst its three pendants were identified long ago and at first sight? To this question we may reply, first of all, that the *mahâ-prâtihârya*, especially in the preaching form which had prevailed, does not lend itself, as we have abundantly experienced, to anything more than a picture almost void of movement, if not of picturesqueness , to effect its instant recognition, it has neither the exceptional role of the monkey or the elephant, nor the characteristic decoration of the triple ladder . and heie we have, doubtless, an excellent reason. There is room, in our opinion, for adding another. We are so accustomed to utilize the archæological information of the Chinese pilgrims in India, that we no longer think of being grateful to them for it, in order to measure the value of their help, we have to be once without it That is the case on this occasion . Fa-hien and Hiuan-tsang, so explicit as regards the three other episodes, scarcely mention the one which interests us here. The places where Çrâvastî and the Jetavana had been, the favourite sojourn of the Master, evoked too many remembrances pell-mell for the « Great Miracle » not to be swamped in the crowd of those which on all sides, through the mouths of the guides, solicited their devout interest. We must likewise reckon with the fact that the story of the rivalry between the Master and the Tîrthyas was on the spot inevitably entangled with the calumny of the novice Ciñcâ, or with the assassination of the courtesan Sundarî : and these dramatic stories could not fail to encroach upon the miracle of Buddha, which was after all so neutral and quasi-passive. Thus, when the pilgrims finally arrive at the temple which marked the locality of the purely doctrinal and magical conflict, they both specify indeed that a statue of the Blessed One was *seated* (¹) there ;

---

(1) We believe, in fact, after careful reading, that the *mahâ-caitya* of Çrâvastî, marking the locality of Buddha's victory over the other chiefs of sects, was the temple (*vihâra*), 60 or 70 feet high, which Fa-hien and Hiuan-tsang both saw and mentioned at the west (that is to say, at the right) of the road leading to the south of the town towards the Jetavana, about 60 or 70 (Chinese, therefore double) paces in front of the eastern gate of the park, opening from the same side upon the same road (trans. BEAL, I, p. XLVII, and II, p. 10, WATTERS, I, p 393) It will be noticed that this situation corresponds fairly well with the indications of the texts (cf

but they both forget to tell us on what kind of seat and
accompanied by what attendants  Accordingly, do not ask
why the connection between the narratives and the representations of the « Great Miracle » has been so tardily realized  Cease likewise to be astonished that we are still even
at the present time posed by the question whether the two
divine acolytes retained to the very last (as we are certain
they did in the representation of the « Descent from Heaven ») their names of Brahmâ  and  Çakra, or whether
they ended by transforming themselves, in the eyes of the
faithful, into Bodhisattvas, and, in that case, at what moment the transformation took place  Fa-hien and Hiuan-
tsang tell us nothing concerning this  One feels how valuable
their testimony would have been to us, by reason of its
mean date as also of the central situation of the country
from which they would have borrowed its elements, forming a bridge between the ancient works of the north-
west and the later, but identified, productions of eastern
India. If we have been able ultimately to dispense with
it, this is because the stele recently discovered at Sârnâth and
immediately published by Mr  Marshall put into our hands
precisely the missing middle of the conducting wire, and
thenceforward all that we have had to do has been to follow
its direction, downwards to the disappearance, upwards to
the sources of Buddhist art  For this let us thank the
Archæological Survey [1]

---

above, p  149, n  2)  it seems that it is expedient to set aside in its favour
the « preaching hall » built by Prasenajit, which was to be found in the
centre of the town, and the *stûpa* next to that of Çâriputra, which is mentioned by Hiuan-tsang only  As regards the latter, Watters states that he did
not know where to place the « tope » of the « great miracle », he forgets
that the eight great *caityas* are not necessarily all *stûpas*, we know, for
example, that that of the *Sambodhi* at Bodh Gayâ is a temple, and the same
is explicity told us by Fa-hien and Hiuan-tsang concerning the *Devâvatâra*

PLATE XIX

Cf. pp 150, 155, 159-60

I — This stele was obtained from the excavations carried out by the Archæological Survey at Sârnâth, near Benares, during the season 1906-1907 Its height is about one metre    We reproduce it from a photograph kindly lent by Mr. J H Marshall, and already published by him in the *J R A S*, Oct 1907, pl 4. It is divided into eight panels, on which are represented the eight great scenes from the life of Buddha (cf p 23), they are.

1  At the bottom, on the left, the Nativity (*Jati*) near to Kapilavastu, at the left of Mâyâ the child Buddha, standing, is bathed by the two Nâgas, Nanda and Upananda, his pedestal, on each side of which two women are kneeling, seems to be composed of seven superposed lotuses, symbolizing the « seven steps » which he is supposed to have taken immediately after his birth (cf for this detail *Ét sur l'Iconogr bouddh de l'Inde*, I, fig 28)

2  At the bottom, on the right, the Perfect Illumination (*Abhisambodhana*), at Bodh-Gayâ, symbolized by the Attack of Mâra (*Mâra-dharshana*), Buddha is seated and makes the classical gesture of the *bhûmi-sparça-mudrâ*, at the top, on each side, are two demons ; at the bottom, on his right, is Mâra, and, on his left, one of the daughters of Mâra.

3 At the top, on the left, the First Preaching (*Dharma-cakra pravartana*), at the Mṛigadāva, near to Benares, symbolized by the gesture of instruction and the Wheel of the Law between the two gazelles facing each other, to which the two lions of the throne (*siṃhāsana*) turn their backs; the two acolytes, who can only be monks, have, under the mechanical chisel of the sculptor, assumed the mien of Buddhas.

4 At the top, on the right, the definite Death (*Parinirvāṇa*), near to Kuçinagara, on the usual bed and in the accustomed position, with the habitual cortège of sorrowing monks.

These are the four chief episodes, let us pass on to the four others.

5 In the second compartment on the right, starting from the top, is the « Great Miracle » (*Mahā-prātihārya*), near to Çrāvastî : for the description cf above, p 159, and for the identification of the two attendants at the bottom, p 164 Note further the two lotus flowers, which bend so as to fill the space underneath the seat of the central Buddha.

6 In the second compartment on the left, coming from the top, the « Descent from heaven » (*Devâvatāra*), near to Sânkâçya , on the right of Buddha, who is standing and whose right hand is in *varamudrā*, is Brahmâ, bearer of a water-vessel and probably of a flyflapper ; on his left Çakra, holding a parasol (cf. *Étud sur l'Iconogr bouddh de l Inde*, I, p 157, and *Art g -b du Gandh* , p 537)

7 In the third left compartment from the top, the « Offering of the Monkey », near to Vaçâlî : he enters by the left of the spectator, holding the bowl of *madhu*, which he places between the hands of Buddha, seated on his throne, and then disappears on the right into a well, above the curb of which only his feet are still to be seen ; at the top, on the

right, is seen what is probably a flying divinity (cf *lc b Inde*, I, p 168 and II p 114, *Art g -b du Gandh* , p 512),

8 In the third compartment from the top, on the right, « the Taming of the Maddened Elephant », at Râjagriha, on the right of Buddha, who stands, with his right hand in *abhaya-mudrā*, the elephant is kneeling beneath a *stūpa*, on his left, Ânanda holds in his right hand his long mendicant's staff or *khakkhara* (cf *lc b Inde*, *ibid*, and *Art g.-b. du Gandh* , p 542)

II — This stele is derived, like the preceding one, from the site of the ancient Mṛigadāva, in the northern suburb of Benares Offered to the Asiatic Society of Bengal by « Captain » CUNNINGHAM in 1835-1836, it is at present preserved in the museum at Calcutta and catalogued under no S(*ārnāth*) 5 (cf ANDERSON, *Catalogue*, II, p 7) Its height is about m 0,90 We believe it to be unpublished, and we reproduce it from a photograph which we took in January 1896

At the bottom, from some bubbling waves, there springs up a large lotus, on which Buddha is seated with his legs crossed in the manner of the Indians, and his hands joined in the attitude of instruction. Around him radiate six other stems, which also branch as they mount higher and open out into tiers of *padmas*, bearers of thirteen other Buddhas, seated or standing, in various *mudrās* At the bottom, on each side of the central Buddha, two attendants, who by their head-dresses and jewels can be recognized as laymen — gods or Bodhisattvas —, are fanning him with fly-flappers ; at the top, two little flying genii fill up the rect angular corners of the slab. It will be noticed that on the part of the three Buddhas of the bottom row there is a tendency to look in different directions (cf above, pp. 160 and 167)

2

AT BENARES

PLATE XX

Cf. pp. 160-1

Plate XX was made from a photograph taken as well as we could manage at Ajantâ, in September 1897, in the gloom of Cave VII It represents a portion of the left wall of the vestibule of the sanctuary We may compare with it a drawing published by FERGUSSON and BURGESS, *Cave Temples of India*, pl XXXI

We limit ourselves to borrowing a description from Dr BURGESS, *Notes on the Bauddha Rock Temples of Ajantâ* (Bombay, 1879), p. 45 « The sides of the antechamber are entirely covered with small Buddhas, sculptured in rows of five to seven each, sitting or standing on lotuses, with lotus leaves between them The stalk of the lowest central lotus is upheld by two kneeling figures with royal head-dresses canopied by the many-headed *nâga* behind each, on the left are a kneeling figure and two standing Buddhas, and on the right a Buddha is behind the *nâga*, and behind him are three worshippers with presents . »

The diversity and alternation of the *mudrâs* will be noticed; true, it is on this wall that the attitudes are the most varied, which is not saying much For the identification of the two *Nâga-râjas* with Nanda and Upananda cf above, p 161

AT AJAṆṬA

PLATE XXI

Cf. pp. 164-5, 166-7

I — Simple sketch made from plate 38 of Mr J Griffiths's great publication, *The Paintings in the Buddhist Cave-temples of Ajantâ* (London 1891, in folio), I (cf pl 39 and p. 31, or Burgess, *Notes R - T A*), p 49, § 4) The original is a very much damaged fresco, decorating the bottom part of the archway of the principal nave of Cave IX, towards the back and to the right, at the spot marked F on the plan published by Mr Griffiths, *ibd.*, pl 36.

In the middle Buddha is seated in the European fashion, leaning against a cushion, on the traditional throne, the back of which is formed of superposed animals, and the front legs carved in the shape of lions (*simhâsana*) His hands are joined in the attitude of teaching, while at the same time he holds with the left the hem of his monastic cloak. His feet rest on a lotus

On his right and left, in the first row, two other Buddhas, likewise sheltered under parasols and with their feet resting on lotuses, stand with one hip projecting and turn towards the central character Their right hands make the gesture of charity, their left hands are turned back to hold up the hems of their robes

On both sides of the throne of Buddha, and behind, two persons in grand lay costume — gods or Bodhisattvas — hold fly-flappers in their right hands Above the group hang garlands (Cf above pp 164-5)

II — Pl XXI, 2, was taken from a photograph brought back by M Ed Chavannes from his last mission to China (1907-1908), and first appeared in the *Bulletin du Comité de l'Asie française*, April 1908, fig 5 From the inscriptions M. Chavannes dates the execution of the original in the Vth century of our era, under the dynasty of the Northern Wei

In its present state the group consists only of the remains of a seated Buddha, and another standing on his left Both are of gigantic size, as may be judged from the man placed between them The attendant one, draped to the neck, like the Gandhâra images, makes with his right hand the gesture intimating absence of fear The splendour of their *tejas* covers the whole rocky wall with a tracery of tongues of flame; from this background stand out nimbuses and aureoles in the form of circular or elliptical bands bearing a quantity of small figures of Buddha seated in the Indian manner in the attitude of meditation Above the head of the acolyte a group of two little Buddhas, side by side in the same niche, seems to materialize what we are told by the texts (cf above, p. 157) of the conversations of the Master with his magic double, or with his colleague in another world-system, the Buddha Prabhûtaratna (*Lotus de la bonne Loi*, trans Burnouf, pp 151-2, etc ), who once came into ours to pay him a solemn visit (Cf above, p 166 )

2. IN CHINA
(IN THE TA-TONG-FOU CAVES)

1. — AT AJANTÂ
(AFTER A WALL-PAINTING)

PLATE XXII

Cf pp 16; 6, 255

Thus photograph, kindly supplied by Major van ERP, compares advantageously with WILSEN's drawing, lithographed on plate CCCLVI, 1, of the great album which accompanies the volume of LEEMANS, *Boro-Boudour dans l'île de Java*. The original is situated to the left of the staircase of the eastern façade, at the height of what LEEMANS calls the fifth gallery, which, since the discovery of the original base of the *stûpa* by Heer YZERMAN, we know to be the fourth, it is, moreover, the last polygonal sculptured gallery before the three circular pseudo-terraces of the summit (cf. our pl XXXII and LEEMANS, *ibid.*, pp 291 sqq and pll CCCLVI-CCCLXXXVIII, especially the first and the last, which form pendants to one another on each side of the eastern entrance)

Two Buddhas, standing on lotuses supported by leaves, enclose two other Buddhas, and are themselves enclosed by six others in various *mudrâs*, all seated on aerial lotuses.

At the bottom are four lay attendants: two of them, the one on the left holding a fly-flapper and the one on the right with his hands joined, seem to be simple worshipping divinities, but in the two nearer to the standing Buddhas we must, according to all appearance, by the flowers which serve as attributes to them recognize two Bodhisattvas; on the right Maitreya, who in his position as future Buddha has an equal right to the honour of a lotus seat, holds a *nâga puṣhpa*; on the left Avalokiteçvara holds a *padma*. Garlands hang down; it rains flowers. (Cf above, pp 165-6)

ON THE BORO-BUDUR, JAVA

PLATE XXIII

Cf pp 167-8.

I — Pl XXIII, 1, which we believe to be unpublished, reproduces photograph taken by us in January 1896 at the Calcutta museum among the sculptures received after the completion of Mr ANDERm's catalogue The original comes from Magadha and measures m.0,70 height

At the bottom, the two *Nâga-râjas*, Nanda and Upananda, whose sts terminate curiously in the curling and scaly tails of serpents (we ay compare with them those on one of the frescoes of Ajantâ, GRIF-HS, fig 16 = *J. Ind. Art. and Ind.*, no 69, 1900, fig 19), encircle, th their joined hands, the peduncle of a great lotus rising from ves, upon which a teaching Buddha is seated in the Indian manner hind each of these Nâgas stands one attendant, and two others her crouch or kneel, the nimbus of the middle one on the left may be ngushed Between the heads of the two outside attendants rise the ms of the lotus stools on which rest the feet of two other teaching ddhas, seated in European manner and looking in opposite direc-ns.

At the top, round the head of the central figure, may be distinguished, t, two little figures of seated Buddhas, then the two traditional rshipping divinities; finally, a Buddha lying crosswise above reflects npletely the words of the texts concerning the four attitudes assumed the emanations of the Master (cf above, p. 159). Before the face of h of the two largest attendant Buddhas (the head of the one on the left is broken) appear, in fact, two little standing Buddhas, one of whom must be supposed to be walking Above, a stem with three branches supports at each side, on three lotuses, a group exactly analogous to the principal composition, a third group, between two flying genii, occupies the summit of the stele (Cf above, p 167)

II — Pl XXIII, 2 is only a reproduction, for the convenience of the render, of the middle part of plate 164 of *Anc. Mon and Temples of India*, published by Dr BURGESS (London, 1897) The original decorates the largest of the twenty-six caves of Kudâ, in the district of Kulâbâ, to the south of Bombay (cf FERGUSSON and BURGESS, *Cave-Temples of India*, pp 206 sqq, *Arch Survey West India*, IV, pp. 12 sqq.)

The two *Nâga-râjas*, Nanda and Upananda, are with both hands supporting the stalk of a large lotus, on which a teaching Buddha is seated in the Indian manner At either side on two other *padmas*, stand two divine personages, both armed with fly-flappers Considering the late date of the sculpture, we must apparently recognize in them two Bodhisattvas, and more especially in the one on the right, judging by the long sinuous stem of the pink lotus which he holds in his left hand, an Avalokiteçvara Padmapâni

Five kneeling worshippers at the bottom are, perhaps, the donors, in the top corners are two flying genii (Cf. above, p. 168)

2.    IN THE KONKAN

1. — IN MAGADHA

PLATE XXIV

Cf pp 170 1. 173-4, 177.

I — Plate XXIV, 1, represents a stele furnished at the top with the handle of a parasol, and at the bottom with a tenon, which must have fitted into a base in the form of a lotus similar to the one on plate XXV, 1 It has already been reproduced in the *J Ind Art and Ind*, no 69, 1900, fig 23 = *Buddh Art in India*, fig 121 The original, which came from the excavations at Loriyān-Tangaï (Swāt), is preserved in the Calcutta museum, in height it measures m 0,45

In the middle, on a lotus which springs from the soil, Buddha is seated in the Indian manner and the attitude of reaching It will be noticed that in Gandhāra — contrary to what takes place, for example, on plate XXI, 1 — it is *the left* hand which holds, between the thumb and index finger, the little finger of the *right* hand (cf pll XXIV, 2-XXVIII, 1) As also on the following plates, his right shoulder is uncovered Garlands of flowers are twined above his head, which was moreover, together with the stele itself, to be surmounted by a detached parasol

Analogous parasols, on the stele seen only in profile, shelter his two acolytes Standing, with their hands broken off, they bear between their eyebrows the mark of the *ūrnā*, which is regarded as a characteristic of Bodhisattvas, but at the same time, according to the customs of the school (cf above, p 175) the rich turban of the one on the right of Buddha designates Indra, as the hair-knot of the one on the left does Brahmā

At the bottom, on each side of the lotus, are two kneeling worshippers, laymen, apparently of different sexes, perhaps Lūhasudatta and his wife, the « mother of Ruddhila » (Cf above, pp 173-4)

II — Plate XXIV, 2, is a direct reproduction of part of a photograph, the plate of which is preserved in the Calcutta museum and has been used previously for plate 98 of the *Anc Mon India* We do not remember having anywhere met with the original of this bas-relief, but from the known dimensions of the sculptures near it in the photograph it must have measured in height about m 0,40

By an exception of which we do not know any other example previous to the recent excavations at Takht-i-Bahaï (cf above, p 172, n 1, and *J R A S*, Oct 1908, pl VI, 3) the pericarp of the traditional lotus is, in this case, covered with a tapestried seat Under the feet of the two acolytes an indication of two other lotuses can be seen. Buddha is seated in the Indian manner, and makes the gesture of teaching Between him and his attendants can be seen the busts of two other figures of Buddha, one of which is broken

The attendant on the right, whose *ūrnā* is still visible, has for his head-dress, after the fashion of the god Indra, a turban enriched with jewelry, the buckle of which resembles the expanded tail of a peacock, he holds in his left hand (broken) what we take to be a bending purse The one on the left, whose head-dress is damaged, holds in his left hand a vase, which in Gandhāra was an attribute of Brahmans and of Brahmā (cf the references, p 175, n 2).

The top of the panel is filled — a rather rare case — by the partly preserved foliage of a tree (cf above, p 163 and pl XXVI 2) and by two divinities throwing flowers For a possible identification of the four worshippers, religious and lay, if, at least, they are of different sexes, see likewise above, pp 173 174

IN GANDHÂRA

2

1

# PLATE XXV

Cf. pp 171, 173-4, 177

I — The stele of plate XXV, 1, which comes from Loriyân-Tangai and is preserved in the Calcutta museum, measures in height one metre; it has been reproduced already by Dr. Burgess (*J. Ind. Art and Ind* , no 69, 1900, fig 25 = *Buddh Art in India*, fig. 152) and in *Art g -b du Gandhâra*, fig. 76.

Here we restrict ourselves to noting the general disposition of the stele in the form of a *vihâra* (cf *ibid* , pp 129 and 138), the fitting of the tenon into the mortise at the base (*ibid.*, p 191), the little columns in the Persepolitan or Corinthian style (*ibid.*, pp 227 and 234), the dog-tooth ornaments, the balconies with figures of women in the different compartments (*ibid.*, pp. 223-224), the Cupid garland-bearers of the lower framework (*ibid.*, pp 239-240), the lion-headed brackets similar to those of plate XXV, 2, etc.

A teaching Buddha, seated on a raised lotus, is outlined against an oblong aureole and a round nimbus : above his head, a twisted garland hangs under a double streamer, under his right foot, which is sole upwards, a knot of stuff forms a round protuberance, which is also to be seen on plate XXV, 2, but which on the following plates is only a puffed out plait. The two Buddhas in the top corners, seated in meditation on inverted lotuses and under little *vihâras*, seem to form an integral part of the composition ; perhaps the case is the same with the three others lodged under the two storied arch of the gable, in any case, the group at the top recalls by its arrangement the other great aerial miracle, that of the Descent from Heaven.

This time the two divine attendants are seated on rattan seats The one on the (Buddha's) right has, unfortunately, his face and left hand broken; his feet are crossed in an attitude often reproduced later in China and Japan The turbaned attendant on the left, leaving his sandal on the ground (cf *Arch. Surv Rep* , *1903-1904*, pl. LXVIII, *b* and *c*), has bent up his right leg and must, as on plate XXV, 2, have rested his forehead on his hand, while at the same time he holds in his left the same looped object as does the right-hand attendant on plate XXIV, 2, — from the analogy of some newly discovered statues we should guess a bending purse.

In the bottom corners two kneeling worshippers, a monk and a lay female devotee — strangers, it seems, to the scene and only inserted for a purely decorative purpose — are, perhaps, the donors, perhaps two of the usual attendants (Cf above, pp. 173, note 1, and 173-4).

II — The original of plate XXV, 2, measuring in height m 0,45, comes likewise from Loriyân-Tangai and is preserved in the Calcutta museum. It has already been published by Dr. BURGESS (*J Ind Art and Ind.*, no. 69, 1900, fig. 22 = *Buddh. Art in India*, fig 147)

Here the lotus which serves as a seat for the teaching Buddha is supported by the two *Nâga-râjas*, Nanda and Upananda, who are visible only as far as the waist The one on the right (in relation to Buddha) is of a curious type of Brahmanic ascetic, with his beard and voluminous chignon, he holds in his right hand an object which reminds us very much of the dolphin similarly carried by certain of his congeners (cf *Art g -b du Gandhâra*, fig 126), but which, in fact, seems to be nothing but the head of a serpent coming out of his neck. As for the one on the left, no less strange with his moustache and his striped hair, we cannot say whether he holds in his left hand a bent paddle or a hooded serpent (cf. *Arch Surv. Rep*, *1903-1904*, pl LXVIII, *b*). On either side of the Nâgas kneel a monk and a nun, perhaps Maudgalyâyana and Utpalavarnâ (cf. above, p. 174)

The two divine attendants are again seated on rattan seats, both rest their elbows symmetrically on their raised knees, while their foreheads, marked with the *ûrnâ*, recline upon the tip of one finger · we know that this pensive pose has been ascribed by Sino Japanese art to Avalokiteçvara The attendant on the right, who, like Brahmâ, has no head-dress other than his hair, holds in his right hand the book (in the form of a palm-leaf manuscript) which will be one of the attributes of Mañjuçrî, the turbaned one on the left holds in his left hand an object which, from its granular appearance and the fold which it makes at the bottom, we believe to be again a purse, fastened by a kind of clasp in the form of a medallion and analogous to those in the hands of the attendants on the left of pl XXIV, 2 and right of pl XXV, 1, but which on plate LXVIII, *c*, of the *Arch. Surv Rep*, *1903-1904* is plainly a lotus

To conclude, let us note the curious porch which shelters the three persons, and which, trapezoidal in the centre and arched at the sides, rests on brackets decorated with lions' heads As usual, birds are represented on the roofs (Cf above, p 171)

1

2

IN GANDHÂRA

# PLATE XXVI

Cf pp 171, 174, 177

I — The stele of plate XXVI, 1, coming from Mohamed-Nârî, bears in the museum of Lahore the number 1134, and measures m. 1,04 in height It has already been published in heliographure by COLE (*Græco-buddh. Sculp from Yûsufzaï*, 1885, pl. I), in outline by Prof GRUNWEDEL (*Buddh. Kunst in Indien*, 2ᴺᵈ ed., fig 63; English edition, fig. 82), in phototype by Dr BURGESS (*Anc. Mon Ind*, pl 112), and in simile-engraving in the *Art g-b du Gandhâra*, fig 77, from one of our photographs.

For the general arrangement and decoration of the stele we must direct the reader to the references given for plate XXV, 1, let us note in addition the atlantes at the bases of the columns (cf. *Art g-b du Gandh*, p 208)

IN GANDHÁRA

PLATE XXVII

Cf. pp. 171-4.

The original of this plate, the exact origin of which is unknown, is preserved in the museum at Lahore (no 572), where we photographed it, it measures m 0.85 in height  As yet it has been published only by Dr Burgess (*J Ind Art and Ind* , no 62  1898, pl 8, 1)

Only the middle part of the stele is devoted to the *Mahâ-prâtihârya*. Under the large lotus two persons, whose bodies are only half seen, but who are not otherwise characterized, and who are leaning back to look at the Master, must be the two traditional *Nâga-râjas*  Above the head of the great central Buddha, which is of disproportionate size, two little genii, flying without wings, hold up a crown of jewellery under ornamental foliage  On each side appear two other small figures of Buddha, analogous to those on  plate XXV, 1, and placed respectively beneath a Bodhisattva in the costume of a Buddha (cf pl XXVI, 2) surrounded by a radiating halo, and beneath a group consisting of Buddha in conversation with a monk  The two usual attendants, standing on lotuses with bent stems, hold up their garlands (cf. pll XXVI and XXVIII, 1)  Above them, on the right of Buddha, is Vajrapâni, bearing his thunderbolt, and having on his head a tiara often worn by Indra (cf *Art g -b du Gandh* , fig 246), and opposite to him, wearing a turreted crown, the *nagara devatâ* of Çrâvastî (cf above, pp 174 5)  About ten other gods are seated in various attitudes, all resting on lotuses, except those (who also have haloes) on the first row at the bottom (the four Lokapâlas, two of which on the right are damaged, cf pl XXVI, 2)

In the top panel a sort of apotheosis of the Bodhisattva corresponds to the transfiguration of the Buddha : the former, accompanied by ten persons with haloes, is seated, with feet crossed and a water-flask in his hand, under a parasol, on a low rattan seat covered with a cushion. From numerous analogies, and notably that of a bas-relief in the Louvre, where this scene immediately follows that of the Nativity (*Art g -b du Gandh* , fig 164), we seem to recognize the *samcodana* of the Bodhisattva Siddhârtha (*Lalita vistara*, chap. XIII), a pendant to the *adhyeshana* of Buddha (*ibid* , chap XXV)  The point to be noted here is the close connection between the types and attitudes of the gods in the upper and lower scenes  On each side of the Bodhisattva are the same garland-bearers on lotuses ; at the two bottom corners are the attendants in the same attitude as on plate XXV, 2 ; the first attendant on the left at the same level is turning round to express to his neighbour his admiration, as on plate XXVI, 2, etc

At the bottom is depicted the adoration of the *pâtra*, or alms-vase of Buddha, placed on a throne (cf *Art g -b du Gandh* , p 419) and surrounded probably by donors

IN GANDHARA

PLATE XXVIII

Cf pp 171-4, 178-80.

I — The stele of plate XXVIII, 1, from the museum of Lahore (no 1135), without any definite indication of its origin, measures m. 1,17, in height. It has already been reproduced from photographs by M. G. LE BON, *Les Monuments de l'Inde* (Paris, 1893), fig 2, and Dr. BURGESS, *J Ind Art and Ind*, no 62 (1898), pl 7,2, and in *Art g.-b du Gandh*, fig 79

The description of the middle section of plate XXVII holds good for this Here, however, it is from a pond, full of fishes and lotuses, that the ornamented stalk of a magnificent lotus rises with well detached leaves Below Nanda and Upananda have as pendants their *Nāgis* Above the head of the central Buddha, which is of disproportionate size, between the crown borne by the two winged genii and the ornamental garlands, are interposed four *Kinnaras* (cf *Art g.-b du Gandh*, p 212), two of whom hold up the handle of a parasol The two Buddhas of the upper angles, instead of being placed under ædicule, as in plate XXV, 1, are sheltered by parasols and aureoled with standing Buddhas (cf above, p 172); a third little Buddha, in conversation with a devotee, by his attitude reminds us very much of one of those on plate XXVII.

At the bottom, standing on each side of the lotus, a male and fem. devotee without haloes are, perhaps, Lihasudatta and his w Riddhila-mātā (cf above, pp 173-4) Beside the two acolyte garland bearers we may count about twenty more divinities

Two of these, at the top, reproduce exactly the attendants plate XXV, 2, including the arches which shelter them Towards the middle of the stele two others, ensconced under two symmetrical edifices, seem to be copied from the top corners of plate XXVI, 1; these are, probably, Bodhisattvas, and perhaps it is the same with the two meditating persons placed obliquely in their frames on both sides of the head of the central Buddha. Among the other gods, two clasp their raised left knees in their arms, as in plate XXVI, 2, two others hold books, as in plate XXV, 2; others, full-face or in profile, hold flowers, take their chins in their palms, raise or join their hands; one of them, towards the top, to the left of the spectator, prepares to throw flowers, which an assistant, likewise with a halo, presents to him in a basket, etc All of them, with their seats and their pavilions, when they have such, are supported in the air on lotuses

2. — AT BARHUT

1. — IN GANDHÀRA

# The Six-Tusked Elephant :

## *An attempt at a chronological classification of the various versions of the Shaddanta-Jâtaka* (¹).

---

The close relation which exists between the written and the figured forms of the Buddhist tradition has no longer to be proved. It is known by experience. Rare indeed are those narratives of Buddha's miracles whereof no illustration has yet been discovered, still more rare are the images which do not at once find their commentary in the texts already published. And thus we have naturally come to speak of the help which, on numerous details of exegesis, the texts and monuments reciprocally lend (²). All the same, it is to be observed that until now we have principally made use of the first to explain the second In fact the two sorts of documents seem to be unequally matched . and the muteness of the stones will never, in the estimation of philologists, be able to equal (as regards the extent and variety of the information which can be derived from them) the verbosity of the writings. However, there is one point in which the sculptures have an advantage over the manuscripts, namely the permanent fixity of their testimony. Such as they were when they left the hands of the

---

(1) Extract from *Mélanges Sylvain Lévi*, Paris, 1911.

(2) Cf *Une liste indienne des Actes du Buddha* in the *Annuaire de l'École pratique des Hautes Études, Section des Sciences religieuses*, 1908, a paper of too technical a character to be translated here.

workman, such are they still to-day ; or at least, if they are
likewise subject to mutilations and susceptible, strictly
speaking, of being counterfeited, no attempt at rifacimento
or interpolation, that scourge of Indian literatures, could
in their case pass unperceived. Guaranteed against the
insidious address of the diasceuasts, they are equally so
against the individual fancy of their own authors, who
are forcibly restrained by the material conditions of their
technique. It results from this that they can be arranged
with perfect assurance in chronological order and dated
with a sufficient approximation It is in this sense that
we are able to say with Fergusson, that « in such a country as India, the chisels of her sculptors are .. immeasu-
rably more to be trusted than the pens of her authors(¹) ».
It is in virtue of this advantage that the figured versions
seem to us able in their turn to render some service to
the written accounts of the same legend. In short, after
having so often applied the texts to the interpretation of the
monuments, we should like on this occasion to essay the
application of the monuments to the chronology of the
texts

I

For this purpose we will direct our attention to a celebrated legend, which, however, it may not be useless briefly to recall to the reader, that of the « elephant with six tusks »
(Skt. *Shaḍḍanta*, Pâli *Chaddanta*, Chinese *Lieu ya siang*).
Of course, this marvellous animal was none other than one
of the innumerable past incarnations of our Buddha, and

---

(1) Fergusson, *History of Indian and Eastern Architecture*, Preface to the
first edition, 1876, p. VIII (2ᵈ edit., 1910, p. x)

he lived, happy and wise, in the company of his two wives and of his troop of subjects in a hidden valley of the Himâlayas However, the second wife, wrongly believing herself slighted for love of the first, gives herself up to death in an access of jealous fury, making a vow one day to avenge herself upon her husband for his supposed want of affection. In the course of her succeeding existence she becomes, thanks to some remnant of merit, queen of Benares, and possesses the gift of remembering her previous birth. She astutely obtains from the king permission to despatch against her former husband the most skilful hunter in the country, with orders to kill him and bring back his tusks as a proof of the success of his mission. The man does, in fact, succeed at great risk of his life in striking the noble elephant with a deadly arrow. But the soul of the Bodhisattva is inaccessible to any evil passion · not content with sparing his murderer, he voluntarily makes a present of the tusks whereof the man had come to rob him. When the hunter finally brings back to the queen this mournful trophy, she feels her heart break at the sight of it.

Such is this touching story, reduced to its essential and most generally reported features · for it is known under multiple forms. We know, in particular, that it appears in the Pâli collection of the *Jâtaka* (n° 514). Since 1895 M. L. Feer has compared with this text, point for point, the Sanskrit account in the *Kalpadrumâvadâna* and two Chinese editions, taken, the one from the *Lieu tu tsi king* (Nanjio, n° 143) and the other from the *Tsa pao tsang king* (Nanjio, n° 1329), but, with perhaps excessive prudence, he was careful not to draw any conclusions from this detailed comparison (¹). More recently the translation of

(1) *Journal Asiatique*, Jan.-Feb. 1895. For the version of the *Kalpadrumâ-*

the *Sùtrâlankâra* of Açvaghosha, so excellently rendered by
M Ed. Huber from the Chinese of Kumârajîva, has made
accessible to us a new and most important version ([1]).
Finally, a publication by M. Ed. Chavannes has placed at the
disposal of Indianists generally both a complete translation of the two texts quoted by M L. Feer, and also a
translation of the corresponding passage of the *Ta che tu
luen* (Nanjio, n° 1169), ascribed to Nâgârjuna ([2]). So
much for the literary sources of our study ([3]). If we now
turn to the works of art, we observe that we have been no
less fortunate in having preserved to us at the same time a
medallion from Barhut ([4]), another from Amarâvatî ([5]), a
lintel from Sânchî ([6]), a fragment of a frieze from
Gandhâra ([7]), and finally two frescoes from Ajantâ, the one

---

*vadana*, cf. the Sanskrit Ms 27, fol 232 v°-240 v° of the Bibliothèque
Nationale and RAJ MITRA, *The Sanskrit Buddhist Literature of Nepâl*, pp. 301-
303 — We refuse to take into account the commentary of vv 26-27 of the
*Dhammapada*, which, as Mr FEER also remarks, has scarcely any feature in
common with the *Shaddanta* legend

(1) Ed HUBER, *Sùtrâlankâra*, Paris, 1908, ch XIV, n° 69, pp. 403 sqq

(2) Ed CHAVANNES, *Cinq cents contes et apologues extraits du Tripitaka chinois* three volumes (1911) The story n° 28 (I, p 101) represents the passage in question from the *Lieu tu tsi king*, the two other extracts will appear
in vol IV Strictly one might connect with it the story n° 344, which also
presents the characteristic trait of the gift of the tusks, but in quite different surroundings We are happy to take this opportunity of thanking
M CHAVANNES, whose great kindness permitted us to make use of the relevant
pages of his work prior to publication

(3) As to n° 49 (not yet published in the *Bibl Indica*) of the *Bodhisattvâvadânakalpalatâ*, we cite it merely for record . for this narrative is missing
from the only ms (*Sanscrit* 8) of the Bibliothèque Nationale (see below,
p 204, n 1).

(4) A CUNNINGHAM, *Stûpa of Barhut*, 1879, pl. XXVI, 6

(5) J. BURGESS, *Buddhist Stûpas of Amaravati and Jaggayyapeta*, 1887,
pl. XIX, 1

(6) Rear face of the middle lintel of the southern gate, cf. J FERGUSSON,
*Tree and Serpent Worship*, 2d ed , 1873, pl VIII

(7) *Art greco-bouddhique du Gandhâra* fig 138 (fragment of the counter-

in Cave X, and the other in Cave XVII ('). The identification of these bas-reliefs and of these paintings is fortunately no longer matter for reconsideration, except, perhaps, in detail (²) From the very fact that the meaning of these images has once for all been recognized, they have taken their place side by side with the texts in the capacity of independent and trustworthy witnesses to the divers forms which the legend has successively assumed. Altogether we find ourselves in possession of no less than twelve versions, of which six are provided by art and six by literature. These twelve versions are, if we may say so, so many successive « stages » of the tradition : the precise problem is to classify these various stages in their chronological order

We must admit that, if we were reduced solely to the historical data relative to the texts, the enterprise would be almost desperate It is easy to contest the orthodox belief, according to which the stanzas of the *Jâtaka* all fell from the lips of Buddha himself; it is much less easy to replace it by more satisfactory assertions concerning the exact time of the composition of these *gâthâs,* which are certainly very ancient, more ancient at times than Buddhism. Their commentary (*atthakathâ*), according to the confession even of the monks of Ceylon, has existed under its present form

---

march of a staircase, derived from the hill of Karamâr, Lahore Museum, n° 1156).

(1) Ajantâ, Cave X J GRIFFITHS, *The Paintings in the Buddhist Cave-temples of Ajantâ,* 1896, I, pl 41 and fig 21, cf J. BURGESS, *Notes on the Buddha Rock-temples of Ajantâ,* 1879, pl. VII, 2, and *Arch Survey of Western India,* IV. pl. XVI — Cave XVII, GRIFFITHS, *ibid* fig 73 and pl 63

(2) Cf for example, *infra,* p 194, n 1 and p. 195. The majority of the published descriptions are in error in speaking of more than one hunter it is, of course, question of the same individual, represented in various attitudes and at different moments

only since the V[th] century A. D ; but in their view this could only be the translation into Pâli of a prose which was quasi-contemporaneous with the verses ([1]). Of the *Kalpadrumâvadâna* all that we can say without imprudence is that this versified amplification does not bear the marks of high antiquity As to the dates at which the Chinese translations were made and which, according to the information kindly communicated by M Chavannes, extend from the end of the III[rd] century to that of the V[th] of our era, they naturally can furnish us only with a *terminus ad quem* Thus, as far as the texts are concerned, practically every extrinsic element of chronological classification is lacking Happily we are a little better served, as regards the images. Each of these forms part of a whole to which either votive inscriptions or technical considerations permit us to assign a determinate epoch. It is established that the bas-reliefs of Barhut and of Sânchî go back to the II[nd] or I[st] century B. C. ([2]) Those of Gandhâra and of Amarâvatî are by common accord attributed to the I[st] or II[nd] of our era ([3]) It is to the same epoch at the latest that, on the strength of the inscriptions and the style, Messrs. Burgess and Griffiths ascribe the archaic paintings of Cave X at Ajantâ on the other hand, the same authorities bring the decoration of Cave XVII down to the beginning of the VI[th] century ([4]). Certainly these are only approximate dates · but it is a good thing to have even so much, and we must consider ourselves fortunate, if we succeed, by using

---

([1]) Cf Rhys Davids, *Buddhist Birth-Stories*, 1880, Introduction, pp. I-II.

([2]) See above, pp 4, 34, 67

([3]) Cf *Art gréco-bouddhique du Gandhâra*, p 42.

([4]) For the « Cave X » see Griffiths, *loc cit*, pp. 5 and 32; Burgess, *Notes*, p. 50, for the « Cave XVII » Griffiths, *ibid*, p 5, Burgess, *ibid.*, p 61 (cf p. 57)

these figured monuments as so many land-marks, in dating
some of our texts with a similar degree of approximation.
Nay, were we not able to call to our aid these hitherto
unutilized auxiliaries, it would be wiser to surrender in
advance every attempt at historical classification.

II

Certainly we should not for that reason remain completely disarmed before the confused mass of these often
divergent versions, and it would be our part to introduce
— by recourse, for want of anything better, to some internal principle of coordination — an order at least theoretical.
It is indeed the favourite occupation of folklorists thus to
draw up genealogical trees of what they have decided to
call « families of tales » But, if the enterprise is possible,
and the pastime permissible, it goes without saying that
the result can be of value only upon a double condition,
namely that we shall have known how to choose the
topical detail which must act as main-spring for the estab-
lishment of the series, and that we shall have well observed
and followed out, in the arrangement of this series, the
natural course of human affairs  Now, in the case of the
*Shaddanta-jâtaka* we are in no wise puzzled to discover at
once the characteristic trait and the way in which to use it
It is a well recognized law that successive versions of narratives of this kind have a tendency continually to outdo
each other in the direction of increasing edification  The
usual effect of this pious inclination is, let us say in passing,
to destroy by degrees the whole salt of the story together
with its probability and its ingenuousness, while substitu-
ting for it compositions whose insipidity is sweetened to

the point of nausea. Nevertheless there is no religious literature, and the Buddhist less than any other, which, its original raciness once evaporated, escapes this deplorable and
fatal invasion of convention and artificiality. Now what, in
the theme with which we are at present concerned, is the
essential point, wherein exactly its edification lies? In
order that we may not be accused of choosing arbitrarily
and to suit the necessities of the case, let us appeal to the
*Lalitavistara,* which happens to sum it up in a verse (¹)   at
the time of his previous birth as the elephant Shaddanta (it
is the Gods themselves who subsequently remind the Bodhisattva, in order to encourage him to follow his vocation)
« thou didst sacrifice thy teeth of dazzling beauty, but morality was saved » This is indeed the point of the story,
which has caused it to be ranged under the category of the
« perfection of morality », or better, « of goodness » (²) :
it is the surrender by the elephant of his beautiful ivory
tusks, as sanction to the pardon granted to the hunter who has just mortally wounded him   But there is
more than one way of returning good for evil, and it can
be done with more or less good grace. In this particular
case the virtuous elephant might have limited himself to
allowing his enemy to work his will, or, better, he might
have facilitated the operation for him ; or finally, which
quite attains to the sublime, he might have done the deed
himself for the advantage of his murderer. It is evidently

---

(1) *Lalitavistara,* ch XIII, 40, ed Lefmann, p 168,1 9 *Parityaji te ruci-
raçubhadantâ na ca tyaji çilam* — Naturally it is this same point that is
emphasized in the résumé of Hiuan-tsang to which reference will be made
below, p 199

(2) *Çila-pâramtâ*   this is the classification of the introduction to the
*Jâtaka* (ed Fausbøll, I, p 45 , trans Rhys Davids, p 55) and of the *Lieu
tu tsi king* (Chavannes, *Cinq cents contes,* I, pp 97 sqq )

in the order of this increasing generosity that, in theory, the various versions will have to be classified.

In fact, if we recur to the written accounts which have been preserved to us, we remark that the protagonist adopts in turns one or other of these attitudes at the culminating moment of the narrative « Rise, hunter, take thy knife (*khura*, Skt. *kshura*), and cut from me these teeth before I die », is the extent of what the elephant says in stanza 31 of the *Jâtaka*; and his interlocutor does not let him repeat the invitation. The *Lieu tu tsi king* considers it only right to add a little moral homily. But with the prose commentary of the *Jâtaka* things become more complicated. The animal has attained a size so monstrous, that it is only with great difficulty that the man succeeds in raising himself up to the root of its tusks, and even there, though instead of the hatchet of a savage (the use of which would, in fact, have been disastrous to the ivory) he now uses a more perfect instrument, the saw (*kakaca*, Skt *krakaca*), he vainly exhausts himself with cruel efforts · his victim himself must come to his aid. In order to make things more pathetic, the monastic editor does not recoil before the most flagrant contradictions The elephant is already so weak that he cannot raise his silver trunk to take hold of the saw, and he has to call all his senses together, in order to beg the hunter to give him the handle of it; after which — as it is generally agreed that the Bodhisattva is by his very nature endowed with supernatural strength — he instantly saws through his two tusks (for here (¹) they are no more in number than two), like the tender stems of a

-----

(1) M L. FEER (*loc cit* p 50 and p 77, note 1) has observed the same thing in the *Kalpadrumâvadâna*, in spite of the persistence in the title of the traditional name of « six-toothed », but it is to be noticed that the word

plantain! In the *Kalpadrumâvadâna*, the *Ta che tu luen* (which besides is simply a very summary résumé) and the *Tsa pao tsang king*, the hero does not even trouble himself to borrow from his murderer any instrument whatever · he himself breaks off his tusks, according to the first two accounts against a rock, according to the third against a big tree. But to the *Sûtrâlankâra* belongs the palm for spontaneity in the action of the martyr . it is simply « by slipping his trunk round his teeth » that this time the elephant pulls them out, not without pain or grief, while the hunter respectfully waits for him to present them expressly to him  Further than this it is impossible to go.

Thus, then, we obtain a first classification of all our texts  Theoretically it is unassailable, practically we must not form any illusions as to its historical value. If notwithstanding we proceed to arrange the figured monuments according to the same criterion, the chances of arriving by their intervention at a less conjectural result assume immediately a better aspect. In fact we are not long in perceiving that the order thus obtained coincides exactly with that already forced upon us by the purely archæological data  At the head of them there always comes, in its simplicity, the medallion of Barhut: on the left the hunter, having put down his bow and arrows, sets about cutting off the elephant's tusks with a rude saw (¹)  The latter has kindly crouched

----

*danta* occurs in the text very frequently in the plural and not in the dual. On the other hand, it is unfortunately impossible to know what was said on this particular point by texts of which we no longer possess more than the Chinese translation

(1) See above, p  39  Perhaps it is worth while to remark that, in the Barhut version, the cause of the drama is evidently the same as in the *Lieu tu tsi king*, that is, the gift of a lotus to the first wife, if at least, as is said in the *Kalpadrumâvadâna*, she did not receive two, one to decorate each of her temples  This reason is cited by the prose commentary of the *Jâtaka*

down to further the wishes of his enemy and to render his task less difficult (pl. XXIX, 1). The case is the same in Gandhâra and at Amarâvatî, where in addition we see represented the episode of the hunter hiding in a ditch, in order to wound the elephant in the stomach with an arrow (pll. XXIX, 2 and XXX, 1). The fresco of Cave X of Ajantâ shows us likewise, in the words of Mr. Griffiths (*loc. cit.*, p. 32), « the huge six-tusked elephant lying down and a hunter engaged in cutting off the six tusks » It is, as a matter of fact, six tusks — more or less distinctly separated, but always carefully noted — that the elephant has in all these representations, except that from Gandhâra But, when we pass on to the painting of Cave XVII, the picture is changed « the huge white Elephant King », says Mr. Griffiths (*ibid.*, p. 37), is standing, « with only one tusk, upon which he rests his trunk, while a man kneels and makes profound obeissance before him ». In reality (cf pl. XXX, 2), the elephant, to whom the artist no longer lends more than his two normal teeth, has already torn out one, and is about, as it is written in the *Sûtrâlankâra*, to twist his trunk round the second, in order to pull that out in its turn. And during this time the hunter, in adoration before him, awaits the accomplishment of the magnanimous sacrifice There is, as we see, a striking parallelism of development between our two kinds of documents ; and it is continued from one end to the other of the two series.

If now we bring the two lists together, we obtain, always

---

only as a subsidiary one of the first, a very ingenious one, that he advances, — and according to which the great elephant one day, unintentionally, by shaking a *çâla* tree in full blossom, caused to fall on his second wife, who was standing to windward, only twigs of wood, dry leaves, and red ants, while the first, who was to the leeward, received flowers, pollen and green shoots — there is no more question at Barhut than in the texts, except this particular commentary by virtue of the same principle and by the simple intercalation of the various versions (') in the position respectively belonging to them, the following combination :

**I  Stanzas of the Pâli Jâtaka**
*The hunter cuts off the teeth with a knife*

**II  Medallion of Barhut (II^{nd} century B C.) .**
*The hunter cuts off the elephant's teeth with a saw*

**III  Medallion  of  Amarâvatî** ⎫
**IV  Fresco of Ajantâ, Cave X** ⎬ **I^{st}-II^{nd} century A. D. :**
**V  Counter-step of Gandhâra** ⎭
*The same version as at Barhut.*

**VI  Lieu tu tsi king (trans by Seng-houei, d  280):**
*The same version (the instrument is not specified).*


**VII. Prose Commentary of the Jâtaka (rendered into Pâli in the V^{th} Century)**
*The elephant himself saws off his teeth*


**VIII  Kalpadrumâvadâna**
*The elephant himself breaks off his teeth against a rock*

**IX  Ta che tu luen (trans by Kumârajîva between 402 and 405)**
*The same version as in the Kalpadrumâvadâna*

**X  Tsa pao tsang king (trans by Ki-kia-ye and T'an yao in 472) :**
*The elephant himself breaks off his teeth against a tree.*

**XI  Sûtrâlankâra (trans into Chinese by Kumârajîva towards 410)**
*The elephant himself pulls out his teeth with his trunk*

**XII  Fresco of Cave XVII of Ajantâ (VI^{th} century)**
*The same version as in the Sûtrâlankâra*

---

(1) It will be noticed that the final list differs slightly from that which we drew up at the beginning of this study  On the one hand, we have had to leave aside the lintel at Sânchî, which, treated too decoratively, did not supply us with any information upon the precise point which we are now considering, on the other hand, the tenor of the commentary of the *Jâtaka* has shown itself so divergent from that of the text that we have had to divide this source into two  On the whole, then, we always reckon twelve versions, five artistic and seven literary.

## III

Such as it is, the chronological table thus obtained is at least worthy, of being taken into consideration , and the hope occurs to us that we may have restored, in accordance with the natural play of the religious conscience, the different phases of the evolution of the story. In fact, it is not that we have thus arbitrarily arranged all the accessible documents : it is they, which, when interrogated on a definite, capital point, have spontaneously and without any violence or solicitation on our part, arranged themselves in the order indicated above. As far as the images are concerned, this series is not only in conformity with their historic succession on the whole : it takes into account, in a surprising manner, their proximity as well as their aloofness in time, grouping together at the beginning the four which resemble each other, and reserving the sole variant to quite at the end  Then, as regards the texts, the impression of confidence and security, which arises from this spontaneous classification, would be still further increased, if we made our inquiry apply equally to such or such other accessory episodes of the legend. It is not, indeed, the  manner of giving the tusks only, it is a whole group of concomitant details, which concur in determining theoretically, for one who knows how to read them, the order of priority of the various narratives. Take the one which comes at the head of the list, that is, the rhymed account of the *Jâtaka*; you will observe that there everything takes place in accordance with the customary rules of elephant-hunting. The hunter hides in a ditch , at the cry of the wounded animal all his companions flee ; remaining alone in the presence of the man, the elephant advances to kill him · the fact that it stops on recognizing on him the colour of the monastic coat is the sole sign of the Buddhist adaptation of the ballad Beginning with the *Lieu tu tsi king* (n° 6), it is no longer sufficient that the clothes of the hunter should be naturally of a reddish-brown, like those of that hunter (¹) from whom Buddha formerly borrowed his first monk's coat · henceforward the man will deliberately disguise himself as a monk, in order to inspire confidence in his prey. But, since he now employs this infallible means of approaching within easy reach, there is no longer need for him to hide in ambush . and in fact, beginning with the *Kalpadrumâvadâna* (n° 8), he ceases to have recourse to this obsolete proceeding. At the same time, as he has approached openly, it will be necessary that by a refinement of pity his victim should defend him against the vengeance of his first wife, if not from the rest of the herd : this is what the Bodhisattva fails not henceforth to do (n° 9-11). Soon — with n° 10 — scruples are aroused in the mind of the hunter, thus protected : he no longer dares to lay his sacrilegious hand on the tusks of the « Great Being », for fear that it may fall from his body Finally, in the *Sûtrâlankâra* (n° 11), to these interested fears is added a real and too legitimate repentance Thus is seen how a striving after increased edification has by degrees modified a whole concordant assemblage of details : and so it is not, as might be imagined, for an isolated reason, but by a whole sheaf of proofs, if we had time to consider them more closely, that the order of the preceding table would be justified.

(1) And doubtless, of all people of low caste for the costume of his order of mendicant brothers Buddha would quite naturally have chosen the coarsest material of the cheapest colour At least we do not see that the tradition relative to the *kâshâya*, if it had any meaning, can at the bottom signify anything else For its variations in form cf. also *Art greco-bouddhique du Gandhâra*, p. 369.

Does this mean that we must blandly accept for the known documents all its features, and that, on the other hand, in order to fix the date of every new version, it will be sufficient to refer it to the corresponding degree on this chronological scale? In the case of a figured monument we should be rather inclined to believe so, provided that it is upon inquiry verified whether by chance it were not a case of some more or less archaizing imitation. As soon as it is a text that is concerned, the question becomes much more delicate, and from the very beginning we fall again into our difficulties. For the most part the table furnishes us with nothing more than simple presumptions, and these need still to be correctly interpreted It affirms, for example, that the *Sûtrâlankâra* represents the state of the legend current from the V$^{th}$ century of our era, and of this fact we have, in truth, two indisputable proofs. The one, of an artistic order, is the fresco of Cave XVII of Ajantâ (VI$^{th}$ century) The other, literary, but by a happy chance dated exactly as belonging to the second quarter of the VII$^{th}$ century, is nothing less than a passage from Hiuan-tsang : the story of the Shaddanta, gathered by the great pilgrim at Benares, is, as M. S. Lévi has already pointed out in his admirable article on the *Sûtrâlankâra et ses sources*, « an exact and faithful résumé of the story of Açvaghosha » (¹). What are we to deduce from these statements ? As the name of the author scarcely allows us to bring the work lower down than the II$^{nd}$ century of our era, must we has-

---

(1) Cf M. S. Lévi, *Açvaghosha, le Sûtrâlankâra et ses Sources*, in the *Journal Asiatique*, July-August 1908, p 175 Stanislas Julien (I, p 360) translates in fact « The elephant tore out his tusks », and Watters (II, p. 53) says exactly the same According to Beal (II, p 49) he « broke off his tusks ». M Chavannes admits that this second translation might literally be pos- sible . but, not to mention that the sense of « breaking » is given in the dic-

ten to conclude, as we might be tempted to do, that the
account of the « white elephant with six tusks » is only a
late addition ? This story forms a part of the XIV[th] chapter.
Now M Ed Huber warns us in his preface « that one of
the first catalogues of the Chinese *Tripiṭaka*, the *Li tai san
pao ki*, drawn up in A. D. 597, gives only ten chapters » to
the *Sûtrâlankâra* Besides, we feel to what a degree this collection of tales (which, like that of the *Jâtakamâlâ*, must at a
very early date have been used by Buddhist sermon-writers
for the needs of their daily preachings) was ill-defended
against interpolations. . — This is all very well and good;
and after all the thing is possible . but surely the place assigned to the *Sûtrâlankâra* in our list by its conception of
the *Shaddanta-jâtaka* does not authorise us to conclude from
it anything of the kind. What, in fact, does it prove ? That
this text already contains the form which the legend had
assumed in the imagination of the artist painters of the
VI[th], and in the memory of the guides of the VII[th], century.
And in what way does it prevent the poetic talent of Açvaghosha from having been the first to put into circulation the
elaborate version which, as we have just seen, was coherent
in all its parts and destined to have great success and definitely to supplant the far too primitive account of the stanzas of the *Jâtaka* ? Two or three centuries may not have been
too much for this literary production to become popular in
its turn , and here we find positively no peremptory reason
invalidating its authenticity. The best course, with a view
to the solution of this question — as of the question how
far the Chinese translation is adequate to the Sanskrit origi-

---

tionary of Couvreur as a secondary meaning, it is that of « tearing out »
which corresponds to the description of the attitude in the *Sûtrâlankâra*,
and its representation in the fresco of cave XVII of Ajantâ

PLATE XXIX

Cf. pp. 39, 194-6

I. — From Cunningham, *Stûpa of Bharhut*, pl XXVI, 2, for the description cf above, pp 39 and 194-5.

II — From a photograph taken by the author at the Madras museum in December 1896 The number and variety of the episodes collected together on this single medallion, among trees and rocks used as frames, give it, in contrast to the simplicity of that at Barhut, an especially entangled and confused appearance — 1 On the lower part, to the right, we see the miraculous elephant with six tusks, standing between his two queens, of whom the first, on his left, holds over his head a parasol, whilst on the right the second flourishes a fly-flapper — 2 He moves in the direction of the lotus pond, which occupies the bottom of the picture, and where we see him sporting with a numerous company , the apparently female pachyderm who is coming precipitately out of the pond on the left and who then seems to crouch in order to throw herself down some precipice, would perhaps be intended to awake the remembrance of the jealous wife and her suicide? — 3. Whatever may be the fact concerning this detail, the story is now continued on the right, in the upper portion of the medallion The great elephant is depicted standing at the moment when he crosses the fatal ditch in which lurks the hunter, whose bust only is to be seen between the animal's legs — 4 A little more to the left the elephant, whose fore part only is shown, is kneeling, in order that the hunter may cut off his tusks by the aid of a saw furnished with a curved spring, much more elaborate than the tool used at Barhut — 5 Finally, right at the top, the latter carries away, on the two ends of a pole balanced on his right shoulder, the *spolia optma* of the Bodhisattva It is curious to observe that the tusks are twelve in number, six (2×3) at each end of the pole ! Here and there indications of antelopes and deer, while lending animation to the scene, only add to the crowding

1    AT BARHUT

2.    AT AMARAVATI

PLATE XXX

Cf. pp. 195-6.

I — A frieze from the Lahore museum (no 1156. height m 0,16), which formerly decorated one of the counter-steps of a staircase on Karamâr Hill, from a photograph taken by the author (cf *Art g -b du Gandh*, I, fig. 158) The elephant has only one pair of tusks — 1 On the left he is wounded in the stomach by the arrow of the hunter hidden in a ditch — 2 He then kneels down, to allow his teeth to be sawn off — 3 Finally, on the right, the hunter, twice represented, brings back on his shoulder his bundle of ivory, and then offers it to the royal pair of Benares We shall note the striking contrast between the distributive order of the episodes according to the ancient Indian school and according to the Indo-Greek school of Gandhâra, there crowded together inside the same pannel, here deployed one by one along a frieze

II — From GRIFFITHS, *The Paintings in the Buddhist Cave Temples of Ajantâ* pl 63 (fragment) For the description and interpretation of the attitude of the great white elephant cf. p 195 The hunter is repret sented twice, first prostrate at the elephant's feet, with his head on the ground, then still squatting, but already balancing on his shoulder the double burden of tusks, which the magnanimous animal has jus-delivered to him

1. — IN GANDHÁRA

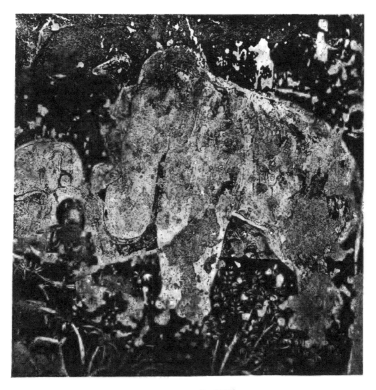

2. — AT AJANTA

nal — is to leave it to the future, especially now that we may hope for everything from the discoveries of manuscripts in Central Asia (¹).

On the other hand, there is a point on which we believe we may already risk a categorical affirmation : we mean the manifest divergence which is seen between the version of the verse text of the *Jâtaka* (n° 1) and that of the prose commentary (n° 7). This divergence is not to-day remarked for the first time(²): what we have here is only one more striking experimental demonstration of it. Read afresh with reference to our list the text of Fausböll's edition (V, pp. 37 sqq.), and you will quickly perceive that the editor of the commentary in its present form knew a state of the legend analogous to that reflected in the works numbered 8 to 11 , that, if he did not follow these latter right to the end, it was because he was hindered at each moment by his text, whose ancient particulars held him back, *nolens volens,* on the incline down which he asked nothing better than to glide; and that finally he applied himself as well as he could to inserting between the lines of the ancient story ornaments borrowed from the later legend. Henceforth you will hold the secret of the strange liberties which he takes with the letter of the stanzas, and you will have only to note point by point, as they occur, the most flagrant of his offences. You will smile at the palpable cunning with which, from the first line (p. 37, l. 1), he transfers the name of the elephant, Chaddanta, to the lake near which the latter dwells, and a

---

(1) It is known that Prof LUDERS has already announced the discovery of fragments (still unedited) of the Sanskrit text of the *Sûtrâlankâra*

(2) It is sufficient to refer here to Prof. LUDERS in *Gottingische Gelehrte Nachrichten*, 1897, p. 119, and M E SENART's article on *Les Abhisambuddhagâthâs* in the *Journal Asiatique*, May-June 1901, pp 385 sqq.

little further (p. 41, l. 23) glosses his « six tusks » by « two tusks of six colours »; for you know that the latest mode was to ascribe to him only one pair. Where the good monk will perhaps seem to go rather far, is when he translates *khura* by *kakaca* (p. 52, l. 9), and unblushingly essays to make you believe that knives are saws, in other words, that chalk is cheese. But soon you will content yourself with shrugging your shoulders before this strange and system-atic perversion of the text which he was supposed to interpret; the fact is that you read his hand in advance and see why, before allowing the hunter to descend into the ditch specified by stanza 23, he believes it necessary to clothe him in the *kâshâya* of a monk (p. 49, l. 8), why, when according to stanza 24 the whole troop is scattered to the « eight cardinal points », he considers it more suitable to detain by the side of the wounded one at least his faith-ful wife (p. 50, l. 9), why, a few lines further down, he has her brutally driven away, for fear she should punish the assassin (p. 50, l. 19), etc And when finally to stanza 32 — which states merely that the hunter took his knife, cut off the elephant's tusks, and departed — he openly opposes (p. 52) the absurd and pathetic account which we have already analysed ('), the measure is heaped up and the cause decisively heard. If the *gâthâs* have all the characteristics of an ancient popular plaint, which the barbarity of the pro-ceeding employed by the hunter to get possession of the ivory forces us to declare anterior to the Barhut medallion,

---

(1) See above, p 193. — It on all these points we have not referred to vol. V of the English translation carried out under the direction of Professor COWELL, it is because the metric version of Mr W FRANCIS (either through blind con-fidence in the commentary or on account of the necessities of the rhyme) seems to regard it as a duty to palliate all the divergencies between the prose and the verse. Thus it is that the beginning of stanza 32 becomes on page 29 « The hunter then the tusks did *saw* » etc

that is to say, to the II^nd century B. C , it is no less evident that their *aṭṭhakathâ* was not merely translated into Pâli, but also accommodated to the taste of the times by a cleric of the V^th century of our era. It is a chasm of at least seven centuries that opens before our eyes between texts which at times some persons have desired to believe contemporaneous.

Thus, whether we arrive at simple points of interrogation or at real certainties, according to the case, it is worth while to take note of these first results. It is well known that in matters of chronology the Indianist is accustomed to be satisfied with very little He can no longer neglect the data afforded by a comparison of the texts and the monuments, wherever they lend themselves to it We have certainly chosen a relatively favourable specimen for our attempt but as regards more than one *jâtaka*, and even more than one miracle of Buddha, it would already be possible to draw up a table analogous to that whose spontaneous generation we have just encouraged. We may augure that these studies in detail, in proportion as excavations and new editions supply their constituent elements, will come to each other's aid, and that by a series of tests chronological data will in the end become more and more precise. From that time it would no longer be of such or such a particular episode, but of the whole Buddhist legend that we should succeed in distinguishing the successive states. If it is permissible even to print prognostications which are still so vague, we should be very much surprised if we did not see reproduced, in a general way, the fact dominating the present list of the versions of the *Shaḍḍanta-jâtaka*. In fact, it is self-evident that these latter divide nearly equally into two large groups, profoundly divergent from one another, between which the Singhalese commentator of the *Jâtaka* vainly endeavoured to construct a bridge. The six first are closely connected with the old native tradition  the five last proceed no less unanimously from a new spirit, which probably filtered into India through its north-west frontier, as a result of foreign invasions. Thus, this table would be before all an excellent illustration of the « crisis » which a succession of great political upheavals at last, a short time after the beginning of our era, provoked in the Indian conscience, and which has already been described in a masterly fashion, by M. Sylvain Lévi, writing of Açvaghosha (¹)

---

(1) *Loc cit* , pp. 73 74  — Since the above article was written Prof. RAPSON has been so good as to have copied by one of his pupils Mr W. H B THOMPSON, under his direction and for our use, the version of the *Shaddantâvadâna* from the *Bodhisattvâvadâna-kalpalatâ*, which is lacking in the Paris ms (cf above, p. 188, n. 3), according to the mss Add *1306* and *913* in the University Library at Cambridge  The kind communication of this copy has enabled us to prove the identity of this version — with the exception of three interpolations — with that of the *Kalpadrumâvadâna*  It appears that the author of the latter collection restricted himself to reproducing, without however (in any way) informing the reader of the fact, the work of Kshemendra, except that on two points he has lengthened the narrative of his predecessor, which in his opinion was too much abbreviated  This fact, however unexpected it may be, naturally does not change anything in our conclusions, as far as concerns the general chronology of the successive forms of the legend . it only causes us to think that the *Kalpadrumâvadâna* and *Bodhisattvâvadâna-kalpalatâ* agree in preserving for us the version of the canon of the Mûla-Sarvâstivâdins, which, as we know (cf. above, p 151, n 2), usually serves as a basis for the poetic lucubrations of Kshemendra  On the other hand, it supplies us with an excellent illustration justifying the reservations expressed above concerning the chronology of the texts  here, in fact, we are dealing with a well-known author, who wrote at the beginning of the XI[th] century, and who yet makes use of a version older than that of the *Sûtrâlankâra*  Thus it was wise on our part to consider as an acquired result only the demonstration of the difference of time between the stanzas of the Pâli *Jâtaka* and their commentary  We are happy to be able on this last point to connect with the already cited evidence of M SENART and Professor LUDERS that of Prof OLDENBERG (*Nachrichten der k Gesellschaft der Wissenschaften zu Göttingen, Phil -hist. Klasse*, 1911, pp 441 sqq.)

# Buddhist Art in Java [1].

I

## THE STÛPA OF BORO-BUDUR.

The ruins of Boro-Budur [1] constitute indisputably the most important Buddhist monument of the island of Java. We know also that they alone can compete, in the amplitude of their dimensions and the profusion of the bas-reliefs with which their walls are covered, with the other gem of Far-Eastern archæology, I mean Angkor-Vat. In beauty of site they even far surpass the rival wonder of Cambodia. Occupying a detached position in advance of a small chain of mountains, which forms a screen on the south, the eminence on which stands Boro-Budur dominates the vast valley of Progo, all covered with shimmering palm-groves and framed on both sides by the majestic summits of great volcanoes. To the west stretch the deep recesses of the Menoreh, flanked by the imposing sugar-loaf of the Sumbing, in height exceeding 10,000 feet, to the east extend the wonderfully pure curves of the twin peaks of the Mer-Babu, the Mount of Ashes, and of the Mer-Api, the Mount of Fire, the latter still active, and in the northern distance, half-way to the sea, whose vapours may be faintly descried, the rounded hill of Magelang represents the head of the nail which, according

---

(1) Extract from the *Bulletin de l École française d'Extrême-Orient*, vol IX, 1909, pp 1 sqq These notes are a result of a too brief stay which the author was able to make in Java during the month of May 1907.

to the native tradition, fixed Java to the bottom of the ocean.
The flat and marshy borders of the Cambodian Great-Lake
have nothing to compare with this sublime scenery; and
yet it is a fact of common experience that Boro-Budur produces at first sight a general impression much less profound
than does Angkor-Vat.

No doubt, we must in the first place take account of
the difference in dimensions. The rectangular base of the
Khmer monument has an exterior measurement of 187 by
215 metres, the lower terrace of the Javanese building
forms a square of 111 metres on each side. The former
attains an elevation of 57 metres, whilst the present summit
of the second does not reach 35 metres above the first steps.
It is well likewise to note that the latter, older by three
centuries or so and exposed to the same destructive agents
— torrential rains and the luxuriant vegetation of the
Tropics — is in a worse state of preservation (¹). But,
after all, we must acknowledge that the two monuments,
even at the time of their unimpaired splendour, had from
an architectural point of view nothing in common. Angkor-Vat deploys on tiers rising above the plain its three
enclosing galleries, intersected by portals, flanked by eight
towers and crowned by a ninth   Boro-Budur encompasses the summit of a hill with the sacred number of its
nine terraces, connected at the four cardinal points by staircases and surmounted by a dome. At Angkor-Vat the eye
ranges through the colonnades or follows in the distance

---

(1) Boro-Budur is commonly ascribed to the IX[th] Century, and Angkor-
Vat to the XII[th]  The leaning walls of the Javanese Stûpa threaten ruin to
such a degree that the Government-General of the Dutch East Indies has
been moved thereby  The friends of archæology will learn with pleasure that
a first grant of 60,000 florins (about ₤ 5,000) is at present being devoted to
works of preservation under the expert direction of Major Van Erp, of the
Engineers

the ever narrowing flight of the porticoes; at Boro-Budur the lower galleries, interrupted by twenty right angles and confined on the exterior by a high parapet, narrowly enclose the visitor in their successive recesses ([1]). In Cambodia, whether from the end of the paved approaches he contemplates the clearly defined silhouette of the towers, or whether from the top of the central group he dominates the widely spaced plan of the enclosures, the spectator always embraces in his view the grandiose scheme of the design. In Java, from the foot as from the top, nothing is ever perceived but a compact mass confusedly bristling with 432 niches and 72 little cupolas forming so many pinnacles. The fact is that Angkor-Vat led the devotee by the perspective of long avenues straight to the dwelling of a god, Boro-Budur, on the contrary, opened no access in its massive sides, which were destined solely as a shrine for relics. In one word, the first is a Brahmanic temple; the second is a *stûpa*, or Buddhist tumulus.

That the architectural form of the temple is infinitely more favourable to the effect of the whole than that of the mausoleum, no one will deny. Still this reason is not entirely satisfying, nor does it suffice to explain what at first sight is « wrong » with the aspect of Boro-Budur (pl XXXI, 1) It is not a dome with simple lines, like the most ancient Indian *stûpas* which are preserved to us, for example at Sânchî and at Mânikyâla. Neither is it a superposition of quadrangular diminishing terraces, a kind of pyramid in steps, such as the Chinese pilgrims describe the « pagodas » of north-western India. Nor has it the lengthy slenderness of its Burmese or Siamese congeners, which point very high into the air as it were the handle of

(1) Cf. pll. XXXI, 2 and XXXII, 2

an enormous bell. To speak candidly, it seems to have been
unable to decide clearly whether to be conical, pyramidal,
or hemispherical. The vertical indented walls of the
first six galleries give the impression that the monument is about to mount up straight towards the sky :
but with the three upper circular galleries this start
is suddenly frustrated, and the whole structure assumes
a crushed and heavy appearance. Doubtless we must
make allowance for the disappearance of the crown and
the depression of the summit under the influence of the
rains. Neither must we forget that the wide band of
masonry which now forms the first terrace was constructed round the edifice as an afterthought and contributes
in no slight degree to the appearance of heaviness ('). But,
all taken into account, the disappointment of the
impartial observer exists none the less. That a great tumulus can never be anything but a kind of huge pudding, he
is quite ready to admit : but there are puddings which
are more or less succesfully constructed. Without irrever-
ence we may say that the *stûpa* of Boro-Budur, with the
endless zig-zags of its passages and the profuse ornamentation of its pinnacles, gives at first the impression of a pasty,
as badly « raised » on the whole as it is minutely carved
in detail (²).

------

(1) We know that the discovery of this peculiarity is due to an engineer,
Heer J. W Yzerman The primitive plinth must have very early been
buried in the new masonry along with the bas-reliefs wherewith there had
been a commencement of decoration Doubtless it was found necessary to
strengthen the foundations, which threatened to give way under the thrust
of the upper stones : at the same time perhaps orthodox tradition found the
addition of a terrace advantageous, thus completing in the most patent
manner the sacred number of nine This addition is indicated on pl XXXII, 1
by the divergent hatchings

(2) In case the reader should be tempted to think that these criticisms
are made by a prejudiced and particularly surly visitor, he is begged to refer

It is not enough to state the fact; we must also explain it. Certainly we cannot question the skill of the architect who conceived the complicated plan of these nine stories, who designed the mouldings and provided for the sculptural decoration, who, finally, by an ingenious arrangement of gargoyles carrying away the rain-water, made sure of an indefinite preservation at a slight cost of maintenance. If, therefore, he pitched so low the summit of his construction, he must have had some reason for it. We confess that this reason revealed itself to us only in the evening, when seeing from the verandah of the neighbouring *pasan-grahan* (¹) the obscure silhouette of the monument stand out against the starry sky. The contours of this dark mass, in which all details were obscured, presented themselves to us as distinctly curved (pl XXXIII, 1) where we were seeking a pyramid, the builder had intended only a dome. Thus we learned our error. It had, in fact, become usual with archæologists to regard Boro-Budur as a *stûpa* erected on superposed terraces after the manner of those of north-western India (²). In reality, it is only a *stûpa* in the form of a dome, according to the old Indian mode, but much more elaborate, being cut horizontally by a series of promenades and itself crowned with a second cupola. The influence which it has undergone, both in its general conception as in the detail of its mural decoration, comes to it not from Gandhâra, but, as is natural, from southern India, where

to the opinion of BRUMUND in LEEMANS, *Boro-Boudour dans l'île de Java*, Leiden, 1874, p. 579

(1) This is the Malay name for the traveller's house, corresponding to the Indian *bungalow* and the Cambodian *sâlâ*.

(2) Such, for example, is the idea expressed in the passage of our *Art gréco-bouddhique du Gandhâra*, I, p. 80, to which the present note may serve as erratum.

its direct ancestor is called Amarâvatî ('). And this theory, imposed on the most uninitiated by observation of the monument, is confirmed beyond all hesitation by an examination of the plans and elevations which have been drawn up by specialists. The ruling lines of Boro-Budur, notwithstanding the right angles and vertical walls of its lower galleries, are all curves

Have the goodness to cast a glance either at the designs contained in the grand album accompanying Leemans' book, or at our plate XXXII The elements of the latter were borrowed from drawings recently executed under the care of Major Van Erp, who was kind enough to communicate them to us We have restricted ourselves to adding to the second, for the purpose of our demonstration, the dotted lines Thanks to this simple artifice, the principles which presided over the construction of Boro-Budur will become quite clear. The plan demonstrates to us in the most evident manner that each of the lower galleries, however angular they may be, is inscribed within a circle, and is itself, at its principal points, tangent to an inner circle. On the elevation we perceive that the initial project of the architect involved the construction of an edifice assuming the general form of a segment of a sphere.

Henceforth nothing remains but to offer him our humble apology and to try to enter into his views. Naturally our observations of fact still hold good; but

---

(1) Cf *Art g.-b du Gandh* , fig 58, a model of a *stûpa* from Amarâvatî, where the procedure in decorating the walls of the monument with the aid of bas-reliefs and the recourse to a promenade intended to facilitate access to the upper row of these latter are already clearly indicated Let us add that the excavations judiciously conducted by Major Van Erp have already borne fruit in the discovery of fragments of the balustrade, furnished with doors, which formerly surrounded the base of Boro-Budur

what we took for defects no longer appear to us anything
but necessities logically imposed by the initial decision.
It was in order to keep more closely to the horizontal
sections of his segment of a sphere that he gave twenty
angles to the parapets of the first four galleries and twelve
to that of the fifth : if, in his desire to furnish his band of
sculptors with plane surfaces, he had made these galleries
simply quadrangular, they would have extended too far
beyond the primordial inner circle. It is because a semi-cir-
cular profile does not mount like a pyramid, that the upper
promenades, themselves circular, are necessarily lowered.
This explains at once the contrast between the steepness of
the first steps and the gentle slope of the last (cf. pl. XXXIII,
2) : not otherwise does one mount the outline of the upper
section of a globe ([1]). Neither is it the fault of anyone, but
rather in the nature of things, if, having once reached the
top of the rounded sides, one can no longer see the foot,
just as from the base it is impossible to perceive the summit  If we likewise reflect that the architect of Boro-
Budur was deprived of our favourite resource of colonnades,
we shall understand why to the use of mouldings he has
added that of antefixes, of niches and cupolas, and we shall
no longer be astonished at the symmetrical multiplication

---

(1) The difference between the steps at the bottom and those at the top
is so great that from the first to the second gallery, for example, thirteen
steps only go back m  3,56 in rising m  3,84, whilst the seven steps
which lead to the first circular gallery, the sixth of the whole, have a depth
of m  3,40 in rising m  1,80, Wilsen (ap  LEEMANS, p  576) asks whether
we must not, in the steepness of the first steps, see a symbol, suggested to
the minds of the faithful by the intermediary of their legs, of the difficulty
of attaining to Nirvâna ! We conjecture, at least, that the impossibility of
imposing upon them still steeper ones is one of the reasons which decided
the architect not to conform in all things to the ancient Indian formula of
the « air bubble on water », and made him recoil before the idea of assigning
to his monument the form of a complete hemisphere

of these decorative elements. On the whole, in every point where we were ready to criticize him, we must now, on the contrary, recognize the ingenuity with which he has turned to advantage the ready-made formula which he had inherited from the ancient religious tradition of India, and to which from the very beginning he was bound as far as possible to conform. We cannot render him responsible for the mediocre architectural effect which his monument must always have had, even at a time before the uneven ruin of the decorations, the subsidence of the summit, and the crumbling of the corners had broken and distorted the lines. Let us add that his first plan, by at once raising the level of the first gallery almost six metres above the pavement, indicated much better and in an incomparably more elegant manner, the form of the edifice. But for the heavy terrace in which he very soon had to bury the original foundation of Boro-Budur, and which still to-day gives the structure an awkward look, we flatter ourselves that we should have made fewer mistakes and felt less hesitation concerning the real intentions of its author.

## II

### THE BAS-RELIEFS OF BORO-BUDUR

#### (PRINCIPAL WALL OF THE FIRST GALLERY)

Whatever from an architectural point of view has been lost to Boro-Budur through the tyranny of religious tradition is abundantly compensated in the decorative aspect. The 2,000 bas-reliefs, more or less, which formerly covered its walls, and of which about 1,600 still exist to-day, are all borrowed from the legend, or from the Pantheon, of Indian Buddhism ; and it was the testimony of these that

from the first established the sectarian character of the
monument. In abundance and variety of subjects the
Brahmanic art and epopee of India have provided for
the labour of the sculptors of Angkor-Vat nothing com-
parable hereto. Neither can these latter vie in skill of execution with their confrères of Boro-Budur While their chisels
could only moderately carve the fine Cambodian sandstone into rather shallow pictures, the artists of Java, not
disheartened by the coarse grain of the volcanic stone
furnished by their island, have drawn from it veritable
high-reliefs of an astounding depth. Their figures, in spite
of the effeminate softness of their lines, are rightly celebrated for the justness of their proportions, the naturalness of
their movements and the diversity of their postures. Above
all, they exhibit a knowledge of foreshortening, which
is totally lacking in the later, but, owing to want of skill,
apparently more archaic works of the Khmer artists. Even
in India, if we except the few chefs-d'œuvre that we still
possess of the schools of Gandhâra, Amarâvatî and Benares,
we find nothing to surpass this final Far-Eastern flores-
cence of Buddhist art.

Among the hundreds of bas-reliefs the first to arouse
interest were those which Leemans calls « of the second
gallery », but which Heer J. W. Yzerman's discovery proves
to have originally belonged to the first. This gallery is a
corridor, having an interior width of m 1,85, which, with
twenty zig-zags, encompasses the whole monument (cf.
pl XXXI, 2). It is enclosed between two stone walls, built,
like the rest of the construction, without any apparent
mortar and interrupted only by the passage of the four staircases, both walls being ornamented by two superposed series
of bas-reliefs. Among those which decorate the parapet (the
« anterior wall » of Leemans), formerly 568 in number,

whereof about 400 remain, Dr. S d'Oldenburg has already
identified a number of *jâtakas*, or previous lives of Buddha (¹) On the wall itself of the *stûpa* (the « back wall » of
Leemans) Wilsen had early recognized in the upper row
scenes from the last life of the same Çâkya-muni, and
Dr C. M Pleyte has recently published a detailed explanation, according to the *Lalita-vistara*, of the 120 panels
which it contains (²) As regards those of the bottom row,
the greater number still await an interpretation. We remark
at once, by the light of the identifications already made,
that these pictures conform in the order of their succession
to the general rule of the *pradakshinâ* (³), that is to say,
they follow the direction taken by the worshipper who cir-
cumambulated the *stûpa*, keeping it on his right hand. It
results quite naturally from this that, on the walls of the

---

(1) S D OLDENBURG, *Notes on Buddhist Art*, St Petersburg, 1895 (in Rus
sian, translated into English in the *Journal of the American Oriental Society*,
XVIII, 1 January 1897, pp 196-201)

(2) C M PLEYTE, *Die Buddha-Legende in den Skulpturen des Tempels von
Boro Budur*, Amsterdam, 1901 in-4° — In general we are in agreement
with Dr PLEYTE as to the identification of the 120 figured scenes, which in
fact follow religiously the text which they have undertaken to illustrate
All the same, his figure 14 seems to us to represent not « Çakra and the
Guardians of the Cardinal Points », which would convey nothing particularly edifying but the Bodhisattva, supposed to be seated in his mother's
womb beneath the « pavilion of precious stone », at the moment when
Brahmâ brings to him in a cup the drop of honey, quintessence of worlds,
which he has just collected in the magic lotus figured in the preceding
scene side by side with the Conception (*Lalita-vistara*, ed LEFMANN,
pp 63-4) — As to figures 47 and 48, not identified by Dr Pleyte, we believe,
paradoxical as the assertion may seem, that they represent twice the episode of the Bodhisattva's wrestling, first with a single competitor, and then
with all his rivals together (*Lalita vistara*, pp 152-3) This is why on
fig 47 we see a single individual, and on fig 48 all the young Çàkyas, standing motionless and facing the Bodhisattva who also is motionless and standing so inveterate was the horror of the sculptors of Boro-Budur for all
violent movements — See below the additional note on p 269

(3) Cf *Art gréco-bouddhique du Gandhâra*, , p 268

parapet, the scenes follow one another from left to right, while, on the building, the succession is from right to left. On both sides they accompany the visitor who makes the round in the only direction compatible with the religious and auspicious character of the monument

It is all the more expedient not to ignore this law, inasmuch as the identification of the bas-reliefs of this first gallery is, as we have said, very far from complete Our attention was immediately and forcibly drawn to the 120 magnificent panels on the right wall, below the scenes from the last life of Buddha Measuring, like these last, from m. 0,70 to m 0,80 in height by *circa* m 2,40 in length, about three quarters of them have until now — partly through the fault of the artists and much more through the imperfections of the only reproductions which have been published (') — resisted all attempts at explanation At the time of our visit we had at our disposal nothing but the text of the *Divyâvadâna* and the excellent *Guide* of Dr. J. Groneman (²). The latter indicates in the series in question only two identifications, both again due to Dr. S. d'Oldenburg: one is that of the legend of Sudhanakumâra, the other, which is connected with the history of Maitrakanyaka, has quite recently been corroborated and developed by Prof. Speyer and Dr Groneman at the cost of an extensive

(1) We would speak of the enormous folio album of 393 lithographed plates, which is annexed to the already mentioned work of LEEMANS and which was so uselessly and so expensively designed at Java by Wilsen and Schonberg Mulder from 1849 to 1853, then published in Holland from 1855 to 1871 under the care of the Government General of the Dutch Indies

(2) *Boeddhistische Tempelbouwvallen in die Prâgâ-Vallei, de Tjandis Bâraboedoer, Mendoet en Pawon*, by Dr J. GRONEMANN, Semarang-Soerabaia, 1907. The venerable archæologist of Jogyakarta was so kind as to accompany us himself into the galleries and even to the summit of Boro-Budur, we cannot thank him too warmly for his trouble

correction of one of Wilsen's drawings. The reading of the
*Divyâvadâna* gave us at once the key to the illustrations of
two other stories, those of Rudrâyana and of Mândhâtar.
Then two or three of these rebuses in stone themselves
bear their own solutions. On the whole, two thirds of the
120 panels in the row are thus clearly elucidated by direct
comparison of the texts and the originals. At a time
when the government of the Dutch Indies is preparing to
endow the world of letters with photographic reproductions
of all the sculptures of Boro-Budur, it is, perhaps, worth
while to publish, without further delay, these first results,
which cannot but open the way to the complete explanation
of the whole (¹)

I. SOUTH-EASTERN CORNER. — We shall begin our *pradakshinâ*, according to rule, at the gate facing the east, which
formerly constituted the principal entrance. The proof, if any
is needed, is given by the fact that here begins on the upper
series of bas-reliefs, the legend of the Buddha Çâkya-muni.
The 30 pictures of this series which are comprised between
the eastern and southern staircases exhibit the very early
events of his last life, from the preparations for his descent
from the heaven Tushita until, and including, his last re-
birth upon earth. Of the 30 corresponding panels of the

---

(1) In order to save the reader all confusion and to facilitate the references to the already published documents, we should explain that we here
treat in detail only the 120 bas-reliefs called by LEEMANS « lower row of the
back wall of the second gallery », which, occupying the base of plates XVI
to CXXXV of his album, are described (but not identified) from page 194
to page 217 of his book We will retain provisionally between parentheses
the numbers 2-240 assigned to them, — the odd numbers 1 to 239 being
reserved for the 120 bas-reliefs of the « upper row » on this same wall,
the row which reproduced at the top of the same plates and described on
pp 121-193, is entirely devoted to the last life of Buddha and has been
studied by Dr. C M PLEYTE

lower row the first twenty are, as Dr. S d'Oldenburg has briefly recognized, dedicated to the legend of Prince Sudhana We propose, with the aid of the text of the *Divyâvadâna* ('), to enter into the details of this identification, which may be regarded as definitive we shall, at the same time, detect the methods of the sculptors.

*Sudhanakumârâvadâna* — 1. (L , pl. XVI, 2). « Once upon a time, says the text, there were in the country of Pâñcâla two kings, the king of the north and the king of the south .. » The former was virtuous, and his kingdom prosperous, with the second it was quite otherwise. Leemans describes the bas–relief in these terms : « A prince and his wife, seated in a pendopo (²) not far from their palace, are receiving the homage of a great number of persons of rank ». Is it the monarch of the north who is presented to us in all his glory in the midst of his court? Is it the sovereign of the south whom we perceive in the act of deliberating with his ministers concerning the means of restoring prosperity to his kingdom? This it is not in the power of our image-makers to specify.

2. (L., 4). What lends more probability to the first supposition is the fact that in the following picture we must in any case recognize as the king of southern Pâñcâla the prince who, sheltered by his parasol and followed by a numerous cortège, is riding on horseback through a conventional rocky landscape. Under a pretext of hunting, as the text tells us, he is making a tour of inspection through his kingdom, which he finds completely ruined and deserted Perhaps he is even now plotting to rob his flourishing

---

(1) S D'OLDENBURG, *loc. cit* , p. 200, *Divyâvadâna*, XXX, ed COWELL and NEIL, pp 435-461

(2) Probably a corruption of the Sanscrit word *maṇḍapa*, which signifies a kind of hall or open pavilion.

neighbour of the young *nâga* Janmacitraka, who resides in
a pond near the capital of northern Pâñcâla, and who by
« dispensing at an opportune moment the exact amount of
rain which is necessary » assures abundance to the country.
But we can hardly rely upon the resemblance between the
Brahman ascetic who goes before him, bearing in his right
hand a kind of bent pruning-bill, and the snake-charmer
whose witchcraft we are soon to witness

3 (L , 6) The following panel represents no less than
three episodes. On the right the young *nâga*— recognizable,
as on the sculptures of India, by his coiffure of serpents'
heads — asks upon his knees, and obtains, the protection of
the hunter Halaka. In the middle (cf. pl XXXIV, 1) the
same Janmacitraka, grieving and under compulsion, is driv-
en from the midst of the waters and lotuses of his pond by
the influence of incantations pronounced (at his right side)
by a Brahmanic ascetic before a sacrificial altar, fortunately
the hunter, standing (on the other side) with his weapons
in his hands, is watching over him. According to the text,
he is about to put the charmer to death, not without first
having made him annul the effect of his charm  In the
third group (on the left) we must therefore, it seems,
recognize the same Brahman, not reporting to the king,
whose agent he is, a mischance which he has not survived,
but at the moment when he receives from this king his
secret mission It follows, therefore, that, by an exceptional,
but not impossible, arrangement, the episode on the
left, like that on the right, must have preceded in time the
one which they both enclose.

4 (L., 8) Next, in the text, comes a brilliant reception
at the house of the father and mother of the young *nâga* in
honour of the saviour of their son. This is indeed what
the bas-relief represents; but then we are forced to admit

that for this occasion the hunter has donned a princely costume, much superior to his caste It is also necessary to
supply the fact that in the meantime he has received from
his hosts a lasso which never misses

5 (L , 10) The following picture transports us to the
Himâlaya mountains. On the right we perceive the lean
ascetic figure of the old anchorite whose thoughtless chat-
ter has guided the arm of the hunter Halaka. The latter, who
is in a squatting posture, holds the *Kinnari* Manoharâ imprisoned at the end of his infallible lasso, while the companions
of the latter, likewise represented in human form, rush
towards the left in their aerial flight over a pond of lotuses

6 (L., 12) At this moment, we are told, Sudhana, the
Royal Prince of northern Pâñcâla, is passing with a hunting
party · Halaka perceives him, and, in order that his captive
may not be forcibly taken away, presents her to him.
We believe we must twice recognize the hunter in the two
persons respectfully stooping down between the prince and
the fairy, who are standing   in the first row he is offering
his captive, in the second he receives the reward for it.
Leemans was wrong in speaking of « a few women of
rank » · Manoharâ is the only person of her sex. It goes
without saying that, as in our stories, love springs up
immediately between the young people.

7 (L., 14). A king, seated in his palace, in the midst of
his court, is in conversation with a Brahman Without the
text we should never be able to guess that this king is the
father of Sudhana, and that the interlocutor is his *purohita*,
or chaplain, the traitor of the melodrama. The latter is in
the act of perfidiously counselling his master to confide
forthwith to the royal prince the perilous task of subduing
a rebellious vassal, against whom seven expeditions have
already failed.

8. (L., 16). The unhappy prince, in despair at having to leave his beloved Manoharâ, obtains permission to say farewell to his mother before beginning the campaign, and begs her to watch over his young wife. That the bas-relief does, in fact, represent an interview between a mother and a son is clearly proved by the higher seat of the queen and the respectful attitude of the prince.

9 (L , 18) Sudhana, as it is written, stopped « at the foot of a tree » near to the rebellious town. Fortunately, Vaiçravana, one of the four gods who reign in the air, foreseeing his defeat, sends to his aid his general Pâñcika with a troup of *Yakshas*, or genii These are the « five giants, or evil spirits », mentioned by Leemans. The latter continues :

10 (L., 20). « A prince, seated in his house with his wife and two servants, is giving audience to six men, perhaps wise Brahmans, with whom he is engaged in a very animated conversation   » Here, again, it is only from the text that we learn that the locality of the scene is transferred back to Hastinâpura, the capital of northern Pâñcâla, and that the father of Sudhana is asking his Brahman astrologers for an explanation of a bad dream. The wicked chaplain takes advantage of this to prescribe, among other remedies forestalling such bad omens, the sacrifice of a *Kinnari* The king seems to make a gesture of protest, and his wife shows manifest signs of sorrow.

11. (L , 22). But in the heart of the king the instinct of self-preservation at last gains the victory. Thus, on the following picture we see the fairy Manoharâ, with the assent, and even the complicity, of the Queen Mother, flee away gracefully through the air (pl. XXXIV, 2)

12. (L., 24). Meanwhile Sudhana, by the aid of the genii, has triumphed, without any shedding of blood. His

mission fulfilled, he re-enters the capital, and begins by presenting to his father the taxes which he has recovered and the tribute of submission from the rebels  We shall not fail to observe on pl. XXXV, 1 the grace and suitability of the attitudes of the various persons.

13. (L., 26). The prince has no sooner remarked the disappearance of Manohârâ and learned the « unworthiness and ingratitude » of the king than he again has recourse to his mother . it is interesting to compare this interview, in respect of variety of attitude, with that at which we were present above (no. 8).

14. (L., 28). Once again a royal personage is presented to us, seated in his palace in the midst of his court, but this time he has a halo. By this sign we shall recognize here, as well as in nos 17 and 18, Druma, king of the *Kinnaras* It is, therefore, his daughter, Manohârâ, who, crouched at his left, is relating to him the story of her romantic adventures on earth. It results, further, from this that the scene is suddenly transported beyond the first chains of the Himâlayas to the distant and inaccessible country of the genii and fairies. The sculptor does all that he can to vary in imagination, if in execution he hardly succeeds, the places and persons.

15. (L., 30). However Sudhana has set himself to search for his beloved. It occurs to him to enquire of the anchorite, whose incautious words formerly led to the capture of the fairy by the hunter. Now it happens that the faithful Manohârâ, bearing no malice, has left with this same *rishi* a ring and an itinerary, which he is respectively to deliver and to communicate to the prince.

16 (L , 32). Without allowing himself to be discouraged by the length and terrible difficulties of the journey, the hero of the story at last succeeds in reaching the city of king

Druma  At this very moment a crowd of *Kinnaris* is engaged in drawing water in great quantities for the bath of the princess — because, they say, of that human odour which she has brought back with her from the earth, and which will not disappear. Sudhana takes advantage of this to throw the ring of recognition into one of the pitchers, which he recommends to the servant as the first to be emptied over the head of Manoharâ. According to the text the trick is played without the knowledge of the *Kinnari*; but according to pl. XXXV, 2, so elegant in its morbidezza, it cannot be that she is deceived concerning the intention of the gesture and the motive for the recommendation of the young man.

17. (L , 34)  The stratagem succeeds · Druma, warned by his daughter of the arrival of the prince, after threatening « to make mincemeat of him », is appeased, and consents to prove him. The bas-relief represents Sudhana standing at the left, his bow bent, ready to pierce seven palms with one single arrow, on the right Druma, seated and with a halo, witnesses his prowess.

18. (L., 36)  Finally he resolves, as is written and as we can see, to grant the prince his daughter's hand.

19. (L., 38).  The newly-wedded couple lead a life of pleasure in the midst of the gynæceum. According to the customary Indian and Javanese formula these delights are provided by a dancing girl, accompanied by an orchestra of musicians of both sexes  As Leemans has shrewdly remarked, the royal couple do not seem to pay great attention to these amusements . they do not, in fact, suffice to cure the prince of homesickness.

20. (L , 40).  And this is why, on the following and last picture, we see him and his wife signalizing by a distribution of bounty their return to Hastinâpura

Here, we believe, ends, both on the monument and in the text, the story of Sudhana-kumâra and the *Kinnarî* Manohârâ, or, as we may translate it, of Prince Fortunate and the fairy Charming. The ten panels which continue the line as far as the southern staircase seem to be devoted to another story, in which the exchange by sea and land of portraits, or models, of the hero or heroine (¹) plays a role sufficiently picturesque to suggest sooner or later an identification. For the present we prefer to abstain from all hypothesis. The example of the first twenty of these bas-reliefs proves clearly that it would be idle to attempt, without the aid of a text, an explanation founded solely on the intimations of the sculptors. Even a text is not always sufficient : it must also be well chosen. We have just remarked that our image-makers have, except for a few insignificant divergences, followed the letter of the *Divyâvadâna*. We should arrive at a quite different result, if we compared with their work another version of the same legend, preserved in the no less ancient and authentic collection of the *Mahâvastu* (²). There we have no more ques-

---

(1) A story, likewise Indian and Buddhist, translated from the Chinese by M CHAVANNES (*Fables et Contes de l'Inde, extraits du Tripitaka chinois*, in *Actes du XIVᵉ Congrès international des Orientalistes*, I, p 94) begins with this double and reciprocal exchange of ideal models but the continuation of the story does not seem to accord with the scenes of our bas-reliefs We may also recall, in the legend of Mahâkâçyapa, the detail of the fabrication of a type of girl in gold (BEAL, *Romantic Legend*, p 317, SCHIEFNER, *Textes traduits du Kandjour* in *Mélanges Asiat de St Péterb* , VIII, pp 296 sqq , or *Tibetan tales*, p 191).

(2) Ed SENART, II, pp 94-115 On the other hand, the version of the Tibetan *Kanjur*, translated by SCHIEFNER (*Tibetan tales*, pp 44-74), follows exactly the text of the *Divyâvadâna*, that is, as has lately been shown by MM S LÉVI and Ed. HUBER, the canon of the Mûla Sarvâstivâdins, we shall have to return to this point Let us again cite two versions of the *Sudhanakumârâvadâna*, the one from the *Bodhisattvâvadânakalpalatâ* (no. 64), the other (pointed out by

tion of a preamble, containing the adventures of the *nâga*
Janmacitraka and of the snake-charmer : also it is not
with an infallible lasso, but thanks to a « truthful word »,
that the hunter gets possession of the *Kinnari* There is no
longer any wicked chaplain, any expedition of the prince
against a rebel, any bad dream of the king : it simply happens
that Sudhana, having in the excess of his love neglected his
duties, is put into prison by his father, and the fairy is
sent home, but not by way of the air. Then it is with
two hunters, and not with an anchorite, that Manoharâ
leaves her ring and her directions to her lover It is a huge
monkey who transports the prince and his three companions to the town of the *Kinnari*, where the best welcome
awaits him, without having to undergo any trial of
strength or skill In short, if we had at our disposal only
the *Mahâvastu*, scarcely two or three out of twenty bas-
reliefs, for example the capture of the *Kinnari* by the hunter
and the throwing of the ring into the pitcher, would be
susceptible of a detailed interpretation by the aid of the
text and yet it is quite evident to us, thanks to the
constant accord between the *Divyâvadâna* and the sculptures, that the identification with the legend of Prince Sudhana would be on the whole none the less just. This
remark deserves to be borne in mind throughout the delicate enterprise of the explanation of these mute stories.

II. SOUTH-WESTERN CORNER — We should be tempted to
apply it without further delay to the bas-reliefs which we encounter immediately after having passed the point where
the southern staircase crosses the first gallery of the *stûpa*.

Dr S d'OLDENBURG, *Légendes bouddhiques*, St Petersburg, 1894, p 43) from
the *Bhadrakalpâvadâna*, no. 29

Thanks once again to the *Divyâvadâna* (¹), we shall there recognize with absolute certainty the biography of the famous king Mândhâtar, as familiar to the Brahmanic legend as to the Buddhist. But it is only from the eighth bas-relief, counting from the southern entrance (no 76 of Leemans), that the text again comes into line with the monument, to march side by side with it thenceforward as far as the twentieth. What does this mean? Are we to suppose that the first seven pictures relate to another story? The analogy of the south-eastern corner seems to supply stronger reasons for supposing that the first twenty bas-reliefs of the south-western corner were likewise dedicated to a single legend, that is to the *Mândhâtravadâna* : only the sculptor must have commenced at a much earlier point than the compiler. The first goes back, it seems, as far as the incidents which preceded the birth of the hero, whilst the second, in an exordium obviously shortened and drawn up in telegraphic style, gives a rapid résumé of his first youth, and proceeds to expatiate at large on the exploits of his reign. Until we have fuller information, everything leads us to believe that the story of Mândhâtar commenced at the corner of the southern staircase and not right in the middle of one of the faces of this twenty-cornered gallery, and that it terminated, like that of Sudhana, at the fourth angle after the staircase.

When we had arrived at this point in our hypothesis, the reading of the *Bodhisattvâvadânakalpalatâ* came to confirm it in a most unexpected manner. The abridged and colour-

---

(1) XVII Ed. Cowell and Neil, pp. 210 228. — Cf a Pâli version in the *Jâtaka*, no. 258 (ed., II, p. 310; trans., II, p. 216), another Tibetan version in the *Kanjur* (Schiefner, *Mél. As. de St Pét.*, pp. 440 sqq , or *Tibetan tales*, pp. 1-20), and a third Sanskrit version in the *Bodhisattvâvadânakalpalatâ*, no 4 (*Bibl. Indica*, New Series, no 730, pp. 123-153).

less version of the Pâli *Jâtaka* no. 258 had been of no
assistance whatever. Neither had we been helped by the
Tibetan text of the *Kanjur* in the translation of Schiefner,
which, in fact, follows with great fidelity the *Divyâvadâna*,
that is the version of the Mûla-Sarvâstivâdins Kshemendra does the same, but for once, in the midst of his insipid *concetti*, he has, at the beginning, preserved for us one
topical detail (st. 8-10):

« One day Uposhadha, anxious to assure the protection of the anchorites by the destruction of the demons,
mounted on horseback, and began to go through the
hermitages.

« There certain *rishis* of royal race were holding a vessel
ready for a sacrifice celebrated with a view to obtaining a
son  very hot with the fatigue of the long journey, the
king drank the contents at one draught.

« No one was there to prevent him, and, because he had
swallowed the contents of the enchanted vessel, the monarch,
on returning to his capital, found that he had conceived.. »

All the versions agree in telling us that there came on the
head of king Uposhadha an enormous tumour, very soft to
touch and in nowise painful When it had matured, there
issued from it a fine boy, for the charge of whose nurture
the 60,000 women of the royal harem disputed. To the
wonderful circumstances of his birth he owes his double
name of Mûrdhaja and Mândhâtar — or even, by confusion
of these two, Mûrdhâtar But what is of special importance
to us is that the Kashmir poet furnishes us with the only
link which was missing in the interpretation of the bas-
reliefs ([1]).

*Mândhâtravadâna* — Henceforth nothing, indeed, prevents

---

(1) Cf nearly the same story in *Mahâbhârata*, *Dronaparvan*, LXII

us from seeing in nos. 1 (L., pl. XLVI, 62) and 2 (L., 64) the
rich alms which King Uposhadha himself bestows and causes
to be bestowed with a view to obtaining a son. The reason
for the expedition represented in no. 3 (L , 66) is no longer
hidden from us it is that undertaken by the king (who in
this case travelled in a litter) for the protection of the
anchorites. No 4 (L , 68) takes us straight to a hermitage of
the *rishis*; and we believe that we can see there the magic
vessel to which Uposhadha owed in such an unusual manner
the fulfilment of his desires. In any case, it is in the following picture (no. 5; L , 70) that the child so much desired is
at last seen. Again, nos. 6 and 7 are probably there simply
as padding, and they represent, the first (L., 72) the horo-
scope of the future *cakravartin* or sovereign monarch of the
world, the second (L., 74) the donation intended to recom-
pense the astrologer These last incidents, like that of the
alms, are very commonplace, it is easily intelligible that the
compiler of the *Divyâvadâna* should have dispensed with a
further repetition of them. On the other hand, the sculptors
of Boro-Budur never fail to emphasize, as hints to visit-
ing pilgrims, these edifying scenes of virtue in practice. But let us proceed · we are now on firm ground,
supported by both a written and a figured form of the tradition in mutual accord.

8. (L., 76) « Having become a royal prince, Mândhâtar
goes to see the country. » We do, indeed, perceive the
young prince at the moment when, starting on his journey, he respectfully takes leave of his father

9. (L., 78) During his absence the latter dies. Among the
marvels susceptible of representation which are adjuncts
of his coronation the text signalizes the sudden appearance
of the « seven jewels » of the *cakravartin*. This is why we
see depicted here among the surroundings of the prince, who

has become king, a disc, a jewel, a horse, an elephant, a woman, a general, and a minister.

10. (L , 80) The *Dıvyâvadâna* tells us, immediately after, that not far from Vaiçâlî there is a charming wood, in which reside five hundred *rıshıs*. Now extraneous noises are the scourge of pious meditations  A surly anchorite, annoyed by the noise of certain cranes, breaks their wings by a curse. King Mândhâtar, angered in his turn by this hardness of heart, requests the hermits to depart from his dominions. The bas-relief also shows us birds placed on the ground between the king, who is standing in conversation with a stooping courtier, and two *rıshıs*, recognizable by their big chignons and their rosaries, who are fleeing by the route of the air

11. (L , 82). Mândhâtar, continuing his tour, decides not to have the fields of his kingdom any more cultivated ; for the corn will rain down from heaven. The peasants do, in fact, gather up before his eyes bunches of ears of rice, which have fallen from the clouds · we expressly say bunches, and not sheaves, because in Java the rice is not cut, but gathered by hand

12. (L., 84). In the same way Mândhâtar decides that his subjects will no longer need to cultivate cotton, or to spin, or to weave. Immediately there fall from the clouds pieces of woven material, which the people have only to catch in their flight and to fold up for subsequent use (pl XXXVI, 1).

13. (L., 86). Somewhat vexed, because his subjects attribute partly to themselves the merit of all these miracles, Mândhâtar causes for seven days a shower of gold, but only within his own palace. This explains why, beside the king and his ministers, we see here only women, engaged in collecting the treasures pouring from jars set amid the clouds.

14. (L., 88). Finally king Mândhâtar, preceded by the seven jewels of the *cakravartin* and followed by his army, sets out for the conquest of the universe . the feet of none of the persons touch the ground

15 (L., 90). Here the text, in order better to depict the insatiable greed of the human heart, enters upon a series of repetitions impossible to reproduce on stone. King Mândhâtar has for a herald *(purojava)* a *yaksha*, or genius, who at each fresh conquest informs him of what still remains for him to conquer. On the monument we are in the presence, once for all, of this periodical council meeting : for the rest, the sculptor has given to the *yaksha* the ordinary appearance of a Brahmanic minister.

16. (L , 92). On the following panel he conducts Mândhâtar at a swoop to the summit of his prodigious fortune. Two kings, exactly alike and both with haloes, are seated in a palace side by side on seats of equal height, in the midst of their court. Without the slightest doubt the moment chosen is that when Çakra, the Indra of the Gods, has, on the mere mental wish of the king of men, yielded up to him the half of his throne : and there was no difference to be seen between them, except that the eyes of Çakra did not blink.

17. (L , 94) If this interpretation were at all doubtful, it would be confirmed by the picture immediately following, which represents a combat between the gods and the Asuras. Thanks to their human ally, the gods triumph.

18-20. But from this moment a certain hesitation begins to manifest itself between the text and the bas-reliefs, and immediately the uncertainty in our identifications reappears. According to the *Divyâvadâna*, Mândhâtar after the battle asks : « Who is conqueror? » — « The king », is the reply of his ministers; whereupon the infatuated king carries his presumption so far as to wish to dethrone Indra, in order to reign alone in his place But this time he has gone too far Scarcely has he conceived this thought than he is thrust from the height of the heavens down to the earth; and he has hardly time, before he dies, to pronounce a few edifying words concerning the excess of his blind ambition Consequently no. 18 (L ,96), which is quite analogous to no. 15, should represent the last consultation of the king with his minister, no. 19 (L., 98) should be dedicated to the last words which he pronounces after his fall, while on the left Çakra, standing and with a halo, should turn away from him, then finally no. 20 (L., 100) should show us his funeral and, as befits a *cakravartin*, the depositing of his ashes in a *stûpa*. But these explanations, plausible though they may be, have not the obviousness of the preceding.

*Çibi-jâtaka.* — We should say the same of those which we might propose for the ten bas-reliefs which continue the series as far as the western staircase, excepting the sixth (L., pl. LXXI, 112) It seems indubitable that this latter represents the essential episode of the *Çibi-jâtaka*, that is to say, that previous life in which the future Buddha ransomed a dove from a falcon at the price of an equal weight of his flesh (¹) At least, nothing is wanting to the scene, neither the Bodhisattva seated in his palace, nor the bird of prey perched on a neighbouring tree, nor the

---

(1) It is well known that we still have no Indian *Buddhist* version of this form of the legend Except for the Brahmanic epopee, it is known to us only from the allusions of the Chinese pilgrims Fa-hien (trans LEGGE, p 30), Sung Yun (trans CHAVANNES, *B É F E -O* , III, p. 427), Hiuan-tsang (trans Stan JULIEN, I, p 137), and from Chinese versions, such as that which was retranslated from Chinese by M Ed HUBER, *Sûtrâlankâra*, Paris, 1908, p 330, and from Tibetan by SCHMIDT, *Der Weise und der Thor*, p 120.

pigeon, which appears twice, once placed on the back of the throne and once in one of the plates of the scales (pl. XXXVI, 2). This time the bas-relief would be sufficient for its own interpretation. We feel how rare is such a case among all these sculptures, and the greater number of those of the upper row — which in the south-west corner extend from the birth of Çâkya-muni to the four excursions which determined his vocation — are not more expressive.

III NORTH-WESTERN CORNER. — The bas-reliefs of the third portion of the first gallery (on the right-hand wall) are known to represent in the upper row the departure of Buddha from his home, that is to say, his entry into the religious life, and all the trials which preceded the attainment of perfect illumination. Out of the 30 in the lower row at least 22, and perhaps 25, are, as we shall show step by step, consecrated to the celebrated historical legend of king Rudrâyaṇa. Again it is in the *Divyâvadâna* that we may read it (¹) In the *B É. F. E -O.* of 1906, M. Ed. Huber gave, in accordance with the Chinese translation and the Sanskrit text, an analysis of it, from which it clearly appears that this *avadâna*, like the preceding ones, is only an extract from the *Vinaya* of the Mûla-Sarvâstivâdins. In this connection M Huber had seemed to discern through the drawings of Wilsen that one of the episodes of the story, viz that of the two cats (cf. below, no. 17), was represented at Boro-Budur, but, justly discouraged by the inexactitudes of the only accessible reproductions, he was obliged to abandon this clue. Direct comparison of the text with the monument has permitted us to follow it up from one end to the other.

_____

(1) XXXVII, ed. COWELL and NEIL, pp 544-586 It is known that BUR-NOUF translated a fragment of it in his *Introduction à l'histoire du Bouddhisme indien*, pp 341-344.

The extremely exact and sufficiently detailed résumé published by M. Huber, to which we refer the reader, will allow
us this time to insist a little less upon the history and a
little more upon the sculptures

*Rudrâyanâvadâna.* — First of all, we must state that we do
not see any way of making the story on the stone begin at
the corner of the western staircase, but only at the first reen-
tering angle after the face intersected by that staircase Do
the three first bas-reliefs on the left of the entrance, in which
Çakra plays his accustomed rôle of *deus ex machinâ*, form a
whole by themselves, or must they not rather be a continuation of those on the right? Or, on the contrary, may we not
some day come to think that the story of Rudrâyana also
comprises a prelude omitted in the *Divyâvadâna*? Only the
chance of reading some Indian text may some day tell us,
even if we have not to await a solution by a Tibetan or a
Chinese translation.

1 For the moment we begin with the *Divyâvadâna* at
no. 128, pl LXXIX of Leemans, where Rudrâyana, king of
Roruka, questions merchants, who have come from Râjagriha, the capital of Bimbisâra, concerning the merits of
their master

2 (L., 130). A king is seated in his palace, on his right
a courtier holds in both hands a rectangular tablet . this
must represent the letter which, in the first fire of his
enthusiasm, the sovereign of Roruka resolved to write to
his cousin of Magadha. Further, two suppositions are permissible if the king represented is the sender, his name is
Rudrâyana, if, as seems more natural, he is the addressee,
he is Bimbisâra. We do not ask our sculptors to decide this
by attributing to each of the two monarchs a characteristic
physiognomy : that would be exacting too much from them.

3. (L., 132) Then follows a grand reception to welcome,

or to say farewell to, the improvised ambassadors, in a royal court no less uncertain. The *Dwyâvadâna* says no word regarding this function . but the meaning of the mise en scéne is not to be doubted; and, for the rest, it is sufficient to compare it with the 112ᵗʰ bas-relief of the upper row (L., pl. CXXVII, 223, or Pleyte, fig. 112), which represents a grand dinner offered to Buddha. There, as here, the table is laid in the Javanese fashion : from twenty to thirty bowls, containing divers seasonings or viands, surround an enormous pot of rice, which constitutes the principal dish — in fact, a regular *rijstaffel* of ten centuries ago.

4.(L , 134). This time the attitudes of the minor persons and the obvious character of the offering define very distinctly the hero and locality of the scene · Bimbisâra is receiving at Râjagriha the casket of jewels which Rudrâyana has sent to him together with his letter.

5. (L , 136) The case of stuffs sent in return by the king of Magadha to his new friend occupies the middle of the scene . but the pensive air of the king and the respectful immobility of the attendants make it doubtful whether we have to do with Bimbisâra deciding upon his present, or Rudrâyana receiving it and already wondering what he can give in exchange (¹).

6. (L., 138). However that may be, the following bas-relief again represents Bimbisâra, receiving from Rudrâyana his precious cuirass. This object has been so terribly maltreated in the representation, where it is absolutely unre-

(1) We were somewhat inclined towards this last supposition  but, all taken into account, it seems impossible to establish a regular alternation between the heroes of these first six bas-reliefs  If we must admit any symmetry between them, we should rather be inclined to think that in nos 1-3 the scene is at Roruka, and in the three following at Râjagriha. Then we return to Roruka until no. 13.

cognizable, that we think it advisable to give a photographic reproduction (pl. XXXVII, 1).

7. (L., 140). The total absence of landscape is sufficiently rare to render it worth our while to direct attention to it here. The whole height and breadth of the panel are occupied by a procession, in which the place of honour, between the arms of a man perched on an elephant, belongs to a kind of rolled up *kakemono*, on which we know that the silhouette of Buddha is painted Doubtless, the scene is taken at the moment when the inhabitants of Roruka, who are come out to meet this supreme gift from Bimbisâra, bring it back with great pomp to their town.

8. (L., 142) This picture is quite analogous to no 1, not to mention that it is likewise placed at the turn of an angle · only, in the interval the subject of the conversation has changed in a most edifying manner. It is no longer the merits of their king which are the boast of the people of Râjagriha, but those of Buddha himself

9 (L , 144). Rudrâyana, as soon as converted, begged to receive instruction from a monk, and the master despatched to him the reverend Mahâkâtyâyana . a monk is, in fact, sitting at the right of the king, and even on a higher seat than he. In the most gratuitous — and also the most perplexing — manner the designer considered it necessary to surmount the shaven head of this monk (cf pl XXXVII, 2) with the protuberance of the *ushnîsha*, which is special to Buddhas Let us add that Mahâkâtyâyana seems, in the midst of the edified hearers, to be making a gesture of refusal  what he refuses is, doubtless, to preach in the gynæceum of the king . that is the business of the nuns

10. (The drawing is missing in L.). Thus the following panel shows us the nun Çailâ preaching from the height of a throne to the king and four of his wives, who are seated on

the ground (pl. XXXVIII, 1). Behind her a servant seems to be ordering three armed guards to forbid anyone to enter the harem during the sermon. It will be noticed that — doubtless from modesty — the nun and, in a general way, the women are seated with their legs bent under them, and not crossed in the same manner as those of the monks and the men (¹)

11. (The drawing does not appear in L.) The scene is obviously the same, except in two points. Firstly, a second nun, squatting behind Çailâ, represents doubtless the *quorum* necessary for an ordination. In the second place, there are now only women in the audience, and the place formerly occupied by the king is taken by a third *bhikshunî* kneeling. Immediately the text invites us to recognize in this novice queen Candraprabhâ, who, conscious of her approaching death, has obtained from Rudrâyaṇa authority to enter into religion (pl. XXXVIII, 2).

12. (The drawing is not to be found in L.). That on the following bas-relief the king is again in conversation with his favourite wife would likewise not be understood, did we not learn elsewhere that Candraprabhâ was born again in the nearest heaven, and that she promised her husband to return after her death to advise him as to the ways and means of reunion with her in another life. Here she is fulfilling her promise (pl. XXXIX, 1)

13 This explains also why the very next morning Rudrâyana decides to go and be ordained a monk by Buddha, and announces to his son Çıkhaṇḍın that he abdicates

---

(1) In the same order of ideas we may again notice that the real *padmâsana*, with the legs closely crossed, the soles of the feet turned upwards and the right foot forward, is reserved by our sculptors for Buddha alone (cf. on the upper corners of our plates XXXVII, 2 and XL, 1 the image of the Bodhisattva, already represented in the form of a Buddha).

in his favour (pl XXXIX, 2). In this case the drawing of
L , pl XCI, 152, reproduces only the upper part of the characters, and commits the very grave fault of making the
king's interlocutor a woman : it is obviously a man

14 (L., 154). If the four preceding pictures are either
totally or partially missing from Wilsen's album, the following one is, in compensation, more than complete The
designer began once more — with the aggravation of an
indication of locks of hair covering an imaginary *ushnîsha*
— the mistake of which he had already been guilty in
no 9 : of a monk with a round, shorn head he made a
Buddha! Furthermore the two scenes nos 9 (pl. XXXVII, 2)
and 14 (pl XXXIX, 3), which are quite symmetrical, bring
face to face with one another, in the customary surroundings of a royal residence, the type of the monk and the type
of the king. Only the continuation of the text reveals to us
that this time the monk is no longer Mahâkâtyâyana, but
Rudrâyaṇa himself, who has just been ordained by Buddha
in person at Râjagṛiha. In a long dialogue he rejects, for his
first round in public as a mendicant monk, the seductive
offers of Bimbisâra. You may well imagine that it was
impossible to pass by so fine an opportunity for reproducing,
both on the monument and in the text, the famous episode
of the temptation of the future Çâkya-muni by this same
Bimbisâra.

15 (L., 156) The bas-relief is divided into two parts
by a tree, and the different orientation of the characters
emphasizes this separation. On the right, at Râjagṛiha, the
monk Rudrâyana (still wrongly represented by Wilsen as a
Buddha) learns from merchants, natives of his country,
that his son Çikhaṇḍin is conducting himself badly on the
throne, and he promises to go and put things in order. On
the left, at Roruka, King Çikhandin is warned by his evil

ministers that there is a rumour of his father's early return,
and he forms with them a plot to assassinate him. In the
background is to be seen already, in her private palace, the
Queen Mother, who in this portion of the story will play
a very important part.

16. (L., 158) The panel is divided like the preceding one,
and the separating tree is, in this case, further reinforced
by a little edicula, which serves as porch to a palisaded
interior (pl. XL, 1) : nevertheless the two scenes take place at
Roruka. On the right king Çikandin learns from several persons (one of whom, being armed, is perhaps his emissary,
the executioner) of his father's death and last words. On
the left, filled with remorse for a double crime, the murder
of a father and the murder of a saint, he comes to seek
refuge with his mother : doubtless this is the moment chosen by the latter to disburden him at least of his crime of
parricide by revealing to him, truly or falsely, that
Rudrâyana is merely his reputed father

17. (L , 160) There remains the task of exonerating him
from the not less inexpiable murder of an *arhat*, or Buddhist saint. Is it worth while to recall the ingenious stratagem
conceived by the evil ministers in order to prove that there
is no *arhat,* or, at least, that those who pretend to be such
are only charlatans? On the left we perceive, each hidden
under his *stûpa* (which Leemans wrongly took for « vases
in the form of globes »), the two cats which have been train-
ed to answer to the name of the two first saints formerly
converted by Mahâkâtyâyana On the right the Queen
Mother and Çikhandin take part in the demonstration,
which to them appears convincing.

18. (L., 162). The frame contains two distinct episodes.
On the right king Cikhandin passes, seated in a litter,
surely he has just ordered each person in his suite to throw

a handful of dust on Mahâkâtyâyana, with whom his relations have never been cordial On the left — for once,
correctly represented by Wilsen — the monk, already
free from the heap of dust, under which he has miraculously
preserved his life, announces to the good ministers Hiru
and Bhiru the approaching and inevitable destruction of
the infidel city of Roruka.

19. (L., 164) Like Çikhandin in his palace, we witness
the rain of jewels which, according to the prophet, must
precede the fatal rain of sand. The eagerness of the inhabitants to gather up the precious objects, cast down from vessels (¹) in the height of the clouds, is painted with a
vivaciousness which seemed to us quite deserving of reproduction (pl XL, 2). In the first row a boat which is
being loaded with jewels proves that the good ministers
have not forgotten a very practical recommendation of
Mahâkâtyâyana (²).

20 (L , 166). The destinies are accomplished : Roruka
has been buried with almost all its inhabitants. When the
curtain rises again, we are in the village of Khara, the first
halting-place of Mahâkâtyâyana on the route of his return
to India. The tutelary goddess of Roruka, who has followed
him in his flight through the air, is detained at Khara by
an imprudent promise : but, on leaving her, the monk presents her with a souvenir in the shape of his goblet, over

---

(1) These vessels, which we have already encountered above (Mândhâtar,
no. 13, L., pl. LVIII, 86), seem to be a current accessory of Indian imagination Compare the passage from the *Jâtâkamâlâ*, XV, 15 (ed. KERN, p 97,
trans SPEYER, p 138), where the clouds pour down « like overturned vessels »

(2) Let us remark in passing that the departure of the two good ministers in ships scarcely fits in with the localization (which was surely already
known to the author of the text, and which M HUBFR recently treated again
in the *B É F E -O* , VI, 1906, pp 335 340) of Roruka in Central Asia.

which a *stûpa* is raised It is the inauguration of this monument which is represented on the bas-relief · on the right is the chief of the village, on the left, with a lamp in one hand and a fan in the other, is the goddess herself, behind them crowd the laity of both sexes and the musicians.

21 (L., 168). We are carried to the next halting-place, Lambaka. Çyâmâka, the young layman, the sole companion who remained with Mahâkâtyâyana, receives from the people of the country an offer of the throne A miracle, which is frequent in the texts, but unsuitable for representation on stone (the shade of the tree under which he stands remains stationary, in order to shelter him), has revealed to them the excellence of his merit.

22. (L., 170). We pass on to the third halting-place, Vok-kâna. Here Mahâkâtyâyana leaves to her who in a former existence was his mother his beggar's staff, a fresh pretext for building a *stûpa*. As in no 20, we are present at the inauguration of the monument At least, the continuation of the narrative accords with the introduction of this subject on the bas-reliefs in too striking a manner for the identification not to impose itself

Better still : just as Leemans' nos. 166, 168 and 170 set before us religious feasts interrupted, thanks to a not excessive desire for variety, by a profane subject, so nos. 172, 174 and 176 intercalate a land scene between two maritime episodes. Now this intervening scene (L., 174) represents the entrance of a monk — notwithstanding the drawing of Wilsen, who lends him hair and jewels, it is indeed a monk — into the palisaded enclosure of a town, whilst a group of inhabitants approaches to give him welcome. Here again, with the text in our hands, it seems difficult not to recognize the return of Mahâkâtyâyana to Çrâvastî. Then, the two pictures in which we see a boat just drawing near to a bank would represent, no less scrupulously than do the texts, the two foundations of Hiruka and Bhiruka by the two ministers Hiru and Bhiru after their flight by water from Roruka  Thus, in spite of the terribly commonplace character of the two disembarcations, we venture to make the following identifications

23  (L , 172) Landing of Hiru and foundation of Hiruka.

24. (L., 174)  Return of Mahâkâtyâyana to Çrâvastî.

25. (L , 176)  Landing of Bhiru on the future site of Bhiruka or Bhirukaccha (¹)

The double repetition of the scene of the *stûpa* and of the ship will be noticed  We do not see any plausible explanation of it, unless we suppose that the sculptor, after having skipped more than one important incident in the history of Rudrâyana, has been obliged, in order to fill up the space for decoration, to lengthen out the epilogue. In fact, we must not forget that the bas-reliefs, which were carved *in situ* and in the very stones whose juxtaposition constituted the monument, could be neither removed nor replaced. There is no absurdity, therefore, in supposing that the artist, on approaching the last angle before the northern staircase, perceived that he still had to fill five or six panels, of which he could not decently devote more than two to the *Kinnara-jâtaka*  he will then have rid himself from his embarrassment by a double repetition, which moreover was justified by the texts, while bringing right to their destination all the few persons who had escaped from Roruka, that is the goddess, Çyâmâka, Mahâkâtyâyana, and the two good ministers.

---

(1) Apparently it is Bharukaccha, the Barygaza of the Greeks and the present Bharoch, or Broach, which is meant.

*Kinnara-jâtaka.* — We may say, furthermore, that the
two last panels of this portion of the gallery (L., 178 and 180)
are likewise duplicates. The only appreciable difference is
that the same prince is standing on the first to overhear —
and seated on the second to listen to — the discourse of
the same pair of *Kinnaras*. Such is, in fact, the name that
we do not hesitate to give to the « human phenomena »,
who are related to the *Gandharvas* by their musical talents (¹)
and who are represented here with birds' wings and
feet (pl. XLI, 1). The Buddhist art of India and the Far
East seems to have taken no account whatever of the
concurrent tradition which claims that the *Kinnaras* are
human monsters with horses' heads (²). When it has not
been considered more suitable to give them, as above
(pll. XXXIV, 2 and XXXV, 2) in the illustration of the Sudhana-kumâra legend, a purely anthropomorphic aspect, it is
usually a kind of harpy that is represented under this name.
This strange combination of the bust of a man or a woman,
with or without arms, grafted on to the body of a bird, is
found almost everywhere. It fits as well into the corners
of the pediments of the temple of Mârtând in Kashmir as
into those of the metopes of the Parambanan temple in
Java. It has continued to be especially frequent in the decorative and religious art of Siam. In India proper it appears
in the paintings of Ajantâ, and we have remarked elsewhere,
in a sculpture inscribed on the « Tower of Victory » at

---

(1) *Gandhabbaputta* they are called by st 7 of *Jât* no 481 (IV, p 252,
l 16)

(2) It is not that monsters of this kind are unknown to ancient Indian
sculpture ; but the woman with a horse's head, who, on a medallion of the
balustrade of Bodh-Gayâ (Râj MITRA, *Buddha-Gayâ*, pl XXXIV, 2) and of
that of the smaller *stûpa* at Sânchî, is carrying away a man, is at the commencement of *Jât.* no 432, which relates her history, simply called a *yakkhinî
assamukhî*

Chitor (XV<sup>th</sup> Century), « a double pair of *Kinnaras* », per-fectly analogous to those of Boro-Budur (¹). Perhaps, under the *Kinnara-jâtaka* rubric, they were not otherwise treated even on the old railing of Barhut : unfortunately we can only judge of this by a wretched sketch from a half-broken stone, and there is at present nothing to prove that, as Cunningham suggests, the leaves, or the feathers, which terminate the busts of the two monsters, « must have separ-ated their human trunks from their bird legs » (²)

We consider ourselves none the less authorized by this inscription to consider the two numbers 178 and 180 as a replica of this same *jâtaka*  what other justification can be given for the edifying character of these scenes and for their introduction into the series? Certainly the subject is once again borrowed from one of the previous lives of the Master  the only question is exactly which « re-birth » is concerned  Here the two prolix pictures of Boro-Budur will be of assistance in determining retroactively the real identification of the bas-relief of Barhut, so poor in details. It is here quite clear, for example, that the scene of the adventure is a rocky solitude ˙ we must at once put aside a certain episode in the *Takkâriya-jâtaka* (no 481), since it takes place in a royal court, where two *Kinnaras*, put in to a cage, refuse to display their talents. Moreover, we cannot fix upon the *Candakinnara-jâtaka* (no 485), although that

----

(1) We brought back a photograph of it  the inscription is *Kinnarayug-mayugma*

(2) CUNNINGHAM. *Stûpa of Barhut*, p 69 and pl XXVII, 12 (cf above, p 53). GRUNWEDEL, *Buddhistische Studien*, p 92 points out that the connec-tion between the *Kinnara-jâtaka* of Barhut and that of Boro-Budur has already been shown by Heer J -W YZERMAN in the *Bijdragen tot de Taal-, Land- en Volkenkunde van Ned Ind* , Vijfde Volgreeks, d I, afl 4, pp 577-579 Since the above was written representations of *Kinnaras* have also been found on the paintings of Central Asia

too has for scenery a piece of jungle   for our king is evidently not thinking of killing the male *Kinnara*, in order to
get possession of the female. It therefore remains for us to
adopt the *Bhallâtiya-jâtaka* (no. 504), in which also we
have nothing but conversations in a mountainous district ('). It is a most touching love story  The king of
Benares, while out hunting, surprises in the depth of the
wood the extraordinary behaviour of two of these marvellous beings, and enquires why they cover each other
alternately with tears and caresses. He learns that 697
years ago they were separated for one single night by the
sudden swelling of a river; and in their life of a thousand
years the loving couple have never yet been able to forget
this cruel separation, or to console each other entirely for
those few hours irremediably lost to their happiness. It will
be observed on pl. XLI, 1, that the sculptor has considered
it his duty to maintain the hierarchical order, and has placed
the male in front of the female, as if he were the interlocutor
of the king: but in the text of the *jâtaka*, just as in the famous
Dantesque episode of Francesca di Rimini, it is the woman,
always the more ready to speak, who relates their common
adventure, whilst her lover stands silent by her side

IV. NORTH-EASTERN CORNER  — Altogether we have offered certain, or at least extremely probable, interpretations
of 27 out of the 30 panels bordering upon the preceding corner  The 30 still to be considered are much more refractory
to all attempts at explanation. After Messrs. S. d'Oldenburg,

---

(1) In other words, relying on the replica of Boro-Budur, we believe we
may for the bas relief of Barhut leave aside the identifications proposed by
CUNNINGHAM (*loc  cit.*) and Prof. HULTZSCH (*Ind  Ant*, XXI, 1892, p. 226)
and advocate that of Mr S J WARREN and of Dr S D'OLDENBURG, who,
besides, is right in believing it as not more demonstrable merely by the aid
of the sole Indian document than the two others (*loc. cit.*, p. 191)

Speyer and Groneman we can quote as certain only the
dentification of the *Maitrakanyakâvadâna* (') For the rest,
it would be useless to launch out into hypotheses, where
we still lack the elements of proof, and even more so to
renew the purely descriptive commentary which Leemans
has given in full . for there is no task more idle than to describe bas-reliefs without understanding them. Let us say in
defence of the Dutch archæologist that access to the sources
was for him almost impossible, and that he had at least the
perspicacity to recognize « that the pictures of the lower
series do not form a continuation of those of the upper ».

On the north-eastern corner these latter extend from
Buddha's attainment of the Bodhi to his first preaching.
Below, the legend of Maitrakanyaka is related to us between
two others, of whose titles we are still ignorant. Our first
care, therefore, must be to determine as exactly as possible
where it commences and where it ends. The texts which
have preserved it for us (²), and to which we are indebted
for the explanation of the meaning of the bas-reliefs, agree
in rendering the story in two symmetrical parts, separated by
a turning-point Maitrakanyaka, the orphan son of a ship-
owner, follows at first various trades, in order to provide
for the needs of his mother, to whom he successively offers
gains increasing according to a geometrical progression

(1) Cf the already-quoted paper of Dr S d'Oldenburg, the Guide of
Dr J. Groneman, pp 66-67, Speyer, *Bijdragen tot de Taal-, Land-en Volkenkunde van Ned Indie*, 1906, v^de Deel , and for the comparison with Burmese
and Siamese images, Grunwedel, *Buddh Stud* , p 97

(2) The *Avadâna-Çataka* (ed Speyer in *Bibl Buddhica*, p 193, and trans.
Feer in the *Ann du Musee Guimet*) gives us, it seems, a canonical version of
it No XXXVIII of the *Divyâvadâna* (ed Cowell and Neil, p. 586) is already
a literary rifacimento Further, let us quote *Bodhisattvâvadânakalpalatâ*,
no 92, *Bhadrakalpâvadâna*, no. 28, and, for comparison, *Jâtaka*, nos 41,
82, 104, 369, 439. A Chinese version has been re-translated by Beal, *Romantic Legend*, p 342.

of 4, 8, 16, and 32 *kârshâpânas*, but, as she wishes to prevent
him from following his father's example and going to sea,
he forgets himself so far as to kick her prostrate head. The
wreck of the ship which he has fitted out marks the culminating point in the story, of which the second part corresponds, point for point, with the first. Having escaped death,
Maitrakanyaka is, as a reward for his works, successively
and amorously received at each halting-place by 4, 8,
16 and 32 nymphs (*apsaras*) . but his adventurous spirit
leads him still further and further, at last into a hell where
sons who strike their mothers are punished. This symmetry must have been welcome to the sculptor, and must
have dictated to him in his turn the arrangement of his bas-
reliefs Now the scene of the wreck is figured on no. 216
of Leemans (pl CXXIII), and the story does not end
until no 224 One might suppose, therefore, that the
four pictures which precede no. 216 are likewise consecrated to Maitrakanyaka. One thing at least is certain, namely
that he appears, already accompanied by his mother, on
no. 212, at the corner of the north and east façades of the
*stûpa*. For the following ones we are entirely in accord
with Prof. Speyer and Dr. Groneman.

1 (The drawing of L., no. 212, pl. CXXI, is almost
entirely missing). Under a *mandapa* Maitrakanyaka, seated
on the ground with his hands joined, is offering to his mother
a purse, which he has just placed before her upon a tray
adorned with flowers (pl XLI, 2). The bystanders are
numerous : behind the mother are seven women, standing
or crouching; behind the son may be counted five of his
companions. Quite at the left a house is seen in outline
We reproduce in plate XLI, 2 only the central group, which
alone is of importance for the identification of the scene.
It will be observed that the left elbow of the mother is as

though the joint were twisted · let us not hasten to cry out that this is a mistake on the part of the sculptor, or even a deformity, at least according to the native taste . the skilfully dislocated arms of the Javanese dancing-girls bend no otherwise in this position.

2. (L , 214) An edifice cuts the panel into two distinct parts  On the right Maitrakanyaka is practising his last sedentary occupation, that of a goldsmith, as is proved by the small balance held by a woman, who may be either his mother or a simple customer  In the foreground a purse, bigger than that of the preceding picture, is doubtless supposed to contain the 32 *kài shâpanas*. The four legendary gifts would thus have been reduced by the sculptor to two. — On the left, in fact, despite the poor state of the bas-relief, we see the mother of Maitrakanyaka vainly prostrated at his feet (pl XLII, 1) Wilsen had given her a moustache, which cut short all identification , and this explains why that of Dr S d'Oldenburg, based upon the lithographs, began only at the following picture, that of the wreck

3 (L , 216) The supplications of his mother failed to restrain Maitrakanyaka, on the right we see the sad end of his sea-voyage, on the left his encounter with the four first nymphs  Here the sculptor seems to have been afraid neither of repeating himself nor of wearying the spectator by the sight of so many pretty women, for we perceive successively :

4. (L., 218) The encounter with the 8 nymphs,

5 (L , 220)  The encounter with the 16 nymphs (in point of fact they are 11);

6. (L , 222)  The encounter with the 32 nymphs (14 in reality)

7. (L., 224). At last the mania for roaming has led Maitrakanyaka as far as a town of hell (pl XLII, 2) · apparently

he is gathering information from the terrible guardian of the
place, whilst in the background we perceive, with a burning wheel upon its head, the condemned soul whose
place, unwittingly, he has come to take. For the rest both
wear the same costume, with the exception of a few details
in the form of their jewels But these differences, slight
though they be, exclude, it appears, the possibility of recognizing Maitrakanyaka a second time in the sufferer There
is every reason for believing, on the contrary, that, owing
to a scruple of the artist, just as we did not see him strike
his mother, so also we are not witnesses of his punishment like his crime, his chastizement is only suggested
We must not forget, in fact, that he is the Bodhisattva in
person. According to the texts, the wheel of fire has scarcely mounted upon his head, than he forms a vow to
endure this terrible suffering for ever with a view to the
salvation of humanity : whereupon he is immediately freed
from all suffering Does the left part of the panel forthwith represent this apotheosis ? Or does the palisading
which intersects the building, while at the same time
determining the boundaries of the interior of the infernal
town, serve as a framework for a new action? This it is
almost impossible for us to decide, so long as we have not
identified in their turn the eight panels of the following
and final story

Let us sum up · the principal wall of the first gallery of
Boro-Budur is decorated with 240 bas-reliefs, arranged in
two rows; all those of the upper row have already been
identified by the help of the *Lalita-vistara* , thanks especially
to the *Divyâvadâna,* the same may now be said of two
thirds of those of the lower row. This recapitulation of the
results obtained not only encourages us to hope for the

fortunate completion of this enterprise in a relatively
near future : it also allows us to discern the ways and
means to the ultimate success, as well as the difficulties
which we shall continue to encounter. Among the first of
these we must naturally place the absence of satisfactory
reproductions. The long series which we have just examined would doubtless have been recognized long ago, as were
immediately the scenes, in two or three pictures, of the *jâtakas* figured on the opposite wall, if the published drawings
had been perfectly exact But a slight inattention — such as,
in the story of Maitrakanyaka, the change of sex of a person,
or, in that of Rudrâyana, the transformation of a monk into
a Buddha — is, as may be conceived, sufficient to put us
off the scent, and forces archæologists who have not
direct access to the originals to abandon the most judiciously chosen clue We must, therefore, rejoice that the
Government-General of the Dutch Indies has recently
sanctioned the project of photographing all the sculptures
still existing at Boro-Budur. Doubtless it will, with its
accustomed generosity, not fail to distribute copies among
the various societies for oriental studies On this condition
alone will the enigmas which still resist, although invaded
on all four sides at once, finally yield to the collective
researches of students of Buddhism, in the meantime we
cannot legitimately reproach the latter for having left so
long unexplained a monument of this importance

Does this mean that it is sufficient to cast one's eyes
upon exact reproductions, or even upon the originals, of
these bas-reliefs, whose narrative aim is not doubtful, in
order to understand their meaning? The preceding identifications prove clearly enough that it is also necessary to
know beforehand the story which they would tell. And,
doubtless, the blame for this belongs to some extent to the

sculptors : still it would be well, before devolving upon them the burden of our ignorance, to have present to our minds the conditions under which they must have worked. Firstly, enormous surfaces were given them to be covered : on the principal wall of the first gallery alone the 240 panels there aligned have an area of more than 400 square metres! In truth, it was not so much sculpture as decorative fresco-work that was exacted from them. Hence we understand why in the 120 pictures of the upper row they should have spun out the childhood and youth of their Master, whilst in the 120 of the lower one they somewhat lengthened out the ten *avadânas* to which they had recourse in order to fill the space. It was materially impossible for them to keep solely to the picturesque or pathetic episodes, that is to those which alone had a chance of being immediately recognized by the spectator, and which were capable of forthwith arousing in the faithful of former days the memory of some tradition and in the archæologist of to-day the recollection of some reading. For them every incident is good, provided that it lends itself docilely to representation. We may even ask ourselves whether the most colourless motifs are not in their view the best. They are really too fond of scenes in which everything takes place by way of visits and conversations between persons whose discreet gestures, such as are becoming to people of good company, tell us absolutely nothing concerning the course of events. If this abuse is, strictly speaking, excusable, they do not, in our opinion, escape the reproach of having more than once evaded the difficulty by intentionally omitting, and replacing by insipid receptions at court, subjects more dramatic and consequently better fitted to make us grasp the thread of the story (¹).

---

(1) It is, of course, understood that we are here speaking from the point

Not only are the characteristic episodes thus drowned in a dull, monotonous flood of pictures without movement, but even in each picture the principal motif is often submerged under a veritable debauch of accessories and details The only excuse here for the artists is to be found in the form of the frame, which is at least three times as wide as it is high. Consequently there is no great personage whose cortège is not spread out to form a wall-covering, sometimes over several rows True, the presence of these numerous dumb actors is quite conformable to Javanese, as well as to Indian, custom, but it is understood that most often they take no part in the action : they confine themselves to crowding it with their stereotyped repetition, which is more or less compensated by the variety of the attitudes, always deftly treated This is not all : the sculptors have made it, as it were, a point of honour not to leave vacant any part of the surface at their disposal. In order to complete the furnishing of their panels, they go so far as to fill the space beneath the seats with coffers or vases (cf. pll. XXXV, 1, XXXVIII, 2, XXXIX, 1, XL, 1), at the top they heap together, according to circumstances, buildings or trees, naturally figured on a reduced scale; or again rocks, treated according to the old Indian convention (cf pll. XXXVII, 2, upper scene, XLI, 1); or, finally, ani-

---

of view of the identification of these bas reliefs All the less must we forget that we are treating of images of piety, the more mindful the sculptors themselves were of this Their evident decision to put aside all scenes of violence (bloody sacrifices, executions, murders, parricide, etc ) offered by their subjects, is justified, like their irreproachable chastity, by the desire to arouse in the mind of the faithful none but calm and collected, in one word, truly Buddhist impressions This they have perfectly succeeded in doing, and we are rather in the wrong to reproach them for it It is not entirely their fault if our western taste, corrupted by an excessive striving for expression and movement, is especially affected by the monotony of these series, whose edifying character remains to us a dead letter

mals of all kinds, cleverly sketched, indeed, from life, with
the single exception of the horses, which are mediocre (cf
pl. XXXVI, 2, upper scene) It may be imagined that the
clearness of the story is not much enhanced by this
crowding, the more so as there is nothing to tell us, for
example, whether the animals play a part in it or not ·
for the worst is that they sometimes do so. Thus the
birds represented in the *Çibi-jâtaka* (pl. XXXVI, 2), or on
such and such a scene from the *Mândhâtravadâna* (no 10),
form an integral part of the story, whilst those which fly
away with Manoharâ (pl XXXIV, 2) are pure decoration.
Finally, we must not forget that the artists of Boro-Budur
did not in any way forbid themselves the use of the ancient
expedients of the Indian school, juxtaposition of two or
three distinct episodes and repetition of a person in the
same picture. Thus it may happen — and on this point the
reading of Leemans' descriptions is particularly edifying —
that in the midst of such confused masses we fail to fix
upon the sole actors, or objects, whose presence is of real
importance for the concatenation of the facts.

But the chief and most evident fault of these bas-reliefs
is the persistent incapacity of their authors, in spite of
their manual skill, to create figures having a characteristic
individuality Assuredly, it would be unfair to regard it as
a crime on the part of the artists of those distant isles not
to have reached a pinnacle of art which remained unknown
to the Indian school and to which Greek art itself attained
only at its best period. But the fact is patent. They are capable
of representing types, but not individuals They possess a
model of a king, which serves without distinction for
gods, as does that of the queen for goddesses; a model of
a monk, which, with the exception of the coiffure, is
equally suitable for Buddhas; a model of a courtier, an

anchorite, a Brahman, a warrior, etc. This stock figure
is used by them on all occasions. According to the circumstances it is capable, by the play of gesture and even by
facial features, of expressing different states of mind :
it is incapable of assuming a physiognomy distinguishing
it from its congeners. Thus it is that, for example, in the
same legend we have seen the same princely personage
called here Dhana, Sudhana, or Druma, there Rudrâyana,
Bimbisâra, or Çikhandin. At a distance of five panels
(cf. pll. XXXVII, 2 and XXXIX, 3) a king and a monk are
similarly engaged in conversation with each other : nothing warns us that in the interval they have both changed
their personalities. It would not appear that in ancient
times the pilgrim who made the *pradakshinâ* of these galleries
was able without the oral commentary of some monkish
cicerone to ascribe different names to figures so similar ·
still less can we, now that the local tradition is completely
extinct, dispense with a written commentary We may
affirm that we shall succeed in identifying on the walls of
Boro-Budur only those bas-reliefs of which we have
somewhere read the legend : and, again, the example of
the *Sudhanakumârâvadâna* proves that we must have read it
in the same work as had the sculptor

This bookish character of the sculptures of Boro-Budur
is from the philological point of view the most curious
conclusion to which we are led by our rapid inquiry directed to the particular point of view of their identification If
these bas-reliefs cannot be understood except by a constant
comparison with the texts, it is because they were composed after the texts and to serve as illustrations thereto.
Through the lithographic reproductions the manner in
which the Javanese artists treated the last life of Buddha
had already given us an inkling of this · the direct study

of the originals and the review of the neighbouring series
only confirm us in this opinion (¹) It follows that these
sculptures not only give us information on many concrete
details of contemporary Javanese life and civilization · they
also reveal to us which version of the Buddhist writings was most readily used in Java at that time. Thus we
know already from the manner in which the artist illustrated the legend of Prince Sudhana, that he followed the
Sanskrit text preserved by the *Divyâvadâna*, and not the
Prâkrit version of the *Mahâvastu*. The three other certainly
identified *avadânas*, those of Mândhâtar, Rudrâyana, and
Maitrakanyaka, likewise attest the current custom of drawing from this canonical fund of which the *Divyâvadâna* is
a kind of anthology. Now the independent researches of
MM. Ed. Huber and Sylvain Lévi have shown simultaneously that this last collection is, for the most part, taken
from the *Vinaya-pitaka* of the Mûla-Sarvâstivâdins, and, on
the other hand, the Chinese tell us that the *Lalita vistara*,
which is followed page after page by the bas reliefs of the
upper row, belongs to the same school (²) The study of
the sculptures of Boro-Budur authorizes, therefore, the
supposition that the canon of the Mûla-Sarvâstivâdins was
that best known in Java. Perhaps this preference was due to
the prestige of the Sanskrit, in which it was edited, and
to what may be called its higher « exportation value »,
as compared with the Prâkrit of the Mâhâsânghikas, or
the Pâli of the Sthaviras. However this may be, the hypothesis is clearly confirmed by the categorical information furnished by the Chinese traveller Yi-tsing; in his
time, he tells us, — towards the year 700 of our era, that is

---

(1) *Art gréco-bouddhique du Gandhâra*, vol. I, p. 617
(2) Cf Ed HUBER, *B. É F E -O* , VI, 1906 and S LÉVI, *T'oung pao*, series
II, vol. VIII, no. 1, BEAL, *Romantic Legend*, pp. 386-7.

to say, scaicely a century before the foundation of Boro-Budur, — « in the Islands of the Southern Sea the *Mûla-Sarvâstivâdanikâya* has been almost universally adopted(¹) ». This agreement in the evidences deserves to be noticed. All taken into account, it does not impair the interest of our bas-reliefs. Assuredly, in spite of the talent of their authors, they were condemned beforehand to lack that indefinable spontaneity and animation which can be communicated to the work of the artist only by labour in communion with a still living oral tradition. The sculptors of Boro-Budur, in the effort to revive an inspiration at times languishing, have had to be content with dipping into foreign and already ancient texts but, on the other hand, they have the merit of having supplied us with several series of illustrations for authentic fragments of the sacred scriptures of Buddhism, treated with a technical skill which would deserve to be studied in detail by those whose métier it is. If our conclusions run the risk of somewhat lessening the æsthetic value of their works, the documentary interest emerges, by way of compensation, considerably increased.

## III

### BUDDHIST ICONOGRAPHY IN JAVA.

*Boro-Budur* — We shall not undertake a detailed review of the bas-reliefs deployed along the upper galleries of the *stûpa*. We restrict ourselves to noticing that, as we mount, they assume a character more and more iconographic, less and less « narrative », and that the edifying story finally

---

(1) I-TSING, *A record of the Buddhist Religion*, trans TAKAKUSU, p. 10. Lit. « there is almost only one »

gives way to the image of piety ('). Buddha, monks, nuns, Bodhisattvas of both sexes file past in twenties, at times seated under trees more or less stereotyped, most often installed under the open porches of temples, just as they are seen on the miniatures, or the clay seals, of India ('). The sculptors weary so much the less of all these repetitions as each one of them represents so much progress in covering the considerable surface which it was their task to decorate. There would be no advantage in noting here and there in passing a few specially characteristic figures, such as, in the second gallery, some Avalokiteçvaras with four or six arms, and a Mañjuçrì carrying the Indian book (*pustaka*) on the blue lotus (*utpala*); or again, in the third gallery, a group composed of a Buddha between these same two Bodhisattvas, etc. The problem is much more vast, and demands a solution of very different amplitude. It would be necessary to make a census of all these images and each of their varieties, to draw up an exact and complete table of them, and to study attentively their graphic distribution; then only, after having allowed for the necessities of decoration and having among this crowd of idols discerned the really essential types, we might attempt the identification of what for the artists of Java constituted the Buddhist pantheon. We must hope that some Dutch archæologist will find time to undertake this delicate and extensive task, it is unnecessary to say that it is forbidden to a simple visitor.

Neither shall we dwell upon the hundreds of statues which decorate this *stûpa* of the « Many Buddhas » (for such would be the meaning of the word Boro-Budur) : but

(1) But see, *supra*, the identification of one of the bas-reliefs of the upper gallery, pp 165-6 and pl XXII (Great Miracle of Çrâvastî)

(2) Cf *Étude sur l'iconogr bouddhique de l'Inde*, I, 1900, pp. 45-6

here the reason for our abstention is quite different. They were, in fact, classified long ago, and W. de Humboldt proposed to recognize among them, in accordance with Hodgson's Nepalese drawings, the images of the five Dhyâni-Buddhas. The identification has since been generally admitted, and in principle we see no reason for contesting it . at the most it would need to be pressed further and completed. The arrangement of the groups must in any case be remade. Among these manifold replicas with heads generally well treated and expressive, but effeminate and bloated bodies, all seated in *padmâsana* and only differentiated by the gestures of the hands, we must, in fact, distinguish

1    in the four first rows of niches (in the proportion of 92 to each façade), to the east, those in *bhûmisparça-mudrâ* ([1]);

2    at the south, those in *vara-mudrâ*,

3.    at the west, those in *dhyâni-mudrâ*,

4    at the north, those in *abhaya-mudrâ*,

5.    in the fifth row of niches, on the four façades (viz. 64 altogethe r),those in *vitarka-mudrâ*,

6.    in the 72 little open cupolas of the three circular terraces, those in *dharmacakra-mudrâ*,

7.    the single image found under the great central cupola.

Whatever identification may be proposed, will, it is understood, have to take into account each of these varieties, without omission and without confusion. Therefore we cannot admit that of Humboldt ([2]), which confuses and mixes up nos. 4 and 5. If we must identify

---

([1]) For the *mudrâs*, or gestures of the hands, cf *ibid.*, p. 68.
([2]) Cf LEEMANS, *loc. cit.*, p 480

1. Akshobhya, by the gesture of calling the earth to witness, 2. Ratnasambhava, by the gesture of giving, 3. Amitâbha, by the gesture of meditation, 4. Amoghasiddha, by the gesture of protection, it is clear that in the last row of niches we must recognize, 5. the fifth Dhyâni-Buddha, Vairocana, by the gesture of discussion, although the gesture of teaching is more usually reserved for him and although, on the other hand, the *vitarka-mudrâ* is scarcely distinguished from the *abhaya-mudrâ* by the fact that in it the index-finger is joined to the thumb. It follows likewise that with the five rows of niches belonging to the polygonal galleries we have, as was natural, exhausted the list of the five Dhyâni-Buddhas.

6. The 72 images of the circular terraces would then all be consecrated to the historic Buddha, Çâkya-muni, and would exhibit him teaching.

7 As for the purposely unfinished statue which was discovered under the great central cupola, it has been the subject of many hypotheses. Dr. Pleyte regards it as the last enigma of Boro-Budur . « The great Dâgaba », he says ('), « was formerly without any opening, but at present one can have access right into the interior, part of the wall having been removed. The removal brought to light a hidden image of Buddha, which represents him seated in *bhûmisparça-mudrâ*. This image of Buddha is thus the centre of the sanctuary. By reason of its incomplete form it is considered by Groeneveldt to be a representation of the Âdi-Buddha. This would be a manner of symbolizing the abstract essence of this supreme divinity of Mahâyânism. Kern, on the contrary, recognizes in this unfinish-

(1) C. M. PLEYTE, *Die Buddhalegende in den Skulpturen des Tempels von Boro-Budur*, Amsterdam, 1901-2, p IX. For the bibliography see *ibid* , notes on pages I-III.

ed figure an embryo Buddha : this would be an allusion
to the Bodhisattva in the womb of his mother... » If these
diverse interpretations fail to satisfy us any more than
they did Dr Pleyte, the short résumé which he gives of
them is at least sufficient for our purpose We do not
indeed pretend to discuss here the greater or less degree
of probability in these theories. Still less shall we stop to
criticize that of Wilsen, who saw in this same statue a rough
model of a future Buddha, prepared for subsequent completion by the cunning priests (¹). In truth, speculations of
this kind are scarcely more susceptible of refutation than
of proof, and it is this which makes us suspicious of them.
If we in our turn venture a new hypothesis, it is because
we should prefer to seek the solution of this problem of
archæology elsewhere than in the messianic, symbolical
or theistic conceptions more or less familiar in such and
such forms of Indian Buddhism

Let us, then, make a *tabula rasa* of all this metaphysics
and consider again, as briefly as possible, the essential
elements of the question  Under the central dome of the
*stûpa* of Boro-Budur, at the spot where we should expect
to find the usual deposit of relics, or at least the upper
deposit — for it happens sometimes that there are along the
perpendicular which joins the summit to the base several
of them, one above the other — was discovered an image
of Buddha, whose emplacement sufficed to prove its specially sacred character  Now this statue was intentionally
left unfinished : « The hair, the ears, the hands and the
feet are not completed », says Leemans, and further on he
adds : « One is forced to admit that the artist who made
the plan of the whole really had a premeditated intention

---

(1) Cf. Leemans, *op cit* , pp  486-7.

of leaving the statue of the central sanctuary in the state in which we possess it ('). » On the other hand, this image shows us Buddha seated, his legs crossed in the Indian manner, the left hand resting in his lap, his right hand hanging down, the palm turned inwards and the fingers stretched toward the ground. Before committing ourselves to any apocalyptical explanation of this figure it is well, in point of method, to ask ourselves, first of all, whether the iconography of India, the recognized model for that of Java, does not comprise any type of Buddha composed in the same attitude and presenting the same peculiarity of incompletion

If it were permissible to judge by the facility of the solution, the question would in this case be well put : at least, in order to answer, it is not necessary to push far our interrogation of the Indian tradition The two most celebrated prototypes of the pretended portrait images of Buddha are that of Kauçâmbî (or Çrâvastî) and that of Mahâbodhi, near to Gayâ. The former is in this case out of the question. Concerning the second we possess two versions of an identical legend, the one reported by Hiuan-tsang, the other by Târanâtha ([2]). Anxious before all to guarantee the authentic resemblance of the image, they naturally attribute its execution to a supernatural artist : on two points they seem none the less in harmony with historic truth. First of all, we learn from the texts, in the most formal manner, that the original work was regarded — rightly or wrongly, matters not — as not being finished, an accident which people were unanimous in explaining as due to an unfor-

---

(1) See the discussion, *loc. cit* , pp. 484-6.
(2) See, for the first, the translation of Stan JULIEN, II, pp. 465 sqq., or of S. BEAL, II, pp. 120 sqq , and, for the second, the translation of SCHIEFNER, p 20.

tunate interruption in the mysterious work of the divine
sculptor. Among the unfinished parts Târanâtha cites especially the toe of the right foot and the locks of hair. Whilst
these material details would be less easy of verification
than might be thought in the obscurity in which, as Hiuan-
tsang tells, the majesty of the idol was hidden, there is some
appearance that this general belief in its state of incomple-
teness was in one way or another well-founded In the
second place, and in any case, it is a fact attested by the
monuments, as also by the descriptions of the texts, that
it represented Buddha « seated, the left hand at rest, and
the right hanging », at the moment when, disturbed from
his meditations by the assaults of Mâra, he touched the
earth with his fingers, in order to invoke it as witness ([1]).
In short, the image of « Vajrâsana of Mahâbodhi », to use
the term under which it was known, made the gesture of
*bhûmisparça*, and was, or — which for us comes to the
same thing — passed for being, incomplete

We leave to experts the task of concluding. To us this
double rapprochement appears sufficiently precise to allow
of our putting forward the idea that the central Buddha of
Boro-Budur, incomplete and in *bhûmisparça-mudrâ*, is, or at
least intends to be, nothing but a replica of the statue of
Bodh-Gayâ. In addition to its simplicity, the hypothesis has
also this great advantage, that it frees us from the necessity of attributing exceptionally to the artists of Java, always
so respectful towards Indian tradition, the creation of a new
model which India would not have known. Finally, if it
does away with one difficulty, in our opinion a considerable one, we do not think that it raises another in its

---

[1] The references are to be found in our *Étude sur l'Iconographie bouddhique de l'Inde*, I, pp. 90-94.

place. It is a fact historically established by Chinese evidence that from the VII[th] to the XI[th] century of our era — that is, during the period covering the construction of Boro-Budur, which is attributed to the second half of the IX[th] century — the « True Visage of the Throne of Diamond », or « of Intelligence », was the most venerated Buddhist idol in India, and even the model most in request for exportation ([1]), whilst the temple of Mahâbodhi had become the greatest centre of pilgrimage. This would explain without effort why a more or less faithful copy of this miraculous image should have been able to assume a character sufficiently sacred to merit being placed by the Javanese architects in the hollow of the great *stûpa* of the Indian Archipelago, just as the original reposed under the arches of the famous sanctuary of Magadha

Such, at least, is the hypothesis which we could not help long ago ([2]) submitting to Indianists, with all the respect inspired by the experience of our predecessors and the reservations imposed by the necessity, in which we still were, of trusting to the descriptions of others. At the time of our visit to Boro-Budur we found nothing to add concerning this statue, inasmuch as it was still in the same state in which Dr. Pleyte had seen it, once again covered up to the neck and left in a state of abandonment very unworthy of all the ink which it had caused to flow. Thus we were obliged to restrict ourselves to reiterating the wish that it might once again be cleared and more closely studied. If we have returned in some detail to this subject, it is because in the interval this wish has been fulfilled, and because the kindness of Major Van Erp allows

(1) Cf Ed CHAVANNES, *Les Inscriptions chinoises de Bodh-Gayâ* in *Revue de l'Histoire des Religions*, vol. XXXIV, 1, 1896

(2) *B. É F. E -O.*, III, 1903, pp 78-80, whence these pages are taken.

us to produce at last a photograph of this famous idol
(pl. XLIII, 1). Perhaps this latter will be for the reader a
disillusionment · in fact it merely sketches in a rather
rough fashion the ordinary type of Buddhas of Boro-Budur,
and it is quite clear that, if a replica of the image of Vajrâsana is really intended, it was executed freely and not
from a moulding. But upon a moment's reflection it will
be seen that this was exactly what was to be expected,
and, in any case, it is well once for all to place before the
eyes of the public the decisive piece of evidence in a dispute
which otherwise would run the risk of being endless

*The Chandi Mendut* — It would be a task more within our
reach to identify, by way of a specimen, the images which
decorate the Chandi Mendut. This edifice, placed in the axis
of the oriental gate of, and at three kilometres from, Boro-
Budur, consists, in fact, of a *cella* only, with a vestibule in
front The whole is, according to the Javanese custom,
perched on a terrace in the same manner as are the Brahmanic temples of Parambanam In Buddhist terminology it is
what is properly called a *vihâra* ([1]) Naturally it shelters statues, and the walls of its entrance vestibule, like the exterior
faces of the building, are decorated with figures whose purely
Buddhist character may be recognized at once by anyone
who is a little familiar with the Indian iconography of this
religion. The building, fairly well preserved, except in the
upper parts, has been the object of a restoration the archi-

---

(1) We know that the meaning of this term (temple of divinity or monk's
cell) has been unduly extended by European archæologists to the whole of
the monastery (Cf *Art g.-b du Gandhâra*, p 99) — We deliberately leave
aside the other Buddhist edifices which we likewise visited in the neighbourhood of Jogyakarta under the guidance of Dr J Groneman, and on
which we may consult his guide, entitled *Boeddhistische Tempel-en Klooster-
Bouwvallen in de Parambanan-Vlakte*, Soerabaia, 1907.

tectural details of which we shall not undertake to discuss.

The three enoimous statues of the *cella* have been replaced on their pedestals ('). They are characterized by a curious detail Wheieas at Boro-Budur, and even on the walls of the Chandi Mendut, the nimbuses of the divine personages retain, as in Southern India, the simply oval form, those of the three figures rise to a point, like the leaf of the Bodhi-tree, in the Sino-Japanese fashion. It would be interesting to date as exactly as possible the appearance of this form in Java. It would, in fact, mark with sufficient certainty the moment when the two great currents of aitistic influence, which, diverging from their common Indian source, had followed respectively the land routes through Central Asia and the sea route south-eastwards, met again in the island and there, so to speak, closed their circuit (')

The central statue, about m 2,50 high, cut out of an enormous block of andesite, represents a Buddha seated in the European manner, the hands joined in the gesture of teaching. Not only the *âsana* and the *mudrâ*, but even the details of the hair, the lotus-stool, the throne with a back, etc., recall in a striking manner the images found at Sârnâth, in the northern suburb of Benares, on the traditional site of the master's first preaching (cf. *Icon bouddh ,* I, fig. 10) Besides, to cut short all discussion, the lower band of the pedestal is still stamped with a « wheel of the law », accompanied by the two characteristic antelopes of the Mrigadâva.

On each side of the teaching Çâkya-muni, on a throne having a back likewise adorned with superposed animals, a Bodhisattva is seated in *lalitâkshepa*, the left leg bent back, the right foot hanging down and resting on a lotus. At the

(1) Cf. *B. É. F E.-O ,* IX, 1909, p 831

right of Buddha Avalokiteçvara may at once be recognized,
thanks to the effigy of Amitâbha which he bears in his
headdress As usual, his right hand makes the gesture of
charity; his left is folded back in the position of discussion,
but without at the same time holding a lotus (cf. *ibid.*,
pl. V, 2). His counterpart, with the palm of his left hand
leaning on the ground and the right hand turned back in
front of his chest, does not present any particular mark
allowing us to determine his identity. It is solely the traditional force of custom which compels us to attribute to
him the name of Mañjuçrî the more so as, after having
despoiled these two acolytes of every characteristic attribute, the sculptor must for a means of recognition have
relied upon their simple presence by the side of Buddha.

The walls of the vestibule bear on the right and left, in
panels of about m 1,90 × m. 1, figures of the genius of
wealth and his wife Hâritî, which have already been published by Dr J Ph Vogel (¹) We shall not insist further upon
them Of the principal façade of the temple — exceptionally
oriented towards the north-west instead of to the east —
only the wall to the left of the entrance is preserved, it
bears a standing Bodhisattva, holding a lotus surmounted
by a *stûpa* : it seems that we must by this sign recognize
Maitreya (cf *ibid*, pp. 112-3)

If we now commence on the terrace the *pradakshinâ* of
the monument, we come first to the north-eastern façade. In
the middle of the central panel, framed by pilasters bearing
atlantes in their capitals, we see, seated on a throne covered
with a lotus and under a stereotyped tree, a feminine divinity with eight arms Unfortunately the head is broken,
but it seems, in fact, that it had only one face; and this

(1) *B. É. F E -O* , IV (1904), pp 727-730 . ct above, p. 141 and
below, pl XLVIII, 2.

suffices to put aside the identification with the Vajra-Târâ with four faces (*ibid.*, II, 1905, p 70) in favour of Cundâ (*ibid.*, I, p. 146 and pl. VIII, 4). Her right arms do hold the shell, the thunderbolt, the disc, and the rosary. Of her left arms, the first from the top is broken, the three others carry an elephant's hook (*ankuça*), an arrow, and some object which we could not distinguish On either side stands a Bodhisattva holding a flyflap · the one on the right has further the pink lotus of Avalokiteçvara, the one on the left the blue lotus of Mañjuçrî. Finally, on the two lateral panels, the same standing Bodhisattva, his right hand in the *varamudrâ*, bears a flower quite analogous to the *nâga-pushpa* of Maitreya (*ibid*, I, fig. 14)

On the next façade the central figure is an Avalokite-çvara with four arms (*ibid.*, I, p 104, etc.) One of its right arms, which is broken, must have been lowered in the gesture of giving, whilst the other holds up a rosary A pink lotus and a book adorn the left hands, the flagon of ambrosia rests upon another lotus on the same side Two feminine attendants, doubtless forms of Târâ, worship him. In the Bodhisattvas figured on the two lateral panels the thunderbolt with which both are armed proclaims Vaj-rapâni.

The principal figure of the south-western, and last, façade is again feminine (pl XLIV). She is seated in the Indian manner upon a lotus supported by two *nâgas*. The two attributes of the upper pair of hands, on the right the rosary and on the left the book, should indicate the Prajñâ-pâramitâ with four arms (*ibid*, pl. IX, 3 and 4). But in that case the normal hands should make the gesture of teaching, instead of that of meditation. Similarly, if she were a four-armed Târâ, the first right hand should make the ges-ture of charity (*ibid.*, II, p. 65). The symbols and the atti-

tudes combine, therefore, to indicate a second representation of the goddess Cundâ, the form with four arms (*ibid.*,
pl. VIII, 3 and figure 24) The two Bodhisattvas, her attendants, reproduce exactly those of her counterpart on the
opposite façade. As regards those of the lateral panels, they
carry on blue lotuses a sword and a book respectively
we must, therefore, see in them two replicas of the same
Mañjuçrî, of whom these are the two traditional emblems
(*ibid*, p 119).

To sum up . in the personages who decorate the exterior of the three unpierced faces of the temple of Mendut we propose at first sight to recognize, in the middle,
two images of Cundâ with four and eight arms, and one
of Avalokiteçvara with four arms, on the sides, two replicas each of Maitreya, Vajrapâni and Mañjuçrî all being important figures of the Buddhist pantheon. But, naturally,
this preliminary review would have to be severely tested.
It would be necessary, in particular, to examine these bas-
reliefs more closely with the help of ladders or a hanging
stage, so that no detail could escape; and, this minute
labour accomplished, it would still be necessary to verify
by comparison with other Buddhist statues of Javanese
origin whether there is not occasion to modify in some
measure, for local reasons, the Indian attribution of these
images At that cost only could these too rapid identifications become reasonably certain

*The Museum of Batavia.* — We have just spoken of a
kind of general confrontation of the Buddhist statues of
Java. The material would not be lacking, in spite of the
relatively restricted number of Buddhist monuments in
the island. Many of them have already been brought
together, both in a building near to the residency of Jogya-

karta and in the museum of the Asiatic Society of Batavia.
Of the first collection a catalogue has been published by
Dr. Groneman The most interesting objects to be mentioned in the second are some inscribed images of the
Dhyâni-Buddhas Akshobhya (no. 224) and Ratnasambhava
(no. 225), of the *çakti* Locanâ (no. 248ª), of Târâ in the
form of Bhrikuṭî (no 112ª), of Hayagrîva (no 76ª), etc.
Every one will appreciate the interest of these names (¹),
taken at hasard from our notes on the lapidary museum.

We must likewise mention as belonging to the museum
of the capital a considerable collection of small figures of
more or less precious metals (gold, silver, or bronze),
which are for the most part already classed (²) Let us cite
among others some very artistic statuettes of Avalokiteçvara, Vajrasattva, Kuvera, Târâ, Mârîcî, etc. All have
this in common, that they are remarkably faithful to their
Indian models.

There is one at which it is perhaps worth while to stop
for a moment, because of the rarity of the type in India
and the success which it has had in the Far East. We have
already had to occupy ourselves with the sole example preserved by chance at Bodh-Gayâ. Now Dr. Pleyte — and
we apologize for not having known this reference at the
time — had for his part published three Javanese replicas (³), one of which is now in London, another at Lei-

(1) Several of these statues have already been published by the late
J L A. Brandes, *Beschrifving van de ruine... Tjandi Djago*, The Hague and
Batavia, 1904.

(2) For access to this collection we are indebted to the kindness of
Dr. C M. Pleyte, who was so good as to take the trouble of opening the
glass-cases for us.

(3) Cf. *Bijdragen tot de Taal-, Land- en Volkenkunde van Ned.-Ind.*, Zesde
Volgreeks, Tiende Deel, afl 1 and 2, pp 195-202, and our *Ét. sur l'Icon
bouddh. de l'Inde*, II, 1905, fig. 4.

den, and the third at Batavia (pl. XLIII, 2). He had likewise
the merit of discovering in Schiefner (¹) a legend which
explained the bellicose pose of this divinity, whose left
foot treads upon the face of a man, and his right upon the
bosom of a woman  This would be a mode of deciding,
with no possible equivocation, the question of the supre-
macy of a simple Buddhist « guardian of the law » over
the great god of the Brahmans. Çiva had the imprudence
to refuse obedience to Vajrapâni under the pretence that
the latter was only a *yaksha* : contemplate for your own
edification the punishment of his crime. We in our turn
may note that on this point the descriptions of the *sâdhanas*,
or magic charms, confirm the Tibetan tradition by likewise
giving to the persons overthrown the names of Mahe-
çvara and his wife Gaurî : while for the genius, instead
of making of him simply a furious transformation of
Vajrapâni, they use the more precise appellation of Trailokyavijaya. Let us add that this last reappears among the
divinities of the Japanese pantheon under the vulgar designation of Gosanze. His pose has not changed, nor his double,
living pedestal ; and, if he has no longer more than one
pair of arms, his hands, at least, continue to execute the
*vajrahûmkâra-mudrâ* characteristic of his anger and common to all his representations (²). On the Javanese statuette we find again the four visages which the Sanskrit
manuscripts and the stele of Magadha ascribe to him, and
even the eight attributes (sword, disc, arrow and bell,

(1) A Schiefner, *Eine tibetische Lebensbeschreibung Çakyamuni s*, p  244.
(2) Cf. J. Hoffman, *Pantheon von Nippon* (vol. V, of the *Beschreibung
von Japan* of Von Siebold), p 75 and pl XIX, fig  164, and *Si do-in-dzou*
(*Ann  du Musée Guimet*, Bibl  d'études, vol. VIII, Paris, 1899), pp. 100-
101 and pl. XII

thunderbolt, elephant's goad, lasso and bow) which they agree in placing in his eight hands.

Any special inquiry would lead us, we believe, to this double conclusion : on the one hand, the close filiation of the Javanese Buddhist images in relation to their Indian prototypes, and, on the other hand, their more or less distant kinship with the Tibetan, Chinese, or Japanese idols, derived from the same origin  If no profound divergence from the composition or style of the common models seems to guarantee to this province of Buddhist iconography any great originality, its interest, on the other hand, promises to extend far beyond the local horizon  It is important for the general advancement of Asiatic studies that it should at last form as a whole the subject of some publication  Not only would the harvest be abundant, but we have carried away the impression that it is ripe and ready to be gathered. It is much to  be desired that the enlightened govern-ment of the rich colony should provide some Dutch savant with the necessary leisure

[Note additional to note 1 on p  214   Upon reperusing M  August BARTH's *Bulletins des Religions de l Inde* ( *Rev  de  l'Hist.  des  Religions*, t  XLV, 1902, p  354 n  1, or vol  II, p  442 n  1, of the edition of his *Œuvres*) we see that  the identification  suggested above for the bas-relief no  14 of Dr  PLEYTE's publication has been already proposed by him. He works out in full  the same  interpretation   « That the maternal womb, the scene of the  central  incident, has been omitted, is entirely  in  conformity with the conventions of this art       »  We are doubly fortunate in finding ourselves *ex post facto* at one with him and in rendering to him the priority as regards the identification ]

## PLATE XXXI

Cf pp. 206-7, 213-5.

I. — View of Boro Budur as it still appeared in 1907, by the care of Major Van Erp the stone seat contrived on the summit with a view to the more comfortable contemplation of the magnificent scenery has since been removed, and the original lines of the top cupola have been partly restored (Cf pp. 206-7 )

II — Our photograph represents the central part of the first gallery on the western face, at the point where it is crossed by the western staircase,

On the right, at the top, we distinguish in the upper row of the bas-reliefs the two last of the Bodhisattva's four promenades, namely, the rencontre with the dead man and with the monk The corresponding bas-reliefs of the lower row have not yet been explained On the other hand, from the place where the view is taken. we cannot see the two rows of sculptures which correspondingly decorate the moulded parapet to the left. (Cf. pp. 213-5 )

1. — BORO-BUDUR: GENERAL VIEW
(FROM THE NORTH-WEST)

2. — BORO-BUDUR: FIRST GALLERY
(PART OF WEST FACADE)

PLATE XXXII

Cf pp. 209 11

The three following drawings (section, plan and outline of Boro-Budur) have been obligingly communicated by Major Van Erp, and they present in consequence every guarantee of accuracy.

I. — The present elevation replaces that published in the *B E F E O*, 1909, fig 3 (cf. *ibid* , p 831), which not being a normal section, had led us into error  The curve *a b* follows the original line of the *stūpa*, the whole portion situated to the right of the point *b* and marked by divergent hatchings represents the terrace subsequently added, under which is at present buried the ancient base with its decoration already half accomplished. (Cf pp. 208 n. 1 and 210.)

II — The plan corresponds exactly in dimensions with the elevation placed above. Just as the elevation shows the arrangement of the decorative architectural elements, niches and cupolas, so the plan enables us to get a clear idea of the distribution of the galleries, both polygonal and circular, of the staircases, and of the gargoyles for carrying off the rain water. (Cf  p  211 )

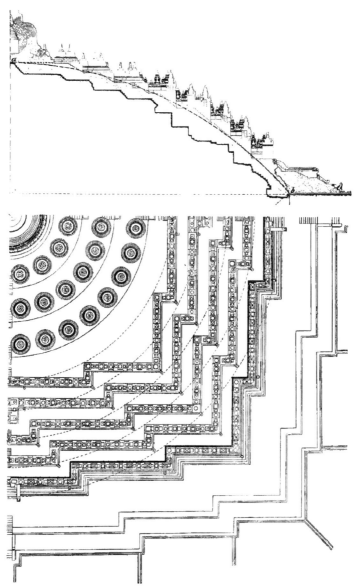

BORO-BUDUR : SECTION AND PLAN

PLATE XXXIII

Cf pp 209, 211.

Plates XXXIV-XLII are reproductions of photographs taken by the author from the bas-reliefs, in the state in which they were in May 1907, with the lichens which in places were eating them away (cf pll XXXV, 2, XXXVI, XXXIX, 1), and their stones sometimes disjointed (cf pll XXXVIII and XLII, 2)

I — This plate and the following belong to the story of prince Sudhana For the description cf. p 218 On the left will be observed the characteristic type of the Brahman, with his beard and large chignon.

II — *Upper scene* Çvetaketu, half recumbent on his throne in his celestial palace amid the paradise of the Tushitas, pays (not, it seems, without a certain melancholy) his adieux to his heavenly companions The latter, ranged on each side of him, manifest, on their part, discreet signs of affectionate regret for the imminent departure of the future Çâkya-muni

*Lower scene* Cf p 220 It will be noticed that the flight of Manoharâ is the only movement in the slightest degree violent that we shall have to encounter in the whole series of these bas-reliefs (cf , however, further pl. XXXVI, 1, lower scene). Scarcely do guards and courtiers allow themselves to betray at the sight of her a gesture of surprise The birds figured on her left have no other object — if it is absolutely necessary to ascribe one to them (cf p. 251) — than to emphasize the aerial character of her flight.

1. — STORY OF SUDHANA, No 3. INCANTATION AGAINST THE NAGA
(CENTRAL PORTION)

2.    STORY OF SUDHANA, No. 11 : MANOHARÂ'S FLIGHT
Above : THE BODHISATTVA'S FAREWELL TO THE GODS

PLATE XXXV

Cf pp. 220-2.

I. — *Upper scene.* That on pl XXXIV, 2 (upper scene) the Bodhi-sattva is, in fact, on the eve of his last re-descent upon our earth, may be seen in this picture, the next in the upper row of bas-reliefs. Seated in the pose of meditation under a much decorated pavilion, which forms a kind of tabernacle, he still floats above the clouds in the midst of his flying cortège of divinities, of whom some are conveying him, whilst others wave banners, fans, fly-flappers and parasols as pledges of his future princely dignity.

*Lower scene* Cf. p 221 Grouped on the right, the royal insignia (parasol, fly-flapper, conical fan, and leaf of *senté* [alocasia macrorrhiza Schott.], the last « still used by the Javanese, says Dr. Groneman, as a provisional umbrella »), will naturally reappear in all the court pictures (cf pl XXXVI, 1, lower scene, etc.).

II — Cf. p. 222 The group on the right duly represents prince Sudhana letting his ring fall into the vessel of one of the attendants, who, stooping down, has just placed it at his feet On the left the spring towards which walk, or rather glide, the other women — have you ever seen the gliding motion of the Javanese female dancers ? — is depicted as a kind of rocky basin, shaded by a tree and overgrown with lotuses

1. — STORY OF SUDHANA, No 12: THE PRINCE'S RETURN
Above THE BODHISATTVA'S DESCENT UPON EARTH

1. — STORY OF SUDHANA, No. 16: AT THE FOUNTAIN
(RIGHT-HAND PORTION)

# PLATE XXXVI

Cf. pp. 228, 230 r

I. — *Upper scene* Prince Siddhârtha, languidly ensconced upon his throne, offers his own ring, as a token of betrothal, to Gopâ or Yaçodâ, who is kneeling with clasped hands at his feet On the left presses the crowd of maidens disdained for her sake, on the right the emissaries of the king with visible satisfaction discover, and discuss among themselves, the significant attitude of the prince, whose heart, to the great despair of his father, had until then remained proof against love

*Lower scene* Cf p 228 On the right, King Mândhâtar, flanked by his court, witnesses the scene from his palace : pieces of woven stuff fall from the clouds, naturally in the same long, rectangular shape which they would have when issuing from the loom Among the people some catch them in their flight, others commence to drape themselves with them, whilst others providently make veritable bundles of them.

II — *Upper scene* Prince Siddhârtha, preceded by his guard and followed by his court, is seated under a parasol on a four-wheeled chariot drawn cy horses, very poorly designed (cf p. 251) he has just met (as may be seen on the left) an old mendicant, leaning on a stick and led by a child, and *à propos* of this unexpected rencontre he learns through the mouth of his squire the existence of old age. This is the first of the four promenades (cf. pl XXXI, 2)

*Lower scene.* Cf p 230 It will be observed that we do not see here, as in Gandhâra and even at Amarâvatî, an executioner lay his obedient, but cruel, hand upon the Bodhisattva, still less does this latter appear. as in Central Asia, with his skeleton almost entirely stripped of flesh Such a horrible sight would jar too strangely at Boro-Budur.

1.   STORY OF MÀNDHÁTAR, No 12 : THE RAIN OF GARMENTS
Above   THE BODHISATTVA CHOOSES HIS BRIDE

2. — STORY OF KING ÇIBI, THE DOVE AND THE HAWK
Above : THE FIRST OF THE BODHISATTVA'S FOUR PROMENADES

PLATE XXXVII

Cf. pp. 233-4

Plates XXXVII XL are consecrated to the story of Rudrâyana

I — Cf pp 2ʒ3-4 Judging by their head-dresses, these are Brahmans who have been charged by Rudrâyana to bring the precious cuirass, which is about to pass from their hands into those of Bimbisâra's courtiers And it is clearly a cuirass, without sleeves and closing, it seems, in front

II — *Upper scene.* On the left the Bodhisattva (already under the aspect of a Buddha) is seated on a throne covered with a lotus, and in conversation with his master Arâda. The latter exhibits all the characteristic marks of the Brahmanic ascetic, as do also his other disciples, who, in the midst of a conventional landscape of trees and rocks, which represents their hermitage, occupy the rest of the picture, meditating or praying, their rosaries round their necks or in their hands.

*Lower scene* It is the ever-recurring court picture that here again appears We have remarked (p 234) that the throne of the teaching monk is higher than that of the king, his disciple It might be interesting to refer the reader to a rule to this effect, explicitly stated in the *Prâtimoksha* of the Sarvâstivâdins, v, 92 *(Journal Asiatique, nov -dec* 1913, p 535, ed FINOT and trans HUBER) But, in fact, this is the general custom in India : it is by an exception, only explained by the prestige of Buddha among later generations, that in the scene above the sculptor has assigned to him a seat higher than that of his master

1. · STORY OF RUDRÁYANA, No. 6  PRESENTATION OF THE CUIRASS
(LEFT-HAND PORTION)

2.     STORY OF RUDRÁYANA, No. 9 : MAHÁKÀTYÀYANA'S VISIT
Above ; THE BODHISATTVA WITH HIS FIRST BRAHMAN TEACHER

PLATE XXXVIII

Cf pp 234-5

I. — Cf pp 234-5 Note in the case of the Buddhist nun the complete tonsure of the head and the total absence of jewels, conformably to the rule of the monastic order to which she belongs. The first feminine person seen full-length on the right of the king is, doubtless, queen Candraprabhâ

II — Cf p 235. It is the latter whom we find again in the following scene, kneeling on the ground in the costume of a nun Between her and the bench on which are seated the two *bhikshunîs* (whose heads have been displaced with the block which carried them) curious utensils of worship will be noticed

1 — STORY OF RUDRÁYAŅA, No 10 : THE NUN ÇAILÁ'S SERMON
(LEFT-HAND PORTION)

2.- STORY OF RUDRÁYAŅA, No 11 : QUEEN CANDRAPRABHÁ'S ORDINATION
(CENTRAL PORTION)

PLATE XXXIX

Cf pp 235·6.

I — Here Candraprabhâ, descending again from heaven, in order to keep the promise which she had made to her husband to come back as a ghost, reappears, quite naturally to our eyes, in the costume of a goddess, and consequently of a queen — that is to say, the same which she wore on plate XXXVIII, 1 Note the cracks in the block on which the king is carved.

II. — Cf pp 235-6 The distinction between the king and the crown-prince is in this scene especially emphasized by the fact that the father alone wears the *mukuta* or tiara, which the son, contrary to custom (see, for instance, prince Sudhana in the lower scene of pl XXXV, 2), here does not wear

III — Cf. p. 236 and, for the sake of comparison, the right part of the lower scene in pl XXXVII, 2

1

2

3

PLATE XL

Cf. pp  237-8.

I — *Upper scene* On the left the Bodhisattva (in the form of a Buddha), seated in meditation among the rocks and in the shades of Uruvilvâ, raises his right hand in order to make to the fifteen gods (one of whom is broken) ranged on his left a polite gesture of refusal. What he declines is the proposal, which they have just made to him, to breathe in through his pores a secret vigour, which may sustain him in the midst of his super-human austerities for he will owe his salvation to himself alone. His well-bred interlocutors receive his decision with a demeanour as discreet as it is varied. It will be observed that the macerations of the Bodhisattva are not in any way shown, as in Gandhâra, by the loss of flesh on his body : so much realism would here be regarded as the height of impropriety.

*Lower scene* Cf. p 237 It will be noticed also in this connection that the sculptor does not make us witness the murder of Rudrâyaṇa (cf. p. 249, n 1) It may be curious to observe the existence in the Musée Guimet of Tibetan paintings whose authors have not troubled themselves with so much delicacy : for there is more than one way of being a Buddhist, in life as well as in art

II. — Cf. p 238 It will be observed — and this trait curiously recalls the pleasantries of our Middle Age concerning the monks — that the Brahmans distinguish themselves by a special degree of cupidity.

1. — STORY OF RUDRÀYANA, No 16: AFTER THE PARRICIDE
Above: THE ASCETIC BODHISATTVA DECLINES THE AID OF THE GODS

2. — STORY OF RUDRÀYANA, No. 19: THE RAIN OF JEWELS
(LEFT-HAND PORTION)

'' PLATE XLI

Cf pp 241-3, 245-6

I — Cf. pp. 240 3 The conventional rocks already met with in plates XXXVIII, 2 and XLI (upper scene) are here still more distinctly seen  they are the same as at Ajaṇṭâ and in Indian miniatures (cf *Ét sur l'Iconogr bouddh de l'Inde*, I, pp. 35, 183).

The three following reproductions belong to the story of Maitrakanyaka

II. — Cf pp 245·6 The respect due to the mother, as well as to the teacher, is here also marked by the higher seat attributed to her (cf p  220, no  8, and pl  XXXVII, 2)

1. — STORY OF THE PAIR OF KINNARAS
(CENTRAL PORTION OF THE SECOND SCENE)

2. — STORY OF MAITRAKANYAKA, No 1: THE PURSE-OFFERING
(CENTRAL PORTION)

PLATE XLII

Cf pp. 246-7.

I — Here, again, it would never be suspected that Maitrakanyaka is supposed to kick his mother on the head : such is, however, the subject (cf pp. 245-6) This portion of the wall shows very serious cracks

II — Cf pp 246 7 The *dvārapāla* is to be compared with those who likewise guard the gates of the Brahmanic temples of Java A palisade of the same kind as that of which we get a side view on the left is seen again from the front on pll XL, 1 (lower scene) and XLIV

1. STORY OF MAITRAKANYAKA, No. 2 : THE MOTHER'S SUPPLICATION
(LEFT-HAND PORTION)

2. — STORY OF MAITRAKANYAKA, No. 7 : IN THE INFERNO CITY
(RIGHT-HAND PORTION)

PLATE XLIII

Cf pp 257 62, 267-9

I — Photograph by Major Van Erp. For the interpretation of pp. 257-262 We must confess that, at first sight, it is difficult to take this figure seriously It would be so simple to suppose, for example, that we have merely a statue spoiled in the execution, so that the sculptor, regarding it as an irremediable failure, had decently rid himself of it by burying it beneath the masonry of the *stūpa* We have, however, to consider, on the one hand, that this imperfect work is unique in its kind and, on the other, that, having been found in position beneath the great central cupola, as were its companions under the 72 encircling small cupolas, it forms part of a finished whole  Only so do we comprehend the importance which the Dutch savants have attached to its discovery

II — Photograph by the author (height m 0,10)  description and identification pp 267-9

2. — TRAILOKYA-VIJAYA.
(BRONZE IN THE BATAVIA MUSEUM)

1. — THE UNFINISHED STATUE OF BUDDHA
(UNDER THE CENTRAL CUPOLA, BORO-BUDUR)

PLATE XLIV

Cf pp 265 6

Photograph by Major Van Erp, for the identification cf pp 265-6
On the plinth stretches the top of a palisade of large wooden stakes
joined by a thin crossbar Behind are seen the waves of a lotus pond, in
which are supposed to grow the lotuses which support the three principal persons. Two Nâgas, recognizable by their serpent head-dresses,
hold up the stem of the central lotus, and thus recall those of the « Great
Miracle at Çrâvastî » (cf pll XX; XXIII, XXVIII, 1) The stereotyped
trees attest a remarkable feeling for ornament At the foot of the two
lateral ones are placed treasure-vases The central tree, surmounted by
a parasol, is further embellished with birds and hanging bells, and,
conformably to tradition, is flanked by adoring divinities, here enframed
in finely chiselled folds of cloud The iconographic motif, carved in
position, thus extends over the whole wall of the temple

THE GODDESS CUNDÂ BETWEEN TWO BODHISATTVAS
(ON THE SOUTH-WESTERN WALL OF THE CHANDI-MENDUT)

# The Buddhist Madonna [1].

The painting reproduced in colours on the frontispiece to this volume comes from the ruins of Yâr-Khoto, at about ten kilometres to the west of Turfan  Discovered on the 13th of July 1905 in the course of the operations of the second German archæological mission in this region of Chinese Turkestan, it is at present deposited in the Royal Ethnographical Museum (Kgl. Museum fur Volkerkunde) in Berlin, under no  T(urfan) II, Y, 69. In shape rectangular, it measures m. 0,35 by m. 0,50, and, according to all probability, was formerly framed in bands of woven material, like a Japanese kakemono  The sanctuary, which it had once adorned, was apparently one dedicated to Buddha : at least, the fairly numerous manuscripts found in its company retain, under the diversity of their Sogdian, Turkish or Chinese languages and scripts, the common characteristic of having a Buddhist purport  we should have to except only some Uigur fragments, which would be Manichean. On the other hand, the final disintegration of the building, constructed of undressed bricks, could not be much later than the ninth century of our era. Only the extraordinary dryness of the climate explains how a thing so perishable should have succeeded in reaching us, beneath the thick accumulated débris of bricks and dust, in a state

(1) Extract from *Monuments et mémoires publiés par l'Académie des Inscriptions et Belles-Lettres (Fondation Eugène Piot)*, vol XVII, fasc. II, 1910.

of preservation relatively so satisfactory. We are indebted
to the kindness of Dr. A von Le Coq and Dr. Bode, the
Director-General of the Royal Museums in Berlin, for the
opportunity of offering to the public a first acquaintance with
this work, one of the most significant, in our opinion, which
have issued from the recent excavations in Central Asia.

I

The reproduction which we publish is sufficiently adequate to enable us to dispense with anything beyond a
succinct description, insisting less upon what is still to be
seen at the first glance than upon what only a close examination reveals. The principal subject is a seated woman,
holding in the hollow of her right arm a child in swaddling
clothes, to whom with her left hand she presents her bosom.
Her head, surrounded by a triple circular nimbus, is covered
as far as the shoulders by a veil, embroidered round the
hems and tied back with a ribbon. She is clothed down to
the feet in a tunic with long sleeves, open at the breast and
quite analogous to those which we have seen worn by the
women of Kashmir This robe is strewn with lozenges —
themselves subdivided into four like figures, each marked
by a red spot — which were probably woven in the stuff,
the collar, cuffs, opening and hem being bordered with the
same embroidery as the veil. The feet are shod in slippers
without heels, depicted in black, and the neck is adorned
with a necklace of the same hue The child is tightly
swathed up to the neck, like a mummy The chair on which
the woman sits, in a very awkward position, is without
arms or back, but very massive and much ornamented.
From the front we perceive only two rectangular uprights,

fitted between two frames of the same shape, the one which rests on the ground being a little wider than that which serves as a seat  The mouldings are repeated symmetrically. Those of the two inner crossbars reproduce the regularly outlined curves of the embroidery : the decoration of the outer framework and of the uprights introduces halves or quarters of the lotus flower into the intervals of the curved undulations or the angular zigzags of a stripe.

This central figure is surrounded by eight little attendants, four on each side. These are so many vigorous and plump little boys. All wear on their shaven crowns tufts of hair : round their necks are necklaces ornamented with medallions, doubtless serving as amulet-bearers, on their feet black shoes; about their loins cotton drawers, forming in front a little pocket which is pierced with a small slit, but projecting in wide pleats behind. The penetrating eye of Dr. A. von Le Coq has already noticed that four of them are about to play a kind of hockey  The first, at the bottom to the left, is raising his two hands, of which the right brandishes a crooked stick, towards one of his companions, who is perched upon the stool, as if to incite him to throw the ball which he clasps tightly in his right hand. The latter also holds upright in his left hand a similar bat, and half turns towards the seated woman, as if she were watching their play, while feeding her latest-born. At the top, on the right, two other little boys are engaged in the same sport. The upper one, who is squatting, with his left hand throws the ball, which is indicated in red; the one standing below receives it with his bat; for, before the canvas was stretched and the drawing distorted, his left arm, which has now disappeared, was, doubtless, long enough to

reach and manipulate the red, bent stick which is to be
seen between the two partners. Below, a fifth child, seated
on the ground, practises playing a sort of guitar with four
strings. Still lower, a sixth is carrying as well as he can, in
a basket too big for his arms, some melons, whole or in
slices — those famous melons of Upper Asia, whose
excellence all travellers unite in celebrating and of which
the scent alone was sufficient to awaken in the heart of
the Great Mogul Baber, even mid the enchantment of his
Indian gardens, a homesickness for his native Ferghâna.
To return to the left portion of the plate, above the two
hockey-players we see another little boy, who seems to be
amusing himself by trying to balance on his head a two-
handled vase. As for the eighth little figure in the top corner,
it is so much injured that we dare not venture any conjectures concerning its manner of amusement · the author
of the tracing which accompanies and supplies what is
missing in the plate, has completed the figure, with infinite
probability, as a little genius perfectly analogous to the one
in the symmetrically opposite corner.

To this summary description we are justified in adding
a few observations of a technical kind The painting is
executed on a piece of coarse canvas, which had previously
been covered with a coating, now partly vanished. The
features (perhaps first sketched by the help of a pounce,
dusted over a perforated pattern, as we know was often
the custom of these image-makers) were drawn in ink,
with great sureness of hand. If the sitting posture of the
woman is unskilfully rendered, we shall remark, on the
other hand, an interesting attempt to make the lozenges
on the dress blend with the movement of the figure. Then
colours, doubtless water-colours, have been applied in
broad uniform tints. Here, it seems, golden yellow was

confined to the seat and embroideries, while for the tex-
tures there is recourse to a series of reds, passing from the
minium of the dress to the carmine of the veil : all
are to be seen again on the various bands of the halo.
Then a light wash in ink, encircling each feature, emphasizes the contours and hollows out the folds, whilst a few
delicate touches here and there give the finishing stroke to
the summary indication of the modelling. These are exactly
the procedures which are found to recur in Sino-Japanese
paintings, as also on Persian miniatures. We know that
Oriental art has continued of set purpose to ignore the
chiaroscuro. As to the date to be assigned to this picture,
it is, provisionally, rather uncertain : for the archæology
of Central Asia has to be drawn from the chaos of its materials, which for the most part are still unedited However,
thanks to the previous excavations of Sir Aurel Stein, we
know that the *rabâb* with four keys, with which the child
musician is playing, the flowers which the mouldings of
the seat encircle, the « wave » or « cloud » motif of the
embroidery were in use at Niya and at Rawak in southern
Turkestan from the third century of our era ([1]). But, on
the other hand, according to the opinion of Dr. A. von
Le Coq, the woman's costume, of a fashion already Uigur
— not to mention the extreme obliquity of the eyes —
would force us to descend at least as far as the beginning
of the seventh.

---

(1) See M A STEIN, *Ancient Khotan*, pl. LXXIII (guitar handle), LXVIII
(seat), LXXXVIII (waves), LXVII (halo), etc , and cf our *Art gréco-bouddhique du Gandhâra*, figg. 162, 213, 243, 246 (encircled flowers), 273
(waves), etc.

## II

So far we have restricted ourselves to a simple statement of the facts furnished by an examination of the document. Now it is time to broach the more delicate question of its interpretation. Inevitably, as soon as we are confronted by this pious design, we are carried back in memory to some familiar picture of the Virgin nursing the Child Jesus For this unavoidable rapprochement we see at least two reasons. Firstly, there are not so many ways for a woman to offer her bosom to her nursling, The second, more topical, reason might chance through long habituation not immediately to occur to us. We remember having heard the ingenuous expression of it from the lips of a young Panjabi Brahman, who, in front of an Italian chromo-lithograph of the Holy Family, could not conceal his astonishment that « the mother of the God of the Europeans should not be dressed after the manner of the Mêm-Sahebs ». He expected, as he explained to us, to see on the head of Mary a hat similar to those worn by English ladies, whereas, in fact, her veil gave her quite an Indian appearance This he could not get over .. After having smiled at his amazement, we shall do well not to forget the exact bearings of his remark It is incontestable that the artistic tradition of the veil does in fact give an Asiatic appearance to the most Gothic of our Virgins. But, if our European images go more than half way to meet this « Notre Dame de Tourfan » — as it had from the first (¹) been christened — it is intelligible that con-

---

(1) This hypothesis was, indeed, put aside by Dr. von Le Coq because of the Buddhist character of the manuscripts found at the same time as the painting (cf *Journ. of the Roy As Soc* , 1909, p 309).

versely our first instinct will be to connect this latter with a Christian prototype. Have not the excavations in fact proved the former existence, in this oasis of Turfan, of Manichean and even Nestorian sects? The unedifying entourage of eight urchins would indeed be ill-explained by this hypothesis, but, with a little good will, all may be arranged, and in strictness one could reduce these little elves to a purely decorative role, analogous to that played by their counterparts, the *putti*, on the paintings of the Catacombs In short, definitely to settle the question of the identity of our figure, we may imagine that it will be sufficient to confront it with the first chance representation, provided that it be somewhat anterior, of the Virgin nursing her child.

It will perhaps surprise more than one reader to learn that we have experienced great difficulty in laying our hand upon such a representation. It is not, indeed, that we ever thought to find thereby the clue to an enigma which seems to us, as will be seen, susceptible of a much nearer solution. But as little as anyone did we think of denying the Christian analogies of the painting of Turfan, and in any and every case it would have been interesting to connect with it a western counterpart. We went therefore, and knocked at the door of the specialists. We must confess that their reply was not what we expected. They told us, to begin with, that the *Virgo lactans* was not shown in the catacombs of Rome ('). Even in Byzantine art, with its well-known horror of the nude, the icons of the Γαλακτοτροφοῦσα, charged, perhaps, at first with some indecorum, do not seem to appear until very late, in the

---

(1) Cf. J. WILPERT, *Die Malereien der Katakomben Roms*, 1903 (not even on his pl. 22).

XV$^{th}$ century, and would be imitations of an Italian model, itself of recent date ('). Finally, in France the first examples would not go back further than the XIV$^{th}$ century, and would translate in our religious art new feelings of familiarity and tenderness (²) But even the best established laws must always have some exception, and in the present case M Gabriel Millet has pointed out to us at least two. The first is furnished by the ivory cover of a Gospel of Metz, attributed to the IX$^{th}$ century of our era (pl. XLVI, 1) . the « Mother of God », thus designated by name in Byzantine sigla, is seated on a raised throne in the form of a coffer, and offers her left bosom, over which she has modestly drawn a fold of her veil, to a child entirely swathed in bands The other specimen, recently obtained from the excavations of the Service of Egyptian Antiquities at Saqqara, is by the gracious permission of M G Maspéro reproduced here (pl XLVI, 2) Seated on a chair with a back, of rather rude construction, the Virgin Mary no less chastely offers the nipple of her right bosom to a little Jesus, already growing, who, installed on his mother's knee, holds her forearm with both hands. According to the published information this painting had once adorned the walls of a convent founded in 470 and probably destroyed soon after the Arab conquest of Egypt (640-641). Whilst the Carolingian ivory would be later than the image of Turfan, the Coptic fresco would, therefore, be earlier. But, since — notwithstanding the analogy of the wholes and even of certain details — we discern at once that none of

(1) KONDAKOV, *Monuments of Christian Art at Athos*, 1902, fig. 68 and p 173 (in Russian); BENIGNI, *La Madonna allatante e un motivo bizantino?* ap *Il Bessarione*, VII, 1900, pp. 499-501 We are indebted for this information to the kindness of our colleague M Gab. MILLET.

(2) E MALE, *L'Art religieux de la fin du Moyen-âge en France* (1908), p. 148

these three figures proceeds directly from either of the other two, their simultaneous existence serves in the end only to induce us to bring a prudent reserve to bear upon our statements. If our short enquiry does not at all result, as we had begun to think, in guaranteeing the entire absence of the type of Nursing Virgin from ancient Christian art, it at least proves the extreme rarity thereof Consequently, it suffices — and it makes no further claim — to divert us from the first trail along which our European prejudices would have started us.

Whoever, in fact, has by his studies acquired a certain familiarity with Central Asian matters, whether he be Indianist or Sinologue, cannot have remained ignorant of the preponderant role played by Indian civilization in « Serindia », at least down to the coming of the Musalmans; and it is a fact no less surely established that the principal vehicle of this influence was the religion of Buddha. It is in this direction that it would be proper, *a priori*, to point our researches : towards the same quarter we are in the case of this particular picture directed by the character of the edifice beneath whose ruins it was discovered. Now, if we look at it no longer with eyes hereditarily Christian, but through Buddhist spectacles, we shall no less infallibly recognize in it, instead of the Virgin Mary nursing the Child Jesus, the fairy Hârîtî suckling her last born, Pingala, whilst some of her numerous sons are playing around her This is a consecrated iconographic theme, of which it will be easy for us to quote numerous examples, spread over nearly twenty centuries and over the whole of the Far East. In face of the scarcity of western counterparts, this abundance of documents would at once weigh down the balance in favour of the Buddhist identification : comparison of the various replicas will bring full confirmation

### III

But, first of all, it is relevant to present briefly to the non-Orientalist reader the goddess whose acquaintance we invite him to make In truth, she was originally only a fairy, and even a wicked fairy By birth she, as well as her troup of imps, belonged to the race, often maleficent, of spirits of the air (*yaksha*), in whom popular Indian belief had, and still has, a habit of incarnating contagious maladies. She herself personified the most pitiless of infantile epidemics. It is well known that in the India of the present day, in spite of the progress of vaccination, small-pox is dreaded to such an extent that it is still the custom not to reckon children among the members of the family until they have victoriously passed through the trial of this terrible disease. This is why the « green » Hâritî still receives from the Buddhists of Nepal the worship which the Hindus of the plains address to the « cold » Çîtalâ That she should have ended by transforming herself from a formidable scourge into a beneficent divinity will not surprise any student of religions. Of course, there was a legend to explain this transmutation of worthless lead into pure gold. Buddha in person had once converted the *yakshinî* who decimated, or (as is metaphorically written) pitilessly « devoured », the children of the town of Râjagriha (now Râjgir, in Behar) In order to convert her to more human feelings, he decided to deprive her for a time of Pingala, the last and most loved of her five hundred sons. Some even relate that the Master hid Pingala under his inverted alms-vase : and on Chinese paintings we do, in fact, see hordes of demons vainly endeavouring by the help of cranes and levers to turn over the huge bowl, in which the little genius is imprisoned (¹) However this may be, the stratagem succeeded. The grief caused to Hârîtî by this momentary separation made her return to herself, or, better, put herself in the place of simple mortals, whom she had at times robbed of their sole offspring : she swore never to do so again. However, every one must live, even the wicked who repent. As soon as she is converted, the ogress mother respectfully calls the attention of the Master to the fact that the first precept of his morality, by interdicting all homicide, really condemns her and her five hundred sons to die of hunger, and Buddha, much struck by the justice of this remark, promises that henceforth in all convents his monks shall offer a daily pittance, of course on condition that she and hers faithfully observe their vows...

This monastic legend, very skilfully composed, endeavours, as we see, not merely to conciliate the contradictory notions attached to this deity, at once both cruel and propitious : in order completely to reassure the faithful, it also stands as a guarantee against any relapse of the converted *yakshinî* into her ancient errors. Last and in regard to decorum most important, it claims to vindicate, under colour of a contract long ago made with the Master, the installation of this former ogress in the convent, and the propriety of the worship offered to her. It is, in fact, only too clear that it is from pure concession to popular superstitions that, according to the testimony of the Chinese pilgrim Yi-tsing, the image of Hârîtî was to be « found either in the porch or in a corner of the dining-hall of all Indian monasteries » There she was, moreover,

---

(1) Cf *Archæologia*, LHI, 1892, pp. 239-244 ; *La légende de Kouei tseu mou chen* (Annales du Musée Guimet, Bibl d'Art, vol. I); Ed. CHAVANNES, *T'oung Pao*, Oct. 1904, p. 490.

he tells us in plain terms, adored no longer as a devourer, but as a « giver » of children  Usually the « genius with the golden bag » was opposite to her — at least, when he was not, as in a number of surviving representations, seated beside her · for the common people had been quick to associate the dispenser of riches with the goddess of fecundity (¹)  We may even be permitted to think that their altars must have been those not least frequented by devout laymen, the more so as both sexes were there plainly provided for. A passage from Hiuan-tsang interests us still more directly by attesting that the worship of Hâritî had been transported early into the north-west of India. While following the same itinerary, we were surprised to encounter, under a name which is nothing but an Afghan translation of hers, the mound, still miraculous, even in the eyes of present-day Musalmans, which marks the location of her principal sanctuary in this country of Gandhâra, where at about the beginning of our era the Græco-Buddhist art flourished (²).

This is sufficient to explain to us the antiquity, number and character, at once classical and benignant, of her Indian images. All answer more or less to the general description given by Yi-tsing : she is depicted « as holding a babe in her arms and round her knees three or five children ». The little genii who are usually playing and worrying each other evidently represent her « five hundred sons »  There is nothing astonishing in seeing them all of nearly the same size : the texts admit that their mother, a true Gigogne, may very well have been able to bring them

---

(1) See above Essay V, *The Tutelary Pair.*
(2) Cf. Yi-Tsing, *Records,* trans TAKAKUSU, p  37 ; Hiuan-Tsang, *Mémoires,* trans. JULIEN, I, p.  120, *Bull. de l'Éc  fr  d'Extrême-Orient,* I, 1901, pp. 341 sqq

all into the world in the same year ('). In the midst of all
this swarm, which often climbs over her person, one
would sometimes say that she is posing in advance as'
an Italian allegory of Charity. At one time she is seated :
her « Benjamin » rests in her lap and childishly plays with
her necklace (pl XLVII, 1), or at times simultaneously
suckles her breast. Then again she is standing; but her
favourite still clings to her bosom. Usually he is placed
astride her hip, in the manner in which Indian women
carry their children ; and two at least of his brothers have
succeeded in climbing as far as the maternal shoulders
(pl XLVII, 2) With these two types — at times partly
combined, as in pl. XLVIII, 1, which in addition shows the
husband of the goddess — may be connected the relatively
numerous images furnished no less by the ruins of the
districts of Peshawar and Mathurâ than by the famous grottoes of Ajanṭâ. The ogress, once the terror of fruitful
mothers, has clearly there become a kind of matron, hope
of barren women It is this auspicious group that, as we
are about to see, has conquered the whole of the Far East.

## IV

For this pacific conquest two ways had been opened by
those pioneers of Indian civilization, leaders of caravans or
master mariners, the one by land and the other by sea. It
was this latter route which must perforce have been followed
in order to reach Java, on the actual confines of the Indian
Archipelago. In preference to the little bronzes of the museum in Batavia — evidence too portable to be unexception-
able, — we reproduce here the Hârîtî actually sculptured on

_____

(1) *Mahâvastu*, ed. SENART, I, p. 253, l 2

the left wall of the entrance corridor of the temple called
Chandi Mendut, near to the famous *stûpa* of Boro-Budur
(IX[th] century), and doubtless almost contemporaneous with
it. Represented on the right wall opposite, an image of
the genius of riches completes the proof of the trans-
plantation of their double worship into the most beautiful
of the « Islands of the Southern Seas » ([1]). Crouching upon
a cushion, her legs covered with a *sarong* and her body
clothed only with jewels, the goddess, who wears a sump-
tuous coiffure, is surrounded by no less than thirteen
« little demons »  One is being presented to her on the
right by an attendant, whilst the others play in the sand,
caper about, or climb trees in order to steal their fruits;
and during this time Pingala, resting in her arms, prepares
to suckle with all the conviction of a nursling charged by
the sculptor to emphasize the identification of his mother (pl. XLVIII, 2).

If, this first mark noted, we return to  our starting-
point, we may follow the same family group on the march
over the sandy roads of Central Asia. It was hardly doubtful that, in order to reach China, they must have pursued
the same routes which the Chinese pilgrims had taken in
order to reach India. Of this probability recent discoveries
have made a certainty. The original of the frontispiece marks
at Turfan precisely the route followed on the outward
journey by Fa-hian and Hiuan-tsang, the northern route
which, footing the chain of the Celestial Mountains, rounds
the great desert basin of the Tarim. As to the southern route,
which deployed along the northern slope of the Kuen-lun
mountains the chaplet of the oases visited by Sung Yun
on the outward journey and by Hiuan-tsang on his return,

(1) See above, p. 264

it was unwilling to be behind its rival in any way, and it also has already furnished us, if not with a canvas, at least with a mural painting of Hâritî.

No one is unacquainted with the brilliant excavations carried out by Sir Aurel Stein, on the occasion of two successive missions, over the ancient alignment of this track across the present-day desert of Takla-Makan. One of them brought to light, in March 1908, at the north of the oasis of Domoko (itself situated at a longitude of a little more than one degree east of Khotan) a large figure of a woman, painted in tempera on a coating of mortar, in the embrasure of the door of a little Buddhist sanctuary. The cell measured on the interior m 2,50 by m 2,45, and its mud walls, decorated with Buddhas and Bodhisattvas, attained a thickness of m. 1,35. The panel, m 1,15 wide, which particularly interests us here, had been preserved almost intact under a heap of sand accumulated by the wind to a height of m 1,20. Only the lower part had in former times, when the entrance served as a passage for worshippers, suffered much from the abrasion of passers-by. However, according to the notes kindly communicated to us by the explorer, there could still be distinguished near the left foot of the woman, who, apparently, is seated, two little figures, clothed and gambolling about, whilst near her right foot a little naked boy seemed to be getting out of the way of a blow struck by a person completely effaced. As to the upper portion, it has reached the British Museum in an excellent condition, and Sir Aurel Stein has very kindly allowed us to give a first and double reproduction of it (pl. XLV). It shows clearly the characteristic features of the principal figure, the dreamy squint of the eyes, the symmetry of the two lovelocks, the perforated and frightfully distended lobes of the ears, the oval of the « moon face », too broad according to our taste, the folds (classic in India) of the neck, the net of pearls in the hair, finally and above all, the triple circular orb of the nimbus  The goddess, since such she is, is dressed to the waist in a short cassock, of a rich greenish hue, spotted with yellow and trimmed with fawn braid, the short sleeves terminating above the elbow in a frill of linen folded in fluted plaits  Underneath are long, reddish sleeves, evidently belonging to the bodice of the dress. A turquoise-coloured scarf, exactly similar to that worn by the Gandharian images (pl. XLVII, 1), hangs in folds in the hollows of her arms  Her left hand, with straightened index, rests on the front of her knee, which is bent in the Indian manner. Meanwhile a naked child clings to her left bosom, as if asking to be suckled, whilst another little boy is seated astride on her right forearm, and two more, one of whom is dressed, ride familiarly on her shoulders  This more than suffices to determine, from analogy with pll  XLVII-XLVIII, 1, the identification with Hâritî and her mischievous progeny  The opposite wall of the embrasure is, unfortunately, destroyed : we should have expected to see there the genius of riches, the usual counterpart of the goddess of children. Let us add that, according to the chronological indications elicited  by Sir Aurel Stein, the decoration of the temple to which this image belonged could not be later than the VIII[th] century A. D., and may be a little earlier.

If, continuing our journey eastward, we at last arrive in China, we are so much the more certain to discover Hâritî there as, according to the evidence of Yi-tsing, « the portrait of the goddess-mother of demon sons (Kwei-tseu-mu-chen) » was already in his time (end of the VII[th] century) to be met with in the country. In fact, under this same surname, pronounced Ki-si-mo-jin, she has

pushed her way much further still, as far as Japan. A simple
inspection of her modern images, whether representing her
under her usual mask or, by a curious survival, in her
proper guise as an ogress (pl XLIX), will prove that the
type has not, any more than the name, been so travestied
by the local interpretation that one can hesitate as to its
identity, even in the absence of any traditional designation,
it could be divined simply from the child nestling in his
mother's lap or walking by her side In China itself matters
are not quite so simple, and a new element seems to have
intervened to complicate the problem. Has the personality
of Hâritî been engrafted upon that same native goddess
who, according to a certain interpretation, had been identified with the Indian Bodhisattva, Avalokiteçvara? Has she
simply been absorbed into the vogue of the feminine
forms of the latter and considered as one of the numerous avatars of his inexhaustible grace? It is not for us to
decide, any more than to unravel the origins of the curious legend which tends to make of « Kuan-yin with a
child » a virgin who is a mother only by adoption. But
what we believe we can affirm, by reason both of the
fundamental identity of the worship offered and' of the
exterior analogy of the iconographic types, is that the
innumerable statuettes, either seated or standing, in which
« the Great Mistress with the white robe... just because she is
the patron of childless people, is represented with a child
in her arms, which makes her strongly resemble the Virgin Mary (¹) », are only succedanea of the Indian and Serind-
ian images of Hâritî (pl. L). Finally, and consequentially,
we must likewise recognize the latter under the exactly

---

(1) De Groor, *Les fetes annuellement célebrées à Fmout* (Ann. du Musée
Guimet, vol XI), p 182

similar features of the Annamese Quan-Am, who, « seated on a rock and draped in a robe with wide plaits, bears in her arms a child, which has caused her to be surnamed by our soldiers the Holy Virgin (¹) »

## V

This time the circle of our pilgrimage of research is closed, but only after having embraced the whole of the Far East We see that the observation of the Christian analogy of these images recurs like a refrain in the mouths of those Europeans whose eyes have once lighted upon them. In case the unanimity of the testimonies should run some risk of impressing the reader, he will quickly reassure himself by reflecting that, if some Egyptian mummy were wakened from its secular sleep, it would not hesitate in the least to recognize in them replicas of Isis suckling Horus, whilst every modern Hindu would with the same certainty see in them Krishna in the arms of his mother Dêvakî or of his nurse Yaçodâ. The type of the woman with a child, the happy incarnation of the wishes of mothers and the natural object of their worship, belongs, in fact, to all times, if not to all countries. Still there are distinctions to be made. Not everywhere do the same images personify the same ideas, far from it : did they so, different civilizations would nevertheless know them under different names. The whole intention of this short study is to assign to the heroine of the frontispiece and pl. XLV her authentic position by restoring to her, if possible, her moral physionomy and replacing her in her milieu. Deified, as witness her halo, a feminine divinity, as witness her forms; goddess-mother,

---

(1) G DUMOUTIER, Les cultes annamites (Extract from the Revue Indo-Chinoise, 1906), p. 30 of the separate print

as witness her progeny ; affiliated to the Buddhist pantheon, as witness the place in which she was found, Indian by origin, as witness her Gandharian prototypes; we have been able, without any shadow of violence, to include her in the group of idols, and the cycle of legends, dedicated to the ancient ogress of smallpox. Of course, she is shown to us only as transformed into a protectress of children and a dispenser of fecundity to women : from the very moment when we catch sight of her in India, this transformation is already an accomplished fact. In the last analysis, the best verification of her identity rests, here as there, in her entourage of urchins : were it not for this suspicious trace of her past, which even in her subsequent dignity continues to cling to her, we should not have been able with absolute certainty to call her by her Sanskrit name of Hârîtî, the so-styled « mother of the little demons ».

All taken into consideration, we believe that we thus arrive at a precise and sure identification    and the interest of this iconographic type is thereby increased. It announces, or recalls, in fact, congeners beginning with India, its fatherland, as far as Japan, the limit of its migrations, to say nothing of Java. Henceforward it would be difficult to choose a better illustration of the recently acquired knowledge concerning the progressive diffusion of Buddhist art throughout the Far East. It was not until 1900 that our public had a revelation of the existence in Japan, since the VIIth century, of a religious art of the human figure — of what was formerly styled the « grand art ». That its origin was to be sought in China, through the intermediacy of Corea, was quickly seen, and can easily to-day be verified by the photographs recently published by M Ed. Chavannes ([1]).

(1) ED. CHAVANNES, *Mission archéologique dans la Chine septentrionale,* Paris, 1909, pll. CV-CCLXXXVII

The productions of the ancient Buddhist art of China are in their turn connected in the most evident manner with those lately exhumed by the Russian, English, German, French, and even Japanese excavations in Turkestan. But these latter had been independently and from the first connected, by a transition no less evident. with the works of the Indo-Greek school of Gandhâra. Thus, thanks to the combined efforts of the latest scientific missions in Asia, we have seen joined again the scattered links, or, better, the broken glimpses, which we already possessed of the long chain of transmission. The most important result of the last explorations will have been definitely to arrange before our eyes in an uninterrupted series the numerous images which, escorting that of Buddha, followed it in procession as far as the islands of the Rising Sun or of the Southern Seas. In this varied train of gracious or furious figures, if there is none more charming, neither is there any more « representative », than that of Hâritî, were it only because we meet her at each step on the road, and this is why, among ll those which have already been brought to the museums of Europe, this one, from the first, forced itself upon our notice

But let us not be misunderstood. We do not in the least claim to base on the frail support of this single image the theory which hundreds of documents continue more and more to reinforce, the theory of the conquest of eastern Asia by Indo-Greek art : we merely say that it remains a signally typical example of a historical phenomenon whereof it formed only a part Were we pressed a little further, we might even be willing to see in it an excellent illustration of a fact still more general. The recent unification of the art of higher and lower Asia has, in fact, a correlative in the fundamental and long recognized unity of European art :

and now it appears more and more clearly that the two
have a common source. If for a moment we disregard the
intrusion of the Musalman Arabs, the history of *religious*
art in the ancient world, from the beginning of our era,
may — when reduced to its essential features and excluding
numerous local variations — be summed up somewhat in
this manner . on the decadent trunk of Hellenistic art
were grafted in nearer Asia two vigorous young shoots,
of which one has been called Græco-Buddhist, and the other
might just as well be called Græco-Christian It is not for us
to ignore the fact that the latter has through Italy and
Byzantium conquered the whole of Europe; but we must
realize also that the former, growing and multiplying like
the Indian fig-tree, has likewise gradually won over the
whole of Eastern Asia. And thus, from the islands of the
Atlantic to those of the Pacific, humanity has by degrees
come to pray only at the feet of more or less distant, more
or less unsuspected offshoots of Greek art But on the most
distant branches of this great evergreen tree never have
there burst forth flowers more beautiful nor more full of
resemblance, if not in regard to the moral perfume
which they exhale, at least in regard to the material form
in which they array themselves before our eyes, than
the images, Christian and Buddhist, of the Madonna.
Even if, as we venture to foresee, the field of artistic
comparisons must habitually be widened from one ocean
to the other, the most universally attractive role will
always revert to those figures which incarnate the maternal — and in some cases at the same time virginal —
grace of the eternal feminine.

PLATE XLV

Cf pp 285-6

We are indebted to the kindness of Sir Aurel Stein for the communication of these two photographs The first (no 1) was taken by him *in situ* and in a slanting position, for want of sufficient space for the camera The second (no 2) was made at the British Museum and slightly retouched on the cheeks Cf. pp 285-6, and *Ruins of Desert Cathay* (London, 1912), II, p 414 and pl XI *b*

For another specimen from Chinese Turkestan we refer the reader to the frontispiece and pp 271-5, — now also to the monumental publication of Dr von Le Coq, *Chotscho* (Berlin, 1913), pl 40

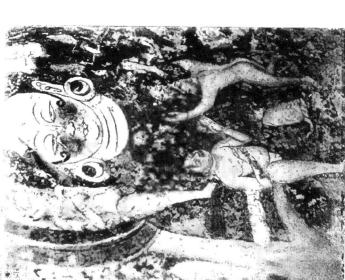

2

AFTER A WALL-PAINTING FROM DOMOKO (CHINESE TURKESTAN)

(AS SET UP IN BRITISH MUSEUM)

1

(SIDE VIEW BEFORE REMOVAL)

PLATE XLVI

Cf pp 278-9

— Lower half of an ivory plaque affixed to a Book of the Gospels, ...ich was transferred in 1802 from Metz to the Bibliothèque Natio-, Paris (Ms latins 10.438, exhibited [cf *Notice des objets exposés*, is, 1851] in glass case XXX under no 472) On the last page of the , in a handwriting of the end of the XVIIIth or the beginning of the XIXth century, there is a note in these terms « Presented to the ...pter of the Holy Saviour at Metz by Bishop Aldaberon II (died 14, 1004), son of Duke Frederic and Beatrix, sister of Hugh ...et » On either side of the Virgin's head are the uncial letters MP ΘY representing MHTHP ΘEOY, « Mother of God » For a descrip...n of the central figure cf p 278 or WESTWOOD, *A Descriptive Cata-ue of the Fictile Ivories* (London, 1876), p 384 Joseph, of smaller ..., sits to the left, deep in thought, to the right stands a female atten-...t, whose hands are hidden under what looks like a swaddling-cloth ...e fact of the nursing Virgin, so unusual in the west till the XIVth ...tury, the crouching Joseph, the presence of the maid-servant, in ...rt, every part in the exceptional design of this « homely *tableau de re* » are so many reasons, adduced by Ad GOLDSCHMIDT (*Die Elfen-skulpturen aus der Zeit der Karolingischen und Sachsischen Kaiser*, ...ln, 1914, pl XXXII, no 79 and p 44), for calling in question the

genuineness of the plaque, which he takes to be a forgery dating about 1800 But a curious passage in the Protevangelium of James, xix 2, to which M Gab MILLET has kindly drawn our attention, would perhaps explain the startling peculiarities, if not completely vindicate the authenticity, of this piece « And they stood in the place where the cave was, and behold a bright light overshadowed the cave And the midwife said And gradually that light withdrew until the babe was seen, and it came and took the breast from its mother Mary And the midwife cried out » (*The Apocryphal Gospels*, by B HARRIS COWPER. 4th Ed , London, 1874 . *The Gospel of James*, c xiv, pp 20-1). The fact that the feminine attendant on the right plays so well the part of the midwife waiting to receive the child renders it highly probable that the ivory-carver had this strange tale in his mind

II The Coptic Virgin of Saqqara is reproduced from the water-colour copy by Mrs Quibbell published in J. E QUIBBELL, *Excavations at Saqqara*, II, 1908, pl XL In the attitude of the child Jesus, holding his mother's fore-arm with his two hands, we must recognize a curious artistic survival; for it is exactly the same as that of Horus nursed by Isis (Cf p 278 )

2. — COPTIC VIRGIN

1. — ROMANESQUE VIRGIN

PLATE XLVII

Cf pp 232-3.

I — From a photograph taken by the author at the British Museum (height of the original m 0.71) The image has already been published by Dr BURGESS (*J. of Ind Art and Ind*, 1898, pl 4, 2)

It reminds us distantly of the type of Demeter The bosoms are placed very high, as is usual in the school of Gandhâra The head of Pingala is partly broken At the bottom, on the goddess' right, ought we to recognize two donors? The other persons — one of whom, on the right, is feeding a parrot, whilst two others on the left, are wrestling, a fourth raises a fruit to his mouth and a fifth is crouched on the front of the stand — evidently form part of the troop of little demons, progeny of Hârîtî. (Cf p 283)

II — From a photograph taken by the author at the Lahore Museum (height of the original 1 metre) it is the statue found by Col Deane at Sikri, published already by M E SENART in the *Journal Asiatique*, febr -march 1890, pl III), and since reproduced by Dr BUR-GESS (*J I A I*, 1898, pl 3, 2) Notice the very ungraceful protuberance formed by the jewelled belt under the drapery The difference of costume between the two figures of the plate arises from the fact that no I, in addition to the long *dhotî* and shawl, wears also a tunic with sleeves, and even sleeves folded into little plaits

INDO-GREEK IMAGES OF HÁRITÍ

(IN GANDHÁRA)

1

2

PLATE XLVIII

Cf pp 141-3, 26₁, 283-4

I — Group, consisting of Pâñcika and Hârtî, now in the Peshawar Museum, and reproduced from a photograph kindly lent by Dr J Ph. VOGEL It comes from the excavations made by Dr. D B SPOONER at Sahrı-Bahlol, and has already been published by him in *Arch Surv India, Annual Report, 1906-7,* pl XXXII, *c* In his hands, both broken, the genius of riches must have held (right) his lance and (left) the purse which Hârtî, apparently, was helping him to exhibit to the gladdened eyes of the faithful (cf pp. 141-3 and 283) In addition to the nursling of the goddess we see also around them five other *putti,* whilst sixteen more play about on the pedestal

II. — This photograph, taken by the author, represents only the central part of the panel, with the image of the goddess (cf. pp. 264 and 284) For a complete picture we may have recourse to the photograph published by Dr J Ph VOGEL in the *B E F E O ,* IV, 1904, p 727

1. — HÂRITÎ AND HER PARTNER IN GANDHÂRA

2. — HÂRITÎ IN JAVA

PLATE XLIX

Cf pp 286-7

These two modern Japanese woodcuts belong (as also does no 2 of pl L) to the collection of Mr. Henry H Getty, to whom we are indebted for the photographs and for permission to reproduce them. We have pointed out above (p 287) the interest of their rapprochement

I — The Hārītī on the left is erect and walking with little Pingala at her side When we observe her frowning eyebrows, her angry features, her wide mouth garnished with its terrible row of teeth, her emaciated and withered bosom, her gesture of seizing prey, everything seems to express the primitive character of the ogress, reappearing under the customary mask of Buddhist serenity

II — The one to the right, on the contrary, has retained not only a pose quite Indian (the same, in fact, which she affects at Ajantā; cf. Burgess, *Notes on the Rock Temples of Ajantā*, pl VI), but also her placid aspect as a stout matron holding her favourite child in her lap.

1                JAPANESE IMAGES OF KI·SI·MO·JIN                2

PLATE L.

Cf p 287.

I — Statuette in white porcelain, belonging to the Musée Guimet, Paris As Prof. Ed CHAVANNES kindly informs us, it represents the *Song-tseu* Kuan-yin, the goddess holds in her lap the child (*tseu*) which she is supposed to bring (*song*) to the faithful Her necklace is cross-shaped. She sits on a rock, encircled by two dragons and lotuses, and on her left is seen a book The child is provided with a writing-pencil and a roll of paper Before the pedestal stand to the right the golden boy (*kin-t'ong*) and to the left the jade girl (*yu-niu*) Height m 0,38 It is well known that this type has been industrially reproduced in thousands of specimens

II — Statuette of painted porcelain, belonging to the collection of Mr Henry H GETTY it appeared in the Exhibition of Buddhist Art at the Musée Cernuschi in 1913 In the Catalogue we read " No 132 China Ceramics Kuan-yin with the child, standing on the *tao-tié* China ware decorated with coral red ". Her polychromy, the sveltness of her proportions, the adorable awkwardness with which she holds the child standing on her left hand, everything, even the grinning monster which she treads under her feet, combines to give her, in spite of her Chinese costume, the bearing of a « primitive » Virgin, and to win for her the keen appreciation of amateurs

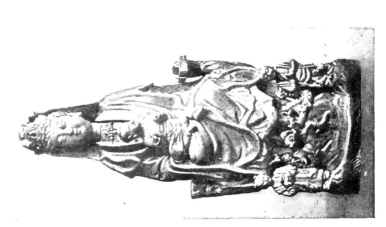

CHINESE IMAGES OF KUAN-YIN

1                    2

# INDEX

---

*(Arabic numerals refer to pages, Roman to the descriptions accompanying the numbered plates)*

Abandonment of Home, Great  See *Mahd-bhinishkramana*
*Abhayamudrd  See* Mudrâ
Acacia sirisa  *See* Çirîsha
AÇOKA, Bodhi-tree provided with railing by, 17, 102
— visited by, 23, 108
— Buddha relics redistributed by, 78.
— Gandhâra a frontier country under, 121
— Râmagrâma visited by, 23
— romance of, at Vidiçâ 79.
— Sânchi connected with, 78.
*Açokdvaddna*, passage in the, figured 79 (Sânchî).
AÇVAGHOSHA  *See* Buddhacarita
— *See* Sûtrâlamkara.
*Açvattha* figured on the gate of Sânchi 94, 102, 104, 107.
— *See also* Bodhi-tree.
AGATHOKLES, coin of, described 126.
AGNES, type of, in Jâtaka 49.
Ajantâ caves, date of frescoes of, 190
— — Great Miracle figured in the, 160 and n 2, 162 5, XXI.
— — Hârîtî figured in the, XLIX.
— — paintings (archaic) of the, 4
— — Shaddanta-jâtaka figured in the, 40,188,195-9,199,XXIX.
AJÂTAÇATRU, visit of, to Buddha figured 19, 179, n. 2 (Barhut)
*Akanishtha* heaven, the highest of the *Rûpadhdtu*, 159, n. 1
AKSHOBHYA figured 267 (Batavia Museum)
— — 256 7 (Boro-Budur)
ALEXANDER, Indian campaign of, 126.
Alms vase figured XXVII (Gandhâra).

AMARÂ, story of, figured 50 (Barhut)
Amarâvatî sculptures, elegant style of, II
— Stûpa, Boro-Budur modelled upon the, 209-10
— — Buddha figures from the, date of, 116
— — Buddha's visit to Bimbisâra figured on the, 102
— — date of bas-reliefs on the, 190
— — four Great Miracles figured on the, 73, 148, II-IV
— — railing of (fragmentary), 4
— — Shaddanta-jâtaka figured on the, 39, 188, 195-6, XXIX
*Amba  See* Mango
Ambrosia, Vase of, figured 91 (Sânchi)
AMITÂBHA figured 256-7 (Boro-Budur)
— figured on head of Avalokiteçvara 264 (Chandi Mendut)
AMOGHASIDDHI figured 256-7 (Boro Budur).
ÂNANDA incarnated in King of Benares 43, XIX (Sânchî)
Anchorite. *See* Hermit.
*Anda*, part of Stûpa, 33
Animals, Buddha in company of, figured 107 (Sânchî)
— Buddha's birth in form of, 35
— throne formed of superposed, XXI (Ajantâ)
— *See also* Antelope, Buffalo, Bull, Camel, Crocodile, Deer, Dog, Elephant, Hamsa, Horse, Lion, Monkey, Quail, Parrot, Peacock, Stag, Swan, Tortoise, Unicorn, Woodpecker.

24

Ankle-rings worn by female figure 89 (Sânchî)

Ankuça See Elephant, goad for.

Annam, Hârîtî figure in, 287-8

Antagiri, Bimbisâra's visit to Buddha at, figured 101 (Sânchî)

Antelope, Buddha's birth as See Kurunga-jâtaka

— figured 97, 107 (Sânchî)

— — xxix (Amarâvatî)

— Woodpecker and Tortoise, story of the, 40

Antelope-horn See Rishyaçringa

— See also Deer

ANTIALKIDAS mentioned on column at Vi-diçâ 82

Antiquities, Indian, materials for Diction-ary of, 80

ÂRÂDA figured xxxvii (Boro-Budur)

Ârâmadûsaka-jâtaka narrated 44

— figured vi (Barhut)

Archer, Buddha's birth as See Asadisa-jâtaka.

— figured on the gate of Sânchî 93

ARISTOTLE, Lay of, cited 48

Armourer workshop of, figured 52 (Bar-hut)

Arms, dislocated, of Javanese women figured 245-6 (Boro-Budur)

Arrow, making of, described 52

Art, Buddhist, abstract character of, 14

— — ceremonial occasions of, 10

— — conflicting tendencies in ancient school of, 18

— — developement of ancient school of, 17, 25-6.

— — Gandharian See Gandhâra

— — origin of See Essay I.

— — routine procedure of an-cient, 17

Asadisa-jâtaka narrated 56

Ascetic, Buddha's birth as See Ârâmadû-saka-jâtaka, Bhisa-jâtaka, Camma-sâtaka-jâtaka Dabbhapuppha ja-taka, Dûbhiyamakkata jâtaka

— See Arada, Brahman Hermit

ASITA, Buddha's presentation to, figured 5 (Amaravatî).

Atlantes figured xxv (Gandhâra).

Aureoles figured xxi (Ta-t'ong-fu), xxv (Gandhâra), xxviii (Gandhara. See also Halo and Nimbus

Avadâna çataka, Maitrakanyakâvadana ac-cording to the, 244, n 2

AVALOKITEÇVARA figured 255, xxii (Boro-Budur), xxiii (Kudâ).

— pensive pose of, xxv (Gandhâra)

— statuette in Batavia Museum 267

— wanting in Gandhâra sculptures, also in Divyavadâna and Mahâ-vastu, 177 8

Axe, hermit's, figured 98

Âyuh-samskâra-utsarjana localized at Vai-çâlî 149 n.

Balconies figured 93 (Sânchî)

— — xxv (Gandhâra)

Balustrade See Railing.

Band round knees and loins See Paryan-ka-bandha.

Banner figured xxxv (Boro Budur)

Barhut railing, remains of, in Calcutta Museum 57

-- stupa, Bodhi figured on the, 102

— -- Buddha represented only by symbols on the, 75

— — Buddha's Conception figured on the, 92.

— — Buddha's figure wanting on the, 117

— — Buddhas, seven traditional, fi gured on the, 72

— — Buddhist Heaven figured on the, 72

— — date of, 34, 190.

— — Elâpatra's visit to Buddha fi-gured on the, 19

— — Great Miracle figured on the, 178-180, xxviii

— — jâtakas figured on the. See Essay II, V, VI

— — Shaddanta jâtaka figured on the, 39, 184, 194 6, xxix.

— — Viçvantara jâtaka figured on the, 57.

— — Kinnaras figured on the, 242

— — monks not figured on the, 76

— — scenes identified by inscrip tions on the, 68

Barhut *stûpa*, sculptures ot, followed a living tradition 58

Bark-garments, Brahmanical, figured on the gate of Sânchi 97.

BARTH, A., scene at Boro Budur identified by, 269 n.

Barygaza *See* Bhiruka.

Baskets figured at Barhut, 50

Bas-reliefs, composition of, at Sânchi, compared with that of altar scenes of Middle Ages, 83.

— *passim*

Batavia Museum, sculptures in the, 266 9.

BEAL, Rev S, conversion of Kâçyapas identified by, 76 (Sânchi)

— view of concerning miraculous trees, 72

Beasts *See* Animals

Bells figured XLIV (Chandi Mendut)

Belt of jewelry, worn by female, figured 89 (Sanchi)

Benares, Great Miracle figured at, 181-2

— king ot, *see* Ruru-jâtaka.

— sculptures from, IV.

— signacula from, 12

— *See also* Mrigadava, Sarnâth

Besnagar, Açoka's romance at, 79

Besom *See* Rajoharana

Bestiaria, Unicorn story in, 48

*Bhadra-ghata See* Vase, Lottery

*Bhallâtîya-jâtaka See* Kinnara-jâtaka.

Bharhut *See* Barhut

Bharukaccha *See* Bhiruka

Bhilsa, Sânchi stûpa near, 63

BHIRU, Minister of Rudrâyana, figured 238 (Boro-Budur)

Bhiruka, foundation of, 240

*Bhisa-jâtaka* narrated 45-6

Bhôpal, Begum of, offers gate of Sânchi stûpa to France 62

BHRIKUTÎ-TÂRÂ, image of, in Batavia Museum 267.

Bignonia flower figured 86 (Sânchi)

— Suaveolens *See* Pâtali.

BIMBISÂRA, visit of, to Buddha, figured 77, 101 (Sânchi)

— visit of Buddha to, figured 102 (Amarâvatî)

BIMBISÂRA mentioned in story of Rudrâyana 232 sqq

Birds figured 100 107 (Sânchi)

— XXV, on roof, (Gandhâra)

— XXXIV (Boro-Budur)

— XLIV (Chandi Mendut).

BLOCH, Dr Th., view of, concerning figure of bull in Lahore Museum 21 n. 2

BOCCACIO, Rishyaçringa-jâtaka transposed by, 48

Bodh-Gaya, signacula from, 12

— *See also* Mahâbodhi

*Bodhi*, emblem of the, employed for miracles of the second rank 19

— figured 16, 77, 103, 108 (Sânchi), 102 (Barhut), IV (Gandhâra and Amarâvatî), XIX (Sarnâth)

— represented by throne under tree 148, n 2

— temple, miracles related by Hiuan-tsang concerning the, 24, n 1.

— tree at Bodh-Gayâ 13

— — Açoka's visit to the, 23, 108

— — Buddha figured under the, 26 (Gandhâra)

— — Buddha symbolized by, 19-20

— — Buddhas, seven last, each symbolized by his special, 72, 104 (Sânchi).

— — figured 72, 102 (Barhut and Sânchi), 89, 90, 102 (Sânchi), 178 (Barhut), I (on coins), II (Sânchi and Amaravatî)

— — railing built by Açoka round, 17

— — Tishyarakshitâ's attempt upon the, 108

*Bodhisattva* figured (?) 162, n 2 (Ajantâ), 255 (Boro-Budur), 263-4 (Chandi Mendut), XV and XVI (Gandhâra), XXII (Boro-Budur), XXIII (Kudâ), XXVII and XXVIII (Gandhâra, XXXV (Boro-Budur)

— *See also* Siddhârtha, Avalokiteçvara, Maitreya, Mañjuçrî

*Bodhisattvâvaddnakalpalatâ*, Boro-Budur sculptures in conformity with the, 225 6

*Bodhisattvdvaddnakalpalatd* Maitrakanyaka story according to the, 244 n 2.
— Mandhâtravadâna according to the, 225 n 1
Book, emblem of Brahmâ 175, of Mañjuçrî 255 (Boro-Budur)
— figured xxvii, xxviii (Gandhâra), l (China)
Boro-Budur, artistic defects of, 207-8.
— conservation work at, 206 n
— designed as stûpa modelled upon Amarâvatî Stûpa 209-to
— Guide to, by J Groneman, 215
— Great Miracle figured at, xxii
— jâtakas at, Essay VIII
— original plan of, 208 n 1, 213
— sculptures, artistic merits of, 212-3.
—     — Bodhisattvâvadânakalpalatâ followed by the, 225-6
—     — characteristics (crowded scenes, avoidance of scenes of violence, failure in individuality, bookish character) of 250-4
—     — edifying scenes emphasized on, 227
—     — insipid scenes figured in, 248-9
—     — Pradakshinâ arrangement of, 214-5
—     — to be photographed 248
— situation, form and dimensions of, 205, 206-7
— view of, xxxi, xxxii, xxxiii
Bowls of viands figured 233 (Boro-Budur).
Boy, golden, figured l (China)
Boys playing a game figured on a painting from Central Asia 273-4
Bracelets worn by female figure 89 (Sânchî)
BRAHMÂ figured 96 (Sânchî), 162 and n. 2 (Ajantâ), xv (Kanishka casket), xix (Sârnâth), xxiv (Gandhâra).
— heaven of, figured 71, 92, 103 (Sânchî)
BRAHMAMITRA mentioned in inscription 4 (Bodh-Gayâ).
Brahman ascetic *See* Cammasâtaka-jâtaka, 44.

Brahman, bark garments of, figured 97 (Sânchî)
— figured 97 (Sânchî), 218 (Boro-Budur), xxv (Loriyân-Tangai), xxxiv, xxxvii, xl (Boro-Budur).
— headdress of *See* Chignon.
— hermitage figured xxxvii (Boro-Budur)
— inferior to Kshatriya according to the Buddhists, 54.
— music of the, 48.
— *See also* Arâda, Asita
*Brisht. See* Mat.
British Museum, signacula in the, 11.
Broach. *See* Bhiruka.
BUDDHA, almsbowl of, worshipped xv (Gandhâra)
— birth of figured 21 n. 1 (later Stelae of Benares), 70 n. 1 (Sânchî), iii (Gandhâra and Amaravatî), iv (Gandhâra and Benares), xix (Sârnâth).
—     — symbolized 20-1 (Amarâvatî), 21 (Buddhist coins).
— Bodhi of *See* Bodhi.
— castes in relation to, 53
— conception of, figured 92 (Sânchî), iii (Gandhâra and Amarâvatî)
— death of *See* Parinirvâna
— descent of, from heaven *See* Devavatâra
— Dharmacakrapravartana of *See* Dharmacakra
— elephant tamed by, at Râjagriha, 150
— farewell of, to Chandaka iv (Benares).
— figure, artistic value of the, 136-7.
—     — composition of the, consisting of monk and prince, 130-4
—     — created by sculptors of N W. India 24
—     — date of, in Amarâvatî 116, Burmah 115, Cambodia 115, Ceylon 115-6, China 115, Gandhâra 117-8, Java 115, Magadha 116, Mathurâ 116, Sârnâth 116, Siam 115, Tibet 115.

BUDDHA figure declared impossible in texts
18
—  — embodies ideals of Olympian
and Mahâpurusha 134-5
—  — Greek characteristics of the,
119 120
—  — Greek origin of the, Essay IV.
—  — Indo-Greek type of, 7.
—  — oldest descriptions of the,
119
—  — omitted in scenes 4
—  — omitted at Barhut 117
—  — Padmâsana posture of, 235 n.
—  — painted on cloth 234
—  — proved by Kanishka casket
to belong to the 1st Cen-
tury B C. 129-130.
—  — related to that of Christ
135-6, XVI
-·  — said to be a portrait 82-3, 259.
—  — tonsure omitted from the,
132-3
—  — uniformity of, 112-3, 114
—  figured 116 n 1 (Turfan Khotan),
128 (on coin of 1st century A D),
172 n 1 (Takht-i-Bahai), 254-
62 (Boro-Budur), 263 (Chandi
Mendut), XI (Gandhara), XV (Kanishka casket), XVI (Gandhâra),
XX (Ajantâ), XL, XLIII (Boro-Budur)
—  footmarks of, III (Amarâvatî)
—  Four Promenades of, hinted at 107
(Sânchî), figured XXXI (Boro-
Budur)
—  Gandhâra said to have been visited
by, 122.
—  Great Departure of. See Mahâbhinishkramana
—  hair cut off by, jewels abandoned
by, 132.
—  Hâritî converted by, 122
—  horse of See Kanthaka.
—  life of, in successive births 35.
—  life of, 113.
—  Mahâbhinishkramana of See Mahâbhinishkramana.
—  monkey's offering to, at Vaisâlî
150

BUDHA, mother of See Mâyâ
—  Nâga of Swât river converted by,
122
—  Parinirvâna of See Parinirvâna
—  portrait statues of, 82-83.
—  preaching of, to the 33 gods, figured 163 n 1 (Ajantâ).
—  Questions of, to Çâriputra 163 n 1
(Ajantâ)
—  relics of, deposited in eight Sanctuaries, 147, in Kanishka casket
129, 130
—  relics of, war of, figured 78 (Sânchî).
—  Renunciation of Life by See Âyuh-
samskâra-utsarjana.
—  return of, to Kapilavastu, figured 93 (Sânchî)
—  squire of. See Chandaka.
—  seven steps of, figured IV (Benares).
—  statue of, sandal wood, 24 n. 1
—  symbolized at Sânchî and Barhut,
19, 75.
BUDDHAS preceding Çâkyamuni figured
XXVI (Mahomed Nari)
—  seven last, symbolized 72 (Sânchî and Barhut), 104 (Sânchî)
—  thousand, at Murtuk and the Great
Miracle 160 n 2
—  See also Çikhin, Kaçyapa, Kanakamuni, Krakucchanda, Prabhûtaratna, Ratnasambhava, Viçvabhû, Vipaçyin.
Buddhacarita, Great Miracle described in
the, 158
Buddhism in Gandhâra, history of, 121-5
Buddhist art, origin of, Essay I
—  monuments abundant in Gandhâra 124
Buffaloes figured 97-107 (Sânchî)
BUHLER, G, Sânchî inscriptions studied
by, 66 n. 1
Bull, symbol of Buddha's Birth, 21 (coins),
1.
Bulls with human faces figured 107
(Sânchî)
BURGESS, J, frescoes at Ajantâ described
by, 162-163, XX

BURGESS, J., photograph communicated by, IV, XXVI.

Burmah, Buddha type not original in, 115

ÇAILA, nun, figured 234-5, XXXVIII (Boro-Budur)

Caityas, Eight Great, 147, Hymn to the, 147 n 2

ÇAKRA See INDRA

Cakravartin, Seven Jewels of a, 227

Çâla tree, symbolizing Viçvabhû, 104 (Sânchî)

Calcutta museum, remains of Barhut railing in the, 57

Cambodia, Buddha figure not original in, 115.

Camel figured 87 (Sânchî)

Cammasâtaka-jataka narrated 44

Campaka (Nagapushpa) flower figured 88 (Sânchî), XXII-III (Boro-Budur)

CANDRAGUPTA, Gandhâra ceded by Seleukos to, 121

CANDRAPRABHÂ, queen, figured 235, XXXVIII-IX (Boro-Budur).

Cankrama figured 93 (Sânchî).

— symbolizing Buddha 19 (Sânchî)

Canoe figured 100 (Sânchi)

Canvas, painting on, 274-5

Capitals, decorations of, 86 (Sânchî).

— Iranian, 87, 91 (Sânchi)

ÇÂRIPUTRA, questions to, figured 163, n. 1 (Ajantâ)

Casket from Kanishka stûpa figured xv

Castes Bodhisattva and the, 53

Catacombs, symbols employed by Christian artists of the, 82

Caves, Buddhist See Ajantâ, Ta-t'ong-fu

Ceylon, Buddha figure not original in, 115-6

Chaddanta-jâtaka See Shaddanta-j°

Chair figured 144 (Gaul and India)

CHANDAKA, Buddha's squire, figured 105 (Sânchî), III (Gandhâra and Amarâvâtî), IV (Benares)

Chandi Mendut, Hâritî figure from, 283-4

— — images in the, 262-6

Chariot figured 93, 100 (Sânchî), 178 (Barhut), XXXVI (Boro-Budur)

Chartres cathedral, carvings on the, 61

CHAVANNES, E., caves of Long-men and Ta-t'ong-fu described by, 115, 167 n 1

— Chinese statue interpreted by, L

— photograph furnished by, XXI.

— Shaddanta-jâtaka translated from Chinese texts by, 188 and n 2, 190

Chignon, Brahmanic, figured 97, 175 and n 2, XXV-VI (Gandhâra), XXXIV, XXXVII (Boro-Budur)

Child figured 139-40 (Gaul), 141-2 (Gandhâra)

Children, goddess of See Hâritî

China, Buddha figure not original in, 115

— Hâritî figure in, 286-7

CHRIST figure based on Lateran Sophocles 136.

— — related to that of Buddha 135-6, xvi

Christian art, Hellenistic origin of, 290-1

— — juxtaposition of incidents in, 83

— — symbols employed by, in Catacombs 82

Çibi-jâtaka figured 230 1, XXXVI (Boro-Budur)

— localized in Gandhâra, 123.

ÇIKHANDIN, son of Rudrayana, figured 235-7 (Boro-Budur)

ÇIKHIN symbolized by Pundarîka, 104 (Sânchî).

CIÑCÂ, calumny of, at Çrâvastî 183

Çirîsha tree symbolizing Krakucchanda 104 (Sânchî)

Civilization of India represented on Sânchî sculptures 80

Cloud figured XLIV (Chandi Mendut)

Cluny museum, signacula in the, 11

Cock, Buddha's birth as. See Kukkuṭa-jâtaka

Coins, Indo-Greek, described 125-8

— — figured XIV

— punch-marked, discussed by D B Spooner 14, 21 n 2

Columns, Persepolitan or Corinthian, figured xxv (Gandhâra)

— supported by Atlantes XXVI (Gandhâra)

Columns *See also* Capitals

Conception, Buddha's, represented 20 (Amarâvatî, Barhut, Sânchî)

Conch figured 93 (Sânchî)

Corinthian columns xxv (Gandhâra)

Cornucopia figured xvii (Gaul), xviii (Gandhâra)

— unclean in India 142

Court scenes figured xxxvi-ix (Boro-Budur)

Çrâvastî, Buddha's birth as son of citizen of, 54

— Ciñcâ's calumny at, 183

— figure (personified) of, 175, xxvii (Gandhâra)

— figured 239 (Boro-Budur)

— Great Miracle at. *See* Essay VI.

— Jetavana scenes figured 77 n 1 (Sânchî) *See* Jetavana

— Sundarî's assassination at, 183.

Çrî (?) figured 70 and n 1, 88 (Sânchî).

Crocodile figured 100 (Sânchî)

Çuddhodana, departure of, from Kapilavastu figured 93 (Sânchî).

Cuirass figured xxxvi (Boro-Budur)

Cundâ figured 264-5, 266, xliv (Chandi Mendut).

Çunga dynasty mentioned in Barhut inscription 4, 34.

Cupid garland-bearers figured xv (Kanishka casket), xxv (Gandhâra).

Çvetaketu figured xxxiv (Boro-Budur)

*Çyâma-jâtaka* figured 74 n 2 (Sânchî)

— localized in Gandhâra 123

Çyâmaka, companion of Mahâkâtyâyana, figured 239 (Boro-Budur)

*Dabbhapuppha-jâtaka* narrated 44-5

Dancers figured 91 (Sânchî).

Davids, T W Rhys, Twin Miracle as viewed by, 157

Decorative motifs at Sânchî 69, 85-90

— — hard to distinguish from Buddhist scenes 84

— — imported from Persia by Iranian artisans 81-2.

Deer figured xxix (Amarâvatî)

— *See also* Antelope, Gazelle

Demetrios, coin of, 126

Demi-gods figured 71 (Sânchî)

Departure, Buddha's Great *See* Mahâbhinishkramana.

Devadatta, monkey incarnation of, 43-4

*Devâvatâra* figured 163 (Ajantâ), 163 n. 1 (Barhut), xix (Sârnath)

— localized at Kanyakubja (Fa-t'ien), Kapitha (Hiuan-tsang), or Sânkâçya (Divyâvadâna and Fa hien) 149 n 1

*Dharmacakrapravartana* confused with Great Miracle 169 n 1

— figured 16 (Sânchî), iv (Gandhâra and Amarâvatî), xix (Sârnâth)

— symbolized by wheel 148 n 2, ii

*Dhotî* figured 85, 89, xl (Gandhâra)

Dhritarâshtra, Gandharva king, figured 85 (Sânchî).

*Dhyâni-Buddha* figured 256 7 (Boro-Budur)

— images in Batavia museum 267

— *See* Akshobhya, Amitâbha, Amoghasiddhi, Ratnasambhava, Vairocana

Dion, father of Heliodoros 82

Disc figured 227-8 (Boro-Budur)

*Divyâvadâna*, Avalokiteçvara and Mañjuçrî wanting n the, 178

— extracts of Mûla-Sarvâstivâdin Vinaya in the, 151 n 2, 223, 253

— followed by sculptors of Boro-Budur 223-4, 225-6, 253

— Great Miracle narrated in the, 151, 173

— Great Miracle described as necessary act of Buddha by, 151

— groups together Birth, Bodhi, First Preaching and Death of Buddha 148 n 1

— Maitrakanyaka story narrated in the, 244 n 2

— Mândhâtar story narrated in the, 225-30

— Pâñcika named in the, 174 n 5

— Rudrâyana story narrated in the, 231-40

— Twin Miracle narrated in the, 156-9

Dog figured 107 (Sânchî).

Dog-tooth ornament xxv (Gandhâra).

Domestic life, scenes from, 80, 95 (Sânchî)
Domoko, Hârîtî figure from, 285-6
Donors to Sanchî stûpa named 67
Dragon figured L (China)
Driver of chariot figured 93 (Sânchî)
Drum figured 93 (Sanchî)
DRUMA, Kinnara king, figured 221-2 (Boro Budur)
DU HAMEL, Constant, story of, 49
Dúbhiyamakkata-jâtaka narrated 43-4.
Dvârapâla figured 71 (Sânchî), XLII (Boro-Budur).
Dzang-loun, Great Miracle narrated in the, 161 n 2

Earrings figured 89 (Sânchî), 144
Edification, increasing, as test of date in religious tales, 191 2
EKAÇRIÑGA See Rishyacriñga.
ELÂPATRA, visit of, to Buddha figured 19 (Barhut)
Elephant, Buddha's birth as, 37-39, 186
— Buddha's conception in form of, figured 92 (Barhut and Sânchî).
— figured 45 (Barhut), 86, 88, 90, 97 (Sânchî), 163, 164 n 1 (Ajantâ), 227 8, 234 (Boro-Budur), XIX (Sarnâth), XXVIII (Barhut), XXIX (Barhut and Amarâvatî), XXX (Karamâr hill and Ajanta)
— goad for, figured 86 (Sânchî)
— savage, tamed by Buddha 150
— six-tusked See Shaddanta-jâtaka
— symbolizing Buddha's birth 20 n. 2
— symbolizing Buddha's conception 21, 1
— wild, figured 88 (Sanchî)
ERP, Major van, Boro-Budur conservation work under, 206 n 1, XXXI
— Boro-Budur drawings executed by, 210
— photograph communicated by, XXXII, XLIII, XLIV
ESPERANDIEU, E , stereotypes lent by, XVII
— work of, on Gallic bas-reliefs 139-41
Eugenia jambu See Jambu tree
EUKRATIDES revolts against Demetrios 126

European literature, borrowing from India by, 50
Existences, previous, of Buddha See Jâtaka

FA HIEN, Great Miracle not narrated by, 183.
— Mahâcaitya at Çrâvasti seen by, 183 n.
Fairy See Yaksha
Fan figured 95 (Sânchî), XXXV (Boro-Budur)
FA-T'IEN, Great Miracle associated with Jetavana by, 149 n 2
FEER, L , Shaddanta-jâtaka discussed by, 187, 193 n 1
FELL, Capt , Sânchî stûpa visited by, 63.
FERGUSSON J , view of, concerning Indian sculptures and texts 186
Ficus glomerata See Udumbara
— indica See Nyagrodha.
— religiosa See Açvattha
Fig tree See Bodhi-tree
Fire cauldron figured 98 (Sânchî)
Fishes in pond figured XXVIII (Gandhara)
Flagstaff figured 90 (Sanchî)
Florence, baptistery of, scenes on the, 83.
Flowers garlands of, XXIV-XXV (Gandhâra).
— rain of, XXII (Boro-Budur), XXIV, XXVIII (Gandhâra).
Flute figured 93 (Sânchî)
Fly-flapper figured, 93, 105 (Sânchî), XIX (Sarnâth), XXI (Ajantâ), XXII, XXVIII (Boro-Budur), XXIX (Amaravatî), XXXV (Boro-Budur)
— holders, Brahma and Indra as, 165 (Ajantâ), 168 (Western India)
FORTUNE, Indian See Çrî
FRANCIS, H., Jâtaka translation by, criticized 202, n. 1
Fresco painting See Painting.

GANDA, GANDAMBA, as name of gardener, 152, n 1
Gandhâra art, Greek details of, 145-6
— — Greek origin of, 145-6
— bas reliefs from, date of, 190.
— Buddha said to have visited, 122
— Buddhism in, history of, 121-5.

Gandhâra, Buddhist monuments numerous in, 124-5
— ceded by Seleukos to Candragupta, 121
— cities of, 118
— columns in Corinthian or Persepolitan style in, xxv
— conversion of, by Madhyântika 122
— frontier country under Açoka, 121
— Greeks in, 125-8
— Haritî story localized in, 122
— jâtaka scenes rare in, 26
— jâtakas localized in, 123
— legendary scenes numerous in, 26
— Madhyântika apostle of, 122
— Mahâyâna flourishing in, 125
— monasteries (1000) of, 124
— Rishyaçringa-jâtaka localized in, 48
— sculptures from, III, XV, XVI, XVIII, XXIV VIII, XXX, XLVII
— Shaddanta jataka figured in, 39, 188, 195-6
— Tutelary Pair commonly worshipped and figured in, 141-2, XVIII.
— See also Karamâr Hill, Kharkia, Mekha-Sandha, Peshawar, Sahri-Bahlol, Takht-i-Bahai, Taxila
Gandharvas as decorative figures 85 (Sanchî)
— king of the. See Dhritarâshtra
Gardener, story of See Ârâmadûsaka-jâtaka
Gargoyles for carrying off water xxxi (Boro-Budur).
Garland as decorative motif, 85 (Sânchî).
— figured 170-2, 172 n 1 (Takht-i-Bahai), XXIV-VI, XXVIII (Gandhâra), XXVIII (Barhut)
— serpentine, in sculpture, 34.
Garments, rain of, figured 228, XXXVI (Boro-Budur)
Garuda figured 107 (Sânchî)
Gate of Sânchî stûpa described 65.
Gaul, Tutelary Pair in See Essay V, xvii
Gazelle figured IV (Gandhâra and Amarâvatî), XIX (Sârnâth)
— See also Antelope and Deer
General figured 227-8 (Boro-Budur)
Genius figured 71, 80 (Sânchî).

Genius, flying, figured xxiii (Magadha and Kudâ), xxvii-viii (Gandhâra), See also Yaksha
GETTY, Henry H., photographs communicated by, xlix
Girl, Jade, figured L (China)
Goat figured 87 (Sânchî)
Gods, Fifteen, figured xl (Boro-Budur)
— Thirty-three, Buddha's preaching to the, 19, 163 n 1
— who dispose of the creations of themselves and others 92
Goddess figured xxxix (Boro-Budur).
Gold, shower of, figured 228 (Barhut).
Goldsmith figured 246 (Boro-Budur)
GOLOUBEW, V, photograph communicated by, iv
Gopâ See Yaçodâ
GOSANZE, Japanese name of Trailokyavijaya (q v), 268
Greek coins 126-8, figured xiv
— influence on art at Sânchî 82
— invasion of India and influence in Gandhâra 125 8
— source of Christian and late Buddhist art 290 1
Gridhrakûta, Saddharmapundarîka associated with the, 149 n 2.
GRIFFITHS, J, Shaddanta-jâtaka fresco described by, 195
Griffons figured 94 (Sânchî)
GRONEMAN, J, Guide to Boro-Budur by, 215.
— Maitrakanyaka-jâtaka verified at Boro Budur by, 215 and n 2, 243-4
Grouping of sculptured scenes 77
GRUNWEDEL, A, Buddhist heavens detected in sculpture by, 71
— frescoes of Murtuk reproduced by, 160 n 2
— Maitrakanyaka figures compared by, 244 n 1
— photograph communicated by, xviii
— sculptures at Sanchî identified by, 71, 76
Guardians of sanctuary See Dvârapâla
Guides, Mess of the, Gandhâra sculptures in, 119, XI

24*

Guimet Museum, Sânchi stûʋa moulding in the, 92

Guitar, boy playing, figured 274

HALAKA, a hunter, 218 9

Halo of Buddhas 172
— figured 173 n 1, XXVII (Gandhâra)
— See also Aureole Nimbus

Hamsa jataka figured 37 (Barhut)

HARITÎ, the Buddhist Madonna, 279 91
— converted by Buddha 122, 280
— figure from Chandi Mendut, 283-4
—      —      Domoko 28, 6
—      —      Annam 287-8
—      —      China 286-7
—      —      Japan 287
—      — universally found in Buddhist countries 290.
— figured frontispiece (Yâr-Khoto),
XLV (Domoko), XVIII, XLVII, XLVIII
(Gandhâra), XLIX (Japan), L
(China)
— images of, in all Indian monasteries 281
—      — described by Yi-tsing
282.
— originally an ogress, goddess of
smallpox, 142, 280-1, XLIX
— reminiscence of worship of, in
Gandhâra 122, 282
— See also Tutelary Pair

Harmikâ, part of stûpa, 33

Harp figured 49 (Barhut)

HARSHA ÇILÂDITYA, poem of, 147 n 2

Hastinapura, capital of northern Pañcala,
220-1

HAYAGRÎVA, image of, in Batavia Museum
267

Head-dress Brahmanical See Chignon

Heaven, Akanishtha See Akanishtha
— Buddhist, figured 71, 91 (Sân-
chî), 72 (Barhut).
— Descent from See Devâvatâra
— Kâmâvacara, figured 103 (Sânchî)
— Mâra's figured 92 (Sânchî)
— Tushita See Tushita

HELIODOROS, column of, at Vidiçâ, 82.

Hell, town of, figured 246-7 (Boro-Budur)

Herald figured 93 (Sânchî), 229 (Boro-
Budur)

Hermit figured 80, 98 (Sanchî)
— See also Ârada, Ascetic, Brahman,
Kâçyapa

Hermitage, Brahmanic, figured XXXVII
(Boro Budur)
— life of a, figured 98 (Sânchî)

Himâlaya, scene in the, 219

HIRU, minister of Rudrâyana, 238 40.

Hiruka, foundation of, 240

HIUAN-TSANG, Gandhâra monasteries esti-
mated at 1 000 by, 124
— Great Miracle disregarded by, 183
— Mahâcaitya at Çrâvasti seen by,
183 n
— Rishyaçringa story related by, 48
— Vajrâsana statue described by, 259-
60

Honeysuckle figured 87, 89 (Sânchî)

Horse, Buddha's See Kanthaka
— figured 93 (Sânchî), 163 (Ajantâ),
227-8 (Boro-Budur), XXVIII (Barhut), XXXVI (Boro-Budur)
— symbolizing Great Departure 148
n 2, 1

Hoti-Mardân, Gandhâra statues in, 119

HUBER, E, Divyâvadâna traced to Mûla-
Sarvâstivâdin Vinaya by, 151, 223
n 2, 253.
— Lûhasudatta and his wife discussed
by, 174 n 1
— Roruka localized by, 238 n 2
— Rudrâvana story analysed by, 231 2
— Sûtralamkara (Chinese) in 10 chap-
ters noted by, 200

HUMBOLDT, W von, Dhyâni Buddhas detected at Boro-Budur by, 256

Hut, Brahmanical, figured 97 (Sânchî)

Idolatry, Buddhism not originated in milieu hostile to, 9
— not mentioned in Veda 9
— rare in ancient India 8

Idols mentioned by Patañjali 9

Images, anthropomorphic See Idolatry
— carved at Sânchi 69
— Indian, discussed by Dr Konow
9 n 2

Indian art, history of ancient school of 18.
— life, details of illustrated by sculptures 29
INDRA, Buddha visited by, 19 (Barhut)
— figured 96 (Sânchî), 162 and n 2 (Ajantâ), 170 n 2, 175 n. 2 (in Great Miracle), 177 (in Devâvatâra), 179 (Barhut), 229-30, 232 (Boro-Budur), IV (Benares), XV (on Kanishka casket), XIX (Sarnath), XXIV (Gandhâra)
— heaven of, figured 91 (Sânchî).
— steals ascetics' food 46
INDRAMITRA mentioned in inscription at Bodh-Gayâ 4
Indraprastha, Vidhura-jâtaka localized at, 55
Inscriptions 34, 92 (Barhut), 66, 86 (Sânchî)
Ionic capital, volute of, imitated at Sân chî 87
Iranian artisans in India 82
— capitals on gate of Sânchî 91.
— influence in Indian art 69, 87, 91
Isis suckling Horus, images of, 288.
Ivory-carvers of Vidiça 67.

Jackal and otters, story of the See Dabbhapuppha-jâtaka 44-5
Jain monk (Digambara) figured 163 (Ajantâ)
Jambu tree at Kapilavastu figured 106 (Sânchî)
JANMACITRAKA the nâga, 218
Japan, Hariti figure in, 287
Jâtaka, antelope See Kurunga-jâtaka.
— Ârâmadûsaka See Ârama°
— Asadisa See Asadisa°
— Bhallâtîya See Kinnara°
— Bhisa See Bhisa
— Cammasâtaka See Cammasâtaka°.
— Çibi. See Çibi°
— cock. See Kukkuta°
— Dabbhapuppha See Dabbhapuppha°
— Dûbhiyamakkata See Dûbhiyamakkata°.
— elephant See Kakkata°, Latukika°, Shaddanta°.
— Hamsa See Hamsa°

Jâtaka Kapota See Kapota°
— Kinnara See Kinnara°
— Kukkuta See Kukkuta°
— Kurunga See Kurunga°
— Mahâjanaka See Mahâjanaka°
— Mahâkapi See Mahâkapi°
— monkey See Mahakapi°
— pigeon See Kapota°
quail See Latukika°
— Rishyaçringa See Rishyaçringa°
— Ruru See Ruru°
— Shaddanta See Shaddanta°
— stag See Ruru°
— swan See Hamsa°
— Temiya See Temiya°
— Unicorn. See Rishyaçringa°
— Viçvantara See Viçvantara°
— Vidhura See Vidhura°
Jâtakas at Barhut See Essay II.
— figured 23 (Barhut and Sânchî), 40 (Barhut), V-VI (Barhut).
— nature of the, 30
— rarely figured in Gandhâra 26
Jâtaka book, age of verses and prose, 189-90, 196-7, 201-6.
— Great Miracle in Introduction to, 152 and n. 1
— Maitrakanyaka story compared with the, 244 n. 2
— Mândhâtravadâna compared with the, 225 n 1
— not complete 58
— Twin Miracle in Introduction to, 155
Jâtakamâlâ, Twin Miracle in the, 155
Java, Buddha figure not original in, 115.
— Buddhist art in, 205
— Buddhist images of, resemble those of India 269
— routes followed by Indian civilization to, 283
— See also Batavia, Boro Budur, Chandi Mendut
Jetavana, Great Miracle not localized in the, 149 and n 2
— Great Miracle represented by wheel in front of the, 180 n 1
— Mahâprajñâpâramitâ associated with the, 149 n. 2
— scenes in the, 77 n 1

Jewels, belt of, figured 89 (Sânchî)
— Buddha divests himself of his, 106
— figured 227-8 (Boro Budur)
— seven, of a cakravartin 227.
Juxtaposition of incidents in art 74, 83 (Buddhist and Christian), 98 (Sanchî)
JYOTIPÂLA, vyâkarana of, figured XXVI (Gandhâra)

KÂÇYAPA, conversion of, figured 76, 97, 100 (Sânchî)
— Buddha figured XXVI (Gandhâra)
— — symbolized by Nyagrodha tree 104 (Sânchî)
Kâkanada See Sânchî
Kalpadrumâvadâna, date of the, 190
— Shaddanta-jataka in the, 187-8, 194, 196, 198, 204 n
Kâmâvacara heaven figured 103 (Sânchî)
KANAKAMUNI symbolized by Udumbara tree 104 (Sânchî)
KANISHKA, Clovis of Northern India, 128
— coin of, with figure of Buddha 128
— figured 129-30, XV (on casket)
— Peshawar winter capital of, 129
— stûpa, and casket of, 128-30, XIV XV
Kanjur, Mândhâtravadâna according to the 225 n. 1
KANTHAKA, Buddha's horse, figured 105 (Sânchî), III (Gandhâra and Amarâvatî), IV (Benares)
Kanyakubja, Devâvatara localized at, 149
Kapilavastu, deity of figured 175, III (Gandhâra and Amarâvatî)
— departure of king from, figured 93 (Sânchî)
— figured 105 (Sânchî)
— gate of, figured 13
— Jambu tree near, figured 106 (Sanchî)
— Mahâbhinishkramana symbolizing, 148
— Nyagrodhârâma at gate of See Nyagrodhârâma
— scenes at, figured 77, n 1 (Sânchî), III
— signacula from, 12.

Kapilavastu See also Lumbini.
Kapitha, Devâvatâra localized at, 149
Kapota-jâtaka figured 37 (Barhut)
Karamâr hill, Shaddanta-jâtaka figured at, XXX
Karlî, Great Miracle confused with Dharmacakrapravartana at, 169 n. 1.
Karma, law of, 31
Kauçâmbî, Buddha portrait statue at 259
— unimportance of, in Buddhist legend, 149
Khara village mentioned in Rudrâyana story 238
Kharkai, Buddha head from, XI
King figured 100 (Sanchî), 232, XXXVI-XL (Boro Budur)
— See also Açoka, Ajâtaçatru, Bimbisâra, Çuddhodana, Çunga, Dhritarâshtra, Druma, Kanishka, Mahâjanaka, Mândhâtar, Milinda, Prasenajit, Royalty
Kings, Four Great See Lokapâla
Kinnara figured 219-24 (Boro-Budur), II (Sânchî).
— form of discussed 241 and n 2, 242
— jâtaka figured 53 (Barhut and Boro-Budur), 241, XLI (Boro-Budur)
— king See Druma
Kinnarî Manohara, story of the, 219-24
KI SI-MO-JIN, the Japanese Hâritî, 286 7
— figured XLIX
Kondivté, Great Miracle figured at, 168
Konkan, Great Miracle figured in the 182
KONOW S, images in ancient India discussed by, 9 n. 2
Kosala king and queen reconciled by Buddha 53
KRAKUCCHANDA symbolized by Çirîsha tree 104 (Sanchî)
KRISHNA suckled by Devaki, images of, 288
Krityâ effigy, in magic rites 8 n 1
Kshatriya Brahman inferior to, according to Buddhists 54
— Buddha's birth as, 55
KSHEMENDRA, Mândhâtar story narrated by, 225 6
— Mûla Sarvâstivadin canon followed by, 151 n 2, 204 n

KUAN-YIN figured L (China)
Kuçinagara, signacula from, 12
— stûpa, Buddha's death commemorated by, 12
Kudâ caves, Great Miracle figured in the, 168
— sculptures from the, XXIII
*Kukkuta-jâtaka* figured 37 (Barhut)
*Kurunga-jâtaka* figured 40 (Barhut)
KUVERA not one of the Tutelary Pair 141
— statuette in Batavia museum 267
KWEI-TSEU-MU-CHEN, the Chinese Hâritî, 286

LA FONTAINE, jâtaka tales reflected by, 45, 48, 50
*Lakshana*, sign of recognition for identifying sculptures, 176, 181
*Lalitâkshepa* posture figured 263 (Chandi Mendut)
*Lalita vistara* versions of stories on bas-reliefs 214 (Boro-Budur)
— Shaddanta-jâtaka mentioned in the, 192
Lamaist images, symbols of Buddha on, 26
Lambaka, scene at, figured 239 (Boro-Budur)
Lance figured 145, XVIII (Sahri-Bahlol)
*Latukika-jâtaka* narrated 28
LE COQ, A von, Hâritî painting discussed by, 273, 275, 276 n 1
— photograph communicated by, XVIII
LEEMANS, jâtaka scenes described by, 217, 222 (Boro Budur)
— Buddha statue described by, 258 9 (Boro-Budur)
Legendary scenes figured 90 (Sânchî).
Leggings figured 144
LEROUX, E, stereotypes lent by, VII-X
Letter figured 232 (Boro-Budur)
LÉVI, S, Bodhisattvâvadânakalpalatâ passage emended by, 174 n 5
— crisis in Indian conscience at the time of Açvaghosha described by, 204.
— Divyâvadâna traced to Mûla-Sarvâstivâdin Vinaya by, 151 n. 2, 223 n. 2, 253.

LÉVI, S, Hiuan tsang shown to reproduce Sûtrâlamkâra version of Shaddanta jataka by, 199 n 1
— Kanishka compared to Clovis by, 128
— poem of Harsha restored by, 147 n 2
— references concerning Panthaka supplied by, 157 n 3
*Lieu-tu tsi-king*, date of the, 190
— Shaddanta-jâtaka in the, 187-8, 196, 198
Life, Buddha's renunciation of See Ayuh-samskâra-utsarjana
*Lilâñj* See Nairañjanâ
Lion, Buddha symbolized by, 1
— figured 87, 90, 107 (Sânchî)
— horned, figured 87 (Sânchî)
— winged, figured 87 (Sânchî)
Lion-headed brackets XXV (Gandhâra)
LOCANÂ image of, in Batavia museum, 267
Loin-cloth See Dhotî
*Lokapâlas* figured 91, 103 (Sânchî), 173 n 1, 174, III (Gandhâra and Amarâvatî), XXVI-VII (Gandhâra)
Long-men, date of caves in pass of, 115
— Great Miracle figured in caves of, 167 n 1.
Loriyân-Tangai, sculptures from, XXIV-V
Lotus as attribute XXII, 255, 264-6
— as decoration 85 (Sânchî).
— figured 86, 88, 89 (Sânchî), 172 n 1 (Takht-i-Bahai), 173, XV (Kanishka casket) XIX (Sârnâth), XXVII (Gandhâra), L (China)
— footstool figured 165 (Ajantâ), 167 (Magadha), 168 (Western India), XXI (Ajantâ)
— seat figured 163, 170-2, 173, 176, XXIII-VIII
— stalks as food of ascetics 46
— symbolizing Buddha's birth 21
—          — miraculous birth 21 n 2, 1
—          — seven steps of Buddha XIX (Sarnâth)
LÜDERS, H, Sûtrâlamkâra fragments identified by, 173-4

Lōhasudatta figured 173 4, XXIV, XXVIII
(Gandhara)
Lumbinî, Buddha's birth at, 13
— Çuddhodana's visit to, 93


Macdonell, A A, photograph communi-
cated by, III
Madhyāntika, apostle of Gandhara, 122
Madonna, Buddhist See Essay IX
—        —      See Hāritî
—   figure explained by M Millet
XLVI
—   figured XLVII (Carolingian and
Coptic)
Magadha, Buddha figures from, date of,
116
— capital of See Râjagrıha
— Great Miracle figured in 167 8
— See also Antagıri, Bodh-Gaya, Gri-
dhrakûta, Mahâbodhı
Mahâbhinishkramana figured III (Gandhara)
IV (Amaravati and Benares), XXVI
(Mohamed-Nari)
—  represented 5 (Sânchî), 20 (Amarâ-
vatî), 21 n 1 (Benares), 105 (Sân-
chî)
— symbolized by horse 148 n 2, 1
Mahabodhi, Buddhist portrait statue at,
259-62
— See also Bodh Gayâ
Mahdjanaka jâtaka figured 52 (Barhut)
Mahâkapi jataka figured 41 (Barhut), 74
n 2 (Sanchı)
Mahâkatyāyana figured 234 (Boro-Budur)
Mahâparinibbana-sutta quoted concerning
the four sacred places 148 and n
Mahâprajñâpâramitâ sutra associated with
the Jetavana 149 n 2
Mahaprâ'ıhdrya associated with the Jetavana 149 n 2
— confused with the Dharmacakra-
pravartana 169 n 1
— confused with the Twin Miracle
156-8
— figured 160 and n 2, 162 5 (Ajantâ),
165-6 (Boro-Budur), 166 7 (Ta-
t'ong fu), 167 n 1 (Long-men),
167-8 (Magadha), 168 (Kondıvté,

Kuda, Western India), 172 n 2
(Takht-ı-Bahaı, Rawak), 178-80
(Barhut), XIX XXVIII
— narrated 159-62
— narrated in Buddhacarita 158, Divyâvadâna 151, 173, Jâtaka and
Mahavamsa 152 and n 1.
— preferred to Twin Miracle in Sârnath stele 153-6
— reasons for tardy recognition of,
182-4.
— symbolized by wheel in front of Jetavana 180 n 1
— versions of the, classified 180 2
Mahâpurusha, ideal of, embodied in Buddha figure 134-5
Mahâvamsa, conversion of Gandhara narrated by, 122
— Great Miracle according to the, 152
and n 1.
— Twin Miracle according to the,
156
Mahâvastu, Avalokıteçvara and Mañjuçrî
wanting in the, 178.
— Twin Miracle according to the,
155-7
Mahâyana, part played by Gandhârian doctors in, 125
Maitrakanyaka story figured 243-7, XLI-II
(Boro-Budur)
—  — narrated in Avadânaçataka, etc,
244 n 2
Maitreya figured 264 (Chandı Mendut),
XXII (Boro Budur), XXVI (Mo-
hamed Nari).
— symbolized by Campaka 88 (Sân-
chî)
— tree of, figured 105 (Sânchî)
Makhâdeva, Buddha's birth as, 55.
Mallas, despair of the, figured IV (Gan-
dhâra)
Mallet figured 140, 144 (Gaul).
Mândhâtâr, story of, figured 224-31,
XXXVI (Boro-Budur)
— story of, narrated in Divyâvadâna,
etc, 225-30 and 225 n 1
Mangifera See Pundarika
Mango tree figured 86, 89 (Sânchî), 162
(Ajanta)

Mango, miracle of the, 152

MAÑJUÇRÎ figured 255 (Boro-Budur), 264-6 (Chandi Mendut), xxv (Gandhâra)
— wanting in Divyâvadâna, Mahâvastu, and Gandhâra 177-8

MANOHARA, flight of, figured xxxiv (Boro-Budur)
— story of, 219-24

MÂRA, assault of, figured 103 n (Sânchi), 161 and n 1, 162-5 (Ajantâ), III IV (Gandhâra and Amarâvatî) xix (Sârnath)
— heaven of, figured 92 (Sânchi)

Mdradharshana See Mara, assault of

MÂRÎCÎ, statue of, 267 (Batavia Museum)

MARSHALL J -H , Kanishka stûpa explored by, 129
— photographs communicated by, 64 n 2 84, II, VII X XIX
— scenes on stele identified by 150

Mat, Brahmanical, figured 97 (Sânchî)

Mathurâ, Buddha figures from, date of, 116
— Great Miracle missing at, 182
— stûpa, fragments of railing, 4
— unimportance of, in Buddhist legend 149

MAUDGALYÂYANA figured 174

MÂYÂ, dream of, figured 70 and n 1 (?), III (Gandhâra and Amaravatî), IX (Sânchî)

Meditation, Buddha's first, 5 (Bodh-Gayâ)

Mekha-Sandha hill, XII

Melons figured on painting from Central Asia 274

MENANDER, coin of, 127
— Nâgasena's conversation with, 6
— Sagala capital of, 127

Mendicant figured xxxvi (Boro-Budur)
— See also Monk

Merchant, Buddha's birth as See Cammasâtaka-jâtaka

MILINDA, Questions of King, 127
— See also Menander

MILLET (Gab ), Madonna figures indicated by, 278
— Madonna figure explained by, XLVI

Minister figured 227 8, 229, 238-40 (Boro-Budur)

Minister See also Hiru, Bhiru

Miracle, Great See Mahâprâtihârya,
— Twin See Yamakaprâtihârya

Mithilâ, Amarâ story located in, 51
— Mahâjanaka story located in, 52
— See also Yavamajjhaka

Mohamed-Nârî, sculptures from, xxvi

Monasteries Buddhist, Harîtî figure in, 281
— Buddhist, numerous in Gandhâra 124

Monk figure in composition of Buddha figure 131-4
— figured 234, 239 (Boro-Budur), xvi (Gandhâra), xix (Sârnâth), xxv (Loriyan Tangai), xxvi (Gandhâra), xxxi, xxxvii (Boro-Budur)
— not figured at Barhut and Sânchi 96

Monkey, Buddha's birth as See Mahakapi-jâtaka
— Devadatta's incarnation as, 43-4,
— figured 45 (Barhut), 100 (Sanchî)
— offering of the, figured 150, xix (Sârnâth)

Moon, crescent, figured 172, n 1 (Takht-i-Bahai)

Mortar and pestle figured 95 (Sânchî)

Motifs, decorative, borrowed from Persia 81

Mrigadava, Buddha's preaching at the, 13

Mudrâ figured 163 (Ajanta), 170 n 2, 181 , 256-8 (Boro-Budur), xv (Kanishka casket), xix (Sarnâth), xx (Ajantâ), xxi (Ta-t'ong-fu), xxiv (Gandhâra)

Mûla-sarvâstivâddin school prevalent in Java 253
— Vinaya and the Divyâvadâna 151, 253

MÛRDHATAR See Mândhâtar, 226

Murtuk, Thousand Buddhas at, 160 n 2

Musicians, celestial See Gandharva
— figured 91, 93, 100 (Sânchî), 239 (Boro-Budur)

Nâga, Buddha relics at Râmagrâma guarded by, 78
— Buddha's victory over the wicked, figured 97 (Sânchî)

*Nâga* figured 167 (Magadha), 168 (Western India), IV (Benares), XIX (Sârnâth), XX (Ajantâ), XIII (Kudâ, Magadha), XXV (Loriyân-Tangai), XXVI (Mohamed-Nari), XLV (Chandi Mendut)
— Janmacitraka, story of, 218 219
— of Swât river converted by Buddha 122
— woman in Vidhura-jâtaka 55
— *See also* Nanda and Upananda, Elâpatra.
NÂGAPIYA, donor of pillar at Sânchî, 67 77.
*Nâga-pushpa* flower *See* Campaka
*Nagara-devatâ See* Town, personification of
NÂGASENA, Menander converted by, 6
Nairañjanâ river figured 96, 100
NANDA and UPANANDA in the Great Miracle 159-161
— figured 167 (Magadha), 168 (Western India), 173, XXIII (Kudâ and Magadha), XXV-XXVII (Gandhâra)
— *See also* Nâga
*Nandîpada* symbolizing nativity of Buddha 1
Nativity, Buddha s *See* Buddha, birth of
Necklace worn by female figure 89 (Sânchî)
Nimbus figured 144 (Gaul and India), 171 n 1, 263 (in leaf form, Chandi Mendut), XXIII (Magadha), XXI (Ta-t'ong fu), XXV (Gandhâra)
— *See also* Aureole, Halo
Nun figured 234-5 (Boro-Budur), XXV (Loriyân-Tangai), XXXVIII, XXXIX (Boro-Budur)
— *See also* Çaila.
*Nyagrodha* tree figured 94 (Sânchî)
— symbolizing Kâçyapa Buddha 104 (Sânchî)
— *Ârâma* figured at Sânchî 94

Ogress (Hâritî) figured XLIX (Japan)
OLDENBURG, S d', jâtakas at Boro-Budur identified by, 214 and n 1, 215, 217, 243-4

*Olla* figured 139 40 (Gaul)
Olympian, ideal of, embodied in Buddha figure 134-5
Otter. *See* Dabbhapuppha jâtaka, 45.
Oxen figured 87 (Sânchî)

*Padma See* Lotus
*Padmâsana* posture, Buddha figures in, 256 (Boro-Budur)
— reserved for Buddha (*ibid*), 235 n
Painting, fresco *See* Ajantâ
— in water colours on canvas 274-5
— Tibetan, XL
Palisade figured XLII (Boro-Budur), XLIV (Chandi-Mendut)
Pañcâla country 217 224
PAÑCIKA, god with purse, 141-2
— in Great Miracle 174 n 5.
— figured 220 (Boro-Budur), 264 (Chandi Mendut), XLVIII (Sahri-Bahlol)
— named in Divyavadâna 174 n 5
— *See also* Tutelary Pair
PANTHAKA, miracles of, 157 n. 3
Paradise *See* Heaven.
*Pâramitâs*, or Perfections of Buddha, 57
Parasol, Buddha represented by, 19
— Buddha's, in the heaven of the Thirty Three Gods 19
— figured 93, 94, 95, 96, 102 (Sânchî), 164 n 1 (Ajantâ), 170-2 (Ajantâ), 172 n 1 (Takt-i-Bahai), XIX (Sârnâth), XXI (Ajantâ), XXIV XXVII and XXVIII (Gandhâra), XXVIII (Barhut), XXIX (Amarâvati), XXXVI and XXXVII (Boro-Budur)
*Parinirvâna* figured IV (Gandhara, Amarâvatî, Benares), XIX (Sârnâth)
— symbolized by Stûpa 16, 89 (Sânchî), 73, 90, I, II, IV (Amarâvatî).
*Parnaçâlâ See* Hut.
Parrot figured XLVII (Gandhâra)
*Paryanka-bandha* posture figured 97 (Sânchî)
*Pâtalî*, symbol of Vipaçyin, figured 104 (Sânchî)
Peacock figured 88, 105 (Sânchî)

Perfections of Buddha  *See* Pâramitâ
Persepolitan columns xxv (Gandhâra)
Persian *See* Iranian
Peshawar, Kanishka stûpa excavated at, 129
—      Kanishka's winter capital 129.
Physiologus, Unicorn story in, 48
*Pishi See* Rajoharana.
Pigeon, Buddha's life as  *See* Kapota-jâtaka
Pilgrimages, four great, as aid to explanation of Buddhist art 10
—      four places of, 148
—      signacula from, 11
PINGALA, Hâritî's youngest son, 279 284
—      figured XLV L
Pitchers figured 96 (Sânchî)
PLEYTE, C M., Boro-Budur sculptures identified by, 214 and n 2, 216 n 1
—      Buddha statue at Boro Budur discussed by, 257
Pond figured xxviii (Gandhâra), xxix (Amarâvatî), xLIV (Chandi Mendut)
Portico figured in Great Miracle 171 179 (Barhut)
—      trapezoidal, figured xxv (Gandhâra)
Portrait statues of Buddha supposed, 82-83, 259
PRABHÛTARATNA, Buddha, figured xxi (Ta-t ong-fu)
*Pradakshinâ* arrangement of bas-reliefs at Boro Budur  14-5
PRASENAJIT figured in Great Miracle 164 n. 1, 171, 174 (Ajantâ), 179 (Barhut).
—      sandal-wood statue of Buddha carved by, 24 n. 1.
Preaching, Buddha's first *See* Dharmacakra-pravartana.
—      symbolized by wheel 90 (Sânchî).
Prince, figure of, 6 (Sânchî and Barhut).
Processions of kings figured 80 (Sânchî).
Promenade *See* Cankrama
Promenades, four *See* Buddha
Pruning-bill borne by Brahman ascetic 218
*Pundarîka* tree, symbolizing Çikhin, figured 104 (Sânchî)

PÛRANA KÂÇYAPA figured 164 and n 1 (Ajanta)
*Purojava See* Herald
Purse figured 139-40 (Gaul), 141-142 (Gandhâra), 145 6 (Gaul and Gandhâra), 246 (Boro-Budur), xxiv, xxv, xLVIII (Gandhâra)
*Purusha*, golden, on Brahmanic altars 8 and n 1
Purushapura *See* Peshawar

Quail, Buddha's birth as. *See* Laṭukika jataka
QUAN-AM, the Annamese, 287 8.
Queen figured 227-8, 235 sqq , xxxviii and xxxix (Boro-Budur)

Railing figured 94, 98 (Sânchî).
—      at Barhut, remains of, in Calcutta Museum 57
—      stûpa surrounded by,33,65 (Sânchî).
Râjagriha, Bimbisâra king of, 232 sqq
—      elephant tamed at, 150, xix (Sârnâth).
—      figured 101 (Sânchî)
—      importance of, in early Buddhism 149 and n. 2
—      *See also* Antagiri
*Rajoharana* figured 163 (Ajantâ)
Ram, story of (Barhut). *See* Jâtaka
RÂMA represented as brother of Sîtâ 45
Râmagrâma, Açoka's attempt upon Buddha's relics at, figured 79 (Sânchî)
—      Açoka s visit to, 23
*Ratna-cankrama.* See Cankrama
RATNASAMBHAVA figured 256 7 (Boro-Budur)
—      image in Batavia Museum 267.
Rawak, sculptures of, 172 n 1.
Relics, Buddha's. *See* Buddha, relics of
Rheims, people of (in La Fontaine), 50
Rice, bunches of, gathered in Java 228.
Riches, god of *See* Kuvera, Pâñcika
RIDDHILA MÂTÂ figured xxiv and xxviii, 174 (Gandhâra)
*Rishis* figured 228 (Boro-Budur)
*Rishyaçringa jâtaka* figured 47 (Barhut), 74 n 2 (Sânchî).
—      story located in Gandhâra 123

*Itshyaçrïnga-jâtaka* narrated 47-8

River figured 98-100 (Sânchî).

Rocks figured XXIX, XXXVII and XL (Boro-Budur), L (China).

Roruka, kingdom of Rudrâyana 232 sqq
— localized by E Huber 238 n 2

Rosaries figured XXXVII (Boro-Budur)

Royalty, insignia of, figured 91 (Sânchî)

RUDRÂYANA story narrated in the Divyâ-vadâna, analysed by E Huber, 231-2
— story figured 231-40 (Boro-Budur), XXXVII-XL (Boro-Budur)

*Ruru-jâtaka* figured 40 (Barhut)


Sacrifice, instruments of, figured 97 (Sân-chî)

*Sad-dharma-pundartka* associated by Wou-k'ong with the Gridhrakûța 149 n 2

Sâgala, capital of Menander, 127

Sahri-Bahlol excavations at, XIII, XIV, XLVIII
— photographs of, XIII
— Tutelary Pair from, XLVIII

*Sambodhi See* Bodhi.

Sânchî stûpa *See* Essay III.
— — bibliography of the, 83-4
— — Bodhi figured on the, 102
— — Buddha figure wanting on the, 117
— — Buddha represented by Can-krama on the, 19
— — Buddha represented only by symbols on the, 15
— — Buddha's Conception figured on the, 92
— — Buddhist Heavens figured on the, 71
— — date of the bas-reliefs of, 190
— — described by Captain Fell 63
— — description of, 64
— — inscriptions studied by Buh-ler 66 n 1
— — Kinnaras figured on the, 11
— — monks not figured on the, 76
— — photographs of, VII-X
— — relics not discovered in the, 64

Sânchî stûpa repaired by Archæological Department 64
— — sculptures, æsthetic value of, 81
— — seven traditional Buddhas figured on the, 72.
— — Shaddanta-jâtaka at, 188.

Sandal-wood statue of Buddha, tradi-tions relative to the, 24 n 1

Sânkâçya, Devâvatâra at, 149-50, 177 XIX (Sarnâth)

Sârnâth, Buddha figures from, date of, 116
— sculptures from, Essay VI, XIX

SÂTAKANI mentioned in inscription at Sânchî 4, 67

Satire against women 46.

Saw employed in Shaddanta-jâtaka 193
— figured XXIX (Barhut and Amarâvatî)

Scarf worn by Gandharvas 85

Sculptures in the round found almost only at Sânchî 66
— Indian, more reliable than texts 186.
— of Sânchî, æsthetic value of, 81
— of Sânchî, observation of nature in, 81
— railings decorated with, 10
— *passim*.

Seat figured XXVII-XXVIII.

SELEUKOS, Gandhara ceded by, to Can-dragupta 121

Serpents figured 107 (Sânchî)

*Shaddanta jâtaka* Essay VII.
— chronology of, versions of the, 196
— figured 39 (Amarâvatî, Barhut, Gandhâra), 40 (Ajantâ), 74 n 2 (Sânchî), XXIX (Barhut and Amarâvatî), XXX (Karamâr Hill, Ajantâ)
— narrated in the Kalpadrumâva-dâna and Sûtrâlamkâra 198-199 n 1

Shorea Robusta *See* Çâla

Siam Buddha type not original in, 115

SIDDHARTHA Bodhisattva figured XXVII (Gandhara), XXXVI (Boro-Budur).

*Signacula* in th. British and Cluny Museums 11

Sikrî, statue of Hârïtî from, XLVII.

*Simhâsana*, Bodhi represented by, 148 n 2
— Buddha represented by, 19
— figured 168 (Western India), 176, xxxvii (Boro Budur)
— formed of superposed animals xxi (Ajantâ)
Sîtâ represented as sister of Râma 45
Sîvalî, story of, 52
Slab, rectangular figured 93 (Sânchi)
Sleeves of tunic xlvii (Gandhâra).
Smallpox, Deity of *see* Hârtî
— infants protected by amulet against, 122
Sophocles, Lateran, and figures of Christ and Buddha, 136 xvi.
Speyer, J S., Maitrakanyaka-avadâna at Boro Budur explained by, 215, 243-4
Spoon, sacrificial, figured 98 (Sânchi).
Spooner, D. B., Buddhist punch-marked coins tabulated and discussed by, 14, 21 n 2
— excavations at Sahri-Bahlol by, xiii, xiv, xlviii
— Kanishka stûpa explored by, 129
Stag, Buddha's birth as *See* Ruru-jâtaka.
Staff of mendicant figured xix (Sârnâth).
Standard bearer figured on capitals of gate 86 (Sânchi)
Stein, M A , excavations in Chinese Turkestan by, 285.
— Hârtî painting discovered and described by, 285-6.
— photograph communicated by, xlv.
Stele from Sârnâth *See* Essay VI.
Stool figured 144 (Gaul and India), 164 n 1 (Ajantâ), 272-3 (Central As a)
*Stûpa*, Açoka form of, 13
— coins marked with, 14
— figured 15, 89, 90, 98 n. 1 (Sânchi), 237-239 (Boro-Budur), iv-xix (Amarâvatî), xix (Sârnâth)
— gate of *See* Torana
— origin and parts of, 33
— prominence of, in Buddhist architecture 10
— structure of, 33-4
— symbolizing Parinirvâna 18 73, 104 (of seven last Buddhas), (Sânchi), 1, 11, 178 (Barhut)

*Stûpa* *See also* Amaravatî, Barhut, Boro-Budur, Sânchi
Subhadra, conversion of, figured iv (Gandhâra)
*Sudhana-Kumâra* figured xxxv (Boro-Budur)
— legend of, 217-224
Sundarî, assassination of, 183
*Sûtrâlankâra*, chapters in the, number of, 200
— fragment of the, discovered 207
— Shaddanta-jâtaka in the, 188, 194-5, 196, 198, 199, 200
— Twin Miracle according to the, 155
Swan, as decoration 85 (Sânchi) xv
— Buddha s birth as *See* Hamsa-jâtaka
Swat River, Naga of, converted by Buddha 122
Symbols 14 (on coins), 69 (Sanchi)

*Ta-che-tu-luen*, date of the, 190
— Shaddanta-jâtaka in the, 188, 194-196
Takht-i Bahai, Great Miracle figured at, 172 n
— photograph of, xii
*Tao-tie*, figured l (China)
Târâ figured on the Chandi Mendut 265
— image in Batavia Museum 267
Taranatha on the Vajrâsana statue 259-60.
Ta-t'ong-fu, caves of, date of, 115.
— Great Miracle figured in, 166 7, xxi
Taurine symbol *See* Nandipada
*Tawîz*, amulet case, 122
Taylor, General, visits Sânchi Stûpa 63
Taxilâ, Heliodoros native of *See* Heliodoros
Teaching, gesture of xxiv (Gandhâra)
*Temiya jâtaka* narrated 56
Throne *See* Simhâsana
Thunderbolt figured 91 (Sânchi)
Tibet, Buddha type not original in, 115
— paintings from, xl
— wheel symbol in, 26
— *See also* Lamaist images
Tishyarakshitâ, wife of Açoka casts a spell upon the Bodhi tree 108

*Torana*, gate of Stûpa railing, 33-4
— *See also* Gate
Tortoise, Antelope, Woodpecker, story of, 40
— as decoration 85 (Sânchî)
Town figured 239 (Boro-Budur)
— gate of, figured III (Gandhara and Amarâvatî)
— of Hell 246-7 (Boro-Budur)
— personification of, figured 174-5, III (Gandhara and Amarâvatî), XVII (Gandhara)
— *See also* Çrâvastî, Kapilavastu, Kapitha
TRAILOKYAVIJAYA figured XLIII (Java)
— statuette in Batavia Museum 267-8
Tree, coins marked with, 14
— figured 15-90 (Sânchî), XXIX (Barhut),XXXV XXXVII (Boro-Budur), XLIV (Chandi Mendut)
— miraculous, in legend of Buddha 72
— *See also* Bodhi tree, Çâla, Campaka, Ficus, Jambu, Mango, Nâgapushpa, Nyagrodha, Pâtalî, Pundarîka, Shorea, Udumbara
*Tsa-pao-tsang-king*, date of the, 190
— Shaddanta-jâtaka in the, 187-8, 194-196
Tumulus, funeral *See* Stûpa
Tunic figured with sleeves, XLVII (Gandhâra)
Turban figured 175 n 2, XXIV-XXV-XXVI (Gandhâra)
Turfan, Madonna figured on painting from *See* Yâr Khoto
*Tushita* heaven, Buddha's descent from the 92
— — figured 91 (Sânchî), XXXIV (Boro-Budur)
Tutelary Pair in Gaul and India Essay V
— — figured XVII (Gaul), XVIII (Gandhâra)
— — reason for worship of, 143-4
— — relative positions of, 144

UDAYANA of Kauçâmbî, sandal-wood statue of Buddha carved by, 24 n 1
*Udumbara* tree symbolizing Kanaka muni 104 (Sânchî)

Unicorn, story of. *See* Rishyaçringa-jâtaka
UPANANDA *See* Nanda
*Upardja See* Viceroy
UPOSHADHA, father of Mândhâtar, 226-7
*Ûrnâ* on forehead of statues 119, 177
— figured 177-8, XXIV XXV (Gandhâra)
Uruvilvâ figured 95 (Sânchî), XL (Boro-Budur)
*Ushnîsha*, on crown of Buddha, figured 119.
UTPALAVARNÂ figured in Great Miracle 174

Vaiçâlî, importance of, in early Buddhism 149, n 2
— monkey's offering at, figured 150 XIX (Sârnâth)
— wood near, 228
VAIROCANA figured 256-7 (Boro Budur)
VAJRAPÂNI figured 174 III, IV, XXVII (Gandhara)
— *See also* Trailokyavijaya
*Vajrâsana* statue of Mahabodhi 259-66
VAJRASATTVA statue in Batavia Museum 267
Vase figured XXIV (Gandhâra), XLIV (Chandi Mendut)
— lottery, figured 88 (Sânchî)
— two handled, figured on painting from Central Asia 274
— *See also* Alms-Vase
Vessels in clouds figured 238 and n (Boro-Budur)
Viceroy figured 91 (Sânchî)
VIÇVABHÛ symbolized by Çâla tree 104 (Sânchî)
VIÇVAKARMAN in Great Miracle 171
*Viçvantara-jâtaka* figured 74 n 2 (Sânchî)
— located in Gandhâra XII, 123.
VIDHURA, Buddha's birth as *See* Vidhura-jâtaka figured 55-57 (Barhut)
Vidiçâ, column of Hehodoros at, 82
— ivory-carvers of, 67.
*Vihâra*, stele in form of, XXV (Gandhâra)
Village life figured 96 (Sânchî).
VIPAÇYIN symbolized by Bignonia 104 (Sânchî)
VIRGIN MARY suckling Jesus, date of earliest representation of, 277 9

VIRGIN MARY, Oriental costume in art types of, 276

VOGEL, J Ph , identifies with Kuvera the god in the Tutelary Pair 141 and n 2

— Lokapâlas identified by, 173 n 1.

— photographs communicated by, XII, XIII and XLVII

Water-vessel figured 175 (Brahmâ's emblem), XIX (Sârnâth), XXVII (Gandhâra)

Wheel, coins marked with, 14

— of the Law figured 15, 88, 89, 90 (Sânchî)

— — — I, II, IV (Sânchî), XIX (Sârnâth), XXVIII (Barhut).

— symbol in Gandhâra, Mediæval India and Tibet, 26.

— symbolizing First Preaching 19, 73, 248 n 2

— — Great Miracle 178, 180 (Barhut), 180 n 1 (Sânchî).

Wise man, Buddha's birth as, 44

Woman, Buddha's birth as, 46

— praise of, 49

— satire against, 46

Woodpecker, Antelope and Tortoise See Kurunga miga-jâtaka, 40

Worship, forms of, depicted 80 (Sânchî)

— utensils of, figured XXXVIII (Boro-Budur).

WOU-K'ONG, Mahaprajñâpâramitâ-sûtra associated with Jetavana by, 149 n 2

WOU-K'ONG, Saddharmapundarîka associated with Gridhrakûta by, 149 n 2

YAÇODÂ figured XXXVI (Boro-Budur)

Yaksha figured 220 (Boro-Budur), III, IV (Gandhâra and Amarâvatî)

— nature of the, 141, 280

Yakshnî figured 70-1, 89 90 (Sânchî and Barhut).

YAMA, kingdom of, figured 91 (Sânchî)

Yamaka prâtihârya confused with the Great Miracle 156-8

— described 152

— hackneyed by use 155-6.

— in Gandhâra 153

— narrated by the Jâtaka book (Introduction), Jâtaka-mâlâ, Sûtrâlankâra, Mahâvamsa, Mahâvastu, Divyâvadâna, 155-9.

— why not preferred to Great Miracle in stele from Sârnâth 153-6

Yâr-Khoto, Madonna figured on painting from, 271

Yavamajjhaka, suburb of Mithilâ, 51

YI TSING, Hârîtî image described by, 281

— reports Mûla-Sarvâstivâdin predominance in Malay Islands 253-4

Yoke pole figured 96 (Sânchî), XXIX (Amaravatî)

YZERMAN, J W., primitive plinth of Boro-Budur as originally planned, discovered by, 208 n 1, 213

— Kinnara-jâtaka identified by, 242 n 2

# ADDENDA AND CORRIGENDA

P 5, l 22  *For* « earthy » *read* « earthly »
P 8, n l 2  *For* « kritya » *read* « krityā »
P 10, n  *For* « suta » *read* « sutta »
P 20, l 15  *Insert comma after* « there »
P. 21, n 1, l 2  *For* « groupe » *read* « group ».
P 26, l 5  *For* « has » *read* « had »
  »  l 22  *For* « at » *read* « in »
P 30, l 14  *For* « owe however » *read* « owe, however »
  »  n 1, l 1 . *For* « éd » *read* « ed »
P 31, l 11-17  Need it be stated that this too summary view of *karma* is not an altogether correct one? If we judge from the numerous *karma*-tales, things were supposed to be much more complicated and less mathematical
P 33, l 21  *For* « was preeminently » *read* « par excellence was ».
  »  l 29  *For* « harmika » *read* « harmikā »
P 36, l 1  *For* « in Indian literature not » *read* « not in Indian literature »
P 37, l 15  *For* « or if » *read* « or, if »
  »  l 16  *Insert comma before* « in »
  »  l 20  *Insert comma before* « under ».
  »  l 21  *For* « whom » *read* « which ».
  »  l 25  *For* « who » *read* « which »
P 40, l 6  *For* « ne-birth » *read* « rebirth »
  »  n l 2  *For* « Saddanta » *read* « Shaddanta »
P 43, ll. 8-9  *For* « only falls to them » *read* « falls to them only »
P 46, l 16  *For* « these » *read* « the above »
  »  l 18  *For* « with » *read* « in »
  »  l 21  *For* « at » *read* « from »
P 47, l 8  *Dele comma*
  »  l 22  *Omit* « back »
  »  l 23  *For comma read full stop*
P 48, l 26  *Omit* « back »
P 49, l 12  *Read* « marriageable »
P 52, l 28  *Omit* « one »
P 56, l 31  *For* « Sēmiya » *read* « Temiya »
P 58, n  *For* « Saddanta » *read* « Shaddanta »
P 66, l 16  *For* « coins » *read* « coigns »
P 68, l 2  *For* « confreres » *read* « confrères »
P 69, l. 25  *For* « according to » *read* « from »
  »  l 29  *For* « only serve » *read* « serve only »
P 70, n  A more explicit statement of the point here mooted will be found in *Les Images indiennes de la Fortune* (Mémoires concernant l'Asie Orientale, I, Paris, 1913, p 131-4)
P 74, l 5  *After* « school » *insert* « in order »
  »  n 2, l 3  *For* « Saddanta » *read* « Shaddanta ».

P 76, l 26   *Read* « explain each other by their propinquity ».

P. 77, l 2   *Read* « in order to pay »

»   l. 18   *For* « this » *read* « the »

P 87, l 23 .  *For* « observe » *read* « obverse »

P 97, l 30   *For* « buffalos » *read* « buffaloes »

P. 98, l 23   *For* « fagot » *read* « faggot »

P 107, l 23   *For* « buffalos » *read* « buffaloes »

P. 116, l 24   *For* « south west », *read* « south-east »

P 119, n   These *Notes on the ancient Geography of Gandhara* have since been translated into English by Mr H HARGREAVES and published in Calcutta (1915) under the care of the Archæological Survey of India

P 129 l 30   The casket is not made of gold but « of an alloy in which copper predominates »  it had been simply gilded.

P 140, l 5-6   *Read* « occurrence ».

P 143, l. 32   *Instead of* « or four » *read* « for our »

P 144, l 15   *Read* « paraphrase »

Pl XVIII (text opposite), l 11   *Read* « Volkerkunde ».

P. 151, n 1, l 1   Read « ibid ».

P. 153, l 21   *For* « besides » *read* « indeed »

P 154, l. 23   *For* « they » *read* « these »

P. 158, l 1 ·  *For* « eye witness » *read* « eye witness »

P. 160, n 1, l. 3 ·  *Read* « which (unfortunately broken) »

P. 162, n 1, l 6   *For* « motifs » *read* « motif »

»   »   l 11 .  *For* « do » *read* « to »

»   n 2, l 5   *Read* « We ».

P. 164, n 1, l 9   *For* « rarety » *read* « rarity ».

P 165, n 2, l 12   *Read* « carved »

P 167, n. 2, l 1   *Read* « provenance »

P 169, l 6   *For* « no » *read* « not »

P 173, n 1, l 5   *Before* « which » *insert comma*

P. 176, l 12   *For* « ands » *read* « and »

P 177, l. 22 .  *For* « beliewe » *read* « believe »

P. 185, l. 8   *For* « on » *read* « concerning »

P. 189, n 1, l 3 .  For « *Buddha* » read « *Bauddha* ».

»   n. 2, l 3   *Before* « question » *insert* « a »

P. 190, l. 13   *Dele comma.*

P. 196, l 5   *Insert* « elephant's » *before* « teeth »

P 201, l 11   *For* « Fausböll » *read* « Fausbøll ».

Pl XXX (text opposite), l 12   *Read* « panel »

»   l 16 17 :  *Read* « represented »

»   l 19   *Read* « just ».

P. 205, l 11   *Before* « Progo » *insert* « the »

P 215, n 2, l 2 ·  *For* « Gronemann » *read* « Groneman ».

P 216, l 4   *For* « Then » *read* « Then again »

P 221, ll 1-2   *For* « begins by presenting » *read* « first presents »

P 241, ll. 4 and 5 .  *For* « on » *read* « in »

P 244, l 2   *Read* « identification »

P 251, l. 8   *For* « on » *read* « in »

P 253, l 13 ·  *For* « this » *read* « the »

P  267, l  19    *For* « rarety » *read* « rarity »,
P  271, ll  11-2 . *Omit commas*
P  274, l  2    *For* « partners » *read* « playmates »
P  275, l  10    *For* « on » *read* « in »
P  279, l  7    *For* « rarety » *read* « rarity »
P  283, l  7    *For* « suckles » *read* « sucks »
P  284, l. 15    *For* « suckle » *read* « suck »
P  285, l  16    *Omit comma*
P  286, l  11    *For* « hangs in folds in » *read* « descends sinuously to ».
P  287, l  30    *For* « consequentially » *read* « consequently »
Pl  XLIX (text opposite), l  1    *For* « wood-cuts » *read* « wood-carvings ». —
These two statuettes and the one on pl  L, 2, have since been published, with three
others belonging to her father's collection, by Miss  Alice GETTY in her very inte-
resting and finely illustrated book on *The Gods of Northern Buddhism* (Oxford, at the
Clarendon Press, 1914), pll XXVI , XXVII *a* , XXIX *b* and *c*, XXXII *a* and *b*

~163

ANGERS  IMPRIMERIE A  BURDIN  — GAULTIER ET THÉBERT Sᵗᵉ

Lightning Source UK Ltd.
Milton Keynes UK
UKHW022119261018
331277UK00011B/78/P

9 781298 948502